OUT OF
THIS WORLD

OUT OF THIS WORLD

Nancy Beck Irland and Peter Beck

ℛℛ

REVIEW AND HERALD® PUBLISHING ASSOCIATION
WASHINGTON, DC 20039-0555
HAGERSTOWN, MD 21740

The author assumes full responsibility for the accuracy of all
facts and quotations as cited in this book.

This book was
Edited by Penny Estes Wheeler
Designed by Bill Kirstein
Cover photo by The Image Bank / © Hans Wendler
Type set: 11/12 pt. Century Light

PRINTED IN U.S.A.

Library of Congress Cataloging in Publication Data

Irland, Nancy Beck, 1951-
    Out of this world / Nancy Beck Irland and Peter Beck.
        p.   cm.
    ISBN 0-8280-0523-0
    1. Devotional calendars—Seventh-day Adventists. 2. Seventh-day Adventists
—Prayer-books and devotions—English. 3. Adventists—Prayer-books and devo-
tions—English. I. Beck, Peter, 1953-
II. Title.
BV4810.I75   1989
242'.2—dc20
                                                                                    89-33719
                                                                                    CIP

Dedication

For the next generation. Including Marc, David, and Holly Irland; Nichole, Carissa, Peter, and Stephanie Beck; and Kristi and Todd Jarnes. Our prayers are with you.

SECRETS OF WINNERS

And Jesus answered them, "Those who are well have no need of a physician, but those who are sick; I have not come to call the righteous, but sinners to repentance." Luke 5:31, 32, RSV.

A certain basketball team with the reputation of winning (after 37 winning seasons in a row) came, at last, to an inevitable loss. You would think that the atmosphere in the locker room would be one of somber gloom at losing; but not this team! Their coach, with the philosophy of a leader, was ecstatic. When asked by a reporter how he felt about his team losing, he said, "I feel great! Now we can concentrate on winning, rather than on not losing!"

To most people, failure feels like the bottom of the barrel. But to a leader, failure is the springboard to new beginnings, a fresh approach, a fresh start. Compare the difference between saying "I am a failure" and "I have failed twice." Failure offers the opportunity to close one chapter and start a new one.

God, I think, is a lover of new beginnings. He gave us a week wrapped up in a package of seven days, with a fresh, new sunrise at the start of every day. When the world was sinful, He cleansed it with the Flood so it could start over. Someday He'll do that again—start over with those who are interested.

In their book *Leaders: The Strategies for Taking Charge,* Warren Bennis and Burt Nanus interviewed and studied 90 successful men and women—executives, coaches, and others. They discovered that successful people don't even use the word *failure,* preferring, instead, to use such words as *setback* or *false start.* One executive said, "If you're not falling down, you're not learning."

Though most leaders don't make an issue of flaunting their mistakes, Bennis and Nanus uncovered the story of a promising IBM junior executive who, several years ago, caused the company to lose several million dollars in a risky venture. Thomas J. Watson, Sr., IBM's founder, called the executive into his office, and the young man blurted out, "I guess you want my resignation."

"You can't be serious," Watson replied. "We've just spent millions of dollars educating you!"

Jesus has the same philosophy. He said, "I didn't come to call the people who know they are perfect, but those who know they aren't." God doesn't want perfect people in heaven—people who don't know the heartache of sin and separation from God! That's the kind of people

Lucifer and his angels were. Rather, God is interested in the sinners —those who have made mistakes, those who can concentrate on winning, rather than on not losing.

Have you suffered a "setback" lately? Just because you've failed doesn't mean you're a failure—you're one of the people Jesus is looking for! This year, 1990, lies ahead of you clean and unblemished. Maybe it will be the year Jesus takes us out of this world!

JANUARY 2

✳ **UNDERSTANDING DISCOURAGEMENT**

Since the Lord is directing our steps, why try to understand everything that happens along the way? Proverbs 20:24, TLB.

The story is told of some old-time mountaineers who were hired to take a load of luggage to a distant town. They had never been more than a mile or two from their home, and surely had never traveled this particular road before. So they were somewhat baffled when they came to a tunnel. It was a long tunnel, so the opening on the other end seemed as small as a pinpoint.

The men discussed the problem among themselves, and finally decided they would not go through. They turned around and went back to the village from which they had come.

The man who had hired them was furious! "I gave you money to take that load to town, and you never got it there!"

"But mister," the men explained, "we looked at that tunnel and we didn't want to risk your possessions. We knew the opening at the other end was too small, and we could never get your luggage through!"

Life is like that sometimes. A new year may seem to hold no hope for happiness. It may seem that you can't go on another day; the future seems impossible. Maybe your parents have separated or divorced. Perhaps you feel betrayed and lonely. Maybe a close friend or loved one has died, and you don't know if you can go on without him. As humans, we are always trying to figure out *why*. But there isn't always a good answer. And when we can't come up with a good answer, we feel angry—angry at life and angry at God. He seems to be picking on us unjustly.

But God doesn't bring suffering or hardship to anyone. It is just the result of living in a sinful world. Satan is the father of trouble, but he wants God to get the blame.

At times I have been so discouraged that Bible verses brought me no peace. I didn't appreciate people quoting them to me, either. But I discovered that the leading cause of discouragement is anger, which is usually caused by real or imagined injustices.

Unlike the mountaineers of this story, we can't always turn around and run from our problems. We have to keep going, one step at a time, till we discover we *can* get past the problems after all.

Here's a challenge for you. Make a list of your problems and check back on them in two weeks. By that time, most of your problems will have solved themselves. It's more trouble to try to come up with a reason that they come than it is to cope with them. And if we're faithful, then someday, when we're out of this world, we'll understand why those problems came.

HOW TO QUIET YOUR CONSCIENCE

These teachers will tell lies with straight faces and do it so often that their consciences won't even bother them. 1 Timothy 4:2, TLB.

"Conscience," said an Indian, "is a three-cornered thing in my heart that stands still when I am good, but when I am bad, it turns around and the corners hurt a lot. If I keep on doing wrong, the corners wear off and it does not hurt anymore."

Another word for *conscience* is *integrity.* It feels good to know that you are a person who does what is right!

A man once bought a pair of shoes from a cobbler, promising to pay him for the shoes on a future day. That day came, and the man took the money to the cobbler's shop and asked to see him.

"I'm sorry," said the man behind the counter. "The cobbler died unexpectedly. I now own the store. May I help you in some way?"

"No! No, thank you very much." The customer smiled broadly at his good fortune and left the store whistling. A free pair of shoes! This new owner would never know of the outstanding debt.

Days became weeks, and weeks became years. The customer moved away. But every time he heard the name of the little town, his conscience pricked him. Try as he might, he just didn't feel right about not paying for his shoes. Finally, the man could stand it no longer. He took a carriage to the little town and hurried to the street where the cobbler's shop had been. It was still there! Before he could change his mind, he dashed into the store and slapped his money on the counter.

"This is yours!" the distraught customer said. "I owed it to the other cobbler years ago. And though I know he is dead, he is alive to me and has been for all these years."

The customer went home. For the first time in years he felt truly happy. He had learned that character is a victory, not a gift. You can strengthen your conscience by listening to it and obeying it.

Your conscience—your sense of "good" and "bad"—is the result of the Holy Spirit's guidance. If you tell the Holy Spirit to leave you alone, He will. Your conscience will eventually stop hurting, but you will be the loser.

JANUARY 4

FROGS IN THE CREAM!

To every one who overcomes—who to the very end keeps on doing things that please me—I will give power over the nations. Revelation 2:26, TLB.

Perhaps you've heard the story of the two frogs who fell into a butter churn filled with cream. "It's cold!" one frog squeaked to the other. "It's deep and cold! And the sides are so slippery and steep, we'll never get out alive!"

"Keep on paddling. We'll get out of this mess some way," the other frog croaked. "Maybe someone will see us." And around and around he swam.

"It's no use!" the other frog squeaked. "Too thick to swim. Too thin to jump. Too slippery to crawl. We're bound to die sometime anyway, so it may as well be tonight." He sank to the bottom of the churn and died.

The other frog blinked slowly, clearing the cream from his eyes. Keeping his nose above the cream, he paddled steadily. "I'll swim awhile," he said to himself. "It really wouldn't help the world if one more frog was dead."

He paddled all night long with his eyes closed. By morning he was perched on a mass of butter that he had churned all by himself. There he was, with a grin on his face, eating the flies that came swarming from every direction.

The little frog had discovered what most folks ignore: if you stick with the task long enough, you're going to be a winner.

Those who keep on believing in God will be winners too. Keep on paddling, never losing faith in God's promises.

JANUARY 5

DO YOU BELIEVE THIS?

Jesus called out to them, "Come, follow me!" Mark 1:17, TLB.

Do you think this story would ever happen? Read on and see. Once upon a time a submarine and its crew lay helpless 243 feet underwater on the ocean floor. Having lost power, there was no way to send radio signals for help.

The only accompanying submarine puttered over to the sub's last-known position. Diving down toward the ocean floor, it attempted to find the helpless sub. But the waters were too dark.

The rescue sub set off flares. A ship on the surface of the water saw these and raced over to the position, lowering a diving bell to rescue the crew.

The first frogman swam to the sub, but the crew wouldn't let him in. "We want to think it over," they indicated by note. "We're in the middle of a card game, and we've got too much money bet on this one. Come back later! We can't understand what you're saying right now." So the frogman returned to the diving bell.

A second frogman swam to the sub and tried to rescue the crew members. A scribbled note was held up against the sub's window from the inside: "Leave us alone; we're fine. We don't have time to study your plan. Maybe we'll have more time next week to work out the rescue." And the card game went on.

The second frogman returned to the diving bell.

A third frogman came.

"We don't know you," the crew members indicated from inside the sub. "Getting out is too difficult, and we might drown. Leave us alone. We're comfortable here."

So the third frogman returned to the diving bell and left the crew members to certain death.

Do you think this really happened? Of course not! The men in the submarine were eager to be rescued. They couldn't get out of that deathtrap fast enough!

This earth is a deathtrap, and Satan has some of us trapped. His most cunning trap is making us believe that Jesus' coming is a long way off and we don't really have to worry about it now.

Satan is dead wrong! Jesus is coming, ready or not. And the only way to be saved is to follow Him.

JANUARY 6

⚡ HOW TO MAKE GOOD DECISIONS

"You have heard yourselves say it," Joshua said—"you have chosen to obey the Lord." Joshua 24:22, TLB.

11

A small-town ice-cream store offered only chocolate and vanilla ice cream. "Why don't you have any other flavors?" a mother asked as her brood milled about, trying to decide.

"Ma'am," the clerk replied, "if you knew how long it takes people to decide just between those two, you wouldn't ask that question."

How good are you at making decisions? Are you sometimes frightened when faced with making decisions and living with the consequences? Decision-making is an important part of growing up, and it doesn't need to scare you if you understand some basic principles.

One of the hardest things about being a teenager is that you must make some decisions that will affect you for the rest of your life. When you're in high school, you must decide whether to take vocational training or go to college. Later you will have to choose what kind of work you want to do for the rest of your life. And one of your friends could very well become the person you marry! That's another decision that affects the rest of your life.

Jim had decided not to take typing in high school. "That's not a very good decision," his teacher warned him. "With all the computers around, typing skills are very important. You can use typing in just about every job available."

Jim thought it over. He'd never thought of decisions as being good or bad. But now he felt confused. It was like coming to a Y in the road. Whichever decision he made could lead to good or bad consequences. "How can I know what to do?" Jim asked his parents. "How do I decide? I don't know what I'm going to take in college!"

"What's the worst thing that could happen if you take typing?" Dad asked.

Jim shrugged. "I'd have to work hard at it and wouldn't have as much time for football."

"OK. What's the best thing that could happen?"

"Well, I could type my own term papers, and I'd be good at it by the time I got out of high school, and maybe I could get a computer job during the summer."

"So what's your decision?" Dad asked.

Jim smiled. "I'll take typing."

Making decisions about the rest of your life can be fun. Be aware of your natural abilities and interests. Talk to someone who can help you. The decisions you make now may be the most important decisions you ever make. If you choose carefully, the rest of your life could be "out of this world."

A HARMLESS BIT OF FUN?

There is a way which seemeth right unto a man, but the end thereof are the ways of death. Proverbs 14:12.

Rita and her friend Julie were sitting in the balcony of their church watching a wedding. Very quietly, Julie began tearing up her program into tiny little pieces and piling them in her lap. "We'll throw confetti down on them as they walk out after the service," she whispered to Rita.

It sounded like fun to Rita, so without thinking, she also tore up her program and gathered the little bits in her lap.

When the organ started playing again and the newly married couple marched out, the girls leaned over the railing and tossed their handfuls of "confetti." It was a harmless bit of fun, they thought, till someone who saw them tapped them on the shoulder and escorted them to the pastor.

With their parents' permission, the pastor had the girls pick up each little piece of confetti by hand! Their backs and fingers were mighty sore when they finished. If they had thought it through, they probably wouldn't have thrown the confetti down in the first place.

Having to pick up the confetti wasn't too bad a consequence; it was mostly embarrassing. Other foolish decisions can have a more serious impact on your future.

A teenager was stopped for a traffic violation. He hadn't stopped at a stop sign. When the officer went up to the driver's window to talk to him, he recognized a peculiar odor wafting out of the window. The teen was asked to get out of his car, and when the officer searched it, he found a few joints of marijuana and packets of other drugs.

The teen's traffic violation had suddenly become more serious. He was convicted of marijuana possession—an automatic felony—and received a suspended sentence.

Maybe you think that was a pretty light punishment, something he could handle. Well, all he lost was his right to vote, the right to own a gun, and the right to run for public office. He also lost the chance to ever be a licensed doctor, dentist, nurse, certified public accountant, engineer, lawyer, architect, realtor, schoolteacher, barber, funeral director, professional pilot, or stockbroker.

He can never get a job for which he has to be bonded or licensed. He can't work for the city, county, state, or federal government. He cannot be admitted to West Point, Annapolis, or the Air Force Academy.

He lost all of that—forever.

Beware of the decisions you make today. One foolish decision can ruin the rest of your life while good decisions will lead to golden gates.

From *The Railroad Evangelist.* Adapted.

THE FACE ON THE CLIFF

The kingdom of heaven is like a man who sowed good seed in his field. But while everyone was sleeping, his enemy came and sowed weeds among the wheat, and went away. Matthew 13:24, NIV.

You've heard it many times, that we are living in the last days of earth's history. It's true. And because the end is near, Satan is trying even harder to shake us from our faith and trust in God. One of the ways he does this is by whispering to us that we shouldn't go to church because the other people there are sinners. We start looking at others instead of Jesus, deciding by their example whether or not we will attend church.

Satan is cunning. It's true that there are sinners in church. We're all sinners! But some of the sinners are sorry for their sins, and some of the sinners are just sorry they got found out. They'll try to be more sneaky next time! These are the people Satan uses to get us to turn away from God. "If that's the way a Christian acts," we say, "then who needs Jesus?" And when we say that, Satan is thrilled.

Jesus said that the good and the bad would "grow up together" until the harvest when He comes to take us home. He also warned us that we can't tell who is a true Christian and who isn't until the end. So the best rule to follow is to go to church for one reason alone—to look to Jesus.

The story is told of a country that was ruled by a kind and gracious king. When he died, the people decided that they would not have another king until they found someone who looked and acted just like their beloved king. To keep the king's memory alive in everyone's heart, stone masons were hired to chisel the king's face high on a cliff.

For years a committee of men searched the kingdom to find a man who was like their king, but without success. Until one day . . .

They came again to study the great stone face on the cliff and stopped in at a little cottage at the base of the cliff for some food and water before going back home. And there, in that humble cottage, they found their next king. He was just a teenager, but throughout his life as he had worked in his garden and chopped wood for his fire, he had gazed at the cliff-side face of the king. As a result, his own face now showed the gentleness and wisdom of the king's, shaped by the thoughts the king's face had inspired.

Have you been discouraged when people in your church say one thing and do another? Look past them to Jesus. When Jesus comes, those who have filled their minds with Him will be taken out of this world. Don't let Satan cheat you by turning your eyes away from the beautiful face of Jesus.

THE PORPOISE GUIDE

Oh, dear children, don't let anyone deceive you about this: if you are constantly doing what is good, it is because you are good, even as he is. 1 John 3:7, TLB.

There is a stretch of water in New Zealand called the "Pelorus Sound" that is filled with treacherous currents and jagged rocks hidden just below the surface. In the 1800s, before there was any radar, many ships were torn open by these rocks and sunk, their crews carried away to their deaths by the strong current.

But all that changed one day in 1871. A ship called the *Brindle,* on its way from Boston to Sydney, was having trouble navigating in the Pelorus Sound. The weather was stormy and foggy, and the captain feared they would be lost. But all at once, through the fog, they saw a porpoise leap out of the water in front of the boat.

"Harpoon it!" a sailor shouted.

"Why not follow it instead?" the captain's wife suggested.

The sailors stiffened. She was just a woman. What did she know about navigating through dangerous waters? On the other hand, the porpoise lived in those waters. He no doubt was more familiar with the position of the jagged rocks than anyone on the ship. And so the captain followed the porpoise, and the ship made its way safely through the sound.

They nicknamed the porpoise "Pelorus Jack," and for the next 40 years he stayed in the sound and leaped out of the water to greet the ships and lead them safely through the dangerous waters. His appearance was always greeted with cheers from the sailors.

Only one ship went down in the treacherous waters of Pelorus Sound between 1871 and 1912. The reason? From one ship, a drunken passenger shot at Pelorus Jack and wounded him. The porpoise didn't reappear for two weeks. When he recovered, he refused to guide that same ship through the waters. And as a result, that ship struck the rocks and went down.

How did the porpoise know that the seamen had agreed to follow him? By their actions, what the Bible calls their "fruit." And how do we know if we are following after Jesus? By our actions, our fruits.

If your heart aches at the sight of a hungry child; if you find yourself wishing that you were older so you could be a missionary now; if you want everyone to be happy; your thoughts are the same as Jesus'. Your fruits are good fruits that will someday take you out of this world.

FEELING GOOD ABOUT YOURSELF

They that go down to the sea in ships, that do business in great waters; these see the works of the Lord, and his wonders in the deep. Psalm 107:23, 24.

How would you get a gravel-filled boat up from the bottom of a river?

In New York State several years ago a group of engineers were commissioned to build a bridge at a certain point across a river. They discovered, to their dismay, that an old fishing boat had been filled with gravel and rocks and sunk to the bottom of the river right where they needed to put the bridge supports. Among other things, they tried using massive cranes to lift the boat out of the water, but nothing worked.

At last one of the newest members of their firm, a young man familiar with the ways of the sea, suggested something. Why not bring in two barges and tie them to the boat at low tide? Perhaps the pull of the water would lift the boat up from the mire.

Finding this suggestion their only remaining alternative, the engineers arranged to have it done. When the tide was out, strong cables attached to the barges were laid under the boat and attached to the sides of it. Then they waited for the tide to come in.

Slowly—almost imperceptibly—the barges began rising. The cables tightened and strained. Then, as the cables were winched in tighter, the engineers saw the top of the old fishing boat rise out of the water. The strength of the sea had done what man-made machines could not do.

God wants to lift all of us out of the mire of whatever bogs us down. He wants us to realize that this world is not our final home. Look up! Someday God will come and take us out of this world. But only those who are attached to Him will go.

How do you get hooked on Jesus? By thanking Him for His love and by believing Him when He says that you are a worthwhile, lovable human being just because you exist.

ANIMAL WISDOM

Father, Lord of heaven and earth! I thank you because you have shown to the unlearned what you have hidden from the wise and learned. Matthew 11:25, TEV.

The coat of arms of the Fitzgerald family of Ireland is the figure of a baboon holding a baby. As you know, a coat of arms is usually a sword and a shield, or something equally heroic. But in this family, the baboon is the hero.

It happened several generations ago. Young Mr. and Mrs. Fitzgerald had no children of their own for a long time. But they did have a rather unusual pet—a baboon who had been in the family for so long that he was almost like their own child. Even after their baby son was born, the baboon was pampered and coddled as before.

One day Mr. Fitzgerald, a wealthy and famous warrior, was away from the home fighting in a war. His wife and newborn son were home alone in the care of the servants. On that day the inevitable happened. Enemy soldiers burst into town looking for the warrior's family so they could take a prisoner for ransom. The person they wanted, in particular, was Fitzgerald's infant son.

In a panic, the servants fled from the home. Mrs. Fitzgerald fled with them, thinking the baby's nanny was bringing him. But the baby was left behind. The nanny was so concerned for her own safety she hadn't even thought about bringing the baby with her!

The soldiers ran through the house, plundering and breaking everything they could find. They heard the baby crying and rushed to the room, only to find him in the arms of a monkey who leaped out the window and swung through the treetops to the highest spot in town—the church steeple.

The baboon hugged the baby to his chest for several hours, peering down at the angry mob below, until Mr. Fitzgerald and his forces came galloping back into the city. Only then did the baboon climb down to give the baby to its father.

In recognition of the baboon's faithfulness to his son, Mr. Fitzgerald immortalized him by making him the figure in his coat of arms.

You are a person worth taking care of, too. And you have that same sense of "safe" and "unsafe" that the baboon did. You know what's right and wrong. Anyone who tries to get you to do something against your conscience or something that makes you uncomfortable is dangerous. If you aren't strong enough to fight someone like this, flee from him. Keep your conscience clear, and when Jesus comes to take you out of this world you can face Him with confidence.

JANUARY 12

GRANDPA'S STRANGE HEART

For even the Son of Man did not come to be served, but to serve, and to give his life as a ransom for many. Mark 10:45, NIV.

A grandpa we'll call George had a failing heart. His heart was so diseased, his doctor had told him he would need a heart transplant or die.

So George's name was placed on the list waiting for a donor, and each night his grandchildren prayed that if it was God's will, a heart would soon be available for him.

Then it happened, but not in the way anyone could have guessed, or wanted.

George's grandson, Scott, was an active teenager, a boy who loved his motorbike and the friends he went riding with. Scott prayed daily that his grandfather would get a heart. But he did more than just pray. He acted upon it, too. He encouraged all his friends to sign organ donor cards as he had, explaining how grateful families were if their loved ones could live healthy lives.

Then one day—a day that Scott's friends can never forget—Scott became the answer to his own prayers. He crashed on his motorbike. Bad. His friends stood around helplessly, waiting for him to get up, or to even open his eyes; but he just lay on the pavement, his body crumpled at an odd angle.

The ambulance soon arrived, its sirens wailing, and sped Scott to the hospital. There tests revealed that though his heart was still beating, Scott was brain-dead. Soon his heart would stop pumping, his lungs would stop breathing, and he would be gone.

Scott's parents raced to the hospital in shock. When they heard that Scott's death was inevitable, they knew what he would want them to do. They signed a form releasing Scott's heart to his own grandfather.

The surgery was completed within a few hours, and in the following weeks Scott's grandfather recovered nicely. He told reporters, "I have a new heart; but it's broken."

Scott's grandfather lives each day to the fullest in honor of the gift his grandson gave to him. "If I waste this life, Scott's gift will have been in vain," he says.

What about you? Somebody died so that you could live forever. That's how very special you are to Him. And that's why He's coming soon to take you out of this world to live with Him. Don't waste His gift. Be there waiting to greet Him when He comes.

JANUARY 13

THE POLICEMAN'S SECRET

For the wages of sin is death; but the gift of God is eternal life through Jesus Christ our Lord. Romans 6:23.

A certain young lady was driving too fast along a residential stretch of road. When she saw the flashing lights of a police car behind her, she pulled over to the side of the road with a groan.

The policeman, a man old enough to be her father, was friendly and polite, but the girl argued that she didn't feel she deserved a ticket, and she gave several reasons that she thought it was OK for her to drive as fast as she'd been going. There was no one else on the road, and it was a sunny day. There were other streets in the neighborhood just like that one with higher speed limits. And most important of all, she was in a hurry to get her hair styled because she was to meet her boyfriend's parents that night.

The policeman was firm. She had broken the speed limit, and she was getting a ticket.

With a pouting sigh, she took the ticket. "You haven't seen the last of me!" she told him.

"I know," the policeman said with a smile. "Your new boyfriend is my son. We'll see you at dinner tonight!"

How do you think the girl felt then? She wanted to vanish. She certainly didn't want to spend an evening with those people—her boyfriend's family! She was ashamed. As she told a friend later, "I just wanted to die!"

The Bible says that "the wages of sin is death." That doesn't mean that God wants to kill sinners; it means that sinners will want to die and God, in His kindness, will allow it. When Jesus comes, sinners will be pleading with the rocks and mountains to fall upon them so they won't have to see Jesus, because they will be ashamed of the things they have done. A guilty conscience is the main thing that separates them from God. And separation from God brings eternal death.

Don't be one of them. Live your life with as few regrets as possible. Jesus offers you the gift of life out of this world. All you have to do is believe in His forgiveness and promises, and love Him back. He doesn't want you to miss out!

JANUARY 14

SATAN'S STRATEGY

Let us draw near to God with a sincere heart in full assurance of faith, having our hearts sprinkled to cleanse us from a guilty conscience. Hebrews 10:22, NIV.

In the process of preparing a sermon, a minister fell asleep over his books. He dreamed that he was visiting a conclave of Satan and his angels. They were meeting to devise ways to get people to turn away from God.

19

One rose and said, "I will go to the earth and tell people that the Bible is all a fable, that it is not divinely inspired by God."

"No, don't do that," another one said. "Let me go. I will tell people that there is no God, no Saviour, and no heaven."

"No, that won't do. People will never believe that," another argued.

Suddenly one rose with a solemn face and said, "Let me go. I will tell God's earthly children that there is a God, a Saviour, and a heaven. But I will tell them that they are too unworthy for God's love. I will convince them that there is no use even trying to be saved."

He was the one they sent.

You hear his words most often in evolution theories. You hear that you were not specially created, that your ancestors just happened, evolved from almost nothing. And if your great-great-great-granddaddy evolved from a single, one-celled animal, then why should you expect God to love you any more than He loves monkeys, or amoebas, or obnoxious flies?

In contrast, God tells us that we were created in a special way by Him. During Creation week, when God created the plants and animals, He simply spoke and the things came into existence. But when God made man and woman, He took His time and carefully and lovingly formed each one. Of course God cares about us! How do you feel about things you have carefully created? You care what happens to them!

The main theme in the Bible is that you are extremely valuable to God. Satan's theme is that you're not. Don't believe him. God wants to take you with Him out of this world forever—because He made you. That's why He loves you. Nothing can change that. Nothing ever will.

JANUARY 15

THE WAITING DEAD

For the living know that they will die, but the dead know nothing; they have no further reward, and even the memory of them is forgotten. Their love, their hate and their jealousy have long since vanished; never again will they have a part in anything that happens under the sun. Ecclesiastes 9:5, 6, NIV.

A Catholic friend of mine was telling me about a rhyme she made up for her 4-year-old son when he was in kindergarten. They had to rhyme a word with the boy's first name. The little boy's name was Kevin, and the rhyme they made up was "Dear Jesus, please take Kevin to heaven."

I thought it was cute, but certainly not a new thought, since we pray that kind of prayer every night in our home. But my friend explained that she felt guilty every time she heard her son saying it, because "it sounds like we want him to die, or something." She believes that when someone dies trusting in Jesus, he goes straight to heaven.

Do you know what the Bible says about dying? Share your thoughts with each other for a moment. The Bible says that people do not go to heaven when they die, for the dead know nothing. Their bodies wait in the grave until the Second Coming. Seventh-day Adventists are among the few Christian churches that believe this. Satan has distorted the Bible's teachings, but many people haven't studied for themselves to find this out.

I can imagine a number of Satan's angels discussing how they can make people turn against God.

"We can tell them God brings death to teach them a lesson," one says.

"But not everyone will believe that," another demon retorts. "For others, we must convince them that God loves them so much He'll take them to heaven when they die."

"Well then, we'll tell them that when their loved ones die, it's because God wants to 'take them home' to be with Him forever."

"That is good," Satan says with a solemn nod. "It will be a comforting thought at first, followed by anger at God for being so selfish. It might even make them kill themselves in an attempt to 'be with God.' That is very good."

And that's what most Christians believe—that when someone dies it is because God wants that person to be with Him. "God must have needed my mother more than I do," a lonely daughter says bravely. How would that make you feel about God?

Yes, God wants us with Him out of this world. But that will only happen after Christ returns. Don't let Satan's lies make you mad at God if someone you love dies. God doesn't kill people. And someday soon God is going to put an end to death.

JANUARY 16

THE JUDGE WHO LOVES ME

If God be for us, who can be against us? Romans 8:31.

You be the judge. What would you say if a prosecuting attorney told you the following story about a 10-year-old child?

"Your Honor, this child is a thief! Last evening he was found leaving the grocery store with his pockets full of apples and cheese. He was apprehended at the front of the store and spent the night in jail."

You look at the child, a dirty waif with greasy hair and torn, soiled clothes. He sniffs and wrinkles his nose, squints at you, and looks back down at the toe sticking out of his worn-out shoes. His hands, clasped behind his back in handcuffs, wriggle restlessly.

21

What are you thinking? How do you feel about this child? Do you like him? Do you understand him? Do you feel like teaching him a lesson?

Now his defense attorney speaks.

"Your Honor, this young child is the sole support of his family. His mother is dying of cancer, and his 4-year-old sister and 2-year-old brother are always hungry. They live around the corner from the grocery store in an abandoned car.

"Usually this boy earns money shining shoes and carrying packages for old people, but the day he stole from the grocery store, his small earnings had been stolen and he had been beaten up by thugs.

"This is the first time he has ever taken anything without paying for it. But he took the apples and cheese to feed his family."

Now how do you feel about the child? Does his crime seem more understandable now? Does his reason for stealing make it OK?

People do things for various reasons. We cannot judge other people's motives for doing what they do. But certainly if we knew why others did what they do, we might not be so hard on them.

Separated from God the Father by our sins, Jesus suffered and died. He would have done it for only one person. But He wants to take as many of us to heaven as He can. He is looking for every reason He can find to take us out of this world to live with Him. Fortunately, He knows why we do what we do. He knows what has happened to us or what is happening to us to make us act as we do. Ellen White tells us it is the general pattern of our lives, not specific incidents, that God judges. He is a judge who gives us the benefit of the doubt. With Him on our side, we have nothing to fear.

JANUARY 17

FINDING YOURSELF

Beloved, I wish above all things that thou mayest prosper and be in health. 3 John 2.

When I was in boarding academy I had a set of wooden Japanese dolls that fit inside of each other. You've probably seen something similar. Each doll is made of two halves that can be twisted open to find a smaller doll inside, which twists open to reveal a smaller doll, and so forth. The largest doll of my set was about six inches tall, the smallest one was only one half inch tall!

Believe it or not, you are just like that set of dolls—we all are. When a baby is born, nobody knows exactly what talents are wrapped up inside that tiny brain inside that tiny person who neither walks nor talks. But soon that tiny person begins to sit up and then to talk and walk, and to express his likes and dislikes with a whole lot of noise!

22

Like climbing a ladder, each of us must develop one stage at a time. I learned in nursing school that very often babies who never crawl have learning difficulties in school because they skipped a step in development. As a result of not crawling, their brains lack an important foundation to build on.

As a teenager, you have two main steps to take in your development: becoming independent, and discovering your own ideas, goals, and values.

How do you know what your goals and values are? Listen to the things you tell yourself silently. What do you think about kids who think a good time is sitting in a parked car "making out"? Does it make you a little uncomfortable? Good for you! That shows that one of your values is to protect your integrity and to find friends who like you for your mind, rather than for your body.

What do you think about people who sleep in on Sabbath morning, rather than getting up and going to church? Or how about kids who want to get married right out of high school instead of going to college or vocational school? Do you agree with them? If not, why not? How do you feel about sharing answers on a test? Or reading X-rated books or magazines?

As you find answers, you will discover what kind of person you are, what you value, what you want the rest of your life to be like.

Dream big. God wants you to prosper and be happy and healthy. The happiest adults are those who took their time to grow up, and enjoyed being a kid while they could. And then, when it was time, they prepared themselves for careers that fit the talents they discovered inside.

As you listen to yourself and find your goals and values, don't forget that your friends, teachers, and parents can help you discover what your gifts are, too.

Finding yourself. It's great fun!

JANUARY 18

WHAT DO YOU GIVE UP IF YOU GIVE IN?

Then suddenly his love turned to hate, and now he hated her more than he had loved her. 2 Samuel 13:15, TLB.

There's a story of a man in Stockholm, Sweden, who was desperately in need of money. Hearing that the Royal Swedish Institute offered large sums of money for dead bodies, this man sold the ownership of his body after death to the institute, for dissecting purposes.

Twenty years later he inherited a fortune. The first thing he tried to do was buy back the contract he had made with the institute for his body. That was not granted.

His next step was to sue the organization for the contract. But he lost the case. The institute owned his body, and when he died they dissected him as he had given them permission to do so many years before.

You wouldn't want to sell your body to anyone, would you? Dead or alive! But sadly, many juniors and teens do. Alone with someone they like very much, they think, *We love each other; we should show each other just how much.* That is the fastest way to get from love to hate.

Being intimate before marriage not only is embarrassing later, when the passion has cooled, but it also makes you lose your integrity. You have lost that feeling of being open with everybody because you have nothing to hide. And "going too far" breaks up many friendships that might otherwise have continued happily.

Your body is a gift from God. You wouldn't intentionally cut scars in your skin, would you? But sometimes kids inflict scars of guilt in their minds by giving away their integrity. A good friend will help you to keep your integrity and therefore keep on feeling good about yourself.

A teenager confided to her roommates that she was "saving herself for marriage."

"You don't know what you're missing!" one of the girls exclaimed.

"I know," the girl agreed. "I don't know anything about a guilty conscience, or a bad reputation. I also don't know how it feels to be afraid of having a baby or being snubbed and embarrassed by the guy I thought I loved. And you know what? I like it that way!"

JANUARY 19

CHEAP THRILLS

But the man who commits adultery is an utter fool, for he destroys his own soul. Proverbs 6:32, TLB.

A father accidentally threw his little girl over Niagara Falls several years ago. He didn't mean to! He was just swinging her out over the water in an attempt to thrill her. But as she swung away from him, her body stiffened and he lost his grasp. She flew out of his arms into the water and down over the Falls. How do you suppose he feels to this day?

Regrets are very hard to live with. They can make people wish they were dead. And don't think the devil doesn't gloat when we have regrets!

With the recent AIDS epidemic, we hear a lot about "safe sex." The world talks about sex as though it is a game, or something everyone must do to stay alive, such as eating and breathing. But there really isn't any such thing as safe sex outside of the marriage commitment to one person. That's another of the devil's lies. Were the Ten Commandments given to us to make us unhappy? Of course not! They are God's printed instructions for being happy and maintaining our integrity.

24

Immorality can result in diseases or even AIDS. It can kill you. And often it results in depression and a guilty conscience. You lose your sense of integrity, the sense that you are right with God, doing His will. It's embarrassing. It can make you hate yourself.

The best way to avoid these devastating emotions is, first of all, to have lots of friends—both boys and girls—not a "steady." After you get married, you'll have the rest of your life to be "tied down" to one person.

And then, when you're with your friends, don't let the conversation drift into suggestive things just for the fun of it.

Like the father who wanted to give his little girl some excitement and ended up killing her instead, you may find yourself dead emotionally (or wishing you were actually dead) if you go too far.

Don't do anything that would keep you from looking your friends in the eye the next day. The only thing you leave behind is your reputation. Guard yours!

JANUARY 20

GOOD AND THIRSTY

You are the salt of the earth. But if the salt loses its saltiness, how can it be made salty again? It is no longer good for anything, except to be thrown out and trampled by men. Matthew 5:13, NIV.

During a discussion period after a Week of Prayer meeting, some young people were discussing the text "Ye are the salt of the earth." Different students had different ideas for the symbolic meaning of the verse, including "salt gives something a better flavor," "salt preserves things," and so forth.

Then a Chinese girl raised her hand. When she was called upon to give her explanation, she said simply, "Salt creates thirst."

A sudden hush filled the room. Everyone was thinking, *Have I ever made someone thirsty for Jesus?*

Does knowing how much Jesus loves you make a difference in your life? Imagine how it would be if you had no hope of a brighter future, no hope of getting another chance at another life someday. If someone came along who was bursting with happiness because he or she had the conviction that there was going to be a second chance at life someday in heaven, wouldn't that make you thirsty to know more?

When Benjamin Franklin wished to interest the people of Philadelphia in street lighting, he didn't try to persuade them by talking about it. Instead, he hung a beautiful lantern on a long bracket before his own door. Then he kept the glass brightly polished, and carefully and faithfully lit the wick every evening at the approach of dusk.

It wasn't long before Franklin's neighbors began placing lights on brackets before their homes. Before long, the entire city awoke to the value of street lighting. By example, not talk, Benjamin Franklin introduced street lighting to the city. And everyone embraced the new idea with enthusiasm.

That's how we make people thirsty for what we have—by showing them that we have something of value.

According to an article in a magazine called *Moody Monthly,* a Christian's garden should contain certain specific things. First, include five rows of peas: Preparedness, Promptness, Perseverance, Politeness, and Prayer.

Next to them plant three rows of squash: Squash Gossip, Squash Criticism, and Squash Indifference.

Then five rows of lettuce: Let Us Be Faithful, Let Us Be Unselfish, Let Us Be Loyal, Let Us Be Truthful, Let Us Love One Another.

And no garden is complete without turnips: Turn Up for Church, Turn Up With a Smile, Turn Up With Determination.

A garden like that is bound to make anyone thirsty! Spread the good news!

JANUARY 21

THE CHOICE IS YOURS!

But blessed is the man who trusts in the Lord, whose confidence is in him. Jeremiah 17:7, NIV.

What is the "good news" of being a Christian? I think it means knowing that Jesus is real, that He truly cares about every single one of us, no matter who we are, where we're from, or what we're doing with our lives. It means that Christians are free from fear of the future. It means having the promise and hope of heaven.

What makes you scared about growing up? Among studies done of college students in America's largest universities, it was found that fear of nuclear war dominated the thoughts of many. Among other things, the students voiced despair about life itself. All it would take to wipe them off the earth would be "the bomb," many mentioned. And then—? Nothing. They had no hope of another life, as we do.

On the contrary, Adventist college students, when asked if they feared a nuclear war, said they rarely thought about it. One student said, "If things got that bad, I'd know the end of the world was near, and I'd start looking in the east for that little black cloud. I'd be rejoicing!"

If you were raised in a loving, Adventist home, you have received a priceless gift from your parents. Don't throw it away. Don't let yourself become blind to how much hope and happiness your parents have given

26

you. Don't let yourself become so obsessed with having fun that you risk losing your relationship with Jesus and eternal life. That would be as ridiculous as the strange custom of a certain African tribe that lived many years ago.

These people elected a new king from among themselves every seven years. Now, that doesn't sound so strange, does it? And while the king was ruling over the tribe, all of his relatives were given anything their hearts desired, and they lived as luxuriously as was possible—for seven years. But then, after his seven years of rule were up, the king was killed.

The strange thing is that even though they knew that death followed the honor of kingship, each man of the tribe tried to beat out the others to be the next king!

Would you be eager for that job? But do you also, by thinking only of today and the fun you can have, live with no thought for tomorrow? And wouldn't it make you afraid to face the future, knowing that you had thrown your hope away?

When you have to make a choice and you don't make it, you have still made a choice. Make a choice to love the man Jesus, who is coming to take you out of this world. God loves you. You deserve to live without fear.

IT JUST ISN'T FAIR!

Let us not become weary in doing good, for at the proper time we will reap a harvest if we do not give up. Galatians 6:9, NIV.

"It just isn't fair!" Have you said that recently? Most everyone feels that way at one time or another. And for Alaska state trooper Frank Johnson, it really wasn't fair!

It happened on a beautiful sunny day at an amusement park in Anchorage, Alaska. As a special feature, the amusement park had arranged for the appearance of a caged, 300-pound lioness named Cleo. She was a beautiful animal and seemed docile enough. But when 11-year-old Elizabeth Lee reached into the lion's cage, Cleo seized Elizabeth's arm in her teeth. Terrified screams shattered the party atmosphere of the park as horrified onlookers shouted for help.

Alaska state trooper Frank Johnson raced to the rescue, grabbed the girl's body in his arms to prevent her from being pulled inside the cage, and with deadly accuracy, he took aim and shot the lion in the head. The lion fell dead. In the same instant, both Johnson and the girl fell backward onto the sidewalk as her arm was suddenly released. Trooper Johnson's gun accidentally went off as he fell, and the girl was wounded in the thigh.

Elizabeth's parents were grateful at the time. But after Elizabeth recovered, they filed a $65,000 damage suit against the trooper, the amusement park, and the state of Alaska because their daughter had been hurt.

If you were on the jury, what would you decide?

The jury decided that the amusement park should pay Elizabeth $15,000 in damages because the cage was inadequately guarded. But it rejected the rest of Elizabeth's claim.

Perhaps you've always been told that it feels good to be kind to others. It usually does, but not always. For not everyone is grateful for well-doing. God understands us so well that He knows unappreciative people might make us bitter or simply afraid to do nice things because we don't want to be rebuffed. So He put a verse in the Bible that says, "Be not weary of well-doing." In other words, we must be careful that we don't stop being kind or doing good to others just because some people don't appreciate it. Angry men and women turned on Jesus, too, even as He gave the ultimate gift.

Next time someone doesn't appreciate your sacrifices, perhaps you can whisper a prayer and let Jesus know that you understand a little bit better how He feels when His gift of eternal life is unappreciated or unaccepted. But whatever you do, don't give up being kind.

JANUARY 23

MAKE IT A GREAT DAY!

This is the day the Lord has made; let us rejoice and be glad in it. Psalm 118:24, NIV.

Are you afraid to die? Why?

As a nurse, I have seen quite a few people die, and the actual process of dying seems quite peaceful. As I watched, my patients' eyes closed as though they were going to sleep, and then they took longer and longer pauses between breaths. Sometimes a long sigh came before a last breath. Finally they breathed no more. They were dead.

One dear old lady I cared for was waiting on a stretcher in the hall of the hospital on a particularly busy night. As we bustled about, preparing a room for her, she asked if the head of the stretcher could be raised a little so she would be sitting up more. I made her more comfortable, and told her it would be just another minute or two till her room was ready. She smiled at me and closed her eyes.

Five minutes later I went back to her and told her we would take her to her room, but she didn't respond. She was dead.

So I don't think it hurts to die. Illness causes pain. In a violent death, the stab or gunshot causes pain. But even that hurts only for a short time before a person passes out.

I think the worst thing about dying is being afraid of it. We don't want to die, because we don't want to miss out on anything here on earth. The death of a much-loved friend or family member causes a terrible sense of loss. Kids want to grow up and enjoy the life God gives them. We want to contribute something before we die. That's good! That gives us something to live for! It should also make us cherish each day and each moment within each day.

Don't waste today. Tell your family you love them. Do it now. And then expand your circle of kindness to those you meet today. As the poet Stephen Grellet wrote, "I shall pass through this world but once. If, therefore, there be any kindness I can show, or any good thing I can do, let me do it now. . . . For I shall not pass this way again." This life is special. Treasure it! And rest assured that after this life comes a life that's out of this world!

JANUARY 24

RISKY BUSINESS

Just as man is destined to die once, and after that to face judgment, so Christ was sacrificed once to take away the sins of many people; and he will appear a second time, not to bear sin, but to bring salvation to those who are waiting for him. Hebrews 9:27, 28, NIV.

Have you ever heard someone say that the Bible is a hoax, that there is no heaven and no God? Have you ever heard someone say that he doesn't believe in heaven because he hasn't seen it? Because no one has ever been there?

The process of dying and being resurrected to live in another world has been likened to the process of birth. Before you were born, you had no way of knowing what life would be like. Even if someone had set up microphones on top of your mother's tummy and explained how you would be born and grow up, you wouldn't have understood, would you? Because learning is like building blocks or chain links. As you learn more and more things, you begin to understand their similarities and link them together, or build on them. Unborn babies have nothing to compare life to, so they cannot understand.

Scientists believe that babies are startled at loud noises even before they are born, and that the process of being born is quite frightening. I would tend to agree, as I have heard babies' heartbeats quicken and even drop during labor and birth. I suppose that if babies could talk before they are born, they might say that they don't want to be born! They just want to stay put, right where they are.

Our next life out of this world will be even more fun and exciting than this one is—just like the baby discovers, after he is born, just how much more fun and love there is in this world than before birth. If he could talk, he might say that actually, life was rather boring before birth compared to what it is like now.

The bottom line is that whether or not the baby believes in life after birth, it still happens to him. And whether or not we believe in life after death, it still will happen to us. Everyone will see Jesus come. Those who didn't believe it would happen will be alive again for a short time and then be forever dead. But those who believed in heaven and accepted Jesus' gift will go on to live forever.

Which people are taking the biggest risk? Those who don't believe the Bible, or those who do? Decide for yourself.

JANUARY 25

IT'S A DOG'S LIFE!

You have put [man] in charge of everything you made; every-thing is put under his authority: all sheep and oxen, and wild animals too, the birds and fish, and all the life in the sea. Psalm 8:6-8, TLB.

Do you have a dog? Dogs make wonderful pets, don't they? They're always there when you need them, and they will do just about anything for a pat on the head. But for some reason, nobody wants to lead "a dog's life." Let's see what a dog's life is like.

Maybe your dog sleeps in your bed, but he probably doesn't. Does he have to sleep in the garage or outside? If he lives in the house, is he dependent upon you to take him outside to go to the bathroom? What if you're busy or tired or still asleep? Does he just have to wait? How would you like it if you had to sleep outside whether it was 90 degrees or 30 degrees? How would you like to be dependent upon someone putting a leash on your collar and taking you to the backyard before you go could to the bathroom?

But, you say, that's silly. The dog doesn't care. How do you know that he enjoys being dependent upon your remembering to feed him and give him fresh water? How do you know that he doesn't mind waiting to go outside until you are ready to take him?

Of course, animals don't reason like people do, and obviously these things don't worry a dog or cat like they would a person. On the other hand, animals don't have the same sense of right and wrong that people do. They do not have the conscience people have. But sometimes we forget that since we are not animals, we have the responsibility to control our natural impulses and stop ourselves from doing things that may be convenient or even good.

Like animals, we are a little like chemical robots. We get hungry when the chemical balance in our blood becomes low on sugar. Our muscles hurt when we have exercised them too much and produced too much of a chemical that makes them sore. Under the influence of chemicals called hormones, our hearts race and we feel a warm rush when a certain somebody we like looks at us.

Dogs and cats and elephants and mice mate when nature tells them to. Many animals feel devotion to each other, but their mating cycles are fixed by the times during the year when certain chemicals flow through their bodies. They have no choice.

Unlike animals, we don't have to be at the mercy of our hormones. We can make good choices and control ourselves. Lots of people may make your heart race just by giving you a smile or standing close. Someday you will choose just one of them to marry. That decision will be based on your age, your education, the amount of income you have, and the qualities you see in the young man or woman you have come to love.

Animals—dogs and cats, elephants and mice—are not promiscuous. They do not wander in and out of each other's beds just because it feels good. They mate when nature demands it, but they have no choice.

Acting on impulse or feeling is not much different than "leading a dog's life." You are one of God's children. You deserve much more than that.

THE MOST HOPELESS JOB THERE IS

You can see that I am not trying to please you by sweet talk and flattery; no, I am trying to please God. If I were still trying to please men I could not be Christ's servant. Galatians 1:10, TLB.

An ancient Persian humorist named Mullah Nasr-Ed-Din and his son were walking along a country road one evening behind the family donkey. The donkey, being in no hurry, was contentedly nibbling grass along the way.

Two men passed by them. Seeing Mullah and his son walking along, sweating profusely, one of them remarked to the other, "Look how foolish they are, walking instead of riding."

Hearing the remark, Mullah and his son climbed on the donkey and rode through the next village. As they passed through the marketplace, they heard an old man exclaim, "Look at those men on the donkey! They ought to be ashamed, making that poor old donkey carry the two of them."

Hearing the remark, Mullah got off of the donkey and walked while his son rode the donkey to the next village.

There Mullah heard someone whisper to another, "Poor old man! That boy should be ashamed, making his poor old dad walk!"

Mullah was ashamed as he thought of it. So he asked his son to get off of the donkey, and let him ride. The son walked beside him for some distance, till they came to another village. There, a villager made this observation: "Look at that old man riding, while his son has to walk. How cruel!"

Mullah rubbed his beard, shook his head, and said to himself, "You can't please all of the people all of the time."

To never offend anyone is the most hopeless job there is. As you grow up, you're bound to offend many people and, from time to time, many people will differ with you. But just because someone disagrees with you does not mean you are wrong or dumb. Jesus, the only perfect person who ever lived, displeased many people. But does that mean He was unlikable? Or wrong? Of course not!

If someone disagrees with you, be agreeable about your differences. Allow others their opinion and ask them to allow you the same. Consider their opinion, for it may have some value. But if it disagrees with your long-range goal of getting out of this world, drop it. For getting out of this world to live with Jesus is the most important decision you can make. Don't let anybody change your mind on that.

JANUARY 27

JUST WHEN YOU NEED IT MOST

Be strong and of good courage; be not frightened, neither be dismayed; for the Lord your God is with you wherever you go. Joshua 1:9, RSV.

Everything was wonderful about summer camp, except one thing. Scott was working toward an Honor in horsemanship, but he was having trouble with the hurdles. He couldn't muster up the courage to make his horse jump the fence like the other boys could.

The instructor tried to help. "Basically, you're a good horseman," he said, "but your horse senses your fear. When she approaches the jump, she feels your hesitation and doesn't want to put you in jeopardy, so she shies away from the hurdle or runs to the side. She's just doing what she thinks you want her to do."

Scott nodded, his head down, studying the toe of his shoe.

"Just keep trying, keep working on it. When you gain confidence in yourself she'll settle down and skim over the jumps. You'll see."

Scott nodded again. Inside, he felt like a sissy. All the other guys could do it, why couldn't he?

One afternoon he was practicing in the corral with his horse, Beauty, trying to talk confidence into himself. A lake lay on the other side of the fenced corral, and Scott waved at Doug, his best friend, trying out a kayak he'd made himself. Then Scott got back to the barrel racing he was working on.

A sudden, shrill scream arrested his attention. His attention jerked back to the lake, and he saw the tip of Doug's kayak nosing straight up into the sky. Doug was beating the water, trying to stay on top of it. "Help!" he screamed. "Scott, help me!"

Without a second thought, Scott pulled Beauty's head around. Pointing her head toward the fence, he signaled the horse to canter. Straight toward the fence they charged. Scott's mouth felt dry as dust. A thrill of fear shot through him. In his mind he could hear the teacher's voice: *Let Beauty pace herself. Keep the reins loose. Grip the saddle with your knees. Keep your heels down!*

All at once Scott's fear left him. The fence grew in size, but that no longer bothered him. Beauty faltered. "Don't fail me. Go, Beauty. Go!" he shouted.

The horse tucked up her legs and soared over the fence, then touched down on the opposite side and splashed into the water toward Doug.

Scott slipped off of Beauty's back and pulled Doug from the sinking kayak. "Hang on to Beauty's tail. She'll pull you in," he said, and Doug hung on.

As they sat beside the lake catching their breath, Doug said, "That was the most beautiful jump I've ever seen."

"Thanks," Scott said modestly. "I guess it makes a difference when you're doing it for a good reason."

Do the "last days" worry you as much as Scott's fence-jumping did him? Hold on to the promise that when you need extra strength, God will give it to you. He wants you with Him out of this world.

Adapted and reprinted by permission from Robert Kelly, *How Do I Make Up My Mind, Lord?* Copyright 1982, Augsburg Publishing House.

FINDING NEW DOORS

Wait for the Lord; be strong, and let your heart take courage; yea, wait for the Lord! Psalm 27:14, RSV.

Everything Gregg had worked for was snatched away from him in an instant. The doctor told him that he had an infection in his heart and while he recovered, he had to stay in bed. That meant he couldn't go to school, he couldn't play on the baseball team anymore, and he couldn't even ride his bike—for at least two months!

"I'm sorry, son," the doctor said gently, patting Gregg's shoulder.

His dad tried to be encouraging. "You're good enough at baseball that I'm sure you can be on the team next year!"

"Yeah, but what about this year? What will I do?"

At first, it wasn't so bad being sick. He almost enjoyed it. He slept until noon every day and when he awoke, his mother brought him his favorite foods on a wicker tray and let him watch TV while he ate. Then he'd sleep some more, have a milkshake in the afternoon, and watch TV until supper.

But after three weeks he was bored with doing nothing. And though he couldn't believe it himself, he was tired of milkshakes!

One afternoon when he awoke, his mother told him that his teacher had stopped by with some schoolbooks she thought he might enjoy reading. One book in particular, *The History of Transportation,* caught Gregg's eye. He read it through in the next couple days.

"Shall I get you some more?" his mother offered.

"No, I'm tired of reading. I want to do something," Gregg said, frustrated. And then he got an idea.

He explained his plans to his father that evening, and when his dad came home from work the next day, he brought several shoe-sized boxes with him, some glue, a pair of scissors, and a large sheet of plywood to serve as a lap desk. Gregg got right down to work.

His friends started visiting, sharing their plans for the upcoming science fair at school.

"I'm entering an exhibit too," Gregg told them proudly. But he wouldn't tell them what it was.

At last the six weeks were up, and Gregg was allowed to return to school. On the day of the science fair, his teacher announced to all the parents and students there that Gregg's display would be preserved permanently in a glass display case so future students could enjoy it too. His exhibit? A set of five model steam engines, showing the development of train travel.

"I'm proud of you, son," Gregg's dad said, squeezing his shoulder. "You couldn't play baseball, but you ended up doing something else with longer-lasting results. You had one door shut in your face, but you found another door and walked right through it."

Disappointment is a part of life. Often it is disappointment that keeps us growing. Don't view disappointment as an enemy. Rather, see it as a chance to explore new areas. Find the open doors—the other options —life has for you, too.

Adapted and reprinted by permission from Robert Kelly, *How Do I Make Up My Mind, Lord?* Copyright 1982, Augsburg Publishing House.

JANUARY 29

WHAT DO YOU LOSE WHEN YOU STEAL?

No temptation has overtaken you that is not common to man. God is faithful, and he will not let you be tempted beyond your strength. 1 Corinthians 10:13, RSV.

Locking his hands behind his head, Tim leaned back at his desk, closed his eyes, and imagined all he could do with $100.

The night before, he'd seen an announcement of a photography contest open to teenagers. The officials were looking for animal pictures, and offered $100 as first prize. Sunday morning Tim took the bus to the zoo and spent the morning snapping pictures. He got a good shot of a lion yawning, then wandered over to the giraffes and caught the mother giraffe licking her baby. Soon he'd used up his roll of film.

As he sat on a bench to reload his camera, his foot bumped against a roll of black-and-white film that somebody had dropped. Tim felt sorry for the person who had lost it. He knew he'd be upset if it were him! With a shrug, he slipped the film in his pocket and resumed taking pictures.

That night Tim developed his pictures. He was pleased with what he had taken. Then he remembered the other roll of film, and decided to develop that one, too, to see what was on it.

He let out a slow, admiring breath as the pictures came out. One especially, of a tiger splashing in the pool, had intriguing contrasts of light and dark and shadows. It would be a winner, Tim was sure. He laid it out to dry and filled out the entry blank for the contest. Then, in spite of his conscience, he slipped the tiger picture into the contest envelope. He wanted that $100 so badly, he would do anything to get it.

He then went upstairs to show his other pictures to his brother, Mark. Mark was busy with pictures he had taken for his own project. He was working on a poster for science class. The other kids had drawn pictures for their posters, but Mark had asked if he could use some pictures he had taken, instead. The teacher agreed, since it would still be his original work.

The next morning Tim was surprised to see his picture of the mother giraffe and her baby on Mark's poster!

"Hey, that's my picture!" he scolded Mark sharply.

Mark grinned sheepishly. "I didn't think you'd mind," he said. "I needed wild animals for my poster, but didn't have any. Since you're my brother and all, I thought it would be OK."

"It's not OK," Tim said firmly. "Passing off my work as your own is dishonest!" He snatched the picture off of Mark's poster, turned, and marched back to his room, falling wearily onto his bed. Why did it bother him so much that Mark was using his picture as his own? Could it be his guilty conscience? He realized he had begun worrying about his own dishonesty.

Quickly and carefully, he opened the contest envelope, removed the tiger picture, and inserted the giraffe picture. He felt better instantly. And as he dropped the envelope into the mailbox on the corner, he smiled to himself. He had regained his integrity. It was a feeling that was out of this world.

Adapted and reprinted by permission from Robert Kelly, *How Do I Make Up My Mind, Lord?* Copyright 1982, Augsburg Publishing House.

JANUARY 30

BIG IDEAS AREN'T ENOUGH

For God sent not his Son into the world to condemn the world; but that the world through him might be saved. John 3:17.

The fable is told of a miller who discovered an old abandoned mill that had not been used for 100 years. He thought the place would be perfect for his work of grinding corn and wheat into flour.

But alas, he soon discovered the place was overrun with mice! Hundreds and hundreds of the little gray creatures scampered over his bags of grain during the night, nibbling holes and scattering the grain all over the floor. They were a nuisance!

So the miller bought himself a cat. A great big orange tomcat who soon began feasting on the little gray mice. He became even bigger and plumper, and the mouse families became more and more distressed that their home had become such a dangerous place to live. They called a meeting one night to decide what they should do about the cat.

Several good suggestions were offered. "We should tie a bell to his neck!" one little mouse suggested. "A great big brass bell."

"With a blue ribbon!" suggested another. They all laughed and cheered at their suggestions, and big plans were made for the cat's bell and how it would aid them in the future.

Finally, the littlest mouse twitched his whiskers and asked in a teeny, squeaky voice, "You all have such excellent ideas. But tell me. Who is going to tie the bell on the cat?"

There was immediate silence. Nobody volunteered.

A similar discussion took place a long, long time ago in a place not of this world. The whole universe discussed the menace of Satan on this earth. Somebody had to do something. Somebody had to "hang the bell" around Satan's neck at the risk of his own life. Somebody had to sound out a warning. And Jesus said, "I will go." He did it for you because you are special.

Don't let His gift be wasted. Instead, when you hear that bell in your conscience ringing, run fast, away from Satan.

JANUARY 31

THE TINY LITTLE HOUSE

When the Roman officer standing beside his cross saw how he dismissed his spirit, he exclaimed, "Truly, this was the Son of God!" Mark 15:39, TLB.

The story is told of a poor man who had many troubles. So he went to the home of a wise man in town who gave out good advice.

"Please help me," the poor man pleaded. "My house is too small. My wife and I and our six children do not have enough room, we bump into each other and have no privacy, and the house is so hard to keep clean! What shall we do?"

The wise man thought for a moment. "How many animals do you have in your barn?" he asked, scratching his head.

"One cow, a horse, two pigs, and three chickens."

"Very well. Bring all the animals into the house with you."

The poor man was surprised. But he went home and did as he was told.

The next day he returned. "That will not work," he cried. "The animals have turned the house into a barn! They've eaten all our food, and we have had to eat standing up. They are into everything! My wife can't do her work with them in the way."

"Very well. Then take the animals back to the barn," the wise man told him.

The poor man went home and put the animals back in the barn. The next day he returned once again, smiling. "With the animals gone it is so peaceful and so much easier to keep the place clean!" he said. "Thank you for all your help. I wish I were as wise and as clever as you are."

And the wise man only nodded sagely.

A foolish story, you say? Perhaps. But how often do we complain about what we have? And only when it is gone do we appreciate it. While Jesus was dying on the cross, a Roman soldier murmured, "Surely this was the Son of God." But it was too late to undo Jesus' pain or take it away.

Look around you at all you have—your family, your religious freedom, food, friends. Cherish each one as though it was about to be taken from you.

Would you spend your last day on earth praying? Would you waste energy being mad at someone? Would you cheat on a test or use dirty words?

Treat others today as if it were your last day on earth, as if it was their last day on earth. Show appreciation to someone right now.

More important, make a choice to believe that Jesus Christ is the Son of God.

FEBRUARY 1

THE LION'S FRIEND

Give generously, for your gifts will return to you later. Ecclesiastes 11:1, TLB.

There's a famous story about Androcles, a good man who lived more than 1,000 years ago. Unfortunately, a jealous person lied about him, so he was forced to leave his home and wander in the forest with the animals.

Androcles took his sentence bravely. To him, honesty was always of prime importance, no matter what it might bring.

One day he heard the distant roaring of a lion. He held very still, so as to learn which direction the lion was going. But the roaring didn't change directions. And as Androcles listened to the roar a bit longer, it sounded more like the roar of an injured animal than an angry one.

Androcles crept up closer, until he could see the lion through the underbrush. Sure enough, the massive lion was injured. His thick mane fell forward and backward as he licked a wounded paw. From time to time he threw his head back and uttered an earth-shaking roar.

Androcles wanted to help. Seeing the foam that dripped from the lion's jaw, he hurried to the nearest stream and returned with some water in his hat. Slowly he inched toward the lion, holding the hat in front of him. Quickly placing it on the ground so the lion could drink, he hurried away. The lion drank thirstily amid roars of gratefulness.

For several days Androcles befriended the lion, bringing him food and water, until finally it allowed him to inspect the paw. Androcles saw the source of the infection—a deeply embedded thorn—and removed it.

In time, Androcles went home and forgot the lion. But it was about this time that Christians were being rounded up and thrown to lions in the Roman coliseum for the amusement of the people. Androcles was captured and taken to Rome.

After imprisonment, Androcles was sent to the coliseum. He stood bravely on the dirt floor of the vast clearing, hearing the hungry roar of the lions. The crowd was restless with excitement. Finally the massive doors to the lions' den were opened, and the lions came bounding out. Androcles stood firm, praying, as a mighty lion ran toward him.

Suddenly the lion stopped and roared. And then he crept toward Androcles and licked his outstretched hand. Androcles saw a scar on the lion's paw. It was the lion he had befriended in the forest.

The "games" were called off for that day, and the Christians were released. Nobody in the crowd could understand Androcles' power over the lion—except Androcles. What was that power? The power of kindness. Why don't you tame a few "lions" today too?

POSITIVELY CHRISTIAN!

For I am not ashamed of this Good News about Christ. It is God's powerful method of bringing all who believe it to heaven. This message was preached first to the Jews alone, but now everyone is invited to come to God in this same way. Romans 1:16, TLB.

Several years ago the state of Oregon was flourishing with tourists and visitors to its beaches. Each of these people was spending money in Oregon, but some stayed and found jobs there. Then someone decided Oregon was growing too fast. The governor asked for negative advertising to discourage people from coming to Oregon.

He got it. Soon bumper stickers were everywhere, proclaiming "Oregonians have webbed feet." "Oregonians don't grow old; they rust." "Oregon: a great place to visit. But please don't stay."

The negative advertising worked. Tourists felt unwelcome and Oregonians became known as being selfish and unfriendly.

In time, a new governor was elected. He had a concern for his state and began a positive campaign in an effort to reverse the negative one.

"Positively Oregon" is the newest slogan. They are trying to get the word out that Oregon is a great state to visit and to live in. But unfortunately, bad news travels faster than good news, and it's going to take a long time to change the bad advertising that went on for so long.

Sometimes we do that to Christianity, too.

Cindy worked in a fast-food restaurant one summer, the only Adventist there. Many of her coworkers soon became friends, and they learned that she was a vegetarian and went to church on Saturday, didn't go to movies, or dances, or bars.

At first they'd say things like "You can't eat meat, can you, so I guess you don't want to share the pizza" or "I'm sorry you can't go to lunch with us on Saturday because you have to go to church."

Cindy patiently explained that no one was putting pressure on her about anything.

After a few weeks some of her friends confided in her that they thought she was lucky. "I hate dances," one said. "They give me headaches. And besides, there's usually a gang of creeps that won't leave me alone, breathing stale air into my face."

"My girlfriend got pregnant after a dance," one girl said ruefully. "The music and sexy movements kind of made her lose her mind, and she and a couple guys danced out of the party into the bushes. She'll probably never finish high school."

Soon the girls started asking Cindy for bites of her vegetarian food. Before too long, one of her friends told her that she'd talked her mom into buying Big Franks rather than meat hot dogs, and the whole family preferred them!

Cindy was happy, because while she was sure she wasn't always the best example, she felt that most of the time she had shown them she was postively Christian instead of negatively Christian.

What about you? Do you give the impression that you are a reluctant Christian? Be a positive one! Let's make the other people just a little bit envious of what we have. It'll reel them in!

FEBRUARY 3

THE TWO SOAPS

For whoever exalts himself will be humbled, and whoever humbles himself will be exalted. Matthew 23:12, NIV.

This is an allegory about two soaps. The first cake of soap was very beautiful. It was purchased at a fine store, where it rested on a bed of white tissue inside a beautifully decorated box. It was shaped like a rose, was rose-scented, and even had a picture of a rose embedded in it! It was the kind of soap you would bring out for company to admire—but never to use!

And so this fine cake of soap was purchased as a gift of love for someone's mother.

As was expected, the mother loved it. And she placed it gently in an exquisite pearl-glazed soap dish on a stand, for decoration only—it was never to be used! Instead, the mother bought a plain white cake of soap and placed it by the sink for daily use.

The beautiful rose soap watched the family's activities quietly as they came into the room to wash their hands, always reaching for the plain white bar of soap. Sometimes she shuddered inwardly when she saw the brown, grimy suds that occasionally remained on the bar. When the mother saw them, she rinsed the soap well until it was clean again, and the rose-colored soap smiled smugly to herself as she saw the white bar of soap slowly shrinking. "I am still perfect," she said to herself, preening in the mirror.

One day she could contain herself no longer. In the silence of the night, she spoke to the white bar of soap. "They're using you up," she warned ominously.

The white bar of soap laughed. "I was made to be used," she said happily. "In time I will be worn away, but in losing myself, I will have made this home a cleaner, fresher, more fragrant and pleasant place to be.

"In time I will be gone; but so will you. It's inevitable. You will be tucked away in the attic, beautiful but alone. A sad way to go, I might say. Your silent beauty is your greatest enemy."

Which soap would you rather be? The one whose only reason for existence was to make things better, or the one whose only reason for existence was to sit arrogantly in a corner and look beautiful? God wants us to be used up—to share ourselves with others and make everyone around us feel cleaner, fresher, and more pleasant than before. That's the way it's going to be, out of this world.

FEBRUARY 4

STICKS AND STONES CAN BREAK YOU

But if any of you causes one of these little ones who trusts in me to lose his faith, it would be better for you to have a rock tied to your neck and be thrown into the sea. Matthew 18:6, TLB.

As little kids, most of us have said, Sticks and stones may break my bones, but words can never harm me. I said it often to boost my spirits. We were overseas at the time. Americans were disliked, and many of the people took out their anger on us. But even as I said the jingle, I wondered why it didn't really make me feel better. Words still harmed me. They made me feel awful.

The fact is, words can harm us. Words can cut like a knife. They can separate friends or families forever. It is better to bite your tongue and just think your anger than to actually say it and regret it later.

If you have younger brothers or sisters, your words have a stronger impact on them than their words have on you. Do you find yourself putting your brother or sister down a lot? Do you call them names? Do you laugh at them critically?

They may hide their hurt, but everything you tell them about themselves is recorded on their brains. For example, if you have told your sister over and over, "You're so stupid," she will begin to tell herself, "I'm stupid . . . I'm stupid." And soon she will believe it. After all, her big brother (or sister) told her so, and he knows more than she does!

Right now you might be saying, "Well, she is stupid." Is she, really? If so, do you want to make things worse? Will it help to tell your friends she is stupid, and have them think of you as "the kid with the stupid sister"?

The more she thinks of herself as stupid, the more stupid she'll act, until you'll really be sorry you ever started saying it.

Do yourself a favor. Find out just how powerful words really are. Grant your sister the qualities you would like her to have, just by telling her good things about herself. Tell her she's neat. Tell her you are glad she doesn't hog your friends when they come over. Tell her you like being with her, and maybe that will make her leave you alone!

Put yourself in her shoes and treat her as you would like to be treated if you were the little sister. Someone has said, "Resolve to be tender with the young, compassionate with the aged, sympathetic with the striving, and tolerant of the weak and the wrong. Sometime in life you will have been all of these."

FEBRUARY 5

WHAT WOULD YOUR SLOGAN BE?

And there is not a single man in all the earth who is always good and never sins. Ecclesiastes 7:20, TLB.

What Bible verse can you think of that best describes you and your friends? Could it be "God loveth a cheerful giver," referring to the time and energy you put into your friendships and into God's work? Or do you have such problems in your life right now that if God had to choose a verse for you, He might choose "Jesus wept"? If so, do you think God can still love you? Do you think you can change?

The Bible is filled with stories of great people whom Jesus loved. Many of these people did foolish things. But because God doesn't hide things from us, He has chosen to include the good and the bad of these great people. I think He did it to encourage me and you when we do something stupid.

When you hear about "David the shepherd boy," what is the first thing you think about? What about "King David"? Jesus spoke of King

David as "a man after his own heart." Jesus identified with David. He was proud of him. David did many foolish things, yet God loved him.

Peter, the disciple, had a name that meant "the rock." He was one of Jesus' closest friends. Yet he betrayed Jesus.

Noah was a great man. He was the only man whom God could trust before the Flood. God saved Noah. But after the Flood, Noah became drunk and sinned. Yet God still loved him.

God could have kept these stories out of the Bible. He could have led us to believe that He loves only perfect people. But I think He deliberately allowed these stories to be included because He wants to give us courage. He wants to show that He doesn't love us because we are good, but because He is good.

After all these years of watching people on this earth, God is not shocked by anything we do. He knows what our struggles are like. He knows that when we do wrong it hurts us terribly. It may hurt others terribly, too. And so God warns us to stay away from sin so we won't get hurt and so we won't hurt others.

Maybe your life has been summed up in our verse for today. Maybe Jesus and your parents have wept over you. Do you know why? Because they love you. Don't make them keep on crying. Do yourself a favor and do what's right. God has never stopped loving you. His love is out of this world!

FEBRUARY 6

WHAT HEATHENS CAN TEACH US

About three o'clock, Jesus shouted, "Eli, Eli, lama sabachthani," which means, "My God, my God, why have you forsaken me?" Matthew 27:46, TLB.

One of the pleasures of life is to travel to other countries and see how other people live. Each country has certain foods that everyone eats, certain things they do for entertainment that are unique to their culture, and so on. Since my parents were missionaries from the time I was a baby till I was 16 years old, I had the opportunity of seeing how people are different, and yet the same, all around the world.

Even though some of the things other cultures do seem strange to us, we can learn from each other. One thing in particular that I have learned from the heathen countries is how much they reverence and obey their gods. They do not worship God as we do. Rather, they worship the things God has created. Some call their gods "the god of the wind," "the god of the sea," "the god of the rain," "the god of the sun," and so forth.

And they respect these gods. They are faithful in burning incense before their home altars every day and saying their prayers, expressing

43

their devotion to their gods. They don't question or get angry at their gods like we sometimes do. For example, when a child gets sick and dies, or when a monsoon storm comes and destroys their crops, they don't ask "Why would the gods do this to me?" They take it as a warning that they must be more faithful in their worship. "I must do more for my god to please him," they say. And they do it.

Have you had a personal tragedy? Did it make you resolve to be more faithful in your worship so that God could bring a blessing out of your trouble, or did you get angry at God and swear not to trust Him again?

As I have thought about tragedy I have come to this conclusion. God has warned us that near the end of the world the angels will not be able to "hold back the winds of strife." More and more disasters will happen. People's hearts will "fail them for fear." We may not be able to find a reason for each tragedy that happens, except this one: maybe the battle is almost over. Maybe God's restraining hand is being lifted from the earth. Maybe we should spend time filling our minds with God's promises instead of whining, "Why?" God doesn't always answer questions that begin with why. He didn't even give Jesus an answer when he asked, "Why?"

Satan's world is on "self destruct," spinning toward the end, like water draining from the tub. We've been warned. We've also been promised God's protection.

Thank God we have the promise that this world won't last forever; someday soon God will take us out of this world. Believe it.

FEBRUARY 7

A GEM OF AN IDEA

When you are arrested, don't worry about what to say at your trial, for you will be given the right words at the right time. Matthew 10:19, TLB.

What on earth are you doing for heaven's sake? What do you think is the most useful or important thing to do to get ready for heaven? Can you do it today?

Two things that I think will help us get through the time of trouble are learning to accept what comes to us without getting angry at God, and believing that God is real. Those two attitudes lead to the very most important preparation we can make—loving and trusting God without question.

This well-known parable bears repeating:

A man was out walking in the desert when a voice said to him, "Pick up some pebbles and put them in your pocket, and tomorrow you will be both sorry and glad."

The man obeyed. He stooped down and picked up a handful of pebbles and put them in his pocket. The next morning he reached into his pocket and found diamonds and rubies and emeralds. And he was both glad and sorry. Glad that he had taken some—sorry that he hadn't taken more.

We can learn something from that parable about religious education. Learn all you can about God now. Load up the computer in your mind for the time when that may be the only "Bible" you have.

How do you "load up your computer"? By deciding what you like best about each Bible story you've learned. How has it made you believe in God more? How has it made you appreciate His love and forgiveness? Before you go to sleep tonight, find a Bible promise that meets a specific need you may have. Memorize it. That's how you collect gems and make the Bible really special.

Write your own Bible. Read a Bible verse and write it down in your own words. That will make the words stick in your mind. By taking the Bible apart and making it a personal book of promises, you guarantee a collection of priceless gems. And someday you will be more glad than sorry about the preparations you have made today.

Jesus is coming, ready or not!

FEBRUARY 8

FACT OR FANTASY?

"You will not surely die," the serpent said to the woman. "For God knows that when you eat of it your eyes will be opened, and you will be like God, knowing good and evil." Genesis 3:4, 5, NIV.

It made a good story, and Kara repeated it without a thought. After all, she got it from Jenny, and a friend of Jenny's mom had known their teacher, Mrs. June Hendricks, back in college when she was June Applewood. This friend's mom said that wild June Applewood had spent some time in jail. If the story had stayed in the eighth-grade classroom, it wouldn't have made much difference, but Jeri Jones told her dad, and he marched right to the principal and demanded to know what kind of person was teaching his daughter.

The principal went to Mrs. Hendricks, who responded with a puzzled shake of her head. Then she began to laugh. "I took a sociology class in college, and while working on a special project I spent several weekends with the local police department, including a night in jail. Could *that* be what someone is thinking about?"

You will remember that Satan told Eve if she ate from the tree of life she would be as God, knowing good and evil. Unfortunately, just as people have done ever since then, Satan mixed just enough truth with his lie so that Eve believed him. The temptation to be like God—to know both good and evil—was too much, and Eve ate the fruit.

Unfortunately, tragically, Satan told the truth. For Adam and Eve, who had known nothing but beauty, trust, and love, became very well acquainted with evil. It began with the chill of guilt, and they hid themselves from their loving heavenly Father instead of welcoming Him when He came for His evening visit.

Their intimate knowledge of evil continued as thorns tore at their flesh, and large animals, former friends in the garden, hid from them in suspicion and fear. As the years passed, their knowledge of evil continued to broaden, reaching a terrible peak when their firstborn son killed his brother and buried his lifeless body in the ground.

And we, the children of Eve and Adam, still suffer with the firsthand knowledge of evil. Sin hurts. Grandparents die, and babies, and friends. Day after day we experience the terrible knowledge of evil. We see it in vivid color on the evening news. We see it in our lives and in the homes of our friends. Alcoholism, drug addiction, divorce, lies, angry words—the lives of families and friends are living proof that Satan told the truth when he said that Eve would be like God, knowing good and evil.

But it's not going to last forever. Someday Satan will tell his last lie. Someday the last person will be hurt, the last tear shed. For Jesus is coming and will put an end to evil forever! He's going to take us out of this world.

FEBRUARY 9

A FRIEND IS FOR DOING NOTHING TOGETHER

As water reflects a face, so a man's heart reflects the man. Proverbs 27:19, NIV.

When Betty filled out a college dorm questionnaire, asking her what she wanted in a roommate, her mother had to laugh. Betty indicated that she didn't care what kind of music the girl listened to, "just so she doesn't play it too loud," and, she wrote, "I can sleep even if her light is on, or sit outside in the hall to study if she wants to sleep. The only thing I ask is that she be reasonably neat."

Reasonably neat. Mom put down the paper with a smile. Betty, who had never cleaned her room without great pressure in her whole 18 years, was asking for a roommate who was "reasonably neat." Maybe there was some hope for her yet.

It's human nature to expect more from others than we expect from ourselves. We sort of spoil ourselves by giving ourselves excuses when we don't measure up to what we would like. "I was born that way," we say, or "I've had a rough life," or "Nobody understands me." Unfortunately, when we don't demand much of ourselves, we lose.

One of the most important friendships you will ever make will be with the person you eventually marry. All people wonder before marriage how they can be sure they're choosing the right person. The best rule of thumb is to marry your "best friend." A test of friendship is this: If you find you can't be with someone unless you're doing something together —skiing, going to a restaurant, watching TV (in other words, a third thing to which you both direct your attention)—then that person may not be as good a friend as you think.

The real test of friendship is this: Can you literally do nothing with the other person? Can you enjoy together those moments of life that are utterly simple? That is the kind of friendship that can last a lifetime. Marriages based only on physical attraction and physical intimacy soon die. Probably because physical intimacy is just a small portion of "forever." And if that is the only glue to hold you together, it's just not strong enough.

Perhaps you have a friend who says he wants to marry a girl who has "saved herself" for marriage, but he doesn't save himself. That isn't really fair, is it? And he'll probably find that the girls with high standards and a good self-image will have nothing to do with him. Become the kind of person you would most like to marry. That is, if you want to marry a girl or a guy who is a Christian, who is not promiscuous, who is educated, and who is kind, then be that kind of person yourself. You'll find you attract the kind of person you would like to spend forever with. And when that happens, it's out of this world.

FEBRUARY 10

THE GREATEST PLACE IN THE UNIVERSE

Now we see but a poor reflection as in a mirror; then we shall see face to face. Now I know in part; then I shall know fully, even as I am fully known. 1 Corinthians 13:12, NIV.

I visited Disney World recently with my family, and we had the good time we expected to have. While we were waiting in line my brother remarked, "I think this is what heaven will be like—marching bands and parades and all kinds of thrilling things to see, but we won't have to stand in line!"

What do you think? Does that kind of heaven sound exciting to you? We usually think of heaven as more of a quiet place, don't we, with beautiful, smiling people in long white robes gliding past each other as they strum their harps. There may be some of that, but I think there will also be more active things we can participate in.

At camp meeting a few years ago, Elder Morris Venden presented the Sabbath sermon. His topic was about God and heaven. One thing in particular that struck me was his suggestion that God is a sensuous God. He went on to say that in heaven our senses will be more heightened than they are now. Imagine your sense of smell being stronger, the flowers sweeter, spices more pungent. Imagine your sight being improved a thousand times more than it is! Your sense of touch more acute. If rabbits and kittens feel soft down here, how much more wonderful are they going to feel in heaven? I wonder.

Perhaps our senses have sort of "faded" because of sin, like trying to look through a smoky glass. But in heaven the glass will be "clean" and our senses will be alive! Heaven will be a fun place!

As I listened to Elder Venden, I remembered how I used to pray that God would postpone His coming until I got married and had babies. I wanted to experience both the pleasures intended for us down here and those I would have in heaven. But marriage and parenthood haven't always been the bed of roses I'd been promised they would be. Along with the pleasures come heavy responsibilities. And with the good times come exhaustion, frustration, and moments of despair. At their best moments, marriage and parenthood are probably very close to the joy we will experience in heaven. But that's the key point. Close friendships, marriage, parenthood, are only substitutes for the joys of heaven. Heaven itself is better!

It's normal for juniors and teens to want to postpone Jesus' coming until they grow up and, perhaps, marry. But no matter when Jesus comes, heaven will be full of wonderful things that we cannot even imagine. Friendships will be deeper and will last forever. In heaven those you love will never leave you or betray you—guaranteed!

I can't wait to get out of this world to experience it, can you?

FEBRUARY 11

NEW AND IMPROVED RELIGION

I the Lord do not change. Malachi 3:6, NIV.

Two advertising agency writers passed each other in the hall. "Hi!" one said to the other. "What's new and improved?"

Nothing seems to stay the same, does it? You may have bought the same kind of peanut butter for years, and then one day you see a label on it that says "New and Improved!" You buy it, wondering how they can possibly improve on it. Your first bite tells you that they haven't. It's still the same peanut butter in a new label.

People are always looking for something new. It happens in religion sometimes, too. Someone tells you, "Join my church. It's new and improved." So maybe you join, and maybe the customs are a little bit different. Maybe they use guitars for song service instead of a piano. Maybe they raise their hands to the ceiling when they pray. Maybe they hug everyone who comes through their doors. And if that's what you go to church for, you'll probably like it. But "new and improved"? If they're teaching the Bible, it hardly seems possible. Because the Bible is a constant. Through the centuries the Bible has told us, "God loves you." The Bible has always said the seventh day is the Sabbath. The Bible has always asked us to love one another. The Bible is our guide, no matter what anyone says.

Many churches teach a "new and improved" religion. Just give the Lord an hour of your time on Sunday morning, and the rest of the day is yours! "New and improved!"

A friend of mine arranged for her Sunday school class to visit my church as part of their comparative religions class. When the teenagers moaned about having to attend church twice in one week—on Saturday and Sunday—she assured them they wouldn't have to attend church on Sunday that week because they would already have worshiped God on Saturday, and once a week is enough. "New and improved."

Someday you may face the temptation to toss aside your Adventist religion and take up a "new and improved" way of worship for the fast pace of life. Be careful. Those three words, *new and improved,* are more often than not a cunning way to deceive you, to make you feel you will miss out on something incredible if you don't try the product. But how can you improve on God's word?

Why should you want to?

FEBRUARY 12

WHAT YOU LOSE WHEN YOU DON'T SMILE

Your own soul is nourished when you are kind. Proverbs 11:17, TLB.

Strange as it may seem, there are many people who perhaps unknowingly send the message "I don't want you to care about me," when inside they desperately long for friendship. It's easy to do. For when a kid is insecure and afraid to reach out to people, he often comes across as snobbish or stuck-up. Melinda, age 11, longed for friends but didn't know how to make them. One day as she sat on the playground slide, several other sixth-grade girls came over and asked her to swing with

49

them. "I didn't do it, though," Melinda told her mother that evening. "I didn't want them to think, *Poor Melinda, she didn't have anyone to play with* so I just didn't go!"

What are some ways we make others think we don't want to be friendly? Scowling at them. Not looking them in the eye. Ignoring them. Looking away when they try to speak. Making fun of them. Sometimes we may seem unfriendly, but we don't really intend to be. Maybe we are thinking about a problem and aren't even aware that we're frowning, or ignoring others. If that happens occasionally, but we're generally known to be friendly, the person we're passing usually breaks into our thoughts with a cheery hello of his own. But maybe you're shy. If so, just smile — at the school principal, the school cutup, and even the senior class president.

It's important to be friendly. It not only makes us happier, but also lightens the loads of everyone we meet! And it's really not hard. Everybody wants to be liked, and just about everybody returns a smile.

Benjamin Franklin said, "When you are good to others you are best to yourself." Try it!

FEBRUARY 13

HOW MANY PEOPLE LOVE YOU?

When a man is gloomy, everything seems to go wrong; when he is cheerful, everything seems right! Proverbs 15:15, TLB.

Sixteen-year-old Wendy was feeling blue, and had been for days. School was rough. She was having problems with her math teacher, and even her folks couldn't understand her. At least she didn't think they did. She was too smart to run away from home, but she was wishing she could just get away from it all when she received a bouquet of carnations. She buried her face in their spicy petals and saw a card. It read only, "Someone who loves you." No name.

Being a teenage girl, her first thoughts were of the guys in her life — old classmates, one or two special guys? Or could it be Mom and Dad? Maybe Grandma? She mentally ran down the list of people who she knew cared about her. Finally she called a girlfriend to help her go over the possibilities again. Something the friend said turned on a little light in her mind. "Janet, did you send the flowers?" Wendy asked.

There was silence on the other end of the telephone. "Well?" Wendy demanded. Janet giggled. "Yes. I'm afraid so."

"Why?"

"Because you sounded so blue the last time we talked, I wanted you to spend the day thinking about all the people who love you."

Sometimes it's easier to think about all the things that are going wrong in our lives, than about the things that are going right, isn't it? But if we stop for a moment and think about all the blessings we have, it may make our problems shrink a little in size.

Can you name three people who love you? People who really care about you, and with whom you can share both your joys and troubles? That's the average number of close friends that most people have. Maybe you consider your mom one of your best friends. Maybe your list of best friends will include a special cousin, an understanding uncle, or roommate. Whoever they are, write down their names on a piece of paper.

Now on the same piece of paper, list three things that have happened, or that you are looking forward to happening—three things you will do today that make you happy. The list will be different for everybody, but it might include having tacos for lunch, finally taking—and passing—your biology test, getting a haircut, listening to tapes, sunbathing, or any three of the thousands of different things that can make us happy. Tuck that piece of paper into your assignment book today, and when the pressure starts to build, read it to yourself. Start counting blessings, not blahs. It's good practice for what we will do in heaven—out of this world.

FEBRUARY 14

PRICELESS TREASURES

Only a fool despises his father's advice; a wise son considers each suggestion. Proverbs 15:5, TLB.

Do you have any idea what it's like to be a parent? Perhaps you've seen home movies or snapshots of yourself as a baby, your young parents smiling proudly as they held you close. Later the pictures show you growing up. There's your first birthday cake, and your first day of school. Sometimes your proud, smiling parents are in the background of these pictures. At other times, they were the photographers. They've obviously invested a lot of love and energy into making you happy!

Now you're a teenager, or very nearly so, and they still think you are priceless! You can never be replaced—not by a brother, not by a sister, not by many brothers and sisters! From the time you were born, your parents have tried to prepare themselves for the day that you'd be old enough to leave them, knowing that if your life went well, they would be happy. If you experienced sorrow, they would feel it too.

Is it any wonder they protect you so much? Watch what you eat, go to church every week with the family, set rules for dates? Midnight curfew? Do they get angry when you're late? Do you know why? Because losing you would devastate them! They don't want to lose you now, or eternally.

When I look at the overall picture of life, I subconsciously divide the things in my life into two groups: those I can take with me to heaven, and those that I will have to leave behind. I try to put more time into the things I can take with me—things like my family, my conscience, my appreciation of God, my faith in Him. These are the things that will last. And these are the things that, if lost, would cause eternal agony.

Did you notice that family is the first thing on my list? I think it's the first thing on every mother's list. Every mother wants her children with her in heaven because she is hopelessly in love with them. Even if she sometimes gets mad, she always gets over it, doesn't she? With God's help, she made you. How could she help loving you?

Over the triple doorways of the cathedral of Milan are three inscriptions spanning the splendid arches. Over one is carved a beautiful wreath of roses, and underneath is the legend "All that pleases us is but for a moment." Over the other is sculptured a cross and the words "All that troubles us is but for a moment."

But underneath the great central entrance to the main aisle is the inscription "That only is important which is eternal."

The next time your parents discuss family rules with you, try not to bristle or get angry. Try to see it as another way they are saying they care about you—now and forever!

FEBRUARY 15

THE TIME TO BE HAPPY IS NOW

Right now God is ready to welcome you. Today he is ready to save you. 2 Corinthians 6:2, TLB.

A champion tennis player was asked how it felt to win the cup at Wimbledon. "I am elated!" she replied with a wide smile. Then she sighed. "But it lasts only two minutes." Then she explained that the rest of her life is filled with hard, sweaty practice on a silent court.

There is a serious myth floating around that "you can't be happy unless you have something exciting going on." A popular slogan is "I'm a party animal!" In an effort to make this myth come true in their lives, people fill their time with endless parties, games, drugs, or booze, and then after each party, they wonder why they feel so bad.

Psychologist William Mounton Marston once asked 300 people this question: "What do you have to live for?" Nine out of 10 were simply waiting for something to happen—a better job, a new house, a trip, an inheritance. They were putting in time while they waited for an uncertain tomorrow.

But happiness is not a misty feeling that we have to sit and hope for. Happiness is a choice. You can be happy right now if you choose to be!

Matthew Henry, a famous teacher, was once attacked by thieves and robbed of his wallet. He didn't fight back, but gave his wallet freely in order to save his own life.

That evening as he related the story to his neighbors, they suggested that he must be feeling very angry at what happened. "It's not fair!" they cried. "If the police ever find those men, you should see that they go to jail for a long, long time!"

Mr. Henry just shook his head. "No, I am not angry; I am thankful." His friends were surprised. "Thankful? But—"

"I am thankful first, because I was never robbed before; second, because although they took my wallet, they did not take my life; third, because although they took everything I had, it was not much; and fourth, because it was I who was robbed, not I who robbed."

What situation can you turn around today from disaster to delight? Challenge yourself to find one! Remember, happiness is a decision.

FEBRUARY 16

WHAT DO YOU GIVE UP WHEN YOU ARE CONCEITED?

There is one thing worse than a fool, and that is a man who is conceited. Proverbs 26:12, TLB.

A sixth grader we'll call Tom was what a lot of kids called very fortunate. His father was a builder, and paid Tom for working for him each summer. Tom had saved up several thousand dollars, with which he bought his own clothes and school supplies. Tom was very pleased with himself, as he very well should be, for saving up so much money. None of his classmates had nearly as much money as Tom had.

The problem was that Tom was more than pleased with himself—he was arrogant! "I'm wearing more than $200," he would brag to his friends. And then he would point out the designer jeans he had on, the expensive shirt and sweater, and the $75 shoes. He bragged about how much everything cost, even his $15 hairstyle! "I spend that much every two weeks to keep it looking right," he said vainly.

You can guess how his classmates treated him. They avoided being with him because he was a braggart, and also a poor sport. When Tom struck out in baseball, he angrily threw the bat away and stalked off the plate. When he played soccer, he sulked if his team didn't win.

One day a new kid came to the school. Tom was the first one to go over to him and talk about how much his clothes cost. The new kid was impressed and flattered that "rich" Tom was friendly with him. But when the new kid realized that Tom's money was all he ever talked about, their friendship fizzled out.

Tom thought he knew why. "He's just jealous because he's not wearing as much money as I am," he told the other guys.

What do you think the problem was? Was it really the money, or was it that Tom was so conceited and didn't really care about anybody else?

It's nice to have enough money to buy whatever you need and then some. But money by itself doesn't bring happiness. And money doesn't make you any more valuable to God than anybody else is. You are valuable to God because of the price He paid to buy you from Satan. Jesus would have died if you were the only person to benefit from it. That's how valuable you really are!

FEBRUARY 17

HOW TO BE HAPPY RIGHT NOW

Keep a close watch on all you do and think. Stay true to what is right and God will bless you and use you to help others. 1 Timothy 4:16, TLB.

The people who are the most discouraged with life are often those who have never learned to cherish the little happinesses that each day brings. It is too bad, for most lives hold little that is dramatic and overwhelming. Most people have fairly routine days with their own quotas of small happinesses.

The trick of really living in the present is to accept each minute as an unrepeatable miracle—which is exactly what it is. Grown-ups may ask you, "What are you going to be when you grow up?" And while it's good to be thinking ahead to the career you plan to spend the rest of your life in, it is also a good thing to remember that you have value now.

Perhaps you should ask, "What am I going to be now?" What kind of friend are you? Are you tolerant? Are you a bully? What kind of student are you? Do you pay attention? Do you do your best? Is your work neat and careful? The kind of person you are now has an influence on what kind of person you will be when you grow up.

Ellen White tells us that our character is the only thing we will be able to take with us to heaven. Character means many things, but the most valuable part is the habit of doing what has to be done.

You are building character when you do your homework before playing, when you are kind to the new kid in school because you know you would appreciate it if you were in his shoes, when you unload the dishwasher without being asked, when you wash your own clothes just because it has to be done, when you make up your bed in the morning, when you do your best to be cheerful, even when you don't get your own way. Building character is never a waste of time.

A good character will make you feel out of this world now—and for eternity.

THE WOMAN OF POMPEII

You can be sure of this: The kingdom of Christ and of God will never belong to anyone who is impure or greedy, for a greedy person is really an idol worshiper—he loves and worships the good things of this life more than God. Ephesians 5:5, TLB

Of the 20,000 inhabitants of Pompeii, Italy, some 2,000 lost their lives when the volcanic Mount Vesuvius, which shadowed their town, erupted almost 2,000 years ago. Among those who died was a woman who treasured her jewels—her riches—above everything else.

As the deadly rain of fire poured down the mountain, she ran to the harbor to escape by ship. Hundreds of people were fleeing by water. However, this woman stayed behind to collect as much jewelry as she could carry.

She grabbed her rings and thrust them on her fingers. There was no time to hunt for a box or a bag in which to cram her jewels, so she picked up as many as she could hold and rushed into the street. Clutching her pearls and diamonds, her rubies and sapphires, her gold brooches and her earrings, she joined the mob of frantic people fleeing the volcano. But she waited too long. The poisonous fumes overcame her as she ran, and she stumbled, fell, and died, clutching the things she prized so much.

There under the ashes of Pompeii she lay. In recent years, excavators discovered her still lovely form, her hands still laden with jewels.

There are many things besides jewels that we might worship and that might rob us of eternal life. The desire to be well liked and to be like others whether or not they're doing what's right can cause big problems. And it's easy for both kids and adults to spend so much on clothes or cars or toys that they don't have any money left over for tithes and offerings or to help the needy.

Obviously our clothes must be clean and neat and we should take care to wear styles and colors that complement our coloring and features. But we must watch out that we don't spend a lot of money on fad clothing that goes out of style and thus looks ridiculous a few months after purchased. It's great to have fun doing things with friends, but we must make certain that we have time for Jesus, too.

If following Him is the most important thing to you, everything else will fit right in place. You'll be happy with yourself and with your friends. And neither money, jewels, clothes, nor anything else will mean more to you than God.

FEBRUARY 19

SOMETIMES I HATE MY PARENTS!

It is better to be slow-tempered than famous; it is better to have self-control than to control an army. Proverbs 16:32, TLB.

Have you ever gotten so mad at your parents that you scared yourself? Did you feel frustrated and angry, yet guilty about feeling so mad at them?

All of us want to have good families. We want to feel safe and loved at home. But we sometimes think that if we get mad at each other, it means we don't love each other. Believe it or not, it's possible to be angry at people you love! We don't get angry at people we don't care about. The opposite of love isn't hate; it is apathy.

So what is anger? Anger is a chemical response to unfairness, fear, or frustration.

All day long your body manufactures and releases different hormones, according to how you are feeling or what you are needing. Your body is programmed to release certain hormones in response to certain events. Like waves in the ocean, the levels of various hormones rise and fall all day long, according to how safe, happy, fearful, hungry, or content you are.

So when you say "I'm angry," you are recognizing that you feel a surge of chemicals that you associate with anger.

How do you know you're getting angry? Does your heart race, your head pound? Do you feel like crying? Next time you feel that way, see if you can figure out why.

Some of the more common things that make us feel angry are (1) a threat, either physical or verbal, (2) an unjust or unfair act toward us, (3) sudden loss of something valued, (4) loss of a relationship because of death, rejection, or betrayal, (5) sudden or chronic sickness, (6) lack of recognition, (7) intrusion into our "property" (most often by a brother or sister), (8) imposed limits on our freedom.

The Bible tells us that feeling angry is not a sin (Ephesians 4:26). This world is unfair, and there are times in all of our lives when we feel angry. But it's what we do with our anger that is important. Part of growing up means learning to understand our feelings and control them.

After your anger dies down—and it will—be sure and make things right again. The Bible says "Be angry—but sin not." Don't do or say anything when you're angry that you might regret later. Remember: "You can't save face if you lose your head."

ARE YOU PERFECT?

Be perfect, therefore, as your heavenly Father is perfect. Matthew 5:48, NIV.

Mother made the absolutely very best, most scrumptious, delicious, blackberry pie! Four-year-old Andrew Wyman eyed his piece eagerly, though he waited patiently for Mother to serve everyone else in the family. He knew this was going to be good!

At last Mother gave him a piece of pie, too. Andrew picked up his fork and began to cut into the slice on his plate. He was doing the best he could, but as the fork broke through the flaky crust, Andrew's anticipated first bite went sliding off the plate, into his lap, and onto the white carpet. Upside down!

Mother gasped.

Andrew felt awful. Wanting to make things better, he decided to clean up the mess himself. Without saying a word, he jumped up from the table and ran into the kitchen to get a towel. He was back almost immediately, kneeling over the spilled blackberry pie, rubbing it with a towel in an effort to clean it up.

Was he helping? Was he doing a perfect job? Yes and no. He was doing a perfect job for a 4-year-old kid. He meant to be helping, but actually he was making a much bigger mess than it would have been had he let his mom take care of it. But his intentions were good.

In the same way, God asks us to be perfect—right where we are—and appreciates our doing the best we can do. For example, some of us find it easy to say just the right thing when a friend is feeling bad, while others of us don't. In our text today, God seems to be asking us to at least try to be like He is. In fact, if we ask for His help, He will help us know just the right words to use when our friends (and enemies) need them.

When we develop the habit of being thoughtful to everyone, we are becoming perfect. What would the world be like if everyone was that way? Today, can you be kind to one more person than you were kind to yesterday? Someone has to start it.

IT DOESN'T FIT HIS IMAGE

[God] does as he pleases with the powers of heaven and the peoples of the earth. No one can hold back his hand or say to him: "what have you done?" Daniel 4:35, NIV.

Has it ever bothered you that the Ten Commandments say "Thou shalt not kill," and yet the Bible contains many stories of battles that God approved of? Why? Why are David and Samson heroes, and why was it OK for them to kill if they were, in fact, "breaking" one of the Ten Commandments?

We probably won't know the full reason until we get to heaven and let God explain it Himself. But until then, we can only offer our guesses.

First of all, we know that God is a God of love. He wants us to be happy. But He also knows us so well that He can tell what kinds of decisions we're going to make, and whether or not we're going to be happy with those decisions. We are not robots. We are not programmed to do whatever God says to do. We can make choices. But only God knows what all those choices are going to be.

It's a bit like this. If you have a brother who is really into model airplanes, you know which magazine he is going to choose if you hold out an airplane magazine and a cooking magazine, don't you? You know his likes and dislikes. God knows them even better.

If God approved of Samson's killing the Philistines, He must have known that they would never change their ways. They would probably always be evil—why let them continue to hurt God's people? The same was probably true for Goliath.

And if it bothers you that when God's people went to war with heathen cities they killed everyone in them—even little children—it might help to know a little about how those people lived. Children in those cities didn't have privileges like you do. Some were offered as living sacrifices to heathen gods! Others were burned alive, molested, and often left to roam the streets as beggars. It was a tragedy for them to be killed, and it certainly caused God great pain. God knew those people would never change, and the cycle of evil had to be stopped.

Parents always say "No" when a baby tries to stick his fingers in electric outlets. But the baby can't understand why. He doesn't understand electricity, but he can learn what no means. And when he's older, he will understand and teach his children the same thing.

The Bible says "Thou shalt not kill." But the Old Testament tells of many times when God allowed and, in fact, helped men and women to kill their enemies. But we know that God has a good reason for everything He does. Maybe, like babies, we can't understand all the whys yet, but God will tell us in time. And it will make sense.

WHAT DO YOU GIVE UP WHEN YOU CHEAT?

Whoever can be trusted with very little can also be trusted with much, and whoever is dishonest with very little will also be dishonest with much. Luke 16:10, NIV

In the school cafeteria, Seth gulped down his lunch without even tasting it. His mind was on the math assignment he had to finish and turn in next period. It was an open-book test, but the teacher had said the students couldn't work together on the answers. Unfortunately, there was no way Seth could finish the test without help. He had an A in the class up to now, and he knew this assignment was going to pull his grade down.

As he scraped his chair away from the table and finally raised his head to look around the room, he saw three of his friends at a table in the back corner, their heads together, obviously working on some assignment. The open-book test?

Seth picked up his tray and walked to their table. "Whatcha doin'?" he asked.

"Working on the test—what else?" one of his friends replied with a laugh.

"But we're not supposed to work together," Seth reminded them.

"Come on, man," the boy said with a laugh. "If we don't work together, we won't get it finished! Sit down! Think about your A!"

Seth's heart raced. If he didn't join the circle, he might be the only one who didn't get the assignment finished. But if he worked with them on it, he wouldn't feel right inside. What would you do?

It doesn't always feel good to do the right thing—not right away, at least. But there are always two consequences: short-range and long-range. The short-range consequences of being honest may hurt a little. Seth didn't get his A. But in the long run, he felt better. He liked himself.

This "liking yourself" can be called "integrity." You are not "shaken," feeling guilty, wondering if you'll get found out. It is something to protect. It is what you lose when you cheat.

Integrity is a gift from God. We can chip away at it bit by bit and feel awful, or we can take care of it and watch it grow. Will your integrity have grown or shrunk five years from now? Ten years? Fifty? It's up to you.

WHAT CAN MUSIC DO TO YOU?

Dear children, keep away from anything that might take God's place in your hearts. 1 John 5:21, TLB.

A large department store was having trouble with employee theft. So a guard was stationed at every door, and each evening as the employees went home, their bags and purses had to be searched.

The guards soon got to know each employee, and could conduct their search rather quickly, as they became familiar with each one's personal belongings. One man, in particular, always left the store pushing a wheelbarrow loaded with trash. He was friendly and waited patiently while the guard searched the trash. At first the guard checked through the trash carefully, but as the weeks wore on, he grew tired of it. He soon just waved the man and his wheelbarrow of trash right out the door.

Still, the store was losing money. Again, the auditor inspected the books and after some study finally discovered the thief.

The next evening, when the little old man passed by the guard with his usual wheelbarrow of trash, he was arrested for stealing—wheelbarrows!

The guards missed the obvious by paying too much attention to the trash and by letting down their standards of scrutiny.

Are there ways that we do this too? Are there some "wolves" you have been getting close to, thinking they are "lambs"? What about the music you listen to? Do you listen to songs that you wouldn't want your folks to hear because of the words and driving beat? Like it or not, the lyrics are becoming part of your belief system. Your brain tucks them away like grooves in a record, making them deeper and more permanent the more you hear them.

Do you watch TV programs and movies that use language that once shocked you? Watch out! As you hear four-letter words and God's name used in vain, these expressions are stored in your memory and will pop out when you least expect it. Emily found this was so one day at school. "Mom, I was so embarrassed," she confided. "I could have died. I never thought I'd say that, but it just came out."

Far too often, music and movies are the trash, the "wolves." You know that you've got to be selective. But the words they contain are the wheelbarrows. Somebody's sneaking something right past your mind, and you may not realize it.

You may have begun to feel helpless or even despair. In fact, some of you may even feel like giving up on life because nothing in your life is pointing you toward God's love. Try giving up your usual music, replacing it with songs of hope and courage and see what a difference it makes in your outlook on life. The best insurance against sin is to be shocked by it. If you're comfortable with it, look out!

WHAT DO YOU GET OUT OF CHURCH?

When you help the poor you are lending to the Lord—and he pays wonderful interest on your loan! Proverbs 19:17, TLB.

Maybe you've heard the story of the greedy monkey who discovered a clay jug in the forest one day. Being naturally curious, he looked inside. There he saw fresh cashew nuts and fragrant slices of mango! He slipped a furry, gray arm into the neck of the jug and wrapped his leathery, black fingers around the fruit. But when he tried to pull his arm back out, he discovered it wouldn't work! You can guess what he should have done—dropped the fruit. But he wanted that fruit, and nothing was going to make him let go of it!

Even when the hunters came a short time later and caught him with their nets, he didn't let go of the food.

A very thirsty blackbird came upon a jug in the forest. Putting his beak into the jug, he smelled water. But the water was too far at the bottom for him to reach.

The blackbird hopped around and gathered some pebbles. Then he dropped them, one by one, into the jug. At last the pebbles raised the water level enough that the blackbird was able to get a refreshing drink.

OK, what's the point of these two stories? Just this: When we go to church, some of us are like the monkey, and some of us are like the blackbird. Like the monkey, some of us expect to "get something" from church. We demand to! And when it doesn't happen, we begin to feel trapped in a hopeless situation. "Who needs religion?" we ask haughtily. "It hasn't done anything for me!"

Others, like the blackbird, have discovered that we don't go to church to "get something"; we go to church to "do something"—to worship God who created us, and forgives us, and who is even now preparing out-of-this-world things for us in heaven! When we go to church with that attitude, wanting to honor God and show Him how much we worship and praise Him, it makes a difference in how bored we feel.

You can almost paraphrase John Kennedy's statement and say, "Ask not what your God can do for you—ask what you can do for your God." Maybe you can be a student missionary, or get a group together to clean up around your town, or paint the house of an elderly or handicapped person. That's how you find that the more you give, the more you get out of life. You'll find the real meaning of why you are here.

YOU'RE WORTH MORE THAN YOU THINK!

But the Lord said to Samuel, "Don't judge by a man's face or height, for this is not the one. I don't make decisions the way you do! Men judge by outward appearance, but I look at a man's thoughts and intentions." 1 Samuel 16:7, TLB.

On the day his wife, Serena, was to begin treatment for cancer, William Scholtz found himself short of money. He didn't know how he was going to pay for his wife's treatment, but he knew he would, somehow.

He suddenly remembered the silver half dollars they had been collecting for 40 years. He hated to part with the collection, but he knew it was his only choice.

With a combination of relief and sadness, Mr. Scholtz took his collection into the bank. The teller advised him he could probably get more money for the coins if he sold them to another collector.

"But I need the money now!" Mr. Scholtz told her desperately. "My wife's life depends on it. I don't have time to find a collector!"

So the teller gave him $251.50, just what the coins added up to. Mr. Scholtz clutched the money appreciatively and hurried out of the bank for the hospital, happy for even a little money to help pay his wife's bill.

Fortunately for Mr. Scholtz, the bank teller didn't let the matter just drop. She knocked on the door of the bank president's office, the coin collection in her hand, and explained the situation to him.

A few weeks later Mr. Scholtz received a check in the mail for $6,856. The bank president had had the coins appraised, sold them at an auction, and then returned all the money—its real value—to Mr. Scholtz.

I think that's how God looks at us. Our friends might not see much in us. Even our family may wonder what talents we possess. If you have a big brother or sister, he or she may call you names and make fun of you. A brother or sister doesn't know your real value. Ask Jesus. He is a "people collector." Jesus stretched out His arms and said, "You are worth this much." And He died for you.

IT REALLY IS THE LITTLE THINGS THAT COUNT

For unless you are honest in small matters, you won't be in large ones. If you cheat even a little, you won't be honest with greater responsibilities. Luke 16:10, TLB.

A young woman waited impatiently in the express line at a super-market, sighing and glancing at her watch every few minutes. All she needed was some cheddar cheese and French bread for the fondue she planned to make that night. But she was not the only person making a quick stop on her way home. Even the "express" checkout line moved slowly. The man in front of the young woman was old and hard-of-hearing, but tried to carry on a friendly conversation. His hearing and his slowness added to the woman's aggravation.

At last the woman exploded. "I have important guests coming for dinner, and dinner won't be ready for them because of this," she fumed to the elderly lady standing behind her.

"My dear," the sweet little old lady asked with concern. "Are you really having important guests for dinner?"

"Yes, I am," the young woman replied, still seething.

"Well, then, I'd better tell you," the older woman said. "Both your bread and your cheese have a spot of mold on them."

The young woman was worried about a really big thing—her important dinner guests. But she worried so much about the meeting that she didn't give much thought to the little details—whether or not the bread and cheese were fresh.

Sometimes we worry a lot about the big "time of trouble," but we don't pay enough attention to the small things that happen every day. Everyone is trying to accomplish something big, not realizing that life is made up of little things. Maybe you won't even be alive during the time of trouble! Stop worrying about it. Pay attention to the little things that make up *today's* life, instead.

Are you on good terms with yourself, or is your conscience nagging at you? Listen to it. Maintain your integrity, that sense of well-being because you have nothing to hide. And when the time of trouble comes, you will just naturally be ready to go out of this world!

YOU DON'T NEED PROOF TO BELIEVE

In the beginning God created the heavens and the earth. Genesis 1:1, NIV.

A demolition team was hired to tear down an old building, and after years of experience they knew just how to do it. Where do you suppose they put the largest sticks of dynamite—at the top of the building? Right in the middle? No, at the foundation. They knew that any structure is only as stable as its foundation. Destroy the foundation, and the structure is gone.

What is the foundation of the Adventist Church? Our foundation is that God is in charge. God owns us. And He makes the rules for our lives, rules that promise our happiness. Many of our foundations can all be traced back to the first book of the Bible—to Genesis. Let's look at a few.

Where do we first learn about God? In Genesis.

Why do we believe in marriage? God gave it to our first parents in the Garden of Eden, as recorded in Genesis.

Why do we keep the Sabbath? God made it for us because He knew that we would need time to stop and rest and remember Him on a regular basis. And as recorded in Genesis, He rested on the seventh day of the week and by so doing made it holy.

Where do we first find how sin entered our world, making it necessary for Jesus to die? Genesis!

Atheists would prefer to live by their own opinions. They don't want to be "owned" by anyone—even by God! They don't want God to make the rules, so they have thrown out Genesis and say that God doesn't exist—that our earth and everything in it just happened. But think about this a moment. Would you believe a computer just "happened" to throw *itself* together? Or a bicycle, or a house?

A few years ago a Russian cosmonaut returned from a mission and announced that God does not exist. He had looked for Him in outer space and didn't see Him. "God is nowhere," he said.

But what would have happened if he had really looked for God, if he had actually stepped out of his space capsule and really looked for Him? He would have found Him, for he would have died and at the judgment found himself looking God right in the face and having to explain why he said God did not exist. Instead of saying, "God is nowhere," he would have had to admit, "God is now here."

There is no proof in the Bible for the existence of God. His existence is taken for granted, as naturally as you do not need proof that you are alive! However, you have proof that God exists, because of the experiences you have that show Him at work in your life. The first verse in the Bible says, "In the beginning God." He was there right from the start. And He is still here now.

FEBRUARY 28

TRUST THE ONE WHO LOVES YOU

I have come that they may have life, and have it to the full. John 10:10, NIV.

"Psst, Eve." The husky voice broke through Eve's reverie. She and Adam had been working in the garden, caring for the animals and flowers, but Eve had wandered off, and now someone was trying to get her attention.

"Psst, Eve!"

Eve looked up in a nearby tree and blinked in amazement. A beautiful winged serpent stared directly at her with a strange and unusual intelligent gleam in his eyes. The serpent's mouth opened, and he hissed her name again. "Eve."

In mindless fascination, Eve stepped closer to the tree. A talking serpent. Amazing!

The serpent lifted his head, arched his back, and took a large bite of fruit. Juice trickled down his long neck as he chewed the delicious mouthful. Then he stared at Eve with a look of mild surprise. "What's the matter, Eve?" he asked. "Can't you eat the fruit of the garden?"

Eve snapped back into consciousness. "Oh, no, serpent," she replied. "We can eat from all the trees of the garden except—strangely enough—the fruit of the tree from which you are eating. God has told us that when we eat of that fruit, we will die."

The serpent opened his mouth and laughed hoarsely, his head bobbing up and down. "You will die, huh?" he said. "Do I look like a dead serpent?"

Eve's hand reaches out slowly, tentatively, toward the fruit. The fruit is beautiful. It has made the serpent wise above all other serpents. It is delicious and juicy, and obviously she won't die from eating it, for the serpent has survived! All the evidence that Eve can see, hear, and touch suggests that she should eat the fruit. What do you think she should do: trust that God has told her the truth, or believe the serpent?

Are you struggling with some temptations that go against what God says you should do? Who do you think is suggesting them to you? God? Or the serpent? What will you do? The abundant, full life comes to us when we trust and obey God, because He loves us.

WHAT'S NEW?

He who loves wisdom loves his own best interest and will be a success. Proverbs 19:8, TLB.

Have you ever tried to tell a joke, only to have someone beat you to the punch line? It's exasperating, isn't it? It's fun to tell a joke only to someone who doesn't anticipate what's coming.

OOTW-3

Tom Brown, a man who loves nature, often leads nature hikes through the Rocky Mountains, where he lives. He says that to really appreciate life we have to stop anticipating what we are going to see and feel before it occurs.

One chilly night when he was hiking in the Rocky Mountains with a group of students, he mentioned that they would soon cross a mountain stream, and the students began grumbling about how cold it would be. When they reached the stream the kids reluctantly plodded ahead. They were almost knee-deep when the students realized Tom had taken them into a hot spring! Then their grumbling stopped, and they were happy.

Life's like that. Sometimes the thought of going to school for years and years makes you want to give up. You feel you'll never be through! You're sure you'll be a student till you die! But still you plod along year after year because you have to. And then you discover that each year of school brings its own rewards and challenges. The more you learn, the more you realize how much there is to learn. And the more fun it becomes.

It becomes even more fun to go to school as you begin zeroing in on the things you really want to know more about. If you've always wanted to be a mechanic or a nurse or a lawyer, you finally get to learn how to be one! And once you graduate and discover you can get a job anywhere, with good pay, it's like finding yourself in a hot spring. You're glad you kept plodding along!

How do you know what you want to do for the rest of your life? You may not discover the hot spring until you get there. You may not know what you want to be until you have spent a year or two in college. That's OK! For example, students who know how to type have a foundation for the computer world; those who are good at math may be engineers; those who enjoy sciences might be doctors, nurses, or medical technicians. Those decisions can be made later. Find out what you like now.

Author Louis L'Amour said, "The best of all things is to learn. Money can be lost or stolen, health and strength may fail, but what you have committed to your mind is yours forever!"

Learn something new today.

MARCH 2

NOBODY MADE IT

In the beginning was the Word, . . . and the Word was God. John 1:1, NIV.

You remember Sir Isaac Newton—the man who discovered and named the law of gravity? Well, the story is told that Sir Isaac had a complete scaled model of the solar system made, with the sun in the center and all the planets revolving around it.

One day a friend of Newton's—a non-Christian scientist—came over to visit. As soon as he walked into Newton's study and saw the model of the solar system, he was amazed. Walking slowly around the model, he whistled appreciatively and looked over at Newton with a broad smile. "This is exquisite! Who made it?" he asked.

Newton looked over the rim of his glasses. "Nobody," he said, the corners of his mouth twitching.

His friend chuckled. "Come on," he said, "I'm no fool! Somebody had to have made this. And he must be a genius!"

Newton walked across the room to his friend and touched his shoulder. "You think you are no fool," he said gently, "but sometimes I wonder.

"This thing is just a puny imitation of a much grander system whose laws you and I both know. Somehow, I cannot convince you that this tiny model did not have a maker," Newton said. "Yet you believe that the great original, from which this design was taken, simply appeared and ran on its own—without designer or maker. How you can reach such an incongruous conclusion escapes me!"

Do you find it hard to believe in Creation? Is it harder to believe an eyewitness or someone who just has an opinion about what happened? I'd take the words of the eyewitness anytime.

God is an eyewitness—a participant—in Creation. He says He made the world and everything in it. He saw it all happen right before His eyes!

Evolutionists base their theories on "what might have been." They weren't there at Creation. They didn't see it happen. They're just guessing! And they change their minds sometimes!

Who are the fools? Those who believe the guessers, or those who believe the eyewitnesses? The eyewitness wins, hands down.

MARCH 3

WHO'S GOT YOUR EARS?

Not one sparrow can . . . fall to the ground without your Father knowing it. And the very hairs of your head are all numbered. So don't worry! You are more valuable to him than many sparrows. Matthew 10:29-31, TLB.

Anthropologist Ethel Alpenfels tells a story about a woodsman who was walking down Fifth Avenue in New York City with a friend. All at once the woodsman said, "Why, I hear a cricket."

"Nonsense," scoffed the city man. "In this uproar? Not a chance."

"But I do," said the woodsman, "and I'll show you." At that he took a dime out of his pocket and dropped it on the pavement. Instantly, people within 30 feet turned around to see whose coin had dropped.

"You see," said the woodsman, "people hear what their ears are tuned to. Mine happen to be tuned to crickets."

The Bible tells us that God is tuned in to us. In fact, though I know God loves us all, I get the feeling that He takes special care with people who are having problems.

Your problems can be divided into two groups: problems that are short-term, and problems that are long-term. If you have a test tomorrow, that's a short-term problem. If your folks are getting a divorce, that's a long-term problem. Sometimes long-term problems need to be set aside until the short-term problems are taken care of.

But with any problem, you'll feel better if you look for any part of it that you can control. Can you tell the teacher what questions to put on the test? No. Can you study for the test so you know most of the material? Yes. Then do it! Can you prevent your folks from divorcing? No. Can you still love them? Can you learn from their mistakes? Yes. Then do it! You won't always be dependent on them. Look ahead to a bright future for yourself as a grown-up.

Satan would love for our problems to permanently overwhelm us so we don't even have the strength to pray. But when we don't pray, God misses us. Like the time a piccolo player stopped playing in the middle of a song as the music swelled loudly and a mighty choir joined in. The director stopped conducting immediately and tapped his music stand to get the musicians' attention.

"And where is the piccolo?" he cried out. His ear was tuned in, even to that tiny little sound of the piccolo.

God is tuned in to you too, no matter how insignificant you may think you are. If you don't spend time sharing your day with God each day, you will be missed. You are special to Him.

MARCH 4

ONLY GOOD THINGS COME FROM GOD

Every good and perfect gift is from above, coming down from the Father of the heavenly lights, who does not change like shifting shadows. James 1:17, NIV.

You can find a text in the Bible that will either deepen your love for God or weaken it. It all depends on whether or not it is taken out of context. This pleases Satan! And one of the often-recited Bible texts that bothers me is the one from Job that says "The Lord gave and the Lord hath taken away; blessed be the name of the Lord." This verse is often quoted at funerals. That bothers me! I don't believe that God takes anything away. Rather, the Lord gives, and Satan takes away.

I think the problem comes when we assume that every single verse in the Bible truly reflects God. Rather, the Bible is a collection of stories about people just like us and their relationships with God. Some Bible verses include misconceptions that those people had about God—such as the one about God taking things away from us. That was only one person's depressed opinion. If you read the whole story, you learn that God didn't take anything away from Job—Satan did.

President Abraham Lincoln, famous for his integrity and love of truth, had a riddle he often asked his colleagues. It went like this: "If you called the tail of a dog a leg, how many legs would the dog have?"

"Five" was the usual reply.

"Wrong," Lincoln would say with a homely smile. "The dog still has four legs. Calling the tail a leg doesn't make it one."

How pleased Satan is when we believe his lies and get angry at God. But God is too good to do evil. I prefer to paraphrase the verse to say "The power of God giveth, and the power of God taketh away." That means that in the long run, the power of God gives us hope and takes away our despair.

Don't let Satan confuse you or plant seeds of doubt and mistrust of God. Just because he says God is unfair doesn't mean it is so—it's just Satan's opinion.

MARCH 5

IS GOD A ROBBER?

And remember, when someone wants to do wrong it is never God who is tempting him, for God never wants to do wrong and never tempts anyone else to do it. James 1:13, TLB.

When the Jackson family returned home one evening they found a note on their front door. "Please accept my apologies for helping myself to your gas can, which I found sitting beside your garage this morning. I ran out of gas on my way to work this morning, and since I didn't want to be late, I borrowed your gas can. You will find it where it was, full again.

"As a token of my gratitude I am enclosing tickets to the theater and $35 for dinner. Please take the family out tonight on me." The note was unsigned.

How would you feel if you found such a note on your front door? The Jacksons were delighted! They only wished they had the person's name so they could thank him personally for his kindness.

They thoroughly enjoyed their evening out and drove home feeling happy. But when they unlocked their front door their happiness disappeared suddenly. Their house was empty—just stripped bare! The police said they had been set up by a professional thief. Theirs was just one of a number of homes that had been stripped in the same manner.

Now how would you feel about the person who left the note?

As Christians, we sometimes confuse the issue with God, too. We give credit to God for giving us blessings—and we should. God is the giver of everything good. But some Christians also say that God brings sadness into our lives, too, to "teach us a lesson." They say that God "takes" our loved ones when they die. The Bible is filled with quotations from other people who wrongly thought that God takes things away from us. If we take those texts out of context it can turn us against God. But the truth is that God gives . . . and Satan takes away.

Everyone has freedom of choice. The thief has the choice to rob us, and we have the choice to protect ourselves. Often we are miraculously protected from harm when the angels step in and perform a miracle. But a miracle is just that—something that can't be explained.

The question should not be "Why do bad things happen to good people?" because bad things happen to bad people, too. Christianity isn't a guarantee against trouble. But rather we should ask, "What do good people do when bad things happen to them?" Good people don't curse God or blame Him. They put the blame where it should be put—on Satan.

MARCH 6

WHEN IS A LOSS A GAIN?

All things work together for good to them that love God. Romans 8:28.

The story is told of an only survivor of a shipwreck who managed to swim to the shore of an uninhabited island. He had a few matches on him when he swam to shore, and decided that to survive, he had to make the matches last as long as he could. He laid the wet matches out in the sun, hoping that when they dried they would work again.

While the matches dried, the man lived on fresh fruit and nuts, which he found in abundance. Every day he prayed that God would deliver him and send a ship to rescue him. And every day he checked the moisture in the matchsticks, eager to start a fire and send smoke signals, but also cautious about not wasting the matches by testing them too soon.

He spent his first days building a small hut for protection from the rain and wind, and managed to eke out an existence while he waited for the matches to dry. At last, he decided to try out the matches. He built a carefully designed circle of stones just outside his hut and laid fine, dry grass in the middle of them. A collection of dry wood was stacked nearby.

If he could keep this fire going night and day, surely someone would see his signal, and he could conserve his matches, as well.

The first match immediately burst into a bright, orange flame and the man sighed with relief. Carefully he fed the flames, and when the fire was burning well, he left it and went into the jungle in search of food.

He wasn't gone long, but a breeze must have spread the fire, because he returned to see his hut engulfed in flames. In fact, everything he had worked so hard on was gone, including all his matches. The horrified man collasped to the ground in tears, ready to give up and die.

A few hours later he was startled to hear the blast of a ship's horn out in the bay. With a cry of delight, he jumped up and down, waving his arms. Sometime later, when he was safely aboard the ship, he asked the captain, "How did you know I was there?"

"We saw your smoke signals," the captain told him.

"And I was so certain that losing my hut was the worst thing that could happen to me, when it was actually the best," the man cried.

YOU ARE MARVELOUS!

Thank you for making me so wonderfully complex! It is amazing to think about. Your workmanship is marvelous—and how well I know it. Psalm 139:14, TLB.

An Asian king wanted to build a magnificent library and art gallery for his people. He summoned all the great builders in his land and asked each man to tell him why he should be chosen for the job and who would be his second choice. The king listened patiently as each man proudly told about his capabilities. And he had little trouble deciding whom to choose. He selected the man who had gotten the most votes as second best.

What is the difference between good pride and bad pride? Is it wrong to be proud of a job well done?

When I was a senior at Auburn Academy, I had a geometry classmate whom I'll call Craig. Now Craig generally did well on every single test and had a right to be proud of himself. But he never gave the rest of us a chance to congratulate him—he busily congratulated himself, waving his corrected test, demanding to know our grades, and bragging that he'd scored the highest.

The rest of us didn't care what our scores were—as long as they were in the A or B category. But the exact score is what mattered to this guy!

Sadly, he was his own worst enemy. The day came when he did not get the highest score, but tied with another student. He demanded that the teacher recheck his paper. Going over Craig's test again, the teacher discovered that one of his answers had been marked as correct when it was actually wrong. Someone had a higher score than he did!

"Bad" pride hurts the owner and others. Craig's pride not only made the poor students in class feel bad, it also hurt him, because nobody liked him. "Good" pride helps people feel good or do better. Studies have shown that successful test-takers think positively. When they sit down to take a test, they remind themselves of past successes and tell themselves they will do well—they have before!

God has given you special talents, or gifts, things that you do especially well. It is wrong to ignore your gifts. Find out what you do well, and then do it—silently. Good pride recognizes that you are a special and unique person. Without bragging about it, good pride helps you be all you can be. And that is what God wants for you.

MARCH 8

BUT I PRAYED ABOUT IT!

And in the same way—by our faith—the Holy Spirit helps us with our daily problems and in our praying. For we don't even know what we should pray for, nor how to pray as we should; but the Holy Spirit prays for us with such feeling that it cannot be expressed in words. Romans 8:26, TLB.

Betsy sat stiffly at her desk, her heart thumping loudly in her chest as she waited for the teacher to hand her test back to her. She was afraid she hadn't done too well. She had studied—and even prayed for God's help as she studied. But still, history was not her best subject—all those wars and everything were confusing!

At last the white sheet of paper floated onto her desk from the teacher's hand. Betsy turned it over with shaking hands to read the score. Only 75 percent—a C grade.

Someone was pulling on her shoulder, and she turned around to see what Linda wanted. "My first A!" Linda exulted in a loud whisper. "I can't believe it! How did you do?"

"C," Betsy replied with a disappointed sigh.

"You should have prayed about it like I did," Linda said confidently.

"I did pray," Betsy returned. "But obviously God didn't answer my prayer." And then she thought, *Maybe He isn't listening to me.*

Does it sometimes seem like your prayers go no higher than the ceiling? Are prayers only a wish list, and you know they've been answered only if something good happens to you?

Someone has said that the biggest mistake Christians make is to use prayer as a spare tire. A spare tire is forgotten for months at a time, until suddenly we have a flat on the road. Then we want the spare tire to be in good condition, ready for use. Just so, lots of people forget God for months at a time when things are going well. Then in an emergency they fly to God and expect Him to leap and answer their prayer.

Just because Betsy didn't get an A doesn't mean God didn't answer her prayer. Perhaps Betsy didn't know certain little "tricks" that would help her memorize the facts she needed to get an A on the history test. She might have even failed the test if God had not helped her remember what she had learned. Perhaps she did have an answer to prayer after all, but didn't recognize it, like the little 4-year-old who asked her father for money. When he handed her a dollar bill, she refused it, saying she wanted 10 shiny pennies instead. She didn't recognize her father's generosity.

If your prayers have been mostly "give me" prayers, try changing your subject matter for a while. Start praying "thank-you" prayers and name your blessings out loud. The more blessings you look for, the more you'll find.

DO YOU REALLY WANT YOUR PRAYERS ANSWERED?

Pray along these lines: "Our Father in heaven, we honor your holy name. We ask that your kingdom will come now. May your will be done here on earth, just as it is in heaven." Matthew 6:9, 10, TLB.

One morning in church a minister noticed a little boy on the very front row mumbling something with his eyes closed. It was a very small church, so the minister could hear the boy whispering "Tokyo" over and over.

The minister was curious. After the service he went to the little boy and said, "Son, I was so glad to see you praying so fervently in church this morning. I think I heard you saying 'Tokyo' much of the time. Is there a reason you were praying for that town?"

The child looked down at his shoes. He twisted inside his shirt and then said, "Well, you see, sir, I took my geography test yesterday. And if God doesn't make Tokyo the capital of France, I'm going to get it wrong!"

What would happen if God answered everybody's prayers in just the way that the boy asked? How long would Tokyo remain the capital of France? How would anyone know where anything was? If you prayed for rain and your neighbor prayed for sunshine, would that mean that God would have to follow you around all day with a little rain cloud wherever you went?

Can you imagine a world in which everyone went around in his own prayer-controlled climate? Some people might be wrapped in a fog blanket, others sunbathing in narrow strips of sunshine, and still others sledding down hills on beds of snow that traveled along under them.

Do you really think God would do that? More important, would you want Him to? Think for a moment of all the prayers you have said in the past week—include all the wishes that have passed through your head. Have you been angry at someone and muttered that you wished that person were dead? How would you feel if he actually dropped dead because of your prayers?

If our prayers were answered immediately in just the ways we prayed, people would be dropping dead and then jumping up alive; getting sick, getting well; feeling good, feeling bad; the weather could change every few inches, and on and on—all at the whim of others. It would be pretty scary to pray if this were the case.

I'm glad that God is in charge. He's fair. And that's why it's easy to pray "Thy will be done." Let Him decide how to answer your prayers.

MARCH 10

WHAT IS FAITH?

What is faith? It is the confident assurance that something we want is going to happen. It is the certainty that what we hope for is waiting for us, even though we cannot see it up ahead. Hebrews 11:1, TLB.

Do you have faith? It's often easier to say you have it than to actually use it.

My dad, a minister from way back, explains it this way. When he is talking about faith, he places a chair on the rostrum in front of everybody.

"Here is a chair," he says. "Now, as you can see, it has four legs, and a nice, sturdy back, and everything seems quite well put together. I have faith that it is going to hold me up if I sit on it. But not until I actually sit down am I exercising my faith. And faith is no good unless we actually use it."

A huge crowd was watching the famous tightrope walker Blondin cross Niagara Falls one day in 1860. He crossed it numerous times—a 1,000-foot trip, 160 feet above the raging waters. Then he asked the crowd if they believed he could take a person across. All said "Yes."

Then he approached one man and asked him to get on his back and go with him. The man refused! What would you have done?

Mental assent or even verbal assent is not real belief.

God asks us to believe a lot of things. He says in the Bible that He loves us and that He is eager to forgive us our sins. He asks us to believe that He is coming again. He asks us to believe that He is real.

Do you believe? If you do, you will treat His name with respect. You will talk to Him throughout each day. You will know that you are special in God's sight, and you will allow that others are special too. And, looking at all the evidence God has given you that He is loving and kind and worthy of your trust, you will have faith in Him.

MARCH 11

THE REAL STAR WARS!

Then there was war in heaven; Michael and the angels under his command fought the Dragon and his hosts of fallen angels. And the Dragon lost the battle and was forced from heaven. Revelation 12:7, 8, TLB.

Have you ever looked around, compared your life to somebody else's, and said, "I'm so lucky to be who I am"?

You are lucky to be you, aren't you? But let's think about the kids who aren't so lucky. Why doesn't God send rain to the people in famine-stricken lands so their gardens will grow? Why does He allow children to be abused? Why doesn't He do something about all the suffering in the world? If you find yourself asking these questions, you are not alone.

Satan has accused God of being selfish and uncaring since before this world was created. The end result of the dispute was that God gave our world to Satan as a "scientific experiment." Created beings on other planets are watching to see what would happen if Satan ruled the universe, rather than God.

The Bible calls this battle between God and Satan a "war." Adventists often call it "the great controversy." And in a war some people are hurt and killed, and others survive almost untouched. During World War II, life in America still consisted of going to work, going to school, preparing meals, having Christmas, and so on. But life in Europe consisted of hiding in bomb shelters, seeing your town blown up, and living in constant, threatening fear. It was the same war, but not all were affected the same way.

If a soldier or a civilian gets killed in a war, is it because his commanding officer killed him? No. The enemy is the culprit. The enemy is to blame.

God is our commanding officer. He's going to end the war soon. And though some people have been hurt by the enemy more than others, it doesn't mean God doesn't love them, or doesn't care. It's just how a war is.

God gives everyone the right to choose his own actions. Tragically, some people make choices that hurt other people badly. We may wish God would step in and zap the robbers and murderers and child molesters, but He doesn't. He must allow people the freedom to follow Satan. There's a war going on, and Satan is trying to do everything he can to make us think it is God's fault.

But Satan is a known liar! Don't be fooled. Don't blame God for disaster. God is love.

MARCH 12

DREAM BIG!

Keep your eyes on Jesus, our leader and instructor. He was willing to die a shameful death on the cross because of the joy he knew would be his afterwards; and now he sits in the place of honor by the throne of God. Hebrews 12:2, TLB.

Way back during Colonial America, when the English fur traders did a lot of business with the American Indians, a certain wealthy Englishman named William Johnson earned a reputation for being very cunning. Mr. Johnson wore his wealth prominently in gold chains and expensive-looking, tailored wool suits. As he was doing business one day with an Indian chief, the Indian said, "White man have very nice suit."

Mr. Johnson looked down at his suit and patted the buttons, nodding. "Yes," he smiled broadly. "It is very warm."

"My suit not very warm," the Indian said solemnly. "But I have dreamed that I had White man's suit as my own."

"If you dream you have my suit, then you must have it," Mr. Johnson said with a smile and a nod. And he promptly went into his bedroom, changed his clothes, and gave the suit to the Indian, even though it was his very best one. That didn't matter to William Johnson. It was part of his larger plan.

A few months later Mr. Johnson visited the Indian's village. He asked about the suit, and the Indian said, "It is very warm."

"I had a dream too," Mr. Johnson said. "I dreamed you owned beautiful fertile land bordering the Mohawk River. I dreamed you gave me five acres of the best land."

With a serious face, the Indian studied the horizon far away for several minutes. And then he said, "It is true. I own much land along the Mohawk River. And now five acres of my best land are yours." Then his eyes narrowed, and he gave Mr. Johnson this declaration. "I will not dream with you again. You dream too hard."

What are some of your dreams? Do you want to be famous someday, or would you rather live a quiet life? What are your talents? How could you best use them to help others?

Whether or not you have dreams, your goals and choices in life are affected by them. Dreams energize. If you keep a dream in mind, you can make choices that will help you realize your potential. Without dreams, you may drift through life without accomplishment or satisfaction.

Our ultimate dream is the second coming of Jesus. So start dreaming. Where would you like to be five years from now? What would you like to be doing in 10 years? Twenty? God's dream is to have you with Him, out of this world.

SOMETHING TO TRUST IN

Since earliest times men have seen the earth and sky and all God made, and have known of his existence and great eternal power. So they will have no excuse [when they stand before God at Judgment Day]. Romans 1:20, TLB.

A college professor found himself puzzled when a certain student enrolled in his algebra class for the fourth year in a row, though she had passed the course the first time she took it. "Why do you take my course every year?" he asked her.

"Because it gives me security," she said. "I'm so tired of arguing about everything with my roommates and discovering that what I learned in biology last year is already out-of-date, along with everything else. I just needed something in my life that was constant."

"What do you mean?" the professor asked.

The student smiled. "Two plus two equals four," she said. "Nobody can argue about it, nobody can change it. Two plus two will always equal four."

There are other things in life that we can always count on, too. These are God's laws. And try as we might, there is no changing them. Can you name some of these laws that never change? How about the law of gravity? If you jump or fall off a cliff, you will go down, possibly to your death. You don't have to wonder if gravity is in effect on weekdays but not on holidays, do you? It always is. Spring follows winter, day follows night. How secure it makes me feel to know that God can be trusted.

The Parks Commission in a small Canadian town was told that certain trees along a road slated to be widened needed to be cut down.

In the lower branches of one of the trees, the foreman noticed a robin's nest. A mother robin sat on the nest, twittering nervously and watching the men with bright, beady eyes.

"Leave that tree till last," the foreman told his crew. The next week he returned to the tree. To his delight, he saw three noisy baby robins in the nest. The wee birds' pink, scrawny necks and overlarge mouths stretched toward the mother robin, who stuffed worms and bugs into their mouths as fast as she could. The foreman smiled and went back to where his men were working on other trees.

A few weeks later the foreman returned to the tree and found the nest empty. The robin family had grown and flown away. Smiling to himself, he lifted the nest gently from the tree, intending to take it home to his daughter. Then something in the bottom of the nest caught his eye. It was a white memory verse card, now brown and stained, but the words were still readable. The words were "We trust in the Lord our God."

You can too. He never changes.

MARCH 14

WHAT TO DO WHEN YOU'RE DISCOURAGED

So don't be anxious about tomorrow. God will take care of your tomorrow too. Live one day at a time. Matthew 6:34, TLB.

There is an allegory about a cave that lived underground, as caves like to do. This cave had spent its lifetime in darkness, and knew nothing else. But one day it heard a voice calling to it. "Come up into the light. Come and see the sunshine!"

The cave retorted, "I don't know what you mean; there isn't anything but darkness." Still, the voice pleaded with the cave to see.

At last, one day the cave ventured forth to see the light. To its surprise, there was light everywhere. There were colors! It was delighted. In a friendly gesture, it invited the sun to its place. "Come see the darkness," it said.

"What is darkness?" asked the sun.

"Just come and see!" the cave replied. And the sun came.

When the sun entered the cave it said, "Now show me your darkness." But that was impossible. Where the sun was, there was no darkness.

If you've ever felt discouraged, you know how dark it feels. Sometimes we get so worried it feels like we're living in a cave. Some kids have money problems. They don't know how much longer they can attend Christian schools because there's so little money to pay for school. Some kids have parents who are divorced or unhappy together, and they're afraid their parents will divorce and break up the home. These are real worries. They are scary. But they don't have to be life-threatening. No matter what happens to us, the sun will always shine the next day, and eventually we will adjust and the crisis will be history.

Life is a continuous series of opposites: joy and sorrow, pleasure and pain, darkness and light. If you expect it to be this way, you will glide through life easier. If your life seems to be on a down-slide, just hang on; something good will happen before too long. Use your down-slides to hang on to Jesus, and cry out to Him all your frustrations and fears. It helps to know that He cares.

Everyone has problems. Jesus knows how it is. He says that living is easier if you take it one day at a time. Find something in the next 24 hours that you can look forward to—a favorite class, a favorite meal, a visit with a favorite person. Maybe just a walk in the sunshine or in the rain. Take the moment, make it an occasion, and enjoy your blessing.

MARCH 15

HOW TO LIVE WITH YOURSELF

If your eye is pure, there will be sunshine in your soul. But if your eye is clouded with evil thoughts and desires, you are in deep spiritual darkness. And oh, how deep that darkness can be! Matthew 6:22, 23, TLB.

Have you ever heard the phrase "It's time to face the music"? Do you know the story behind the phrase?

Long ago in China, a young man signed up to join the emperor's orchestra. Because he seemed so confident about his abilities as a flutist, he was taken on without an audition. The truth was, he couldn't play a note.

For a few years life was good for the young man. He attended orchestra rehearsal every day, holding his flute to his mouth and moving his fingers busily. But he didn't blow on the flute or make a noise, for fear of divulging his secret.

His income from being in the orchestra was quite comfortable, and he was a happy man. That is, he thought he was happy until the day the emperor decreed that he wanted to hear each of the orchestra members play a solo for him.

The lying flutist began to worry. He couldn't sleep, and he couldn't eat. On the day of his solo, he told the royal doctor that he was sick, but the doctor declared him well, and insisted he play for the emperor.

He never showed up. Instead, he killed himself with poison because he couldn't "face the music."

Is there anything that makes you uncomfortable about yourself? Make it right. True happiness comes from maintaining integrity, from having a sense that you are right with man and God and have nothing to hide. In short, true happiness comes from being a moral person, doing what you know is right.

MARCH 16

FAITHFUL DONKEYS SOLVED A MYSTERY

Even the animals—the donkey and the ox—know their owner and appreciate his care for them, but not my people Israel. No matter what I do for them, they still don't care. Isaiah 1:3, TLB.

Once you finish a book, do you read it again? How many times have you reread your favorite book?

Many people who have gone to church school all their lives have a hard time being interested in reading the Bible because they know the stories so well. Perhaps you are one of them. You know how the story of Daniel begins, and you aren't worried when you hear that he is captured, then thrown into jail, and then into the lions' den. You aren't worried because you know he's going to be OK. But because you aren't worried, the story doesn't capture your attention. This doesn't mean the Bible is worthless. It only means that you need to learn how to use your knowledge of the stories to help you personally.

A policeman in Haifa got on the trail of a gang of smugglers. He knew they used donkeys to carry the packs, and he and his men had been able to capture some of the donkeys, though the smugglers got away.

The clever officer, a man familiar with the Bible, kept the donkeys in a stall without food for several days and then turned them loose. Then, just as the Bible verse said, "The ox knoweth his owner, and the ass his master's crib," the donkeys led the policeman straight to the smugglers' hideout.

Rather than reading the Bible for entertainment, read it like a gold miner and sift through it carefully.

Are you discouraged? Find a story about someone in the Bible who was discouraged—David, Esther, Joseph—and see what he or she did to get out of discouragement. Are you worried? Look up *worry* in the concordance and find a promise you can use. Make a color chart, highlighting "worry promises" in one color, "heaven promises" in another color, "forgiveness promises" in another, and so forth. The New Testament books have a lot of promises in them! Then you can find what you need in a hurry. Memorize a verse that speaks to you and repeat it all day long. Believe it or not, there are stories in the Bible that you haven't heard yet, stories that are considered "adult reading." Can you find them?

If you don't have any problems of your own, perhaps you have a friend who needs some encouragement. When you identify what is bothering you and then look for a specific Bible story for help, the Bible becomes what it should be to you—a source of encouragement, peace, and hope.

MARCH 17

WATCH OUT!

Watch out! Don't let my sudden coming catch you unawares; don't let me find you living in careless ease, carousing and drinking, and occupied with the problems of this life, like all the rest of the world. Keep a constant watch. And pray that if possible you may arrive in my presence without having to experience these horrors. Luke 21:34-36, TLB.

Can you find a verse in the Bible that says "And the disciples had a boring day"? Probably not. The Bible, like any good book, includes only incidents of importance in people's lives. But just like you, the disciples and probably even Jesus had their share of boring days. Can you imagine what it was like to pound along a dusty path under a burning sun day after day, followed by beggars and sick people? Or to walk alone for miles? More often than not, that was the daily grind of the disciples.

When we read about the exciting experiences the disciples had with Jesus, it can seem like a movie plot—unreal, yet exciting. And our lives can seem just plain dull in comparison. But people in Bible times were real people with the same feelings that we have, and their own versions of "boring days." Life's like that.

But imagine what it would have been like if those humble peasants and fishermen had had the benefit of our knowledge? If they had known all we know about geology, for example, their lives might have been different. Great pools of oil lay underground, but they weren't aware of it. They didn't have any way to get it out, either, and wouldn't have known what to do with it if they had. But long before, God used that natural resource—and the world will never forget it!

Some years ago Israeli businessman Xiel Federmann began to brood over the account of the destruction of Sodom and Gomorrah ("And, lo, the smoke of the country went up as the smoke of a furnace"). As Mr. Federmann pondered what might cause a city to burn like a furnace, he wondered if there had been a source of underground gas at the site. Underground gas means oil. And Mr. Federmann was right. In 1953 Israel's first oil well went into operation near the ancient site of Sodom and Gomorrah.

So when God destroyed Sodom and Gomorrah, He may have sent fire down from heaven, but He knew it would burn a long time because there was also natural gas below the city.

Even hard-nosed scientists who often work backward from fact to religion acknowledge that the Bible is a book of historical facts. That God was there in the middle of these natural resource catastrophes to warn His people and keep them safe shows me that He was and is still in charge. And when the Bible says that more natural catastrophes will happen just before He comes, but that He will still be with His people, I believe that, too.

MARCH 18

ALWAYS READY

Who then is the faithful and wise servant, whom the master has put in charge of the servants in his household to give them their food at the proper time? It will be good for that servant whose master finds him doing so when he returns. I tell you the truth, he will put him in charge of all his possessions. Matthew 24:45-47, NIV.

Have you ever knitted a scarf with several colors? Some of the colors may not be much to look at by themselves, but when you blend them all together, the result is very attractive. You can knit all the good and bad events in your life into a beautiful ending, too. You have the power. You have the choice of making your life story a happy one, or a sad one.

When Jesus was here, He told a story that could be yours or mine. Being an excellent storyteller, Jesus also provided two possible endings to the story—one happy, one rather scary. Here's the story.

It seems that a certain fabulously rich man had several mansions scattered around the world. He was looking for one good manager to be in charge of one of his smaller estates. The job was a big one. It involved making sure the gardener kept the lawns mowed and the flower beds weeded; seeing that the maid polished the doorknobs; and assuring that the cook kept the freezer clean and stocked so that at any moment the owner of the house could come home to everything being perfectly in order—as though he had never left!

A man we'll call Jake applied for the job. He met with the house owner, Mr. Rathbone, and promised to keep things in perfect order so that Mr. Rathbone would never be disappointed.

Mr. Rathbone was pleased with Jake. "I know you'll do a good job," he said. "I'm not sure when I'll return, but I will be back. So long."

For the first few months Jake did his job well. Every day the house was perfect, the floors swept and polished, the gardens raked, the kettles shining. The servants bustled about as though the boss would be back for supper that very evening! Then a year went by. Mr. Rathbone did not return, and Jake began to do some thinking.

Maybe Mr. Rathbone will never come back at all. He has many luxurious estates. This is one of the smaller ones. Mr. Rathbone probably won't come back for a long, long time. Why waste time cleaning the place every day like this? Once a week should be fine.

Jake began goofing off. He began swimming in the pool every day. Not wanting to swim alone, he invited the cook and the gardener to join him. Jake organized volleyball teams, and they had playoffs. Playing became the most important thing the servants did. The house was cleaned once every two weeks at first, then once a month, and after a while the servants didn't do their work at all. They forgot that they were not here to play, but to keep the place ready for the owner's return.

One day while Jake was sunning himself by the pool, oblivious to the weeds in the flower beds and the spider webs holding the bushes together, he realized with a start that the big iron gates of the estate were creaking open. Jake was surprised! He was the only one who had the key to the gates!

Then his surprise turned to cold fear. There, coming through the gates, was a long, black limousine. Mr. Rathbone was home! Jake tried to hide under the chaise lounge, ashamed.

Jesus said that unless we expect His return every moment of every day, we will be surprised at His coming. We will want to hide when we see Him.

But Jesus offers us another ending to the story.

Every day Jake looked for Mr. Rathbone. And when Mr. Rathbone came home, Jake swung the massive front doors open with a huge smile. He felt good! He was proud to welcome the owner home.

Which ending do you like the best? It's your choice!

MARCH 19

DON'T DIG UP THE DEAD

Where is another God like you, who pardons the sins of the survivors among his people? You cannot stay angry with your people, for you love to be merciful. Once again you will have compassion on us. You will tread our sins beneath your feet; you will throw them into the depths of the ocean! Micah 7:18, 19, TLB.

In the November 1987 *Cornerstone Connections*, Gordon Bietz relates an interesting modern-day parable about a boy and his dog, and about loss.

As you are shoveling snow one evening, your little dog, Fluffy, is running in excited circles around you. Suddenly Fluffy spots the neighbor's cat, an archenemy, and bolts out of the yard toward the street. With horror you see the oncoming car and hear the screech of brakes. Poor Fluffy lies motionless in the dirty, brown slush.

"I am so sorry!" The driver of the car slams the car door and rushes to Fluffy's side.

"You couldn't have helped it," you say past the tightness in your throat. "Fluffy was chasing a cat. She doesn't usually go in the street."

"Is there anything I can do?" the man asks. "I feel so terrible."

"It's OK, really," you try to reassure him. "I forgive you. But maybe you could help me bury her."

"Sure. Anything." He seems relieved.

You dig through the snow and bury Fluffy beneath a favorite tree. Then after reassuring the driver that you've forgiven him, you go into the house for supper.

An hour later the doorbell rings. You're surprised to see the driver standing on your porch, poor, dead Fluffy in his arms. "I am so sorry," he says. "I feel so terrible about killing your dog."

"I know that. But why did you dig her up again?"

"I wanted to show you how awful I feel."

"Well, digging up Fluffy isn't going to do any good. I've already forgiven you. Come on, I'll help you bury her again."

The next morning you're on your way out the door when you nearly bump into someone coming around the corner of the house. It's the driver again. And once more he's holding the dead and dirty Fluffy in his arms.

At your wits' end, you grab Fluffy from the man. "Look," you say, "I don't know what you're trying to prove. I've forgiven you. But you won't believe me. You just go home and let me bury Fluffy myself."

You decide to bury Fluffy where the driver won't be able to find her again.

Have you ever dug up past sins to convince yourself that you are worthless, that God can't possibly forgive you or want you in heaven? Don't do it anymore. This is the good news of the Bible—God wants you to give your past mistakes to Him. He will bury them where you can both forget about them. Forever.

MARCH 20

THE SECRET KEY

The evil man gets rich for the moment, but the good man's reward lasts forever. Proverbs 11:18, TLB.

It was the day before Molly's thirteenth birthday. Her father had asked her to go with him to a fancy restaurant the next evening—her first date—to celebrate the arrival of her teen years. "I have something special to give to you tomorrow," he said.

The next evening Molly dressed for dinner nervously, wondering what in the world her father was going to give her. She was both excited and a little scared to be turning 13. She hoped her father wouldn't get too sentimental and make her cry.

After a magnificent meal, Molly's father took out a small, wrapped box and handed it to her. "Go ahead. Open it," he said with a smile.

Feeling a little uncomfortable, Molly slid the ribbon off the box and then carefully loosened the tape and the paper. A gray, fuzzy box slid gently into her hand. When she unfastened the tiny gold clutch on the side, the box opened to reveal a small gold heart with a key. "It's beautiful," Molly said. "Thank you."

"You're welcome," her father said softly. And then he explained. "Now that you're 13, Molly, you are on the verge of adulthood. You will have many friends—girlfriends and boyfriends."

Molly nodded and smiled, a bit embarrassed, as her father continued. "This heart represents your body, your purity. I hope you will guard it carefully until you find the lucky man who will become your husband. Save yourself for him, Molly. He will be the only one who gets the key."

Molly nodded again and said thank you. Then, as soon as she could, she turned the subject to lighter things. But when she was 19, she realized that her best friend had become a man she loved. She wore the key on her watch chain, and two years later, on the day of her wedding, she gave the key to him.

Growing up. When you take care of yourself in the short-term decisions, the long-term results are out of this world!

WHY CHRISTIANS ARE HAPPY

Your own soul is nourished when you are kind; it is destroyed when you are cruel. Proverbs 11:17, TLB.

You have heard that by helping each other, Christians help themselves. Recently I heard an allegory that illustrates this fact remarkably well.

The story is told about a man who went to heaven. As he stood at the gates of heaven, he asked God if he could see hades before he actually went into heaven, so he could fully appreciate how wonderful heaven was. God agreed, and an angel took the man down to hades.

The air in hades was rank with the smell of rotting food and the sounds of moaning. Everyone sitting around the long tables was thin as a rail and obviously starving—even though the tables were covered with delicious food.

"What's the matter with them?" the man demanded of the angel. "There's plenty of food! Why are they starving?"

The people turned long, drawn faces toward the visitor, with expressions of pain and hunger.

"They can't eat," the angel replied. "Look closely. Everyone is required to use spoons that are four feet long, but they can't feed themselves because their arms aren't long enough. The spoons take the food past their heads. So they starve."

The man watched in dismay as the starving people wildly scooped up spoonfuls of delicious food, then groaned, twisting and contorting their bodies in an effort to make the spoons meet their mouths. But the food fell on the ground behind them and immediately spoiled.

"I've seen enough," the man told the angel, and immediately they returned to heaven.

When they walked through the gates of heaven into the city, the man saw bountiful tables of food just like the tables in hades. But the people sitting around these tables were smiling and talking, looking very well fed and happy. And—this was hard to believe—each one held a four-foot-long spoon.

"What's going on?" the man whispered to the angel, not wanting to attract attention. "These people have the same food and the same eating utensils as the people in hades. How is it that they're not starving?"

"Because," the angel smiled, "they feed each other."

Real Christians look out for each other. Real Christians look out for those who need help. Why don't you find someone who needs you to look out for him today?

MARCH 22

"THE DAY I MET JESUS"

Jesus answered: "Watch out that no one deceives you. For many will come in my name, claiming, 'I am the Christ,' and will deceive many." Matthew 24:4, 5, NIV.

He could have been anybody's grandfather, peering in at me through the car window. Thin face, graying hair, a sharp nose. His eyes were a mysterious steel blue. His clothes were clean and neat, but tattered and worn. His shabbiness seemed out of place when he spoke. "Excuse me," he said in a cultured and dignified manner. "Could you please take me in to town? I have a doctor's appointment, and I need a ride."

A few minutes later we were riding side by side into town. He sat quietly with a sense of dignity and calm. I turned to him and asked, "What do you do for a living?"

Without looking away from the road he replied, "I am a shipbuilder." His reply struck me as strange, because we lived in the mountains and the nearest ocean was more than 100 miles away. Why would a shipbuilder live away from the ocean? When I asked him about this, he turned to me and gravely answered, "I am the greatest shipbuilder in the world. I don't worry about living near the ocean."

I looked over at him with a strange feeling in my stomach. Something about him was not quite right.

When we pulled into town I let him off by a printing shop. He stopped as he got out and asked me if I would wait one minute. Soon he was back clutching a stack of pamphlets. He slid onto the seat beside me and handed me one of the pamphlets. I looked at it, trying to make sense out of the bizarre jumble of pictures, texts, and poems. The man leaned close to me, opened his eyes wide, and stared at me. When our eyes met, he spoke ominously. "I am Jesus Christ," he said slowly. "Fate brought us together this morning. God the Father is over us right now in a spaceship, and in 10 days the world will be destroyed."

I didn't believe him.

If you met someone who claimed to be Jesus, would you believe him? Suppose he worked miracles right before your eyes, healing people and telling people things about the past and the future—then would you believe he was Jesus?

Jesus knew this would happen, and He warned us about it. Take a few minutes to discuss with your family how you would know if someone was or wasn't Jesus. You'll find a clue in Matthew 24:23-27. Don't let 1990 find you deceived.

BELLY-BUTTON CHRISTIANS˙

Listen! The virgin shall conceive a child! She shall give birth to a Son, and he shall be called "Emmanuel" (meaning "God is with us"). Matthew 1:23, TLB.

A little girl asked her father, "How will I know who Adam is when I get to heaven?"

"Well, he'll be the tallest man there," Daddy replied.

"But everyone is tall to me," the little girl complained.

"Well, he'll be the first person Jesus welcomes into heaven with a hug and a crown," her father said patiently.

"But I might not be at the front of the line when Jesus does that," the little girl reasoned.

"Well then, I guess you can ask Jesus who Adam is. He'll tell you."

"No, I have a better way," the little girl said with a smile. "I'll just look at everyone's tummy. Adam will be the man without a belly button!"

Clever little girl. Adam and Eve are the only people who were never babies. But more things than having belly buttons and babyhoods will make us different from Adam. Can you name a few? How about our knowledge of the Bible? It wasn't written when Adam was alive. He doesn't know about Noah, or Daniel, or how bad Jesus was treated because of sin. We can tell Adam all of that, or maybe heaven has a sort of videotape that Adam can watch with us to see the results of sin.

Ellen White says that not even the angels can understand how it feels to deserve nothing, but to be given everything. Forever and for always, those of us on earth have a relationship with Jesus like none other in the entire universe. Angels cannot understand it. And beings on other worlds, who have never sinned, cannot understand it either.

Jesus came to be one with us, "God with us." He is the only Creator who knows just what it's like to be human—He is so human, He even has a belly button!

MARCH 24

MAN-CHILD

"Why are you angry?" the Lord asked [Cain]. "Why is your face so dark with rage? It can be bright with joy if you will do what you should! But if you refuse to obey, watch out. Sin is waiting to attack you, longing to destroy you. But you can conquer it!" Genesis 4:6, 7, TLB.

"You don't know what it's like to have a little brother!" the teenager shouted at his father. "You don't even know what it's like to be a kid!"

The boy's father swallowed hard and ran a hand through his hair. He nodded. "I guess you're right," he said softly. "I don't know what it's like to grow up." He had never had a mother, never had a brother or a sister, never had been faced with anything he couldn't do—except one thing. He couldn't say no.

How would you like to have a father like Adam? Think about it for a minute. Adam didn't know what it was like to be a kid, because he was created a man. He didn't have to learn to walk or talk—he just did it right away! Do you suppose he told Cain and Abel to quit playing and get to work? Or was work so enjoyable to him it was the same as playing?

Unfortunately, Adam was kind of like a kid in a grown-up's body. He did not know how to stand up for what he knew was right. He caved in when Eve coaxed him to take a bite of the fruit. And then when God called to them in the garden that evening, Adam and Eve hid from Him like little kids who know they're in trouble. When they did answer God, they blamed their disobedience on somebody else.

You know that feeling—everybody knows that feeling. It doesn't feel good to know you've done something wrong, does it? Your self-worth, or self-esteem, falls way down. Satan smirks. But God doesn't want you to feel bad.

I kind of like the Adam story, for there's a good side to it. Even though Adam acted foolishly and was very immature, God loves him. Ellen White tells us that Adam will be among those Jesus is going to welcome into heaven. Adam will realize that the unhappiness in our lives and the death of Jesus are the result of his sin, and he'll blame himself and fall down to kiss Jesus' feet.

In heaven Adam will be grown up. Being grown up means making decisions and living bravely with the consequences. It means taking responsibility for what you have done. Perhaps you can share with Adam what you've learned about growing up and making good decisions. Fortunately, all decisions will be good ones once we get to heaven. Won't that be out of this world?

HOW LUCKY ARE YOU?

Always be full of joy in the Lord; I say it again, rejoice! Let everyone see that you are unselfish and considerate in all you do. Philippians 4:4, 5, TLB.

Dry, choking heat blew in the windows of our car as we drove along a country road in Ceylon. My father was driving, and beside him sat a national pastor. Even though he had grown up in the heat, that particular day was so oppressive that even the pastor commented on it. He held his shirt away from his chest with the tips of two fingers and tried to cool himself off that way.

"In America we have air conditioners in the cars," my father told him wistfully. "We also have air conditioners in our houses, so when it's hot in the summertime we hardly feel it." He sighed, considering the heat. "Air-conditioned houses, air-conditioned cars, air-conditioned stores."

The pastor shook his head with a wry smile. "You Americans have so much," he said. "You don't need to go to heaven; you probably won't even appreciate it like we will, because you already have it."

Does your life seem like heaven on earth? Few of us think we are that happy. And yet, to thousands of starving people, or homeless people who sleep on dusty cardboard or city grates, or hungry Filipinos who live in cardboard houses at the edge of the city dump, or children in Beirut who live in bombed-out houses, your life would be like heaven! Imagine! They would give anything for soft, clean beds; enough food that they could throw some away; a family vacation; a chance to get an education, and with that, a good-paying job and a house of their own; a hot shower!

Count your blessings today. Write them down, and see how many you have. It'll make you feel out of this world.

MARCH 26

THE ROWBOATS THAT TAUGHT A LESSON

Dear brothers, how can you claim that you belong to the Lord Jesus Christ, the Lord of glory, if you show favoritism to rich people and look down on poor people? James 2:1, TLB.

A resort hotel owner in Canada has a very unusual way of sharing his faith. Each set of oars that he rents with his rowboats is imprinted with the words Faith on one oar and Works on the other one.

When asked why, the man said, "I think it illustrates so well the necessity of both faith and works. Come on, I'll show you." He took his friend to the middle of the lake. "OK, pull on the 'faith' oar," he said.

His friend pulled, and they began going in circles.

"No good! No good! Use the 'works' oar!" he cried.

His friend did so, and they began going in circles the other direction. "Still no good! Now pull on both oars at once."

When his friend did so, they went in a straight direction. "You see," the hotel owner explained, "how faith and works must pull together. One without the other only makes you go in circles."

What do you think it means to have faith and works? Faith means believing in God and Jesus' power to forgive you and take you to heaven. Works means reaching out to others to share what you know about God and showing them His love.

Some people say they believe in God, but they don't live like they do. They swear and gossip and avoid others who don't look like them or dress like them. They have no works.

Unless our faith in God results in love and concern for others, it will die. Exercise your faith today. Find someone who needs your friendship and concern. You'll be glad you did!

JUST WAIT TILL YOUR FATHER TAKES YOU HOME!

Humility and reverence for the Lord will make you both wise and honored. Proverbs 15:33, TLB.

Do you tend to skip the Old Testament when you're reading the Bible, because it has so many stories of murder and death and you can't understand why God would allow it? Does the Old Testament God seem like a mean and terrible God who frightens you and makes you feel sure you'll never be saved? Many grown-up Christians struggle with the killings recorded in the Old Testament. If God is love, why did He allow or even order it? Some people have given up Christianity because of the Old Testament.

We will probably never have an answer to the question "Why?" God usually doesn't answer "why" questions. He didn't answer Jesus when He cried from the cross, "Why hast thou forsaken me?" Usually, when we ask "why," we only want an argument, and God doesn't argue with us.

The best answer I have found is to tell God that from what I have seen of His fairness throughout the Bible, He must have had a good reason for what He did, even though I may not understand it right now. We are promised that when we get to heaven and God explains things to us, it will all make sense.

There's a place in Canada where the snow never stays on the ground. Even though there may be six-foot drifts of snow all around this acre, green grass always covers this place. The reason? A coal fire that began underground in 1919 still rages underneath, keeping the ground warm. Grasses and flowers grow abundantly all year long because of the heat.

If we have a close friendship with God, if the fire of devotion and trust burns in our hearts, we will believe that He is fair, even though events all around us seem very cold and unfair.

You wouldn't accuse your best friend of robbery, would you? You wouldn't even believe it if someone said he saw your friend robbing a store. You would be sure it was a case of mistaken identity. Your friend just wouldn't do that! It's the same with God. Because we know that God is love, we won't accuse Him of being unloving on account of the Old Testament killings. We will continue to think the best of Him and wait patiently until He explains, knowing it will all make sense then.

YOU'RE SO LUCKY TO BE YOUNG!

Young man, it's wonderful to be young! Enjoy every minute of it! Do all you want to; take in everything, but realize that you must account to God for everything you do. Ecclesiastes 11:9, TLB.

When I was in college, I was often touched by news stories I heard about people starving in other countries, needing to know about a better life. I wanted to help, but I couldn't. I had to go to school. And it bothered me sometimes!

Now I'm a mother, and I'm "out there" in the working world, but it still doesn't seem enough. Yet I can't just leave everything and everybody and live in a tent in Africa. I must stay here and be responsible to the people around me.

Do you ever feel that way? Do you ever feel like you just aren't growing up fast enough?

Billy Graham was once asked if he ever felt that way. He said he did. But he held Bible studies and Youth for Christ meetings while he was in college as a way to meet that need. Now, however, he says he wishes he had spent more time on his studies instead, because he realizes how short the school years are, and how long the years that come after.

It's often hard to find the balance between meeting all our obligations here on this earth and preparing ourselves for our future life out of this world in heaven, isn't it?

So what can you do? Perhaps the best advice is Billy Graham's. Concentrate on the present. Be the best student you can be, for that is your job now.

Football coach Joe Kapp has this to say about achieving: Success is living up to your potential. That's all. Wake up with a smile and go after life. Don't just show up at the game—or at class. Live life. Enjoy it, taste it, smell it, feel it! There are few second chances in the game of life.

HOW TO KNOW WHEN TO BE SELFISH

The Lord is close to those whose hearts are breaking; he rescues those who are humbly sorry for their sins. The good man does not escape all troubles—he has them too. But the Lord helps him in each and every one. Psalm 34:18, 19, TLB.

A little boy was playing on the floor as his aunt was trying to teach him his alphabet. But he seemed unable to keep his mind on his work.

Suddenly he asked, "Auntie, may I ask God to help me find my marble?"

His aunt nodded her consent, and the little boy kneeled down and prayed. Then he sat in a chair next to his aunt, and they continued with the lesson.

The next day, almost afraid of asking the question in case the little boy had not found his toy and would lose his simple faith, the aunt said, "Well, honey, did you find your marble?"

"No, Auntie," the little boy replied. "But God has made me not want to."

Praying about our problems gives us hope and courage to accept whatever comes, doesn't it? No one ever has a life without problems. Jesus never promised that Christians wouldn't have problems. What we do have is the assurance that whatever problems Satan throws our way, God can turn them around into something useful. He can make good things out of them—in the long run.

As humans, we usually look for short-term benefits, but God works in the long-term.

If your parents are divorced, it hurts. But you will not be dependent on them forever. Parents are not born married. Some of them make poor choices. Eventually you're going to be a grown-up yourself, and look how smart you will be, realizing the importance of carefully choosing whom you marry. You know how important it is to wait until you know your own values before you make that choice.

When it comes to choosing a life's partner, you have to be "healthfully selfish." You can't marry someone just because you hate to say no and hurt his feelings. Do you hurt yourself, or hurt him? In this case, it's better to think about your own happiness.

Keep in your mind a vision of yourself as a grown-up. Where do you want to be five years from now? Ten years? What will you be doing then? Enjoy life, but keep in mind it always changes. The time to be happy is now. And you can be happy if you maintain your integrity with God and man and yourself.

HOW TO BE SURE YOU'LL BE SAVED

And now, my little children, stay in happy fellowship with the Lord so that when he comes you will be sure that all is well, and will not have to be ashamed and shrink back from meeting him. 1 John 2:28, TLB.

Young Eddie was the youngest brother of nine children. He had a little sister who was younger than he was, but nobody did anything mean to her, because she was "the baby." But Eddie's big brothers often got him into quite scary situations and then laughed at him about them.

One day, when Eddie was about 9 years old, his big brothers rolled him up inside the large rug lying on the floor of their dormitory-like bedroom. First they made him lie down with his arms over his head. Then they began rolling him over and over, tightening the rug around him. They told him they'd unroll him whenever he asked, and he trusted them. But once he was rolled up tight, his brothers ran downstairs laughing and snickering at Eddie's hollers for help.

Eddie thought he was going to die. The rug was heavy, and there was no way he could get himself unrolled. He was the rug's captive. Terrified, he screamed and yelled until he was hoarse. His arms, held tight above his head, began to tingle. It was dark and dusty inside that rug, and at last Eddie's screams gave way to tearful pleas for help. He felt doomed, convinced that he would not live to be found.

But all at once he heard footsteps pounding up the stairs. Moments later strong arms unrolled the heavy rug and lifted him up into the fresh air. His muffled cries had brought his mother up to rescue him. She had heard when no one else had cared.

In a way we are all trapped. This world has some glorious beauty and a lot of love, but it also has its share of pain and fear. It's not perfect, and won't be until Christ makes a new earth for the saved. We certainly don't want Satan to get us all wrapped up in this earth, do we? Time and time again, we find ourselves calling to Jesus to save us. There's no way out of this world except through Him.

We could try to jump to heaven, but it won't work. We could try to take a spaceship to heaven, but we'd never make it. And besides, we wouldn't know which direction to go.

We need Jesus! He has the power to save us from sin and to take us to heaven, where we will live forever—out of this world!

MARCH 31

THE ELEVATOR WHO WANTED TO STAY AT THE TOP

For all these worldly things, these evil desires—the craze for sex, the ambition to buy everything that appeals to you, and the pride that comes from wealth and importance—these are not from God. They are from this evil world itself. 1 John 2:16, TLB.

An elevator in a skyscraper, as the story goes, felt bored with life. All he did, day after day, was go up and down. Whining his way to the top of the building one day, he complained to the topmost stones that he wanted to stay up there with them. "You're right," the stones told him. "We are the most important. We're at the top and have the best view."

Just then the elevator's bell summoned him to the basement, where the basement stones had some advice for him. "The stones on the top are unstable," they said. "The best stones, the strongest, are down here."

The elevator snorted in disgust and began to climb away. Just then the building shook, and the topmost stones lay broken on the basement floor.

The elevator was speechless, but the basement stones were not. "So you see," they said wisely, "the most solid stone in the structure is the lowest one in the foundation."

What does that mean in people terms? It can mean that it's lonely to be "at the top." For one reason, people often get jealous of you. Whether it's because your grades are always above every one else's, because your family is well-to-do, because you have a good build or long, beautiful hair, anything that sets you apart from other kids can become a reason for jealousy.

It can be lonely to be class president or a school senator, for example. As soon as you get into a position of leadership, some kids will be hanging about just to be seen with the top person. They're not true friends, because they're after whatever benefits the crowd can give them.

But the best friends are the ones who like you for who you are, not for how popular you can make them seem. The most solid friends are people who are genuine and warm, and count quality of friendship more than quantity. This doesn't mean you shouldn't do your best in class and try to get good grades. It doesn't mean you shouldn't run for class president. Just be warned that if you think you won't be happy until you accomplish those goals, you may be in for a surprise. You may be more stressed out than you are now.

The best goal is to do your best. Compete only with yourself. Beat your own last score on the next test. Find friends you just enjoy being with, whether or not they're popular. Find happiness in whatever situation you find yourself in right now.

APRIL 1

THOROUGHBRED HORSES

But if anyone keeps looking steadily into God's law for free men, he will not only remember it but he will do what it says, and God will greatly bless him in everything he does. James 1:25, TLB.

Arabian horse trainers have one goal in mind: to train their horses to obey them and to look good in the show arena.

As with everything else, there are good horse trainers and bad horse trainers. The best trainers take several months to train their horses to keep their focus on the goal and not be distracted by anything else. When it comes time for the show, these horses are self-disciplined. They keep their eyes straight ahead and do very well.

But the bad trainers are in a hurry. They use painful bits to make their horses obey them and keep their eyes straight ahead. Whenever the horse turns its head, the trainer pulls on the bit, and it cuts into the horse's mouth. What would you do quickly if you were the horse? You would keep your eyes straight ahead, wouldn't you, so you wouldn't get hurt.

This works well during training. But the trainers are not allowed to use the painful bits in the shows. And since the horses have not learned to keep their eyes on the goal for any other reason except to avoid pain, they don't do well without the bits. They don't do as well as the horses who have learned to keep going without getting distracted or sidetracked by everything else going on—the horses who take their job seriously.

One reason parents take their children to church and send them to church school is because they want them to be like the well-disciplined horses. They want them to be well grounded, to have a good foundation of trust and love for Jesus. If this trust begins when children are small, it will continue throughout adult life.

If you are a Christian only when it's convenient, you won't do well under pressure. You must know and trust Jesus for yourself.

The most important desire of every Christian parent's heart is to have his children in heaven with him in an unbroken family circle. Your parents are doing everything they can to make that happen. And they do it for one reason: because they love you. You are very, very special.

APRIL 2

WHAT YOU ARE SPEAKS LOUDER THAN WHAT YOU DO

If you are wise, live a life of steady goodness, so that only good deeds will pour forth. And if you don't brag about them, then you will be truly wise! James 3:13, TLB.

There is one thing that makes life exciting. It is the knowledge that something is "just around the corner."

There's a clock in Strasburg, Germany, that has the inscription "One of these hours the Lord is coming."

Billy Graham says that there is an inscription in the dome of the Capitol in Washington, D.C., that few people know about. It states, "One far-off divine event toward which the whole creation moves."

A visitor saw this inscription and asked the guide what it meant. He said, "I think it refers to the second coming of Christ." When the dome was erected, some God-fearing official ordered that inscription to be put there to remind us that this life is not all there is.

So if Jesus' coming is "just around the corner," why is it important for you to go to school and "waste" your time studying math and English? Shouldn't you be out giving Bible studies? How does a student do God's will?

The Bible tells us that everyone has different gifts. Not everyone is called to give Bible studies. Some of us give the best witness by daily activities.

A Christian family invited their new neighbor to go with them to their Christmas program at church. He had lived next door to them for just a few months, and had refused every other offer they had made, so they were a bit hesitant to invite him again. But they gathered up their courage and did.

To their surprise, he accepted the invitation happily. "I'd be happy to come," the neighbor said. "I know I haven't accepted any other invitations you have given me, but I wasn't sure about Christianity before. I've been listening to your family. I don't know your religion, but I've heard your family's laughter, and I want what you people have."

So maybe you don't always have to give Bible studies to share your faith. It's true that what you are speaks much louder than what you say.

Take a few moments right now and discuss what you can do today to be an extension of Jesus' loving hands. You can work for Him and go to school. And as you share His love with others, He fills you up with even more love and happiness. Try it and see!

APRIL 3

HOW TO BE A SUCCESSFUL PERSON

Whatsoever thy hand findeth to do, do it with thy might. Ecclesiastes 9:10.

Thirteen-year-old Bobby Hill, son of a U.S. Army sergeant stationed in Italy, loved to read biographies about famous people. One biography in particular impressed him. It was about Albert Schweitzer, Nobel Peace Prize winner and medical missionary. Bobby wanted to do something to help. If he could do his small part, he would be happy.

As he thought about what Dr. Schweitzer might need the most, Bobby decided to send him some aspirin. He knew that if he was a patient, he would like to feel comfortable. His mother always gave him aspirin whenever he hurt himself really bad, and it always made him feel better. So probably other people would like a little aspirin too, if they were hurting. Bobby didn't have much money. But he bought the largest bottle of aspirin he could afford.

Now the problem of how to get it to Dr. Schweitzer. Where was his jungle hospital? Bobby didn't have the address. But at his father's suggestion, he mailed it to General Richard Lindsay, the Commander of the Allied forces in Southern Europe. "This is for Dr. Albert Schweitzer," Bobby wrote in his letter. "I would appreciate it if any of your airplanes could parachute it to Dr. Schweitzer's jungle clinic in Africa."

Commander Lindsay was touched. He told a local radio station what Bobby had done. After hearing about the young boy's gift, a radio station in Italy aired Bobby's desire to help. Within a few weeks, more than $400,000 worth of medical supplies were donated. But that was not all. Both the French and Italian governments provided airplanes to fly the supplies, as well as Bobby Hill and his parents, to Dr. Schweitzer's hospital.

"I never thought a young boy could do so much for my hospital," a grateful Dr. Schweitzer remarked.

There are seemingly little things that you can do to bring much happiness to others. You can organize a singing band for a nursing home. The lonely people there love visits from young people like yourself. They are starving for a warm handshake or a hug.

You can take soup and sandwiches to the homeless people in your town who live on the streets. Recently one young boy who did that was featured on the news, and so many donations have come in for his business that his parents have quit their other jobs and feed the homeless on a full-time basis.

But it doesn't matter whether or not you get on the news, or even whether or not thousands of dollars pour in to help your cause. Someone has said, "If I cannot do great things, let me do small things in a great way." People who are successful are those who put forth that extra effort.

Find someone you can help, and help this person in a great way! His happiness—and yours—will be out of this world.

APRIL 4

WHERE TEMPTATION COMES FROM

Temptation is the pull of man's own evil thoughts and wishes. These evil thoughts lead to evil actions and afterwards to the death penalty from God. James 1:14, 15, TLB.

A minister knelt, praying over a desperately ill little boy. The doctor had said it wouldn't be long till the child died. "Dear Lord," the minister prayed, "if it is Your will, please let this child live."

The grieving mother looked up at the minister with frightened eyes. "It must be His will," she explained. "I cannot bear 'if's'!"

The minister stopped praying and quietly left the house.

The mother continued to watch her son in his illness, never leaving his side. In time, contrary to expectations, the little boy recovered. He grew to be a man. But as he grew older, his mother knew that something terrible was wrong. Twice he even tried to kill her. He seemed demented.

Often his mother thought back to the time he had been so sick and she had told the minister to stop praying for him. What sort of monster had he become?

Before he was 22, this boy's mother saw him hanged for murder. She must have wondered time and again why she had insisted on her own will when he was a little boy, instead of letting God's will be done.

We could ask, "Was it God's will that the boy become a murderer and be hanged? Why did the boy do these things? Why did God allow it?" Why not ask, "Why did the boy make such bad decisions?"

Evidently he allowed himself to think evil thoughts, and his thoughts resulted in evil actions.

Our aim should be to know God so well that our thoughts are like His. Then we won't question Him. We will just trust that under His loving care, things will work out for good in the long run. You can get to know God just like you get to know people—by reading their letters and messages to you, by observing what they have made, and by talking to them about what their interests are.

God's love letters in the Bible tell us that His most pressing interest is to show us that He loves us and that we are special to Him. They also tell us that He is coming soon—to take us out of this world.

During the Holocaust, when millions of Jews were tortured and killed, a message was found scrawled in bold black letters in an abandoned synagogue in Germany. It said, "I believe in God . . . even when He is silent."

APRIL 5

HANGING BY A THREAD

Consider it pure joy, my brothers, whenever you face trials of many kinds, because you know that the testing of your faith develops perseverance. James 1:2, 3, NIV.

Many years ago a tall chimney in England had been completed, and the scaffolding was being removed. At that point, the supervisor of the project climbed up to the top to oversee the process and to make certain that everything was in order.

Noting that everything was well, the order was given to remove the scaffolding. Only when it had been taken away did workers notice that something had been forgotten. A rope should have been fastened at the top of the chimney for the supervisor to come down with. Now he was stranded at the top of the tall chimney with no way to get down, and no way to get a rope to him.

The man's young son, who had been below watching the excitement, dashed back to his house as fast as his little legs would carry him. "Mother! Mother!" he cried, breathless. "They've forgotten the rope, and Dad's going to throw himself down!" Whispering a prayer, the supervisor's wife left her washing and dried her hands on her apron, hurrying out the door after her son. It was a heart-stopping sight to see her husband at the top of the chimney, white-knuckled, with only a toehold ledge to stand on.

"George!" she called up desperately, hoping her husband could hear her over the din of the milling, murmuring crowd. "George! Unravel your sock and tie a piece of mortar to the end, and lower it down!" Since she had knitted the socks herself, she knew they would unravel easily.

Her husband heard her and did as she had asked. As the yarn came within reach, the woman told the men to tie some twine to the mortar. Then she called to her husband to pull the yarn back up.

At the end of the yarn was the twine. And as the man pulled the twine, he discovered a strong rope fastened to the end of it. Gratefully, he fastened the rope to the top of the chimney and lowered himself down, as he should have been able to do from the start.

It was only a small thing—a length of thin, weak yarn—that they first used to get the rope to him. And that's how our faith is too. When we first acknowledge that God is love and that He is in charge of our lives, it doesn't feel very strong. But every time we sense God's leading, every time we have an answered prayer, our bond with Him becomes stronger.

Get started talking to God as a friend. Tell Him you trust Him and that you love Him. You don't have to kneel every time you pray. You can talk to Him all day long. Tell Him what makes you happy. Tell Him what makes you sad—or mad. The more you get to know Him, the more you find to love.

HOW TO KNOW IF YOUR FAMILY IS HEALTHY

But the wisdom that comes from heaven is first of all pure and full of quiet gentleness. Then it is peace-loving and courteous. It allows discussion and is willing to yield to others; it is full of mercy and good deeds. It is wholehearted and straightforward and sincere. James 3:17, TLB.

A child we'll call Mike was abused by his father every time they were alone. He told his mother that he didn't want to go on trips with his dad because he was scared to be alone with him, but his mother said, "Don't be silly. He's your father. Go along with him and keep him company."

So Mike had to go, though he was terrified. And his father abused him each time they were alone. Mike soon came to believe that he deserved to be abused, that if he was better-looking, or more obedient, or smarter, his father wouldn't hurt him. He thought, wrongly, that abuse was something a father had to do to a bad son.

When he became a teenager and went to boarding school, Mike was surprised to hear his friends talk warmly of their fathers. Some of the guys actually enjoyed being with their fathers! Their fathers sent them letters saying how proud they were of the boys! Mike's father had never said he was proud of him. He always said he was ashamed to be known as Mike's dad. Mike began to feel like he had missed something he could never have—a father who was proud of him. That realization hit him hard. He became depressed, but few people knew it, because Mike always acted as though he didn't have a care in the world.

Then Mike met and married a girl who didn't know about his family. She didn't know how abused Mike had been as a child. She and her family loved Mike, and for the first time he discovered what it was like to be loved for no other reason than that he was Mike!

His father continued to belittle him and tell him he was worthless, but Mike's wife and her family and all of the friends Mike had made told him otherwise. Fortunately, he saw for himself that his father's problem was just that—his father's own emotional problem. Mike was a neat person. He didn't deserve to be abused. Nobody does!

Your value does not come from what you look like, or what kind of grades you make, or whether or not you are cheerful all the time. Your value comes from just being alive. You are valuable because you were created by God.

Professionals tell us that families of alcoholics and/or abuse have a common motto: "Don't think, don't act, don't feel." In these families, nobody talks about anything but the weather. They avoid each other.

They don't share feelings, and it's too risky to talk about problems. A family like that is headed for trouble, and its members need to get help immediately.

If you think your family needs help, don't just talk to anybody. Talk to a trusted adult friend. If that friend can't help you, find someone who can; maybe your pastor or school counselor. They don't judge. They are there to help you bear your burdens. Don't be afraid of "ruining the family's reputation." If you get help, your family can change and become happy! In the long run, your parents will most likely thank you for helping them.

APRIL 7

WHAT MAKES PIGEONS SO SMART?

I will instruct you (says the Lord) and guide you along the best pathway for your life. Psalm 32:8, TLB.

Have you ever seen a desert in real life? Have you ever walked very far in a desert? Deserts are easy places to get lost in because there are no landmarks, and the sand dunes can change shape continuously—almost like magic!

There was a certain guide in Arabia who never got lost in the desert. This man was incredible! People talked about him in awe. Regardless of the time of day or the time of the year, this man could lead anyone out of the desert with amazing accuracy—and all because of a secret companion. What do you suppose that secret helper was? A homing pigeon.

The guide would take his homing pigeon with him on every trip into the desert. He tied a long length of fine twine to the bird's foot, and whenever he was in doubt as to which direction he should go, the guide simply tossed his pigeon into the air and told it to fly home.

Without fail, the pigeon would tug at the cord, flying in the direction of home. And following the pigeon, the Arabian guide made it safely home each time. He knew that he could trust the pigeon's instincts to find its way home.

Who has given pigeons such a superb sense of direction? That's right—God has. We can trust Him to guide us, too, if we listen to Him on our journey out of this world to heaven.

HOW TO MAKE TIME FOR YOURSELF

Finishing is better than starting! Ecclesiastes 7:8, TLB.

Scott threw his books on his bed with a tired sigh. His best friend had just called to invite him to go swimming, but he had had to turn down the invitation. "I've got to finish my homework," he explained. "I still have yesterday's to do."

"OK! See ya!" his friend said and hung up.

Scott plopped down beside his books, folded his hands behind his head. Why was he the only one who never got his papers in on time? he wondered. Why didn't he ever have time to go swimming after school? Perhaps if he got started on his homework now, he could get a little bit of swimming in with the boys. No, he didn't feel like starting on it yet. First he had to get something to eat.

Ambling down to the kitchen, he made himself a peanut butter sandwich. Then he poured a glass of milk for himself and started for his room. No—Mom had a rule that he couldn't eat anywhere but in the kitchen.

Scott turned back and started toward the table, flipping on the TV as he passed. He could watch a little while he ate.

But he finished his sandwich before the program was over, and by that time he was involved in the story and didn't want to turn it off. So he didn't. When the program was over, he started back toward his room again.

He had to stop and tease his little sister, and then noticed his mom had bought a new kind of air freshener for the bathroom. He had to spray it and try it out, of course! Once he got back to his room, he had to change his clothes before he started on his homework. Then he fiddled with his radio and took his time finding his favorite station. By that time his mother was home from work, and told him to hang up the clothes he had taken off and come down to help her fix supper.

He did. And then after supper his favorite TV show was on, which he couldn't miss, and after that there wasn't enough time to finish his homework before bed. He complained to his friends the next day. "I never can finish my homework," he said. "I wish I was smart like you, so I could get it done on time. Some guys have all the luck!"

What do you think? Was intelligence his main problem? Or was it procrastination? If you have the same problem Scott did, I would suggest two things for you.

First, set limits and make a "homework hour." Decide, for example, that you'll do homework between 3:30 and 4:30.

Second, get started. This is the hardest part of getting work done, but it's the most important. You can't finish unless you start.

The Bible tells us that lazy people lose out in the long run. If you've been lazy, do something about changing. It sometimes means hard work. But "happiness, I have discovered, is nearly always a rebound from hard work" (David Grayson, in *Adventures in Contentment*).

APRIL 9

HOW TO GET THINGS DONE

In the beginning God created the heavens and the earth. . . . And there was evening, and there was morning—the first day. . . . And there was evening, and there was morning—the second day. . . . God saw all that he had made, and it was very good. And there was evening, and there was morning—the sixth day. Genesis 1:1, 5-31.

"I'm depressed." Susan sighed and flopped into the nearest chair.

Her mother watched her silently from the dining room where she was setting the table. "What's the matter?" she asked gently.

Susan gestured toward the stack of books on the floor. "I've got a paper to write on England, and I just don't know where to begin."

"What notes do you have so far?" her mother asked.

"Nothing! That's the problem! I don't know where to begin!"

"You have to decide on a topic before you can begin," Mom suggested. "That's the first step in writing a paper. Choose a topic, do your research, write your rough draft, polish it, and then write the final copy. When you divide the assignment into smaller parts, you get a feeling of accomplishment as you finish each one. First you finish choosing your topic, then you finish doing your research on that topic, then you finish your rough draft, then you finish editing it, and then you actually finish the job!"

Susan darted her eyes toward the ceiling helplessly. Mom was so organized.

Mom continued. "What interests you about England? The temperature? The royal family? Buckingham Palace?"

"Well, the royal family kind of interests me," Susan admitted.

"Then why don't you look up the history of the royal family, or what their duties are, or how they live, or some of the more interesting characters? Get started! That's the only way you'll get finished!"

Susan nodded and began gathering up her books. She eyed her mother with an interested look in her eye. "How is it that you know how to make it sound easy?" she asked.

"It's in the Bible," Mom replied. "God took Creation one step at a time, one day at a time, and as He finished each part He said, 'That's very good.' "

104

She waved Susan away. "Go on. Start your research. Do each part carefully so you can say to yourself, as you finish, 'That's very good!' "

If you don't have a plan—a vision—how do you know where you're going? Goals are good for us. Goals are like the top of a mountain. To reach the goal, we have to take one step at a time, but as we keep looking at our goal, we know which direction to take.

What is your most pressing goal for today? For your life? What little steps can you take, in ascending order, to achieve that goal? Write them down and enjoy the feeling of satisfaction when you reach the goal at the top of that mountain and can say with a smile, "I did it!"

You'll feel out of this world!

WHAT YOU GAIN WHEN YOU LOSE

If you cling to your life, you will lose it; but if you give it up for me, you will save it. Matthew 10:39, TLB.

"Why me?" Darcy wailed. "Why should this happen to me? Just when I need time to study, my mother gets sick, my boyfriend breaks up with me, I've been signed up for flute lessons, and I have to do all the cooking and cleaning for the family! Why me? It just isn't fair!"

Have you ever said that?

One of the best ways to guarantee that you'll be disappointed in life is to let yourself think that life is fair and that you will always enjoy it. Life is not fair. Life isn't always fun. Life is about learning how to give up things. But rather than being something to dread, giving up things can be something to look forward to!

You've been giving up things for a long time, already. When you were born, you gave up being attached to your mother inside. As you continued to grow, you gave up letting your mother feed you, and you learned to feed yourself. You learned to walk so you could give up being carried and could go where you wanted to go. You learned to dress yourself and choose your own clothes. You have been making more and more of your own decisions, giving up dependence for independence. Eventually, you will learn how to make your own money and get your own job so you can live by yourself! Look at how much you will have given up at that point! But think how much you will have gained by it!

In *The Treasure Chest* Ralph W. Sockman says, "There are parts of a ship which, taken by themselves, would sink. The engine would sink. The propeller would sink. But when the parts of a ship are built together, they float.

"So it is with the events of my life. Some have been tragic. Some have been happy. But when they are built together they form a craft which is going someplace, and I am comforted."

God's promise is that you are going someplace. As you continue to give up things in this life and concentrate on talking to Jesus as a friend, you also keep on gaining. You gain a life that's out of this world!

APRIL 11

GOOD, BUT ALONE

I have given them your word and the world has hated them, for they are not of the world any more than I am of the world. John 17:14, NIV.

Sometimes when you refuse to do something others are doing because you know it is wrong, they get mad at you. When this happens, it is very easy to feel that you don't have any friends and that you don't belong.

Jesus must have felt very lonely the night before He was killed. His friends slept as He pleaded with God for strength. Then His friends ran away when the soldiers came to arrest Him. Finally, Christ's arms and feet were stretched out on the cross and soldiers drove sharp nails through His limbs, pinning Him to the cross. He had nothing to dull the pain. And He had no one near to hug and comfort Him as the pain flashed through the nerves of His body. Even God, His Father, drew away from Him then, and Jesus cried, "My God, my God, why have you forsaken me?" (Matthew 27:46, TLB).

Sometimes you and I feel lonely like Jesus did. But even though people who don't love God are cruel to us, we are not really alone. You see, we only *feel* alone. In reality there are many more servants of God than servants of Satan.

Imagine that you are in the middle of the desert and you pick up one grain of sand between your fingers. That grain of sand represents our world. In this world, the majority of people don't respect God or His children. Look, however, at the endless rolling hills made up of countless grains of sand. These grains of sand represent other worlds throughout the universe whose inhabitants are true to God. These many worlds contain countless beings who love and serve God.

Remember that the next time you feel alone. As a child of God, you are never alone or outnumbered. There are others, out of this world, who believe and trust God as you do.

THE DREAM

For the wages of sin is death, but the gift of God is eternal life in Christ Jesus our Lord. Romans 6:23, NIV.

It's a wonder I grew up at all, considering the environment I grew up in! I have two older sisters who were both very mean to me—you brothers with older sisters understand what I'm saying, don't you? Not only were my older sisters mean, but my parents were mean too! They would never let me eat all the ice cream I wanted, and when we went to a fair my father would allow me only three rides on those exciting roller coasters. Now do you see how difficult it was for me to grow up? Of course, I'm only joking. But sometimes when I didn't get my own way, I pouted and thought bad thoughts about my family.

One night I had a dream—a dream about Jesus' coming! In my dream, I was standing beside my "mean" family. The wind was howling and the earth was shaking. We were scared. Suddenly we noticed a small cloud on the horizon. The cloud got bigger and bigger and—yes!—we could see Jesus on the cloud!

I glanced over at my "mean" sisters. They wouldn't be going to heaven, I was sure of that. I looked at my "mean" parents. They wouldn't be going to heaven either, I knew. Of all the people in our family, I was sure I'd be the only one taken to heaven.

As I stood there lost in thought, I saw, out of the corner of my eye, my sisters becoming taller. I looked over at them and gasped as I realized they were actually floating up into the air! My parents were going up too! I was left behind.

Frantically, I bent my knees and jumped—hard. But I fell back to earth. I tried again. And again! But I kept falling back down. My own efforts just weren't good enough to get me to heaven. That's when I began to understand the meaning of our text for today. Going to heaven was not a "right" I had somehow earned. Eternal life was a gift from Jesus. He earned it and He gave it to me! The good news is that He earned it for you, too.

Go ahead. Take His gift. Just reach out and say "Thank You. I believe You." Let 1990 be the year that you confirm your future in heaven!

WHAT IT MEANS TO FORGIVE

I am still not all I should be but I am bringing all my energies to bear on this one thing: Forgetting the past and looking forward to what lies ahead. Philippians 3:13, TLB.

They were the best of friends. As president and vice president of their eighth-grade class, Alan and Chester had hours of fun planning class outings and working together like a real team!

But one day after a field trip, the principal called Alan into his office. He told him that because some of the students had been seen in a theater that afternoon, the entire eighth-grade class had to be punished. There would be no more field trips for the rest of the year. "I want your support when I break the news to the class," the principal said.

Alan took a deep, helpless breath. He thought the principal was being unfair. But he respected the man's authority. "Yes, sir," he responded.

After the principal broke the news to the class someone directed a question to Alan. "Whose side are you on? Why didn't you stand up for us innocent ones?"

"Impeach him!" came a taunt from the back of the room. "Elect a new president!" Others joined in noisily.

Alan looked over at Chester for his support, but Chester just looked down at his shoes. When the principal calmed the students down, he explained that Alan would not be removed as president. "And the decision to discipline all of you is just as final," he said.

For the next few weeks nobody talked to Alan. When the students had a suggestion for the graduation program, they took it to Chester. Chester made decisions without checking with Alan.

At last Alan got Chester to talk to him. "Why are you doing this?" he asked in desperation. "I thought we were friends!"

"We were," Chester replied, "but the kids want someone who listens to them and stands up for them. They don't want a noodle for a president."

That did it. Alan felt betrayed. And he couldn't forgive Chester for what he had done. At last his sister told him, "Carrying a grudge is hurting you more than it hurts Chester. You need to forgive him."

"But I can't! He hurt me!"

"Forgiving him means doing yourself a favor," his sister persisted. "Forgiveness doesn't mean saying 'Do it again! Hurt me some more!' Sometimes people do things to us that make us unable to trust them anymore. Sometimes friendships break up because of it. But forgiveness means you choose not to think about it anymore. You close the chapter and let your wounds heal."

Alan admitted he was hurting more than Chester was. He didn't want to think about Chester's betrayal anymore. So Alan forgave Chester and stopped reminding himself how he had been hurt. But he wasn't comfortable being with Chester anymore, so he found other friends. By the end of the summer he had almost forgotten the pain. He even felt like maybe he would be ready to make friends with Chester again when the new school year began.

His sister had been right. "Forgive" and "forget" were one and the same thing.

THE MOST AMAZING BIBLE TEXT

For in the days before the flood, people were eating and drinking, marrying and giving in marriage, up to the day Noah entered the ark; and they knew nothing about what would happen until the flood came and took them all away. Matthew 24:38, 39, NIV.

In my opinion, our text for today is the most amazing text in the Bible. Yes, it looks like an ordinary text. As you read it, you nod your head and say, "Yes, that's right." But when you think about what Jesus is saying, the text is amazing! For Jesus tells us that the people of Noah's day "knew nothing about what would happen until the flood came and took them all away." Do you see what's so amazing? They knew nothing until the Flood came!

It wasn't as though they should have been surprised. There were plenty of clues that should have warned them the Flood was coming. Noah kept on preaching to them every day about the Flood. Some of them believed and planned to be in the ark. I can picture Ham, Shem, and Japheth singing "Just as I Am" while Noah called for commitments. I can see the people coming forward saying, "Yes, I want to be saved in the ark!"

Year after year passed as the huge boat took shape under Noah's direction. Ten years. Twenty years. And the sun came up every morning, the sun set every evening. People went to work and came home. Young people fell in love, married, and started families. Babies were born, grew up, and some even died. People grew old. And still Noah kept on preaching; he and his sons kept on building. Everything seemed so ordinary and predictable that no one could believe there could ever be a flood! Gradually people became blinded by time and delay.

The people became so blind that they failed to see the significance of wild animals marching miraculously into the ark. They didn't even wonder when that huge wooden door creaked as it was slammed shut by unseen hands. Jesus says that they didn't know the Flood was coming until it was already there.

According to Jesus, this is how it will be when He comes. People won't know He's coming until it's too late. How many years have we been saying that Jesus is coming? It's been more than 2,000 years, ever since Christ returned to heaven. Some people who thought it would be soon have begun to wonder if it will ever happen.

Yet things keep on happening in our aging, weary world that should alert us to the fact that Christ is coming soon. Unfortunately, as we go about our busy lives we don't notice. Just like the people who lived during Noah's time, we are blinded by time and delay.

Look around you. Don't be surprised. Christ is coming soon!

APRIL 15

WHAT WAS IN JEREMY'S EGG?

But the fact is that Christ did actually rise from the dead, and has become the first of millions who will come back to life again some day. 1 Corinthians 15:20, TLB.

Sometimes we wonder how much retarded persons understand about life. It's easy to just assume that much of what we say and do goes "right over their heads." Some people treat retarded or handicapped people like animals, laughing at them and making fun of them. But inside those hearts are the same feelings we all have—and sometimes a deeper understanding of things that we just take for granted.

Miss Jones taught a special education class at the elementary school in her town. Her students all had learning disabilities of one kind or another. Some of them had cerebral palsy and couldn't communicate very well, others had Downs syndrome and couldn't learn very well. Sometimes she wondered if they actually understood what she taught them. There were days when she went home discouraged. But there were other days when she went home with a broader understanding of life because of those children.

Near Easter, Miss Jones gave each child an assignment. They were all to bring a plastic egg to school. Inside the egg they were to include something that represented what Easter meant to them.

Miss Jones hoped they understood what they were to do. She wondered what they would come up with.

At last the day came. As she called their names, each child came to stand beside Miss Jones and showed what he had brought. One girl opened her egg to reveal a tiny candy heart. Someone else had included a chocolate Easter egg. There were also some tiny yarn chickens and fluffy, white bunnies, all miniature, to fit inside the plastic eggs.

Finally it was Jeremy's turn. Of all the children in the class of 20, Jeremy was the most disturbed. Miss Jones wondered if he actually understood the assignment. She called Jeremy's name, and he hurried up eagerly to stand beside her.

"Go ahead, Jeremy, show us your egg," Miss Jones urged him.

With a big smile, Jeremy opened his egg. It revealed—nothing.

"But Jeremy, your egg is empty," Miss Jones said gently. "There's nothing inside."

"I know," he said with a smile. "And Jesus' tomb is empty too!"

Miss Jones was silenced.

Jeremy died three months later. On top of his casket—as a testimony to Jeremy's faith in the empty tomb—lay 19 plastic Easter eggs—all empty.

That is the foundation of the Christian's faith—the power of God.

From Ida Mae Kempel, "What Was in Jeremy's Egg?" *Focus on the Family,* April 1988. Adapted.

CHICKEN!

But none of these things move me, neither count I my life dear unto myself, so that I might finish my course with joy, and the ministry, which I have received of the Lord Jesus, to testify the gospel of the grace of God. Acts 20:24.

All the guys leaned in closer and leered at Jerry. "Why won't you try a drink, Jerry?" Bill asked with a sneer. "Are you chicken or something?"

Jerry was in a bind. If he refused the can of beer, the guys would think he was a wimp and perhaps beat him up or exclude him from their group. But if he drank the beer, he'd feel awful about not having the courage to do what was right. What should he do? What would you do?

In life, we have to make tough choices. Some choices are harder than others. Jerry was faced with the choice of friendship or a clear conscience. Which is more important to you?

I remember reading a book called *Foxe's Book of Martyrs*. It made me sad, but it also inspired me. It is a book about different people who were willing to give their lives for their faith in Christ. One story that has always remained with me tells of a girl, about 18 years of age, who loved Jesus more than anything else in the world. She was arrested and told to give up her faith, but she refused. She was threatened, but still she resolutely refused to deny her faith.

Finally, she was tied to a pillar in the bay. The tide was out but when it came in it would slowly rise above her head and drown her. She was told that at any time she could give up her faith in Jesus and be rescued, but if she refused, she would be left to die. The story describes this beautiful young girl's courage as she began singing praises to God. The water began to swirl around her feet, but still she sang. The water rose to her waist, but she kept on singing. Finally the waves swirled above her upturned lips. She stopped singing, struggled for a moment, and peacefully fell asleep in Jesus.

Jerry was facing the same type of situation in miniature. His life wasn't in jeopardy, but something important to his life was in jeopardy —his circle of friends. Would he have the courage to do what was right, to be his own person without letting others decide what he should do?

You and I face situations like Jerry's every day. We have choices to make. Are the choices you are making the right ones?

APRIL 17

GOD IS LISTENING

If you, then, though you are evil, know how to give good gifts to your children, how much more will your Father in heaven give good gifts to those who ask him! Matthew 7:11, NIV.

Every month the Baileys had $300 for household expenses, kept in a white envelope above the kitchen cupboard. One day as Mrs. Bailey was hurriedly cleaning up the kitchen, she absentmindedly put the envelope in a K Mart bag, which she then threw into the garbage. Busy, as mothers always are, Mrs. Bailey didn't think of the envelope or the money until the next day. She reached above the cupboard where the envelope should be, and didn't find it. Only then did she vaguely remember the K Mart bag, and she realized that the money might be in it. Not finding the bag anywhere in the house, she ran outside to the garbage cans only to find that the garbage had just been hauled away.

Mrs. Bailey became frantic. She dropped to her knees, then raced to the garbage dump. Pulling into the dump, she saw a garbage truck and driver. The man told her he had not picked up garbage from her street, but his friend had, and he would look for the bag and the money.

Later that afternoon the garbage man drove in the Baileys' driveway. He handed Mrs. Bailey an envelope—the envelope—with $300 in it. He said, "You know, it was the most amazing thing. As my friend was dumping the garbage in his truck, this K Mart bag kind of fell to the side. So I looked in the bag, and there it was!"

Have you ever asked God to help you find something you'd lost?

Five-year-old Tommy raced around his bedroom, hunting a little red tractor. Unable to find it by his frantic searching, he dropped to the floor on his knees. "Dear Jesus, please help me find my tractor. Amen." He leaped to his feet and began charging around the room, kicking aside toys, throwing the pillows from the bed, but the tractor was nowhere to be found. At that point, Tommy ran to his dad. "Daddy, Daddy, I don't believe there's a God," he wailed. "I prayed to Him to help me find my tractor, and He didn't find it for me!"

Do you think God heard Tommy's prayer? Even though God didn't put the tractor back into the little boy's hands? Do you believe God hears your prayers? Even when you don't see an answer right away? I do! Don't forget, He is your Father. And when you don't seem to get an answer right away, you can still know that God is watching over you. He cares about you today and every day.

APRIL 18

COULD YOU DO WHAT JESUS DID?

I tell you the truth, whatever you did for one of the least of these brothers of mine, you did for me. Matthew 25:40, NIV.

In many parts of the world you see them everywhere. They are homeless people. They are beggars. They lie on the street corners showing their crippled or missing limbs and beg for you to help them by giving them a little money for food. Some beggars are missing their tongues, others are ill with crippling diseases, and some are just barely alive.

Beggars usually have no homes. They eat on the street, they seldom bathe, and they don't have any places to wash their clothes. When you see a beggar—skinny, filthy, helpless—it is easy to walk by in disgust. The matted hair and missing teeth coupled with clawlike, clutching hands, and the stench of filth make you and me want to ignore beggars and walk away. I wonder, though, what Jesus would do with beggars.

Jesus left Paradise to come to our world and experience its violence and selfishness. Would we be willing to leave our homes and live with beggars on the streets? Jesus gave everything He had so that we could live with Him in heaven. Are we willing to give what we have so that beggars can learn to live a better life?

There may or may not be beggars where you live, but there are people who need help. You may see the so-called street people, the homeless who sleep on sidewalks. Or maybe there are simply acquaintances who need you. Do you see them? The kid that everyone laughs at—can you stick up for him whenever possible? The new kid in school—can you invite him into your group? The kid who has trouble with a subject you do well in—can you give him some tips that you've learned?

Whether or not you think you have something to give anyone else, let me assure you—you do. Everyone needs your smile.

To live a life like Jesus means to be sensitive to the needs of people around us. Let's make this the year that we treat others like Jesus did. We are His hands; we are His voice; we are His smile.

YOU ARE THE IMAGE OF GOD

So God created man in his own image, in the image of God he created him; male and female he created them. Genesis 1:27, NIV.

Sometimes we say what we don't mean. Some people talk about how special we are to God, but then spend a lot of time telling us how bad we are, and that we are worth nothing. Sometimes we start thinking that God must be disgusted with us, or at the very least, extremely disappointed. We don't like to go to church because we know that when church is over, we'll feel terrible about ourselves. We won't feel like we're worth much at all.

The truth is that God created you in His own image and you are special and valuable to God, because He doesn't make junk. When Christ was on earth, sinners loved to listen to Jesus—to be near Him—because He made them feel loved and important. Children flocked to be around Jesus because He made them feel happy. And one reason Jesus came to earth was to show the whole universe—for then and for eternity—how God really feels about us.

A student was working on his doctoral thesis. Part of his thesis was a research paper dealing with the customs of Navajo Indians in the Southwest. As he did his research, he lived with a Navajo family. He ate with them, slept with them, worked alongside them. In short, he lived the life of a twentieth-century Navajo Indian.

There was an old grandmother in the Indian family. She spoke no English, yet she learned to love this student as one of her own children. The young man also enjoyed his friendship with this wise old woman. They communicated with sign language and intuition at first, but as the months went by, the graduate student learned some phrases of Navajo and the grandmother learned some phrases of English.

When it was time for the student to return to the campus and write his thesis, the tribe held a going-away celebration. The celebration was both happy and sad since the young man had become a good friend to everyone in the village. They would miss him.

As the graduate student prepared to get into his pickup truck to leave, the old grandmother came to tell him goodbye. With tears in her eyes, she placed her hands on either side of his face, looked directly into his eyes and said, "I like me best when I'm with you."

People liked themselves better when they were with Jesus. People like themselves better when they are a friend of God. His friendship is out of this world!

UNFAIR BOSS

But many who are first will be last, and many who are last will be first. Matthew 19:30, NIV.

Did you ever think that someone was unfair? Did his unfairness make you mad? My first job involved doing odd jobs for a fruit market. I was 14. One day we had to unload two large truck trailers full of watermelons. The easiest way to do this was to form a line, standing about eight feet apart, and throw a watermelon from person to person, until the last one caught the melon and placed it in the special display bin.

It was a hot day, and sweat poured down our faces as we worked. Catch the eight-pound melon on the right, turn left and throw it to the next man, then look right again because the next melon is already on its way. We worked until our arms ached and our backs were sore. Yet we kept on working because we were promised $30 at the end of the day!

Jesus told a story about some men who worked hard all day, much like I worked. Some were hired early in the morning. Others began working at noon. The boss even hired some new recruits during the last hour of work—just before quitting time!

To complicate the story even more, the men who began early in the day didn't know how much money those new workers were going to get. The boss had just said he would pay them a fair wage, and nobody thought much about it until quitting time. "OK," the boss called out. "I want those that began working an hour ago to line up here. The rest of you line up according to when you came in." When the men were in line, the boss began handing out the pay, giving a full day's wage to those who had arrived only an hour before.

"Hey, this is great," the other workers told each other. "If those guys get a full day's wage for just working an hour, there's no telling how much we're going to get."

But then they watched, puzzled, as the boss gave the same amount of money to the men who had begun work at noon. And their puzzlement turned to anger when they realized that the men hired a mere hour before quitting time were paid the full day's wage that they had been promised.

"I paid you what we agreed upon," the boss said. "Why should you expect more?"

Jesus told this story to illustrate how "unfair" God is when He forgives and loves us. God has the same amount of love for everyone! Jesus is telling us, "See how generous My Father, and your Father, is with His forgiveness!" He forgives those who deserve more the same as He forgives those who deserve less. There is always more forgiveness than there is sin! All you have to do is ask for it! I'm glad that God is "unfair" with His forgiveness, aren't you?

APRIL 21

FOOLISH LITTLE LADIES

There is neither Jew nor Greek, there is neither slave nor free, there is neither male nor female; for you are all one in Christ Jesus. Galatians 3:28, RSV.

What stereotypes do you have? What do you think of when you hear that one of the kids in your class is very rich? Do you automatically think he or she will be stuck-up? Is it fair to assume such a thing when you don't know the person?

What do you think of when you meet a preacher's kid? An automatic "goody-goody" or automatic "wild guy"? What do you think when you meet someone dressed in expensive clothes, or in poor, out-of-style clothes? What do you think of someone who says he is Mexican? Or Indian? What about someone who can't see or hear? Do you have an automatic reaction to someone who is different from you?

It's common to be afraid of others who are different from us. We often have wild ideas about them and what kind of people they are. We don't trust them. And sometimes, because we expect the worst, that is just what we get.

One day three timid elderly ladies from Nashville, Tennessee, decided to venture to New York. They were afraid of being hurt, even mugged, in the big city, but their sense of adventure helped a little to master their fears.

They had heard about the Black gangs in New York, and worried that they would be victimized by one. Sure enough, moments after they had left their car and stepped into their hotel elevator, a big, tall Black man entered too. The women moved closer together and braced themselves in a corner. Eyes squinted, eyebrows knit tightly in frightened arches, the little ladies kept their hands on their purses and stared at the man's back.

As soon as the elevator door closed, the man growled, "Sit down."

The three ladies were terrified! Immediately they squatted on the floor, waiting for his next command, expecting to die. But nothing else happened! They rode for a silent eternity until the elevator stopped at the next floor and the man got off.

That night when the ladies returned to their room, a dozen red roses were waiting for them. A card explained, "Please accept these flowers and my apology. You must not have seen my dog when I told it to sit. I was embarrassed and did not know what to do, so I just got off. I'm sorry." The card was signed "Reggie Jackson."

Why is it that we don't trust the opposite sex, people from other countries, or people with skin color different from ours? Paul is saying that Christians don't need to be afraid of each other any longer. They look past their differences and become one family in Christ. Christians are not prejudiced against one another. They accept, love, and forgive others.

Give up your stereotypes in 1990. Don't look at people; see their souls.

GOD MUST BE MEAN

I know that You are a gracious and merciful God, slow to anger and abundant in lovingkindness, One who relents from doing harm. Jonah 4:2, NKJV.

Gary leaned into the pastor's face and sneered, "Some God! He gets mad if you don't do what He wants, and kills you off. The Bible is full of those stories. I don't need a God like that!"

Have you ever felt that God was unjust, or have you known someone who thought God wasn't fair? Is it unfair that God loves both "good" and "bad" people, or should He love only those who are always "good"? Is it unfair for God to "kill" mean and dangerous sinners who don't care about others? Is it unfair for God to change His mind when He sees that sinners have changed from "bad" to "good"?

Jonah had a problem with God's loving nature. When the people of Nineveh changed their ways, Jonah was embarrassed because God changed His mind and didn't destroy their city. Jonah complained to God that the reason he hadn't wanted to go to Nineveh in the first place was that he knew God would change His mind. "That's just like You," Jonah told God. "I knew You'd be gracious and compassionate, slow to anger and overflowing with love for these people. You made a liar out of me, God, and I'm angry about it!"

Imagine being angry at God because He is full of love. Would Jonah have felt differently if he had been a repentant Ninevite?

How is it that some people read the Bible and see an angry God, while others read the same Bible and see a loving, kind, forgiving God? Does God have a split personality? Or do people simply misunderstand God because they are not really listening?

I know of a man in Mexico who cut off a girl's legs—just went into her house and cut off her legs!

"How cruel!" I hear you gasping.

But it wasn't cruel. The girl was trapped in her home after it collapsed during an earthquake. She was grateful that her rescuers cut off her legs, for it was the only way she could get out alive.

When you read the Old Testament stories about people dying because they didn't obey God, it sounds like God is mean. But like the story of the man who cut off the girl's legs, it seems like a cruel thing to do until you know "the rest of the story."

There is a lot we don't know about Old Testament times, a lot of explanations God will be eager to give us when we watch the "videos" of our histories with Him. Don't let anyone change your mind about God. God isn't a mean, supernatural tyrant. God is love! His love is out of this world.

APRIL 23

HOW TO FIND GOD

Stand silent! Know that I am God! I will be honored by every nation in the world! Psalm 46:10, TLB.

Nature seems to unfold its secrets to people who watch and wait. Are you a watcher? What type of clouds were in the sky the last time you were outside? Which way was the wind blowing? How many kinds of wildflowers can be seen from your front door? How many different birds have you heard today? How many shades of gold are there in a buttercup? Which tastes sweeter, the nectar from clover or honeysuckle? Have you even tasted either one?

In our fast-paced, busy lives, we often forget to take the time to be still and listen to nature. But we should. It is so easy to find God there. We sense His tremendous powers when we realize that He simply spoke and millions of flowers suddenly appeared. He spoke and created thousands of varieties, each one exquisitely beautiful—instantly! Nothing is insignificant to God. Even the wildflowers, which we so often trample underfoot without a thought, are exquisite. Many wildflowers bloom and die in the desert and forest and arctic without ever being seen by human eyes. Yet each is as perfectly exquisite as if it were destined for a king's table, as if God created it individually just for you!

That's how God created you—individually. And that's how He loves you, too—as an individual of value just because He created you.

God is real. He is the unseen force that holds our universe together. And whether we acknowledge Him or not, He just keeps on being there, making the flowers bloom season after season, keeping each star in its special place, holding things together.

BACK-SEAT DRIVERS

For God sent not his Son into the world to condemn the world; but that the world through him might be saved. John 3:17.

"Watch out! Slow down—and I mean now! You're going to hit him. Put your turn signal on. . . . Are you going to turn or not? Drive this thing right or let me get out of this car. Don't stop so fast! Your tires are squealing! Where'd you get your driver's license—K Mart? . . . Stop!"

I don't know about you, but back-seat drivers drive me crazy! They distract me. They embarrass me. They grate on my nerves. Are they good drivers? N-o-o-o. Most of them don't have a car, or if they do, it's being repaired from their last accident.

They either have glasses and can't see out of them, or they don't have glasses but desperately need them. They either want you to drive 25 miles per hour in a 65-mile-per-hour zone, or 90 miles per hour in a 30-mile-per-hour zone. Then they complain about the wind that's blowing their hair, or the heater that's making them sneeze, or the air conditioning that's drying out their skin. Rock music makes them nervous, and country music puts them to sleep. Classical music makes their teeth hurt, and they don't understand the social implications of bluegrass.

Back-seat driving is a disease. We need a Back-Seat Drivers Anonymous. Maybe these people can help each other. They definitely deserve each other! There ought to be a law against back-seat driving! Also, back seats should be equipped with back-seat driver headphones that play 200 watts per channel and are tuned in between stations at all times.

Am I kidding? Of course I am, but let me ask you a question: Are you a spiritual back-seat driver? Do you complain about others and point out their faults?

Here's an idea. Let's stop complaining about others. Let's stop putting our own selves down, too. Let's start focusing our attention on Jesus and what He means to us. Let's concentrate on how bighearted and wonderful He is. The Holy Spirit is the one God designated to convict of sin, and we're little better than a back-seat driver when we make it our business to do so. Let's do the work that Jesus began on earth when He said, "For God did not send his Son into the world to condemn the world, but to save the world through him" (John 3:17, NIV).

OVERCOMING THE IMPOSSIBLE

But whoever lives by the truth comes into the light, so that it may be seen plainly that what he has done has been done through God. John 3:21, NIV.

I'm almost embarrassed to suggest it. I'm sure that you don't have any bad habits. Or maybe just one or two?

Maybe you don't always tell things just like they really happened. It's so easy to add a little spice to a story, or when it would make things easier, to subtract from the truth. Or maybe you do things when you're by yourself that you'd be embarrassed to admit to other people. Maybe you're like me and just love a good thing too much. You see, I love to eat! Give me a pizza or tacos, and I'm the happiest man in the world.

The problem with bad habits is that they make your life unhappy, and many can kill you. They can get you in a lot of trouble if you don't find some way to stop letting them control you. It only takes being caught in one or two lies, and people won't trust you anymore. You're ashamed of your ragged, bitten-down fingernails. And if I'm not careful to watch how much I eat, I'll get so heavy I'll risk serious physical problems.

Steve Silva weighed 435 pounds, but he was dying because he was so heavy. His doctor told him that he wouldn't live to see his newborn daughter's sixth birthday if he didn't learn to control his appetite. Six different times Steve tried to lose weight. Each time he lost more than 100 pounds, only to gain it back again when he began to eat in the way that was normal for him. At last he put diet together with exercise. He began climbing steps—hundreds of steps every day. And he concentrated on eating fruits and vegetables, and other nutritious foods. Ten years later Steve had won his battle with his bad habit. He weighed only 190 pounds.

You may not know it yet, but your bad habits are hurting you too. The first thing you can do is admit that you need to change, then ask God to make you want to change.

The next thing you can do is to go to your parents or someone you trust and ask for help. If the habit is lying, ask the Holy Spirit to convict you every time you skirt the truth. If biting your fingernails is the bad habit, you may be helped by chewing sugarless gum for a while, or by learning a hobby that keeps your hands busy. If the habit is too many TV programs, you may need to change what you do in the evening.

Your parents or other trusted adult will encourage you. Together with their help and God's help, you will overcome your bad habit. Remember, having bad habits only means you are normal, for everyone has them. But don't let your bad habits control your life. Team up with someone who cares about you. And above all, team up with God. You'll have success that's out of this world.

HOW TO BE REALLY CLEAN

How can a young man stay pure? By reading your Word and following its rules. Psalm 119:9, TLB.

Eddie Croaker saw his first "dance floor" back in 1960. He was only 10 years old, and that's the best way he can describe his aunt Gerry's floors. The floors in her house looked like they were covered with polished glass and had lights shining up from underneath. They were the shiniest, prettiest floors he had ever seen.

But he felt uneasy in his aunt's house, because the welcome mats began 10 feet from the door and didn't stop until three feet inside the entrance. A mat just inside the doorway held two pairs of shoes on it. Their owners exchanged the shoes for slippers when they entered the house. When Eddie walked on those floors for the first time, he almost wished he'd shined the bottoms of his shoes, because he could see Aunt Gerry's eyes following his every step to see if he was leaving any tracks.

Aunt Gerry had a huge, beautiful sofa. It would have been comfortable except for the clear plastic covering that stuck to you until you got sweaty and began to slide around on it. The first time Eddie visited, he took time to admire the aluminum foil wrapped around the chrome pieces that were under Aunt Gerry's countertop cooking units. She'd spent quite a bit of time trying to get the wrinkles out of the foil. Especially neat was the little paper mat that stayed under the car in the garage. There wasn't a spot on it, and he couldn't decide if they kept it changed frequently or if their car didn't leak and the mat was just there for safety's sake.

Magazines were neatly displayed in the bathroom and the den, but they were so clean and perfect that Eddie didn't dare touch them. He figured Aunt Gerry must have another set she used for reading.

You ask, "What's the message here? There's nothing wrong with having clean floors, stoves, carports, and sofas." You're right. Cleanliness is good, but it involves more than just avoiding dirt or covering it up, like closing the barn door after the horse escapes. Cleaning is an ongoing process. And religion involves more than just avoiding sin or covering it up after it happens. Religion involves action—continued action—repeated decisions for right. Religion is made up of actively seeking God's will and doing it! You know in your own life where you're just covering things up. Only God can make you really clean.

BEE ALERT

Do not set foot on the path of the wicked or walk in the way of evil men. Proverbs 4:14, NIV.

"Daddy! Daddy! Bees are everywhere in our house! What are we going to do?"

"Just calm down, Cassandra, and tell me what you mean," Eddie Croaker said to his 6-year-old daughter.

"There are bees all over the living room flying around the lights," she said. "It looks like a giant beehive in our living room!"

The bees were indeed having a housewarming in their new home, which would have been OK had their new home not been the Croaker family's old home. There was a hive in the crack between the first-floor brick wall and the second-floor siding.

"What are we going to do?" Cassandra asked, jumping up and down with a little squeal.

"What do you think we should do?" her father asked. They discussed the options, which ranged from burning the house down to asking the bees politely if they would please move. Obviously, neither of those would work.

At last, after careful thought and a few stings, somebody thought of the vacuum cleaner solution. Of course! They could just vacuum up the bees that flew out of the hive! Mr. Croaker fastened a long pipe to the end of the vacuum cleaner hose. He placed the other end right at the opening of the hive. Then, hurrying to the vacuum cleaner while swatting at persistent bees, he turned the machine on.

The bees returned to their hive entrance. Some flew into the house from outside to see what was going on. But when they neared the vacuum cleaner pipe, their fragile, beating wings were no match for the sucking power of the machine. One by one, and sometimes in clusters, the tiny wings folded and the fuzzy, yellow bees disappeared into the fatal pipe.

The bees found out too late that it is dangerous to be on someone else's turf. Had they been out somewhere in God's nature, they probably would still be buzzing in and out of their doorway in safety.

Sometimes we Christians set up housekeeping in dangerous places too. We find a nice comfortable corner that at first glance looks innocent enough. But later—sometimes too late—we find out who our landlord is. Or we make friends with someone who seems so friendly and accepting ... until we say no. And then that "friend" turns on us until we give in or run away.

Solomon warns us not to set foot in the path of evil men. If you aren't strong enough to say no, don't sit in a parked car alone with your girlfriend or boyfriend. If you're not strong enough to say no, don't spend time with a friend who smokes or drinks and keeps trying to get you to join him. If you aren't strong enough to say no, don't put yourself on Satan's turf. It can be fatal.

TOO BAD, SO SAD, BE GLAD

Even though I walk through the valley of the shadow of death, I will fear no evil, for you are with me; your rod and your staff, they comfort me. Psalm 23:4, NIV.

"How did we get into this mess?" Carol screamed, trying to be heard above the thunder.

"Beats me," Todd shouted back as he fought the boat's steering wheel. "I'm sure I don't love to fish this much." Their eyes met in horror as they saw the funnel cloud streaking from the south, blocking their return.

"It looks like a giant ice-cream cone with bends in it twisting across the sky," Carol said, clinging to her brother's soggy coat.

"Is food all you ever think about?" Todd yelled back. "Here we are in a killer storm, five miles from land, with a bilge pump that's about as worthless as a random opinion, and there's only 20 feet of worn-out fiberglass between you and the bottom of the Gulf of Mexico." The wind whipped the words out of his mouth, but he kept on. "The captain here is on his maiden voyage in a borrowed boat and scared to death, and you're thinking about 31 flavors."

Carol smiled. "Just trying to enjoy even a bad situation," she said. "You know, a lot of people would give their next five years' Social Security checks for this much excitement." She hugged her brother close. He looked down at her and saw the same face that he'd been looking at for 18 years, except now she was teaching him.

"Let's see now," he said, fighting the steering wheel to keep on course. "Five years times 12 months equals 60 times $378.50 —"

"Stop it!" she squealed. "Don't you make fun of me anymore. And start being more positive."

Just then they noticed the storm moving away from them, and the water growing obviously calmer. After a few "I told you so's" from Carol, they made their way back home.

We live in a day and age when the fear of nuclear destruction is old news. A new disease seems to crawl right out of the woodwork with every new high-pressure system that comes through, and just making a living in the financially unstable future is enough to send you to the funny farm. Millions of people are starving, and millions more couldn't care less.

In spite of all this, you are lucky! You have the opportunity to see history unfold as none before have seen it. You have the opportunity to help others. You have the opportunity to change lives, to influence people for good in bold, new ways. And you may very well have the opportunity to see your Saviour coming in the clouds to set you free! No more fear then. No more griping. No more complaining. So look around you and make the best of the troubles that come your way. Ask God to help you use them to fertilize your spiritual growth.

APRIL 29

UNIMPORTANT PEOPLE

Then they called the blind man, saying to him, "Be of good cheer. Rise, He is calling you." Mark 10:49, NKJV.

Day after day, year after year, he sits by the road, listening, dreaming. *What would it be like to see?* he wonders.

What does the sky look like? What is the difference between blue and green? What is it like to be able to go someplace by yourself when you want to—alone—without worrying about getting lost? Oh, how nice it would be to have a regular job, to meet a nice girl, to have a family, to feel valuable and valued.

His sensitive ears pick up some unusual sounds, excited sounds. People are hurrying by, their voices edged with awe. His skin tingles from electricity in the air. He reaches out, trying to stop someone, but people are moving too fast. His voice sounds strangely hoarse as he calls out, "What's happening? What's going on?"

No one seems to notice him as he wanders helplessly in the crowd. Then he hears part of a conversation. Just a part—but what he hears sends chills up his spine.

"Jesus is coming to our town."

Jesus! The name brings hope to his heart. He has heard of this Teacher from Nazareth. He has power to heal, power to heal anything . . . anyone.

Now blind Bartimaeus joins the excitement. He begins yelling at the top of his lungs, "Jesus, Son of David, have mercy on me."

Someone pushes him from behind. "Be quiet, blind man. The Teacher doesn't have time for you."

But Bartimaeus refuses to be quiet. He is a nobody, but deep inside he believes that Jesus is a friend of nobodies. He won't stop, he won't be quiet, because he knows that Jesus cares about him. Suddenly a hush falls over the crowd. Jesus is speaking. Bartimaeus feels hands around his arms and waist. Caring hands. People are helping him forward.

Someone whispers in his ears, "Jesus is asking for you. He heard you calling." Jesus is about to make Bartimaeus' dreams come true.

Do you feel like a nobody sometimes? Everyone does at one time or another. But the Bible says—over and over—that you are somebody to God. And you can be sure that Jesus will hear you when you call to Him. Don't hesitate to call Him. Jesus listens extra carefully for those who think they are nobodies, to those who think nobody cares.

APRIL 30

BEING GOOD IN A BAD WORLD

Don't let anyone look down on you because you are young, but set an example for the believers in speech, in life, in love, in faith and in purity. 1 Timothy 4:12, NIV.

Are you bad enough to get along with your friends? What's that? You don't know what I mean about being bad enough to get along with your friends? Let me explain.

You are with two of your best friends, and you stop at a pop machine to get something to drink. Your friends drop in their quarters and punch the Coca Cola button. As they open their cans, they joke about drinking these "bad" drinks. They laugh about how some silly people refuse to drink Coke just because it has a little caffeine in it.

You step up to the machine and drop your money in it. You don't usually drink Coke. You know that caffeine makes your heart race and causes other problems. Now, however, you face a problem. Will you choose the Sprite or root beer, or will you get Coke and save being embarrassed? Will you be "bad" enough to get along with your friends? What will you do?

Let me share a secret with you. If you want to be admired, if you want people to notice you as being special, don't be afraid to stand for something. Don't be afraid to do what you feel you should do regardless of the consequences. Sometimes your friends will tease you, but if you are firm, they will secretly admire you. And someday you will receive their admiration and respect.

People used to laugh at Elvis Presley. Everybody else wore his hair short, but Elvis wore his long. He looked different and didn't always fit in. However, Elvis didn't change in order to please the crowd. He continued to be who he was, a Mississippi kid with an unusual voice, and soon the crowd changed and began admiring him. Elvis was a trendsetter. He didn't set the best of trends, but you can.

It's an old trick, but one Billy enjoyed pulling. He'd stand on a street corner and point to the sky, saying such things as "Wow, just look at that" and "Hey, I can't believe it." Within minutes a crowd would gather, all looking at absolutely nothing, and Billy would slip away.

There's a power in leadership, even when it's silly. And there is tremendous power in good leadership. Why don't you decide to be a trendsetter in 1990? All the kids are complaining about the new teacher? Look for something good in her. Everyone tries to top the other in telling dirty jokes? Take yourself out of the crowd. The kids on the back row goof off during Sabbath school? Sit back there and give the leader your undivided attention. No one studies his Sabbath school lesson? Study yours anyway, and contribute to the class discussion.

It takes courage to stand on the side of right. Don't change in order to please others, but be who you know you must be and let others follow your lead.

MAY 1

FAST CARS

As a prisoner for the Lord, then, I urge you to live a life worthy of the calling you have received. Ephesians 4:1, NIV.

Lee Gray had a 1965 Ford Mustang. It was shiny and black with sport wheels and a fancy "Pony" interior. His tires weren't just tires; they were *tires*, with raised, white letters that really looked sharp! When Lee drove by, others couldn't help staring, speechless, their mouths hanging open in awe. It was partly because of that noisy engine — when Lee thundered by, you thought a storm was threatening!

Lee raced with everyone he could, but he had one small problem: his engine. It was just a little 289 cubic inch engine without any performance equipment at all. The car didn't have much power! No matter how many races Lee entered, he always lost. The other fellows had engines built for performance, so they easily outran him. Lee's big dream was to save enough money to one day have his engine built for performance. In fact, he spent most of his time wishing for a bigger and better engine. So great was his desire for a faster car that he didn't enjoy the beauty of his car. He was never satisfied with it because he wanted more speed, and his car didn't have it.

Lee was not unusual. Have you noticed that most people are a lot like him? If they play the guitar, they wish that they could play the piano instead. If their gift is programming a computer, they don't appreciate it; they want to be something else.

Perhaps you feel like the things you are good at are not important. Do you wish that you could be good at something else? When you are

126

enthralled with someone else's talent, do you sometimes wonder why God couldn't have let you have that talent too?

Well, don't despair. It has probably happened to every person in the world at one time or another. Remember, God has given you your special talents. You have a unique place that no other person in the world can fill. No one else will see the world exactly as you see it, and no one else's life will be exactly like yours.

In the parable of the talents, the man who buried his one talent wanted to have some of the other guys' talents. In his desire for what was not his own, he saw his talent as worthless.

Lee had a beautiful car, but he never entered it into a car show. Forgetting the beauty and wanting only to race, he not only missed enjoying what he had, but the racing soon ruined the beauty of his car.

Don't bury your talents under a desire to be what you are not. Polish your talents, and when you are ready you will be given more. Remember, God made you what you are, and as someone has said, God doesn't make junk.

MAY 2

ARRIVING AT HEAVEN'S GATE

This righteousness from God comes through faith in Jesus Christ to all who believe. Romans 3:22, NIV.

"We're going to need a horn and turn signals on this thing if we get down much lower," shouted Captain McIntyre. "I don't believe we can make it to the runway. I hope the traffic lights on Highway 41 are green. I'd hate to get a ticket."

Captain McIntyre worked feverishly to restart the dead engine, but none of the tricks he'd seen or heard in his 30 years as a pilot could produce the needed miracle.

"Well, Mac, back in Scotland if we couldn't pull the wagon, then we left some of the load," the flight engineer suggested.

"Good idea." The captain turned to the crew. "That's your job. Everything that's not tied down goes out the door and everything that's tied down gets untied. The only exceptions are things that yell and scream when you try to throw them out."

In a quiet panic, the crew threw out everything they could, trying to save their seemingly doomed mission. A brand-new silver Mercedes-Benz rolled from the cargo bay and hurtled into the ocean, landing with a silent splash before sinking to the bottom. Designer suitcases with their contents followed. Videocameras and lights broke on impact with the ocean surface. Their value was nothing compared to human lives.

Still, the plane dropped ever closer to the earth, unable to soar, yet not crashing.

"Cap'n, what about the musical instruments and your guitar?"

Captain McIntyre gulped as he thought of his beautiful stringed friend of 40 years splintering as it hit the water.

"No exceptions," Mac yelled. "It's it or me." Those words echoed in his ears.

At last, after interminable minutes of uncertainty, the plane gained a little altitude and the captain brought it down safely on Highway 41.

How often we fly with excess religious baggage. "I've got to be good."

"God can't love me like I am."

"He can't accept me until I give up some yelling or swearing, or doing bad things."

"How can He possibly forgive me?"

"I can't go to church because the church is full of hypocrites."

Jesus not only forgave sins while here on earth, but He ate and drank with sinners. He wants you just like you are. You don't have to change yourself before you come to Him—He'll change you!

There's only one plane that will fly all the way to the golden runway. It's a plane with plenty of power. Get that power, and you'll be in heaven. That power is in Jesus. Why not leave your excess baggage at the counter? The flight will be safe and your destination sure. There's only one name under heaven given among men that will save us—Jesus Christ. Don't leave home without Him this year or any year!

MAY 3

THE HANDS AND HEART OF GOD

The poor are shunned even by their neighbors, but the rich have many friends. He who despises his neighbor sins, but blessed is he who is kind to the needy. Proverbs 14:20, 21, NIV.

Shaquana McManus, 8, is separated from her parents more than half the time now. She stays with friends whenever possible so that she won't miss school. In the past four months her family has moved 27 times. They stay in filthy, decaying hotels provided for them by welfare. Once Shaquana's mother had to use a bottle to fend off a rat in their room. They are allowed to stay a few days, then they have to go to welfare and get another room. They have no home, no warm cozy place where they can feel secure.

Two-year-old Joey is a sullen child who never speaks or smiles. At night his mother, Esther, hears him babble and punch at the air. She tries to understand what he is saying, but she can't. Then one night she lies down next to him and hears him muttering, "I'll kill you! I'll kill you!" all the while punching furiously at the air. Apparently he has been threatened in the halls of the old hotel where he and his mother live. Older kids threaten to beat him up, and he's scared.

A month later Joey and his family move to another shelter for the homeless. This one is much nicer and quieter. Joey is a different child now. He has blossomed. He sleeps quietly and peacefully.

Today, while you enjoy a warm breakfast, children are starving. You have nice clothes, but there are children whose only clothes are dirty and worn out. You live in a comfortable home, but they have no homes to live in.

Here's my question for you. Do you have any responsibility to help people who are hurting like this? What would Jesus do about these people if He were here on earth? How can you be the hands and heart of God?

One family I know doesn't spend Thanksgiving Day in front of the TV set. They spend it serving food to the homeless at a shelter home in their town. They come home feeling really full—full of joy.

A little boy in our town had his picture in the newspaper for asking his friends to bring canned food to his birthday party instead of presents. Instead of playing games after they ate cake, the kids packed the cans into paper bags and delivered them to a shelter home.

Shaquana McManus is helping her parents beg on the subway. A bum comes up and asks Shaquana for change. She reaches into her pocket and gives him what she has—all that she has.

What can you do to share your blessings?

MAY 4

I GOTTA HAVE PIZZA!

And do not be conformed to this world, but be transformed by the renewing of your mind. Romans 12:2, NKJV.

Nothing is as good as pizza when you are really hungry! Can't you just smell the hot cheese and tomato sauce? Do you hear it sizzling as it comes out of the oven? Olives, peppers, onions, perhaps some mushrooms on top.

Seth was craving pizza. He hadn't eaten for hours, and his stomach was grumbling and moaning. He could almost hear it saying, "Send down some pizza."

So Seth raced down the steps and out to his car, almost tasting the hot pizza already. But as his car rounded the corner he saw . . . golden arches. A hamburger stand! He was starving! A chocolate shake and some fries would hold him over till he got to the pizza place. Impulsively, Seth zipped his car into the drive-through lane and ordered his snack.

OOTW-5

Five minutes later Seth again headed across town for pizza, munching on the fries and sipping the milkshake as he drove. Ahh, that pizza would taste good!

Suddenly Seth slammed on his brakes and skidded his car to a stop in front of a taco stand. *Ummmm,* he thought, *a couple of tacos would taste great right now!*

Seth was soon driving down the road crunching his tacos. The shells were crisp. The lettuce and cheese spilled onto his lap. What a great way to whet his appetite for pizza.

Before he knew it Seth's tacos were gone, and it seemed almost providential that at the moment he was swallowing the last of the tacos he spotted a sandwich shop. *Oh,* Seth thought. *I'll just have a little sandwich to keep me until my pizza is ready to eat.*

At last Seth pulled slowly into the pizza parking lot. He was finally here. He'd been dreaming about this moment all day long. Soon he could sink his teeth into a hot, spicy pizza. Strangely, however, Seth didn't feel like eating pizza anymore. The pizza hadn't changed—but his appetite had.

We know that heaven is going to be more than we could ever hope or dream, but it's easy as we journey through life to get involved in study and parties, sports and TV. Pretty soon our time is taken up with so many other things that we don't have time for Jesus anymore. Heaven doesn't seem so important. Jesus hasn't changed—but we have.

Our text today says that you become what you think about. You are transformed by renewing your mind. What direction is your mind taking you in 1990? Is it out of this world?

MAY 5

I LOVE YOU

Be imitators of God, therefore, as dearly loved children and live a life of love, just as Christ loved us and gave himself up for us as a fragrant offering and sacrifice to God. Ephesians 5:1, 2, NIV.

Her blue eyes grew large as she leaned close to Terry's ear and whispered, "I love you." He watched her turn and walk away. Boy, did he feel good!

"Susan," he called after her.

She turned, her eyebrows raised in question. "Yes?"

"Could you take about 10 minutes to just sit down here and talk?" Terry asked. "I'd like to talk with you, to just spend time with you."

Susan smiled that beautiful smile of hers again. "Oh, Terry," she cooed, "I'd love to, but I can't. I'll find time later to sit down with you, and we can talk and share then. It will be such fun!" Then she smiled and walked away.

Terry's face fell. He was disappointed. He wanted her to stay. But the promise of time together the next day brought a smile to his lips. Tomorrow she'd spend some time with him.

The next morning Terry called Susan on the phone. "Susan," he said gently, "when can we get together today?"

"Oh, Terry," she whispered, "I've been thinking of you since I got up this morning. I'll be thinking of you all day long. But unfortunately I just don't have time today to spend with you."

"Susan—" he said, running a frustrated hand through his hair.

She silenced him with her light laugh. "Don't be upset," she coaxed. "There's nobody else! And I promise to spend tomorrow with you."

Now, Terry wasn't the smartest guy in the world, but on the other hand, he wasn't a dummy, either. It didn't take him long to realize that Susan was very quick to say "I love you," but very slow to show it.

If Susan had never said "I love you," but had spent time talking and sharing with Terry, he would have believed she loved him. Because it's not so much what you say but what you do that shows how you really feel.

God showed how He felt about us by coming to our world and dying for us. He not only told us He loved us; He proved it by His actions. He loves me, He loves you. Do you love Him? The person who really loves God is always available to Him and takes time to talk to Him. There's no better time to start than today!

MAY 6

LITTLE THINGS

Catch us the foxes, the little foxes that spoil the vines, for our vines have tender grapes. Song of Solomon 2:15, NKJV.

Did you ever say something that you didn't really mean? Something that sounded funny or that you didn't mean seriously, but was taken seriously? Little things that we do that seem insignificant can spoil our lives.

He hadn't eaten all day, and he was starved. The big and brawny man had been tracking deer through deep woods. His legs were tired from vaulting over fallen trees, climbing rocks, and swimming rivers.

He'd pushed himself since daybreak, but all day long things had gone wrong. Early in the morning he had a perfect shot at a large buck, but as he carefully drew back his powerful bow, the bowstring snapped. The arrow snapped backward, and the sharp stone arrowhead sliced a gash in his left arm. Right then the man knew it was going to be one of those days!

After that, everything seemed to go wrong. His aim was slightly off, and he didn't seem to be able to stalk through the forest as quietly as usual—he had one problem after another. Now the man started toward home, giving up the hunt for the day. It would soon be dark, and he was tired, cold, and hungry. He rounded the last turn in the trail and stopped in his tracks. His mouth began to water as he smelled the delicious aroma of stew.

His brother was cooking again. His brother was a bit odd—not a man's man—but the hunter really appreciated his cooking. And right now the hunter knew that he had to have some of that stew, and he had to have it now!

You know how the story ends, don't you? Esau said, "Jacob, give me some stew." Jacob was a little smarter than Esau, and so he replied, "Not till you give me the right to your inheritance as firstborn."

Esau didn't really care about the inheritance right then. He was hungry and tired, and needed food. In the next moment Esau gave away his birthright without a thought for the significance of what he was doing. "Sure, sure, take my birthright," he said. "What good will it do me if I die of starvation now?"

Esau didn't think that it would make any real difference in the future. But God heard and saw. God had a record of that conversation, and in that careless moment Esau gave away his future.

The little decisions that you make and the little things that you do in 1990, and in every year of your life, will shape your future. Make it a future that's out of this world!

MAY 7

THE JUDGE

Moreover, the Father judges no one, but has entrusted all judgment to the Son. John 5:22, NIV.

"Yee-hah, ride 'em cowboy," Donald yelled as Teddy hung on with all his might to the calf he was trying to ride. The calf kicked and bucked all over the barn stall, trying to rid itself of its unwanted burden.

Why, this is better than any rodeo I have ever been to, Teddy thought. *Probably because I'm in it.*

About that time he tumbled to the floor, and now it was Donald's turn to ride. You see, Donald, Gary, and Teddy had slipped into Teddy's grandfather's barn and secretly began to play rodeo with his very young calves. Grandpa would have had a fit if he'd known what they were doing, but he wouldn't be back for hours, and the boys were going to have fun while they could. They each took turn after turn with the calves.

After a while Teddy wasn't sure who was winning—the calves or the boys. They grinned at each other and at the calves while they leaned against the stalls, their sides heaving.

About that time Donald and Gary's dad strode toward the barn. They hoped he wouldn't guess what they had been doing, but like all fathers, Mr. Jones knew that his boys had been up to something.

"Stop that and come here right now!" he yelled.

So Teddy and his friends began the seemingly endless walk from the stall to the gate. Teddy was the last in line. Mr. Jones had a big stick in his hand, and as Donald and Gary walked through the gate, he whacked both of them harder than Teddy had ever seen a father hit a boy. Teddy's weak knees began to bang together. His feet were sweaty and squeaked in his shoes. His backside was braced for the worst, when he suddenly realized that he was through the gate. Mr. Jones and his boys were heading home, leaving Teddy to the mercy of his own family.

With a sigh of relief, Teddy kept on walking to the house. "I saw the whole thing," Granddad told him. "It's a good thing Mr. Jones didn't hit you. He has no right to punish any member of my family," Grandpa said, "even though you did wrong."

After a stern and long lecture about the dangers of calf riding, Grandpa said he thought Teddy had learned his lesson already. So Teddy didn't get a whipping, as his friends did.

Someday God is going to judge our lives. It's reassuring to know that our Judge is a family member. We don't have to worry about an outsider judging us harshly. Our Judge is our Father, God, who made us. Our brother, Jesus, is just like us. He understands and loves us, just as God does. And when our Judge looks at our cases, it will be with love and mercy. Just like Teddy's grandpa, God is on our side.

MAY 8

TO BE OR NOT TO BE LOYAL

Then Judas, which had betrayed him, when he saw that he was condemned, repented himself. . . . And he cast down the pieces of silver in the temple, and departed, and went and hanged himself. Matthew 27:3-5.

"How much do you want for him?"

"I don't know," she answered in her childish tone. "Herman is my favorite rooster. He follows me everywhere I go."

"Two dollars," Big Ben offered. Greed stirred in Elaine's veins. Why, with two whole dollars she could buy that doll she had been wanting.

"Will you take good care of him?" she asked.

"Of course," Big Ben replied. "Here. Take the money."

The money had a warm glow to it as Elaine clutched it in her hand. But that neat feeling left her and the money began to feel cold as Big Ben left with Herman hanging upside down, clucking out an SOS. Butterflies turned great big loops in her stomach as she thought of what she had done—she had sold her best friend! Then the butterflies gave way to giant whales churning and flopping within her when she thought of the loyalty that she had betrayed. She felt sick.

Chasing after Big Ben, her short legs finally caught up with him down at the catfish pond.

"Big Ben, here's your dirty old money back," Elaine yelled. "I want Herman. I miss him!"

"Sorry, darlin'," he drawled, "Herman's gonna catch me that big 50-pound catfish right out of the bottom of this pond."

Then she saw the blood on Big Ben's hands and the feathers, feet, and other assorted parts from what had been Herman, her very best friend. Tears stung her eyes, then poured down her cheeks in torrents. Turning, she ran home, bitterly weeping and mourning the loss of a true friend.

So it was with Judas when he thought to sell a friend. He was promised that his friend would not suffer. In fact, Satan convinced him that this would help Jesus assume the greatness He deserved as King and Messiah, while it assured Judas of a prime position in the new order. Besides, the 30 pieces of silver would add a nice jingle to his pockets.

And we too are sometimes asked to sell our most prized possession —our integrity, otherwise known as a clear conscience. Sometimes we sell it for as little as a few hours of "fun" or one experience of the forbidden that we desire so much.

Satan tells us not to worry, that nothing will change if we "cut loose" and sow a few wild oats. What he doesn't tell us is that after a decision to sell, it may be impossible to buy back the pain and hurt that follows.

Have you sold out on a friend for popularity? Not all friendships can be bought back. Not all reputations can be changed. You can't change history, but you can change the future. Starting today, be a loyal friend to yourself and to others. Don't sell out.

MAY 9

DECISIONS FROM A DISTANCE

But God demonstrates his own love for us in this: While we were still sinners, Christ died for us. Romans 5:8, NIV.

Eddie stretched out languidly in the backyard hammock. His mind drifted back to a conversation he remembered clearly from just four years before.

"Just wait until you get in the eighth grade," Mary had said. "That Mrs. Paris is a killer. She is so tough that she could make hardened criminals cry."

"How do you know?" Eddie asked. "Are you in her room?"

"No," Mary answered, "but Susie Marx is, and her sister told me that she heard what was going on in her room one day as she passed by in the hallway. It was awful! She said that old battle-ax was yelling and screaming, and that everyone was scared to death and just crouched down in his seat. How any learning takes place in that room is beyond me."

"I have noticed that she doesn't seem to smile very much," Eddie said. "In fact, I've never seen her smile."

"Well, she never says a word out of the classroom," Mary snapped, "and her clothes look like something found in the closet of an old folks' home. And her hair. I'll bet you if she ever dies, they'll make cleaning brushes out of her hair."

Young Eddie thought a minute, flattered that his big sister would confide in him. "Her house does look a little spooky. Do you reckon all her rubber meets the road?"

Just then a gust of wind blew some twigs down on Eddie's face, and he jerked out of his daydream and looked around the yard. He couldn't believe that he and his sister could have said those things about Mrs. Paris. They didn't know the Mrs. Paris he knew! She was his favorite teacher. In fact, he'd nominated her for Star Teacher of the school! Funny how his attitude had changed once he got to know her for himself. She had a good sense of humor, was quiet and fair, and loved to see the kids having a good time.

Have you ever dreaded a certain teacher, yet when you got in his room you found him to be loving and kind? Sometimes we think of God in the same way. We listen to the misinformation that people have about God. "I'm too bad to love. God can't love me until I stop sinning, and I can't ever stop," they may say with a laugh. "Why try?"

In time, we find ourselves believing what they say.

Many people have never gotten to know Jesus for themselves because nobody has told them anything good about Him. They judge Him by what other people say about Him—people who don't really know Him, but are only echoing what others have said.

But others can be wrong. Jesus died for us, knowing we were sinners. He sees our potential. Get to know Jesus for yourself before you write Him off. It's only fair. And you'll always be happy you did.

THE BURNING BRUSHPILE

Honor your father and your mother, so that you may live long in the land the Lord your God is giving you. Exodus 20:12, NIV.

"What are you doing?" Eddie Croaker's dad asked in alarm as he walked around to the backyard and spotted Eddie with a gasoline can beside a pile of brush. "That much gas is enough to burn you completely up!"

Eddie shrugged. His dad was so picky! It bugged him that his dad didn't trust his judgment. When was he going to trust him?

"I'm going to burn a brush pile for Laura," Eddie answered. Laura was the widow who lived across the street. "She desperately needs me to help her, Dad, and besides, I know what I'm doing. I'll just use this gas to get the fire started. It's so damp today, I'm having a tough time getting that brush to burn."

Dad walked away after making sure Eddie understood the danger of using gasoline to start a fire. "Those fumes can ignite, you know," Dad warned him.

"I know, I know." Eddie carried the gas to the pile of brush. He moved away from where he had been trying to start the fire before. He was smart enough to know that any spark that might still be in the brush could ignite the gasoline. He tried to slosh the gas onto the brush, but the top of the can was closed. There was just one little hole for the gasoline to pour out of.

So intent was Eddie on doing his good deed that his reasoning was a bit impaired. He climbed onto the pile of brush to get the gas where it was needed. But he forgot about a little smoldering flame, the size of a candle flame, that was burning about 25 feet to his right. Suddenly he heard a giant V-A-R-O-O-M and felt himself blown up into the air, then landing on the hard ground with a dull thud. Fire blazed over his body, and he moaned in desperate pain.

A little ditch had led the gas fumes directly to the small, flickering flame.

After a rushed trip to the hospital and a month of agony while the second-degree burns over one third of his body healed, Eddie was almost back to normal—but much, much wiser. And his dad seems to have learned a lot too. They think more alike now.

We sometimes think that God is picky. Why does He worry about such little things as white lies or stealing the golf ball at the end of a game of miniature golf? People are starving to death and even killing each other. Why doesn't God worry about things like that?

Eddie has learned from his own experience that God has seen what little mistakes can lead to, and He wishes to save us the pain. God reminds Eddie of his dad.

PLAY IT SAFE

Submit yourselves, then, to God. Resist the devil, and he will flee from you. James 4:7, NIV.

"Puh-lay ball!" the umpire yelled as the last warm-up pitch came from the pitcher. John grabbed his bat and banged the dirt off of his spikes. He stepped into the batter's box and pointed the bat directly at the young right-handed pitcher. John was a switch hitter, and even though he threw with his right hand, he loved to bat left-handed because it put him a giant step closer to first base.

I'll swing away at the first pitch, he thought to himself. *That ought to back that first baseman up.* No first baseman wants to play close when a hot ball might come right at him.

"S-s-strike one!" bellowed the ump after John swung at a hard, low fast ball. He noticed the first baseman take a couple of steps back, and grinned in approval.

Now to bunt and run, he thought. *They'll never catch me while the first baseman is playing that far back.* He eyed the pitcher. The pitcher went into motion and threw the ball. John could see it spinning, and he knew it was a curve breaking down and inside. It was the perfect pitch for a bunt.

John squared around and laid the bat on the ball. At the same instant he ran for first base. The ball rolled up chalk dust under his feet as he outran it to first base. Those two steps backward had put the first baseman out of the play, and he had no chance of putting John out.

Have you noticed how some of us, as Christians, often play too far back? "Satan's too powerful," we say. "He's a real heavy hitter." So we back up, away from where we know Satan is.

That's fine; we should stay away from Satan. But Satan is cunning, isn't he? When we step back from what we know is wrong, thinking we're safe from any of his "hot shots" at home, he makes a play and wins because we're not expecting it.

In the past 24 hours, have you said something you regretted? Have you disappointed yourself in any way?

You can't stand up against Satan by yourself. You need Jesus to coach you, for He knows Satan and all of his tricks. When you stand up to Satan and call on God's power for help, the devil flees. He doesn't just walk away—he flees, legs pumping.

So the next time Satan surprises you with a bunt, ask your coach, Jesus, to play interference and put the devil *out!*

THE RIGHT STUFF

Do not conform any longer to the pattern of this world, but be transformed by the renewing of your mind. Then you will be able to test and approve what God's will is—his good, pleasing and perfect will. Romans 12:2, NIV.

She was tall and gray-haired, and had interesting glasses. Her voice was powerful and clear. When her third graders heard it, they knew she meant business. Mrs. Kemp was not their favorite teacher, but they knew she cared about them. Sometimes, though, the way she got the kind of behavior that she wanted was mysterious. There was that matter of eating squash.

The school cook served squash every Thursday. The kids thought it was awful! Usually there was one garbage can for the leftover food, but on Thursdays they brought in two more garbage cans for all the thrown-away squash.

Mrs. Kemp took notice of this. One day, to everyone's surprise, she called the class to attention. "There are too many people going hungry to let all that squash go to waste," she told them.

Good, Eddie Croaker thought, *let them have the squash and maybe we can have something really good.*

Mrs. Kemp continued, "Starting next Thursday, there will be recess only for those people who eat their squash. The first week you must eat one fourth of your squash. The second week you must eat half of your serving, the third week you must eat three fourths, and the fourth week and on, you must eat it all."

The kids were shocked and surprised! They felt doomed to die by gagging. Eddie hoped against hope that when he woke up on Thursday it would all be a bad dream.

Thursday came, and all but seven students ate at least one fourth of their squash—and lived to tell about it! The next week all but four students ate their squash. In the third week all but two complied. The final week all the class except Wesley Duke ate all of their squash.

Squash was a big, big subject at school for at least six weeks as the kids gagged it down. Then one day about three months later, Eddie realized that he wasn't gagging on the squash any longer. No one talked about it much, either; they had found other things more important. Eddie wondered why Mrs. Kemp had slacked off on them about squash. Then, like a thunderbolt, he realized that she hadn't forgotten it at all. But the whole class, like Eddie, had learned to actually like their squash!

When you taste squash, where do you taste it? In your mouth, with a little help from your nose? Dead wrong! You taste it with your brain. The taste buds in your mouth and the fragrance sensors in your nose send signals to the brain. Whatever continually goes into your brain is gradually accepted as true and good. Eddie and his friends had told each other over and over again that squash was terrible. Finally they believed it. When they decided to eat the squash anyway, they found out that squash is good.

So it is with our spiritual lives. The things that we let into our brains tend to change us, little by little, until we become what we have seen and heard. Let's decide to let only true, wholesome, honest, and upbuilding things go into our minds. What we think is what we will become.

MAY 13

WHY MOTHERS LOVE THEIR KIDS

The greatest love is shown when a person lays down his life for his friends; and you are my friends if you obey me. John 15:13, 14, TLB.

One morning a mother made a platter of steaming pancakes for her husband and small son. When she lifted her plate to hold it closer to the platter while she served herself, she discovered a little note, neatly folded, lying underneath her plate. It was a bill from her 8-year-old son. It said: "Mother owes Johnny 25 cents for emptying the dishwasher, 55 cents for taking piano lessons, 15 cents for picking up his room, 10 cents for feeding the dog. Total: $1.05."

Mother smiled but said nothing. Breakfast was finished with the usual light conversation.

At lunch Johnny found an envelope under his plate, with the requested $1.05 tucked inside. But along with the money was another note: "Johnny owes Mother: for sitting up with him while he had chicken pox—nothing; for clothes and food and a warm bed—nothing; for hugs and kisses and being good to him—nothing; for toys and a brand-new bicycle—nothing. Total: nothing."

How would you have felt if you were Johnny? Would you have been able to keep the money without feeling guilty? How is it that moms are able to love us even though we're sometimes unkind to them and say awful, hurtful things or tell them we are embarrassed by them?

It's easy: our moms have invested a lot of time and dedication in us. They made us. And that's why we are so special to them.

God made you. And Jesus has invested a lot of pain and suffering in you. That's why He loves you so very, very deeply.

You don't owe Jesus a thing—but you can give Him your life. That's the greatest gift of all.

MAY 14

BETTER THAN SIX FLAGS

Then I saw a new heaven and a new earth, for the first heaven and the first earth had passed away, and there was no longer any sea. Revelation 21:1, NIV.

Only a few miles from where I live is a fantasyland—a place where roller coasters scream around corners and drop into gullies, only to soar up again while riders pale in breathless wonder. This place has Ferris wheels that lift you to the stars and merry-go-rounds with brightly painted wooden horses that prance and dance in tireless circles. It is a place of lights and rides and fantasies without end. It is a place you never tire of visiting; you only wish you could be there every day, all day, forever.

This fantasyland was built by people—that's why it is so fascinating. You see, people know what other people will enjoy. People understand each other, because they share so many joys and fears. People know what will please other people.

The only thing wrong with this fantasyland near my home is the price of admission. It costs so much to go in that I can't afford to enjoy it very often. Every day I drive by and often think of the fun I have had there. Every day I wish I could be there again, but I can't. I can't afford it.

I know of another land. A land that makes my neighborhood fantasyland seem dull in comparison. In this land, you can soar with the birds, diving and twisting in the air, relishing the freedom of flight. All the animals are harmless and tame. Instead of a stuffed teddy bear, you can cuddle up to a real live one (and it won't have bad breath). You can swim in the river, playing games with friendly fish. Then you can crawl out of the river onto the bank and curl up next to the soft furry belly of a lion. The sun is warm on your face and stomach, and you fall asleep.

People won't call you names there. Others won't have anything better than you; in fact, you wouldn't mind if they did. Friends won't disappoint you. You will be yourself, and you will be accepted and loved for just being you.

You can travel to distant planets and stars, exploring civilizations older than our own. You can climb into deep underground caves in perfect safety with your friends and be gone for months! You will not be sad, you will never be hurt, you will never have to leave, and you can be there forever. Parents won't fight in this land. People won't hurt each other and they won't hurt you.

Would you like to go to this place with me? What's that? How much does it cost? Good question, but that's the best part of what I have to tell you. Your way there has already been paid. The trip is a gift from Someone who really thinks a lot of you. This place is a gift from Jesus. He is very fond of you! He just asks that you be ready to go when He comes.

SO PROUD

Humility and the fear of the Lord bring wealth and honor and life. Proverbs 22:4, NIV.

You are sitting in class. You're nervous. Your palms are sweaty. You've taken a test, and the teacher is handing the tests back. You take yours from her with a trembling hand, and then breathe a sigh of relief to see that you have a pretty good score. Now the teacher begins to write all the scores on the blackboard. You almost stop breathing when you see your score at the top of the list—your score is the highest one! The second-highest score is 10 points lower than your score. Not only did you beat everybody else, you blew them all away! Now how do you feel?

I remember a class in college in which my score was 11 points above the next-highest score. Around me I could hear my classmates enviously discussing who could have gotten the highest score. I felt smug and good.

Casually, I put the test on my desk, faceup. I leaned back in my chair so that everyone could easily see the score on my test paper. I yawned and stretched my arms out, trying to draw people's attention. It felt good doing better than everybody else, and I wanted the world to know.

At the end of the school quarter I took my final test in that class. Immediately after taking the test I left on vacation. I couldn't wait to get back and compare my final test score with the scores of my classmates. I knew I had done well, but wondered if I'd beaten everyone else again.

I was in the teacher's office when I saw my test again. There was no one else around, just the teacher and me. My score was on the paper, but I needed to know how I compared with the others to be satisfied. Had I done better than the rest? How much better?

I think my teacher knew what I was thinking. He just stood there looking at me. I was too embarrassed to ask him how my test compared with the others'. I began to see myself through his eyes.

When we compete with others, we are never satisfied. We beat someone else today, but there's always a new challenge to our superiority tomorrow. Our victories are short-lived. Satisfaction lasts only for a moment.

There's another way of living that brings deep satisfaction along with great success. It calls for competing against yourself instead of others.

Have you done your best? Were you more patient today than you were yesterday? Can you be proud of your effort? Were you courageous? When you strive to do your best and forget about the other guy, you will find lasting satisfaction as well as success. God doesn't judge you by how you compare to others. He loves you because He created you and He wants you to be the best you can be.

MAY 16

OUT OF CONTROL

Better a patient man than a warrior, a man who controls his temper than one who takes a city. Proverbs 16:32, NIV.

Where I grew up, almost everybody else had brown skin. Usually that wasn't a problem, but once in a while some boys would tease me about being White. They would chant "Whitey, Whitey, Whitey."

One day I was outside the church when three boys began following me around, chanting "Whitey, Whitey, Whitey." I tried to ignore them and walk away, but they were persistent. They followed me everywhere. To make fun of me, they mimicked what I did, and then laughed and laughed.

I was beginning to get angry. I wandered around the corner of the church, only to be followed by these boys. I wasn't so angry by their teasing as I was hurt by feeling like an outcast, a freak, someone who didn't fit in.

Suddenly my anger boiled over. I picked up a small rock and drew my hand back, as though I was going to throw it at the most obnoxious of the boys. He ducked down, and just as he ducked I sprang at him like a wildcat, knocking him to the ground. I was so angry I didn't care if I hurt him. I didn't care if he got hurt bad. I was just angry!

I remember kneeling over him, straddling his chest and glaring into his frightened face. I remember grabbing his hair and slamming his head back onto the ground. I remember muttering something about him leaving me alone.

Suddenly my anger was gone. I stood up and watched him run away with his friends, crying. I didn't feel good. I didn't feel victorious. I felt bad. I hadn't been able to control myself. I had been out of control. I had let those boys control me.

Years later I held Sabbath services in a state penitentiary. I became acquainted with murderers. I expected them to be horrible people, but they weren't. They were men very much like you and me. The only difference between us is that they lost control of their tempers and killed someone, while I lost control of my temper and only wanted to kill someone.

You will be in situations in which you will be ready to explode in anger. Are you going to let the situation control you, or are you going to stay in control of yourself?

Sometimes you have to talk to yourself to calm down. Sometimes you have to say out loud, "Stop!" And then quietly, "Relax. Keep cool. Keep quiet. Don't stoop to their level."

God wants you to live your life in control of yourself—this year and every year. There's no better time to start than today!

THE DREAM

Through him everyone who believes is justified from everything you could not be justified from by the law of Moses. Acts 13:39, NIV.

Fear gripped me. I was standing in a large room surrounded with great, high walls. On the tops of the walls were bright beings, looking over documents while talking among themselves in somber whispers. Occasionally I could hear a comment like "But right here I think he meant well, don't you?" or "This was totally uncalled for." Then I heard the clicking of an adding machine. It was as if totals were being added and compared.

I remember being so scared that I felt like running, but there was no place to run. Suddenly I realized that I was in a judgment hall, and it was my case that was being decided. I can still feel the chills running up and down my spine, as I knew that my eternal destiny was being decided that very moment.

"What do you have to say for yourself?" the one in charge asked me.

"I—I—" I cleared my throat, trying to think of something that would make me sound good. But it was difficult.

"Well," he said again, "it's now or never. Speak up!"

I wished that I could say I had been good or that my wrong acts were accidents, but as hard as I tried I could not get one word out.

"Well, you have not met the standards that are required for eternal life. Your record is not perfect. But we have noted—"

I woke up with a start. My bedroom was warm and I was sweaty. The summer night seemed far away from any kind of eternal judgment, and I could hear the frogs and katydids singing.

I still remember that dream well, but now without fear. I have learned the great secret of Jesus' good news. I know now that when the judgment comes and the questions are asked, I won't have to answer. I won't stand there before the universe and God's throne all alone, because Someone will be right next to me, holding up scarred hands and answering for me.

"I died for this man, Father. I have made him perfect. He is Mine. There is a place for him here in Our home."

Jesus can say the same for you if you let Him. Don't go it alone. You can't make it out of this world without Jesus.

MIND YOUR OWN BUSINESS

For God did not send his Son into the world to condemn the world, but to save the world through him. John 3:17, NIV.

Have you ever felt that your parents were a pain? Sometimes parents can be so nosy, always telling you what to do or what you shouldn't do. Wouldn't it be nice if they would leave you alone? Wouldn't it be nice if God would leave you alone? If everyone would mind his own business and just let you go on with your life for a change!

The low bridge hung not more than 10 feet above a wide, slow river, a river perfect for swimming! And Bill's family, after traveling all day, finally stopped to rest. Bill's dad looked at the river, then at the bridge, and broke into an interested smile.

"Bill," he mused, "wouldn't it be fun to jump off that bridge into the river?" Bill's eyes lit up with excitement. What a great idea!

Dad and Bill changed into their swimsuits and walked to the middle of the bridge. Dad looked carefully at the river. It didn't seem to hide any dangerous rocks, and the water seemed deep enough to dive into. Dad climbed up on the rail and balanced precariously, preparing to dive.

Just then an old pickup began driving across the bridge, honking loudly. When it got to Bill and his father, the pickup stopped. A weathered old farmer peered out of the pickup window, looked at them for a second, and then said, "Mister, I wouldn't dive in there if I were you! Just a few feet under the surface are some rocks. I know you can't see them, but they're there. Trust me and don't dive in!"

Bill's dad smiled. "Go away, you old goat," he said. "Can't you see that my boy and I are having some fun?"

The farmer's mouth dropped open as Dad went on. "Leave us alone! Stop interfering with our lives! We're old enough to make our own decisions."

Let's stop the story and ask a question. If you had been the farmer, would you have warned Bill and his father about the rocks? Would you have tried to save them from breaking their necks? Would you consider that interfering?

When you care about people, you try to help them avoid painful mistakes. Your parents are not trying to interfere in your life; they are trying to help you avoid trouble. Sometimes they get carried away a little, but talk to them about it. Let them know how you feel. Let them share with you how they feel and why they feel that way.

Your parents are like God in a sense. They aren't here to condemn you, but to save you. They are not the enemy; they are your friends.

Oh, what about Bill and his father? Well, I made this story up, so you can make up your own ending. How would you like the story to end? Did they listen to the farmer? Or did they go ahead and jump?

MAY 19

GERMS AND JESUS

So we fix our eyes not on what is seen, but on what is unseen. For what is seen is temporary, but what is unseen is eternal. 2 Corinthians 4:18, NIV.

Do you believe in things you have never seen? Is it hard for you to believe in something if you've never seen it? Do you believe in things that nobody has seen?

He was a pastor's small son. He'd been playing outside and had just come in for dinner. He was a mess! Dirt covered his cheeks and nose. His hands were caked in mud, and his feet left a trail of brown on the floor.

Mother took a horrified look at him and told him to wash up. She explained that there were germs in the dirt. The little boy protested, complaining as he trudged down the hall to the bathroom, "Germs and Jesus! Germs and Jesus! That's all I ever hear around this house, and I've never seen either one!"

We don't see germs, but they are real enough to make us sick. We don't see radio waves, but when we turn on the radio we hear the music that they make. Television signals are invisible, but your TV can convince you that they exist.

Angels are all around you right now. You can't see them but they are beside you. Heaven is a real place. You can't see it, but it exists. God is caring for you. You can't see Him, but you can see His work all around you. And if you ask God to be a part of your life, you will experience His love and support, as well as His work to help you be everything you want to be. Why not make every day in 1990 a day when you enjoy the friendship and companionship of God?

145

THE POWER OF LOVE

There is no fear in love. But perfect love drives out fear. . . . We love because he first loved us. 1 John 4:18, 19, NIV.

What kind of person do you imagine God to be? Are you afraid of Him? Is He someone you are excited about introducing to others?

God wants you to know the truth about Him. He loves you, and when you know that He loves you it will change you. When your parents and friends are convinced that God loves them, they will be changed too.

A pastor by the name of Fred Craddock tells the story of a cat to illustrate the power of love.

A family is taking a drive on a beautiful Sunday afternoon, relaxing and singing as they cruise down the highway. Suddenly the two children start shrieking at their father to stop. They pound on his back, crying, "Daddy, Daddy, stop! You must stop! There's a kitten back there on the side of the road."

Father is unimpressed.

"So there's a kitten on the side of the road. I'm sure he has a home somewhere," Dad replies.

The children won't be put off. "Daddy, you've got to stop now! The kitten will be run over. Daddy, I'm sure it doesn't have a home. It is so skinny. Daddy, Jesus would stop because He loves that kitten."

Finally Mother joins in the requests to stop, so Daddy pulls over, turns around, and drives back to the place where they'd seen the kitten. Daddy stops the car and says, "You kids stay here. I'll see about it." Then he goes out to pick up the little creature. It is just skin and bones, sore-eyed, and covered with fleas. Daddy reaches down to pick it up, but the little kitten growls, then hisses. Daddy picks the kitten up by the back of the neck and brings it over to the car. "Don't touch it," he grumbles. "It's probably got leprosy."

When they get home the children give the kitten a warm bath, about a gallon of warm milk, and then ask Dad if they can keep it in the house, "just for tonight."

"Just for tonight," Dad warns them. "We'll fix a place in the garage tomorrow."

Several weeks later Daddy walks in the house and feels something brush against his leg. It is a cat. Making sure that nobody is watching, Daddy carefully reaches down to pick it up. Again the cat arches its back, but this time it is purring instead of hissing. It is arching its back to receive a caress.

Is this the same cat Daddy found by the side of the road? No, it is not the same as that frightened, hurting, hissing little kitten by the side of the road. Do you know what made the difference?

Love, of course. Loving care made the difference. And just like that family did with the kitten, God reaches out His hand to you and your family. His hand is covered with scratches. It is the hand of love. Let it change you.

MAY 21

DANGER IN YOUR MOUTH

Their tongue is a deadly arrow; it speaks with deceit. Jeremiah 9:8, NIV.

In Bible days the bow and arrow was a frightening weapon, comparable in those days to a rifle or machine gun today. An arrow could fly through the air and kill you before you had time to react. It could pursue you and strike you dead when you tried to run away. It could pierce armor and allow someone to kill you from a great distance. It was a feared and formidable weapon. In the right hands it was deadly and accurate.

If you read the next verse of our text today, you will discover that God is talking about people who say one thing but really mean another. They say kind things to their neighbors, but in their hearts set traps for them. Do you do this? God says in Jeremiah that people who do this will not survive the destruction of the world. Your mouth is a powerful and dangerous weapon. If you use it carelessly, it can hurt you today or in the future.

Mrs. Johnson was a godly woman who had a simple trusting faith in God. Her husband was unemployed, and so they prayerfully asked God to help him find employment. Each day Mrs. Johnson walked the streets with her husband trying to help him find work.

One day she saw a group of men working at a railroad crossing. She quietly approached one of the men and in broken English asked him if her husband could work with them. The man was irritated and told Mrs. Johnson that she would have to talk to the foreman, whom he called a son of a so-and-so.

Mrs. Johnson did not understand that the man was insulting the foreman. She thought that the names he had called the foreman were names she should use when addressing him.

She confidently walked up to the foreman and in her broken English addressed him as a son of a so-and-so and asked him if there was a job for her husband. The foreman immediately realized that she didn't know what she was saying. His eyes grew cold as he began to understand what had happened. Shrewdly he asked Mrs. Johnson who sent her to him, and she pointed the man out. Within a moment the foreman fired the man and gave his job to Mr. Johnson.

Luckily, or maybe unluckily, the punishment for shooting off your mouth usually isn't as quick as that. But it is sure. Today and every day, take care that your mouth doesn't hurt you or anyone else. Your mouth can be more dangerous than a gun. It can maim; it can hurt. It can even kill.

MAY 22

IT'S AWESOME TO BE LOVED

And I pray that you, being rooted and established in love, may have power, together with all the saints, to grasp how wide and long and high and deep is the love of Christ, and to know this love that surpasses knowledge—that you may be filled to the measure of all the fullness of God. Ephesians 3:17-19, NIV.

It is awesome to be really loved! It overwhelms us. We give in to love and joyfully surrender to its peace. Paul is talking about this kind of overpowering love. God loves you—that thought is your security, your roots. When you know for sure that God loves you, a sense of peace and security floods your life. You give up and simply relish the love of God.

The Reuben Donnelly Company of Chicago is one of the world's largest printers of magazines. They have a machine that sends out notices to people whose subscriptions have expired. One day the machine was purring along when a tiny spring broke and the machine typed the same subscription notification 9,734 times. All those notifications were addressed to one rancher in Powder Bluff, Colorado. He was overwhelmed with 9,734 notices that his subscription to *National Geographic* magazine had expired. The poor man drove 10 miles into town and sent his money to National Geographic with a note that read "Send me the magazine. I give up!"

God wants you to give up. He is telling you over and over again that He loves you. The birds that you hear singing today are telling you of God's love. The trees and flowers all are a sign of God's devotion to you. People who care are showing you what God is like. Everywhere you look, you can see messages of God's love for you.

It is awesome to be loved, especially to be loved by God. I pray that this year you will begin to understand more clearly how wide and deep and overpowering the love of God is. And then rooted in this love, you will become a messenger to all you meet, showing them how great the love of God really is.

148

HONEST PRAYERS

Man looks at the outward appearance, but the Lord looks at the heart. 1 Samuel 16:7, NIV.

Are your prayers honest prayers? What I mean is, when you make a mistake, are you honest with God about how you feel? Too often we try to lie to God, forgetting that it doesn't do us any good. God reads our hearts.

Have you ever done something wrong and then prayed to God, "I'm so sorry—I hate what I did, and I'll never do it again," yet knew in your heart that you enjoyed doing it, were sorry only because you feared losing out on eternal life, and expected to commit that sin again? If you have ever prayed a dishonest prayer like this, then you know what it means to be a normal human being.

You see, we humans have an instinct that helps us cover up our mistakes. We shy away from admitting the truth. A little girl was in the school library looking through a preschool primer. She was a cute little girl, and also very wise for her age. The principal came strolling through the library and sat down beside her. He pointed to the picture on the first page and asked what it was. The girl quickly replied, "That's a cat." As the principal pointed to the following pages, the girl answered quickly and correctly, "That's a boy, that's a dog, that's a wheelbarrow."

The principal pointed to a picture of a hatchet, and the little girl said, "That's a hammer." The principal didn't say anything, but as the smart little girl turned the next page she saw a picture of a hammer. She turned the page back to the hatchet, then ahead to the hammer. Without hesitation she closed the book and, smiling sweetly at the principal, chided, "This is the library, and we really shouldn't be talking."

It is instinct to avoid saying "I was wrong," "I was dishonest," or "I made a mistake." We can sometimes get away with being dishonest to people, but never to God.

Why not begin praying honestly? When you're mad, tell God how you feel. When you're not sorry, admit that to God. Let Him know where your heart really is. He will listen, He will love you, and He will accept you. But most important, He will work in your heart to change you. He will take away the instinct to cover up your mistakes, and will change your outlook and your thoughts until honesty is second nature.

ONLY A SHADOW

He who overcomes will not be hurt at all by the second death.
Revelation 2:11, NIV.

There are two deaths. The first one is only temporary, because everyone who dies this death will live again. The second death, which occurs after the millennium, is one from which no one wakes up. It is final.

Our text today promises that if we stay close to God, we will not experience the second death. That's some promise! It's worth taking seriously.

Donald Barnhouse, a great preacher, was widowed while a young man and left with a heartbroken 6-year-old daughter to console. It was difficult enough for him to deal with his own grief, but to attempt to explain to his daughter why her mother died was harder than anything he'd ever done in his life. All his education and theological training had not prepared him for this.

One day he and the little girl were standing on a busy corner at a downtown intersection waiting to cross the street. Suddenly a large truck careened around the corner, momentarily blocking out the sunlight and frightening the little girl. Dr. Barnhouse picked his daughter up to reassure her and suddenly a flash of inspiration hit him.

"When you saw the truck pass it scared you, but let me ask you, had you rather be struck by the truck or the shadow of the truck?"

"The shadow, of course," she said.

Dr. Barnhouse went on to explain that when her mother died she had just been hit by the shadow of death. However, Jesus had been hit by the truck, which is the second death. The shadow brings darkness. It may frighten, but it cannot truly harm.

TOO MUCH OF A GOOD THING

Follow the ways of your heart and whatever your eyes see, but know that for all these things God will bring you to judgment.
Ecclesiastes 11:9, NIV.

Did you ever wish you could overindulge? You know, eat as much ice cream as you want or swim all day every day. Certain things are so much fun that we wish we could do them forever. Unfortunately, or fortunately, there are rules that keep us from doing exactly what we long to do. Are you ever frustrated by this?

A little boy named Bobby went to visit his aunt Alice. When he had settled into his room, Aunt Alice asked him what he would like to do. He thought for a minute, then said, "Well, I love your pancakes, and whenever we have pancakes at home I'm allowed to eat only three. So I'd like to have as many as I can eat." The next morning Aunt Alice made pancakes. As soon as Bobby gobbled up the last of the pancakes, Aunt Alice piled more on his plate. Bobby was in paradise! He kept eating, and eating, and eating. His stomach kept stretching, and stretching, and stretching.

When Bobby had finished over a dozen pancakes, he began to slow down. It wasn't long until Bobby's face was screwed up in a "I'm sick" expression. Aunt Alice was concerned and asked, "What's wrong, Bobby, don't you want any more pancakes?"

Little Bobby slowly shook his head in distress. "No, I don't want any more," he groaned. "I don't even want the ones I've already had."

Solomon, who wrote today's text, knew what Bobby was talking about. Sometimes the things we love aren't good for us. Staying up till midnight night after night, driving fast, and eating everything that tastes good to us are just a few examples of some of the things that are easy to love doing. Solomon knew this. He had wealth, wives, everything his heart desired. At the end of his life he counseled us to enjoy the desires of our hearts, but to realize that someday we will reap the rewards of our choices.

What choices are you making? Will your future life bring happiness, or heartache? You are choosing your future, today and every day.

MAY 26

PROTECT YOUR VALUABLES

Love the Lord your God with all your heart and with all your soul and with all your mind. . . . Love your neighbor as yourself. Matthew 22:37-39, NIV.

Imagine that your house catches on fire and you have time to take only one thing out with you. What would you choose? Would it be your pet hamster or fish? Maybe you have a football or baseball signed by big-league players. Perhaps you would grab some award you've won, or maybe your piggy bank. A bride might grab her wedding book. Others would snatch up a much-used Bible. When asked this question, many people say that they would save their pictures, because pictures cannot be replaced. What is really important to you? What do you value the most?

If you stop to think about what you do day after day, you begin to understand what is important to you. What do you spend most of your time thinking about? Getting rich? What do you dream of? Whom do you make time for? The tragedy of life is that many of us spend little time on the people and things that are most important to us. We have our values mixed up.

It was a dark night when the hoodlums broke into the department store. Mischievous rather than dishonest, they didn't steal anything. They simply changed the price tags on everything. They had a wonderful time switching price tags! The next morning, customers were excited to find fur coats selling for $5 dollars. However, cold cream was $150 a jar. Umbrellas were $1,000 each, and diamond rings were priced at $2.

Have the price tags been switched in your life? Are you placing a high value on things that really don't matter that much? What is more important to you, getting an A or B in math, or the methods you use to get the grade? Is a new bike or a new dress more important than your parents' feelings? Do you value the approval of your friends over what you know to be right? Are you more interested in what you can have on earth than in what is waiting for you in heaven?

Make 1990 the year you begin valuing things that are really important to you.

MAY 27

ASHAMED NO LONGER

My dear children, I write this to you so that you will not sin. But if anybody does sin, we have one who speaks to the Father in our defense—Jesus Christ, the Righteous One. 1 John 2:1, NIV.

They were destined to be ashamed forever! Veddas! Their name was spoken with contempt. Years ago they had been noblemen to the kings of Sri Lanka. One day these noblemen had been asked to hunt venison for the king's feast. But these Veddas took their job lightly and wasted the day drinking and talking, having a grand time. Toward evening, when it was almost time for the feast, they had not even tried to hunt meat for the king's table.

According to legend, these Vedda hunters did a terrible thing. They took the child of a low-caste family, killed him, and prepared him as meat for the king and his guests.

Eventually the deed was discovered, and the Vedda tribe was sentenced to live as the lowest of all people. As part of the punishment, their only income would be from making and selling baskets.

I met a Vedda man once. He was tall, quiet, and dignified. He had grown up ashamed, but he was ashamed no longer. The man, Sompathi, had realized that Jesus died for him. It no longer mattered that society despised his people, for Jesus was his personal friend. The God of the universe was his constant companion.

Have you done something wrong? Are you ashamed? Do people look down on you for one reason or another?

Have you forgotten that the greatest Inventor and Creator in the universe made *you*? Have you forgotten that there is only one of you, that Jesus died for you? That you are irreplaceable? Special?

No matter what you or anyone in your family has done, Jesus forgives when you ask Him to. And He forgets. It doesn't matter anymore. Find dignity this year in your friendship with Jesus.

MAY 28

LITTLE THINGS MAKE A BIG DIFFERENCE

I tell you the truth, anyone who gives you a cup of water in my name because you belong to Christ will certainly not lose his reward. Mark 9:41, NIV.

A little thing like a cup of water makes a big difference. Not because of what it is, but because of why it is given. The person who gives this cup of water gives it in the name of Christ. He gives it because of a heart that overflows in love. This little act then becomes vitally important.

Today and every day, you will do countless little things. Many of these little things may seem insignificant, but they could turn out to be vitally important to you or to others.

In Elmer Bendiner's book *The Fall of Fortresses,* he describes one bombing run over the German city of Kassel: "Our B-17 *(The Tondelayo)* was barraged by flak from Nazi antiaircraft guns. That was not unusual, but on this particular occasion our gas tanks were hit. Later, as I reflected on the miracle of a 20 millimeter shell piercing the fuel tank without touching off an explosion, our pilot, Bohn Fawkes, told me it was not quite that simple."

On the morning following the raid, Bohn had gone down to ask our crew chief for that shell as a souvenir of unbelievable luck. The crew chief told Bohn that not just one shell but 11 had been found in the gas tanks— 11 unexploded shells where only one would have been sufficient to blast us out of the sky. It was as if the sea had been parted for us. Even after thirty-five years, so awesome an event leaves me shaken, especially after I heard the rest of the story from Bohn.

He had been told that the shells had been sent to the armorers to be defused. The armorers told him that Intelligence had picked them up. They could not say why at the time, but Bohn eventually sought out the answer.

Apparently when the armorers opened each of those shells they found no explosive charge. They were clean as a whistle and just as harmless. Empty? Not all of them.

One contained a carefully rolled piece of paper. On it was a scrawl in Czech. The Intelligence people scoured our base for a man who could read Czech. Eventually they found one to decipher the note. Translated, the note read: "This is all we can do for you now."

It seems that some Czech prisoners of war had been put to work making shells. Probably they filled most of the shells with explosives. But obviously whenever possible, they left the shells empty and inserted at least one note so that someone, somewhere, would know what they had done.

That little act saved lives. What little act that you do today will turn out to be important? Why not do everything as though someone's life depended on it?

MAY 29

A GOD FOR BELIEVERS

I know whom I have believed, and am persuaded that he is able to keep that which I have committed unto him against that day. 2 Timothy 1:12.

Do you believe in God? Sometimes people begin questioning God. They can touch their cars and homes, they can touch their parents and their dogs, but they can't touch God, and so they begin to wonder if God is real.

If they would stop in a quiet place to think about God, they would see His footsteps everywhere. They would see God in creation, and they would see God in miracles. Today's story will help you believe in God. It's a story of God's power, even when some doubt that He exists. The story happened to C. Roy Angel, and can be found in his book *Iron Shoes.*

"I had set up camp in a dangerous tribe of cannibals. Day after day I pleaded with the old chief to let me preach to his people. I would speak his language, and I told him the story of Jesus with all the fervor of my heart. He listened attentively but was not convinced.

"I had not paid much attention to his son, who sat just behind him, until one day the son came to my tent with questions that were so penetrating they startled me. The weeks wore on, and I was a virtual prisoner. Then one day toward sunset the tom-toms began to beat, and the tribe began to gather, and the huge fire was built. Two rough young giants led me into the center of the ring and tied me to the stake. The old chief held his powwow, and a death sentence was passed on me.

"Wild dancing and carousing followed way into the night. Finally it was stilled by the old chief's standing and holding out both hands. He made a speech to me and added at its end this question, 'Where is your God? If He is able to deliver you, I will believe on Him.' My answer was drowned out in the wild yells of delight as the dance was resumed.

"Then suddenly the old chief's son, a tall young giant who carried a long sword that had been taken from a pirate boat, walked into the middle of the circle and stood with his back to me. He whipped his long sword out of its scabbard, and a hush fell over the orgy. In a clear unfaltering voice he said, 'The missionary's God is busy tonight, so He sent me to deliver him. There will be no feast tonight. The missionary lives. If any of you objects, I am waiting.'

"A long silence followed, broken only by quiet whispers among the braves. The old chief stepped forward into the circle. The young giant pointed the long sword at the ground in front of his father, and his voice was quiet but lethal. 'You may come two more steps. No farther.'

"The old chief stopped and stood looking at his son. There was admiration written all over his face. He lifted both hands and turned back to face his tribe, and he said: 'Tonight I abdicate as chief in favor of my son. From now on he is your chief. Obey his commands.' He turned and faced his son and said, 'May I have permission to cut the ropes that bind the prisoner?' "

God is alive. I know that if you think for just a minute, you will remember many times when God answered your prayers in a special way.

MAY 30

FORGIVEN

If you, O Lord, kept a record of sins, O Lord, who could stand? But with you there is forgiveness; therefore you are feared. Psalm 130:3, 4, NIV.

One of the most terrible feelings you will ever have is the feeling of guilt. Guilt is the result of doing something wrong, and not being forgiven. Guilt changes to peace when we know that the person we wronged has forgiven us.

The magazine *Parables, Etc.* ran a story about a seminary professor who began his New Testament class with this story about forgiveness.

Apparently, years before, this professor had told a lie that greatly hurt his father. As time passed, the guilt did not go away, but grew deeper and deeper. He had hurt his father. Had his father forgiven him?

One day the professor could stand it no longer. Tearfully, he wrote his father a letter describing again what he did, so that his father would remember, and then asking his father for forgiveness.

The days dragged by. Finally the reply came. Yes, his father remembered the incident and the hurt. Yes, he was forgiven. A great weight fell off the son's shoulders. He was forgiven. He felt free. It made all the difference in his life.

Several years later the professor had a chance to experience again the joy of forgiveness. Both his mother and father died suddenly within a few months of each other. As he sorted through the attic of their house he came upon a box of keepsakes. Treasures from their marriage filled the box as well as little items that were precious because they belonged to their son. The professor's mind flooded with memories as he discovered the things his parents had treasured. Then he saw the letter that he had written to his father asking for forgiveness. Tears streamed down his cheeks as he began to read it again. He turned the letter over, and saw that his father had written "Forgiven" in large letters on the back, underlining it several times.

He knew then, without a doubt, what he had known all along—that his father had relinquished all the pain and hurt. He had been forgiven. What a gift it is when we forgive and are forgiven. Don't live with guilt. Find the peace of forgiveness.

MAY 31

A LEAP OF FAITH

Now faith is being sure of what we hope for and certain of what we do not see. Hebrews 11:1, NIV.

It's all right to not have all the answers. Sometimes we have to leap out in faith. Sometimes we have to trust others, to listen to them when we don't have answers for ourselves.

Early one morning a father woke up with the acrid smell of smoke burning in his nostrils. The fire alarm in the basement was ringing its warning. Quickly the father woke his family, and they began making their way out of the house. The father carried his daughter and held his 4-year-old son's hand.

Confused and frightened by the chaos and fire as the family ran to safety, the child pulled away from his father and dashed back into his room. He thought he would be safe in a special corner where he kept his stuffed animals.

Soon the family was outside. The father called to his son, and the little boy appeared at his bedroom window on the second floor, crying. Smoke was blowing out of the window, engulfing the frightened little figure.

"Jump, jump," the father called. The little lad stopped crying long enough to answer, "But I can't see you."

"That's all right," his father called back reassuringly. "I can see you."

Sometimes God asks you to do things you can't understand. You are frightened. Sometimes your parents ask you to do things that you can't understand. You're not sure. At times like this you need to trust. Trust and leap, because even though you can't see where you are going, others can. You can trust those who love you.

JUNE 1

KEEP SMILING

Rejoice in the Lord always. I will say it again: Rejoice! Philippians 4:4, NIV.

Roller coasters are great, unless you have to live on one. Some people go up and down on an emotional roller coaster. They are either happier than they have ever been, or they are more depressed than ever before. Life is lived best when it is lived with a positive attitude through all circumstances. You never know when something great is going to turn bad, or when something bad is going to turn out to be a blessing.

Paul suggests that you get into the habit of being constantly joyful in God. You can be at peace and joyful with God because He is in control. He has a plan for your life. You are not just wandering out of control. What seems to be bad can turn out good, and vice versa.

Here is a little story of life called "The Lost Horse," by Liu An.

"A man who lived on the northern frontier of China was skilled at interpreting events. One day, for no reason, the family's horse ran away to the nomads across the border. Everyone tried to console him, but the father said, 'What makes you so sure this isn't a blessing?' Some months later the horse returned, bringing a splendid nomad stallion. Everyone congratulated them, but the father said, 'What makes you sure this isn't a disaster?' Their house was richer with such a fine horse, which the son loved to ride. One day he fell off his horse and broke his hip. Everyone tried to console him, but his father said, 'What makes you so sure this isn't a blessing?'

157

"A year later the nomads came in force across the border, and every able-bodied man took his bow and went into battle. The Chinese frontiersmen lost nine out of every 10 men. Only because the son was lame did the father and son survive to take care of each other. Truly, blessing turns into disaster, and disaster into blessing: the changes have no end, nor can the mystery be fathomed."

Live life on an even keel. Trust in God; He loves you.

LOOKING FOR THE BEST

Do not judge, or you too will be judged. For in the same way you judge others, you will be judged, and with the measure you use, it will be measured to you. Matthew 7:1, 2, NIV.

Jimmy looked strange. His jeans were ripped, and his tennis shoes were in desperate need of relief. Just by looking at Jimmy's lower half you might be shocked, but then when you looked up toward his head, well, you needed a strong stomach. Jimmy was constantly trying new things with his blond hair. Sometimes he'd dye it green, sometimes red. Sometimes he would combine both colors. Then he would shape it in spikes, mohawks, rat nests. You name it, he did it. And he even did some things that people couldn't find names for.

People looked at Jimmy and they thought, *What an angry young man! He must be a hoodlum! He's probably a dope pusher.* Do you know what? The more people thought those thoughts, the more they treated Jimmy like he was an angry, hoodlum dope pusher. The more Jimmy was treated like an angry, hoodlum dope pusher, the more he acted like one.

Sometimes parents and teachers actually create problem behavior in children by constantly telling them they are a problem. "You are so lazy! You never learn! Can't you do anything right?" Have you heard these lines before? If you have, chances are you are fulfilling them.

You don't enjoy being put down. It hurts. Why not try doing your best to lift up the people around you? Why not try looking for the best in people rather than looking for the worst.

Your parents may bother you at times, but don't concentrate on that. Think about what you appreciate about them. They are, after all, only human. They are allowed some faults, aren't they? Your teachers can have some annoying habits, can't they? Think about this for a minute: your teachers also have some fantastic gifts that they share with you. They take time for you; they care for you. Can't you forgive a few faults?

Can you accept and forgive faults in your friends? Is it all right if your pastor isn't perfect? Can you look past the mistakes others make and appreciate the beautiful in them? Isn't that how you want others to treat you?

BELIEVE THE BEST

Love is patient, love is kind. 1 Corinthians 13:4, NIV.

So much of what we believe is a matter of judgment. Different people look at things through different eyes, and see things differently. It is unfortunate, then, when people choose to argue and fight over things that are really a matter of perspective.

A friend of yours shows you a poster that he has drawn. He explains its meaning and shows how the harsh lines and pictures of people partying depict despair. It is a poster describing the emptiness of life without Jesus Christ.

Now your friend takes the poster to Sabbath school to show it to his teacher. Before he can explain it, the teacher begins to judge the poster. The teacher sees people partying, drinking, smoking, and taking drugs. She is shocked. How could one of her students bring such a poster into Sabbath school? Your friend tries to explain that the poster is against all of that, but his teacher disagrees. Then they turn to you and ask for an opinion. What will you tell them?

Since your friend drew the poster and explained it to you, you will probably see it his way. You will probably think bad thoughts about the teacher for being so closed-minded about the poster. You will be ready to criticize the church and older people in general for thinking the worst of young people. They will seem so negative and critical!

Now, suppose that you saw the poster for the first time in Sabbath school. You were surprised that your friend would bring something like that to Sabbath school. The pictures seem to glorify things that you don't believe in. You agree with your teacher that your friend is wrong. Who will you think is being closed-minded now? Your friend will argue that the poster doesn't mean what you see, but it will be obvious to you that it does. How can your friend be so blind to the truth?

In the situation above, your perspective is changed because of your perception and understanding of the poster. The poster hasn't changed, but it means different things to different people. People see the world differently. They have different opinions about art, music, history, food, and even God.

Next time you run into someone with different opinions, don't argue, listen. Try to understand why that person feels the way he does. You don't have to agree with him, but maybe you can learn to accept him without falling into the trap of judging him.

THE MIRACLE THAT IS YOU

If you believe, you will receive whatever you ask for in prayer. Matthew 21:22, NIV.

You are a miracle. Do you believe it? God has created within you special gifts and abilities. You may occasionally get in trouble. OK, so you get in trouble a lot. Still, God created you for a reason; you are a miracle. It doesn't matter what people tell you. It doesn't matter how you feel; you are a special miracle. Admit it! When you begin believing in God's great will for your life, then you will see the miracle take place.

Zig Ziglar tells a story about the great magician and escape artist Houdini. Apparently Houdini issued a challenge everywhere he went. He promised that he could set himself free from any jail cell in the country in very little time. He always kept his promise, but one time something went wrong.

Houdini entered the cell in his street clothes. As he walked to the center of the cell, heavy metal doors clanged shut behind him. From a concealed pocket at his belt, Houdini whipped out a short piece of metal. It was strong but flexible. Houdini sprang to the door and began prying the lock.

Something was wrong. This lock was different. For 30 minutes Houdini worked on the lock, but he got nowhere. An hour passed, and still the lock had not been opened. Houdini was bathed in sweat. He was breathing heavily. Never had he worked on so difficult a lock. He could not figure the lock out.

Finally, after two hours of feverish work, Houdini collapsed against the door in frustration. As he fell against the door, it began to creak open. It had never been locked! In his mind it was locked, and that was all it took to keep him from opening the door and walking out of the jail.

Have you locked away your potential by not believing in God's plan for you? Believe in who you are—a child of God. Believe in your destiny—God's great plan for your life. Let the doors of your mind swing open, releasing you to become all that God has in mind for you to be.

YOU'RE FORGIVEN

If you, O Lord, kept a record of sins, O Lord, who could stand? But with you there is forgiveness; therefore you are feared. Psalm 130:3, 4, NIV.

Often the toughest person to forgive is yourself. How do you see yourself? When you look deep in your heart, are you ashamed of yourself, or can you accept and forgive yourself?

How you feel about yourself will affect every aspect of your life. If you have experienced someone telling you, over and over again, that you are slow, or dumb, or ugly, or nasty, chances are you have begun to believe that about yourself.

Of course you aren't perfect. The problem you have is that you are too much like everyone else—too imperfect. The good news is that God loves you and forgives you. He takes you just as you are and makes you His child. When you discover this, you will find room to forgive yourself, and to become all God has in mind for you to be.

There was a man who could never seem to accomplish anything. He was a failure. One day his life turned around. Here's his story:

"When I was in college I belonged to a fraternity initiation committee. My job was to drive my car at a tremendous speed straight toward some new members who were lined up in the middle of the road. They could not jump until they were told to, which would be at the last minute. It was a dark night, and my car reached 100 miles per hour. At the last minute, all the fraternity pledges jumped, except one. He was killed instantly.

"I left college after that. I married and had two children. But the look on that boy's face as I passed over him at 100 miles per hour stayed in my mind all the time. I became inconsistent and moody, and finally I became an alcoholic.

"I was drinking at home one morning when there was a knock at the door. As I opened the door I saw a woman who looked vaguely familiar. She introduced herself to me as the mother of the boy I had killed. She said that she had hated me for years, and had wanted revenge. Recently she had given her life to Christ, and had experienced forgiveness. She said, 'I am here to let you know that I forgive you.'

"I looked into her eyes and saw deep in her eyes permission to forgive myself, to be the kind of person I could be had I never hit her son. Forgiveness changed my life."

You are not perfect. You've made mistakes. But God forgives you. He has a plan for your life. Look to God and become everything He has in mind for you to be in 1990.

OOTW-6

LOST IN THE WORST WAY

For the Son of Man came to seek and to save what was lost. Luke 19:10, NIV.

Being lost is bad enough, but you are lost in the worst way when you don't realize you are lost.

A lady took her two young grandsons to Disneyland. The two boys, ages 4 and 6, were fascinated by the rides and pageantry around them. They especially loved the marching band of "toy" soldiers. Whenever the band would come marching by, the boys would smile and wave their little flags. Suddenly Grandmother noticed that the 4-year-old was missing. Where could he be? There were so many people, so many things happening. How could she ever find him? Nevertheless, she looked everywhere. Frantically she searched through the crowds of people, but her little grandson was nowhere to be found. Grandmother was exhausted. She sat down on a bench to think of what to do next. She felt like crying.

Grandmother heard a commotion to her right, and looked up in time to see the "toy" soldier band marching by again. This time, though, there was something different. At the end of the marching band was a little boy—her grandson—marching proudly and waving his little flag. He was unconcerned, because he didn't realize he was lost.

Sometimes people go through life unconcerned, even though God, our Father in heaven, is frantic about them. They don't realize their danger. They don't know that they are lost.

Where is your life going? Are you a friend of God, or are you wandering through your life, oblivious to your danger?

HEALTHY FRUSTRATION

Indeed, it is easier for a camel to go through the eye of a needle than for a rich man to enter the kingdom of God. Luke 18:25, NIV.

It has long been thought that when students get frustrated, they don't learn as well as they could. What do you think? Columbia University psychologist Herbert Terrace believes this theory is wrong. His experiments with pigeons seem to show that it is not frustration, but the complete lack of frustration, that blocks learning and makes us unstable. Here's what he did.

You have, no doubt, seen "trained" pigeons, or "trained" mice that have learned that when they punch a certain button or lever, they get fed. By contrast, when they punch the wrong button, they get a small electrical shock or something else that they don't enjoy. They soon learn to be accurate.

Dr. Terrace's experiments were done on 200 pigeons. The testing cage had a green light and a red light. Whenever the green light came on, the pigeons were to peck at it. If they pecked at the sight of the red light, they were not fed.

Half the pigeons were fed consistently each time the green light came on and they pecked at it. Their lives were very structured, very secure.

The other half of the pigeons were fed at random. Sometimes they were fed when they pecked at the green light, and sometimes they weren't. They learned not to panic. When the correct peck failed to produce food, they just tried again, knowing the food would come later.

In contrast, when the consistently fed pigeons were treated the same way, they went to pieces, banging their heads against the walls, flapping their wings, and pecking wildly at anything in the cage!

So what does this have to do with you today? The Bible says that those who have had it easy all their lives, who have never needed anything from anybody because it's been provided, may find it hard to make it to heaven. For one thing, they have no reason to desire any better way of life than they have now. In the future, when things get rough, they may not have the stamina to stick by their beliefs, come what may.

In contrast, those of us who are not rich are learning that we can make it through hardships. Our values are based in trust and respect. Perhaps, at first, heaven interested us because we were intrigued by the thought of living in a mansion and having anything we want. But as we learned more about heaven, we discovered the big picture—the battle between God and Satan—and the agonizing sacrifice Jesus made for us just because He loves us! We couldn't help loving Him back, and it's that love that will take us out of this world.

JUNE 8

SOME FRIEND!

Do not look at wine when it is red, when it sparkles in the cup. . . . At the last it bites like a serpent, and stings like an adder. Proverbs 23:31, 32, RSV.

Satan has a lot of notoriety for being sly and cunning and cheating us out of the really good things in life like a happy conscience and self-esteem. He has ways to take these things away from us. But he is not alone. He has many helpers who are willing and eager to take these things from us, helpers we may not suspect.

In the 1930s, a certain man invited a well-known doctor into his home for a consultation. This man had been bothered by intestinal problems off and on for several months and wanted some relief.

The doctor nodded pensively and prescribed some medication. Much to his patient's relief, the medication worked! And the patient vowed to follow the doctor's every suggestion to the letter, even though the doctor began prescribing strychnine and hormones and belladonna and, eventually, what we know today as "speed"—28 different drugs in all.

In time the patient was totally dependent on the doctor and his drugs. The doctor would later say that his patient was never really sick—until he began taking the medications.

The name of the doctor has dropped into obscurity. He was obviously not a doctor, but a sinister drug pusher. But history will never forget the name of the patient—Adolf Hitler!

People are still dying and hurting because of drugs and alcohol. Don't let these chemicals push you around. You're much too special for that. And besides, you're getting ready for heaven. There will be no drugs there. Instead, we will be "high" on self-esteem and friendship and being with Jesus. Don't miss out. You can have that kind of happiness even now. That kind of joy is for you!

JUNE 9

JOEY'S SECRET MISSION

And he said unto me, My grace is sufficient for thee: for my strength is made perfect in weakness. 2 Corinthians 12:9.

The July 19, 1948, edition of *Time* magazine listed Mrs. Josefina Guerrero, a society figure from Manila, a heroine. During World War II, Mrs. Guerrero, affectionately known as "Joey," was a spy for the Americans. She had a secret weapon that aided her in her job, for though she was often seen and not always in hiding, she was never searched.

Before the war began, Joey's husband was a wealthy medical student. Joey was young, pretty, and vivacious. But when the Japanese invaded the Philippines, Joey joined her other prominent women friends and they helped the American soldiers by sneaking them food, medicines, maps, and messages.

On her first assignment Joey drew a map of the locations of enemy antiaircraft batteries along the waterfront. Armed with only a paper and pencil, she prowled the restricted areas, sketching all that she saw. And from Joey's drawings, the Americans were able to pinpoint their targets.

Many near-impossible tasks were completed by Joey. On one mission she tramped through 56 miles of Japanese encampments and check-points on foot, a top-secret map taped to her back. Though she was questioned at every checkpoint, she was never searched.

Joey's secret weapon? She had what other people might call a handicap, for Joey suffered from leprosy. And because of that, she was never searched.

Many of us, aware that we have the dreaded condition called "sin," might just give up. But God says it is that "handicap" that can make us strong. We can do great things if we know we are sinners, for that observation takes away our pride. It causes us to reach out in faith to Jesus and ask Him to change us. And He will! The next time you are tempted, reach out of this world to Jesus and ask for His strength to resist. You will receive it and far more.

JUNE 10

THE LIMITS OF FREEDOM

But the fruit of the Spirit is love, joy, peace, patience, kindness, goodness, faithfulness, gentleness and self-control. Against such things there is no law. Galatians 5:22, 23, NIV.

Do you have much freedom? Well, you may think you don't have enough freedom, but do you have more freedom than you did when you were a baby? Would your parents have let you crawl down the street to play with a baby there? Of course not! They kept a strict eye on you! You may have spent a few hours of each day in a playpen, and even in that limited space you learned that there were limits on what you could do. If you wanted to play with your toys for any length of time, you had better not throw them outside the playpen, or your mother might not give them back to you! You learned to exercise self-control in order to maintain happiness.

Then you became a toddler, and your freedom increased. Perhaps you were allowed out of the playpen, to roam the house or even the fenced backyard! Here, again, you learned that there were limits to your freedom. If you smeared the walls with crayon pictures, your mother got angry and you were unhappy too. Outside, if you dug up Mother's flowers, you got into trouble. So you learned to control yourself and make good choices about what to do with your freedom. You remembered the limits that were set.

Then you went to school—more freedom—and you learned that you had to be quiet and listen when the teacher was talking. You learned that if you didn't do your homework, or if you didn't turn in neat papers on time, you and your parents were unhappy. So again, you learned to

165

control yourself, and you sat quietly in your seat without whispering and turned in neat papers on time, and both you and your parents were happy.

Someday you will be a grown-up. Grown-ups have limits on their freedom too. Grown-ups have to show up for work every morning and accomplish their goals, or they may not have a job! They learn to control themselves and do what has to be done, whether it's fun or not! So we are never totally free of limits in this world.

But, praise God, there is one area of our lives in which there are no limits. There is no limit on being kind. Paul tells us that there are no laws or limits on love, joy, gentleness, patience, or any of the other fruits of the Spirit! You don't have to control yourself to keep from being too thoughtful. So get out there and experience true freedom—the freedom to be joyful, gentle, patient, and kind!

JUNE 11

MYSTERY OR MIRACLE?

The things which are impossible with men are possible with God. Luke 18:27.

Sometimes God uses miracles to get our attention; to make us sit up and take notice that He is in charge here, whether we may realize it or not.

The following story happened more than 100 years ago. It may seem incredible, but "a stack of sworn statements and legal documents say that it was so."

The Methodists in the town of Swan Quarter, North Carolina, had no church. They had scraped the money together to build one, and had approached a shrewd and prosperous landowner about building on one of his choice sites in the middle of town. But he had turned them down.

The only other site available for a church was in the lowlands, where flooding was a common problem. But they wanted a church building so badly that they went ahead and bought the land and built their little white-frame church on top of brick pilings.

On Sunday, September 16, the little church was dedicated. Three days later a terrible cyclone blew in, ripping off roofs and drenching the town with heavy rains.

The next morning the rains had stopped, and the residents of the town looked out on total devastation—except for the brand-new Methodist church. The floodwaters had lifted it intact off its brick pilings, and it was floating silently in four feet of water down the street toward the middle of town.

166

Efforts to fasten it with ropes failed against the strong current, and after struggling for some time, men simply gave up and let it float. At last the church, still floating, made a sharp right turn as though it had a mind of its own. And then, another turn into the middle of the choicest plot of land in the middle of town—the congregation's first choice of property. There the church stopped. And there it is today.

The next morning the prosperous landowner, who had originally refused to sell his land to the Methodists, visited the Methodist minister. With trembling hands he presented him the deed to the land.

God can do anything. He keeps on trying to show you how special you are, how much He loves you and wants the best for you, but it's up to you to believe that.

JUNE 12

CLINGING VINES

Jesus wept. Then the Jews said, "See how he loved him!" John 11:35, 36, NIV.

At what point is a tunnel the darkest—at the beginning, the middle, or at the end? A tunnel is darkest in the middle, when you can see neither one end nor the other.

If you had to be all alone in a tunnel, would you rather be at the beginning, at the middle, or at the end? Why, I would rather be at the end. Somehow, seeing that light at the end would give me the energy I needed to get through it.

All our hard times are like tunnels. When we are in the middle of them and can see no end in sight, we wonder if we will ever pass through them. The hardest thing about troubles is not knowing when they will end.

As I write this, my very good friend, Pastor Laverne Schlehuber, has just died of cancer. He wasn't even 40 years old, and he had lived a healthy life, free of meat, alcohol, cigarettes, and coffee. He was a good and kind man, and he didn't deserve to die. His children don't deserve to have to grow up without him. He was like a brother to me, and I will probably never understand as long as I am on this earth why this tragedy happened to him and his family. Perhaps you know of a similar tragedy. How did it affect your trust in God?

When faced with the tragedies of life, we all have two choices to make: We can wrongly decide to blame them on God and hate Him. Or we can more accurately decide to blame them on sin and cling to God for comfort.

Have you ever seen a tree with ivy climbing up its trunk? Ivy is astonishingly hardy. Once it decides it is going to be attached to a tree, it stays attached, tiny tendrils clinging tenaciously to the bark. It is next

167

to impossible to completely remove ivy from around a tree. If the vine grows on the side of the tree opposite the wind, the trunk protects it and it flourishes. If the vine grows on the exposed side of the tree, the wind only serves to press it in closer to the tree for support. Either way, that vine stays with the tree, come what may!

Pastor Schlehuber's family and friends are being buffeted by the winds of sorrow right now. Right now, those of us living in this sinful world are on the exposed side of the tree. We are hurting. But hopefully we all will use this sorrow to be good vines and press in tighter to God—our solid support, who is suffering too. Hopefully our suffering will help us get things in perspective and remind us that the only thing we can take with us from this life is our love for God. And the most precious things we will find in heaven are people we love.

JUNE 13

IF ONLY THEY KNEW!

Seek ye the Lord while he may be found, call ye upon him while he is near. Isaiah 55:6.

It has been said that "life has to be lived forwards, but can only be understood backwards." Sometimes things seem so clear when we look back on them. Decisions we should have made seem so obvious from afar.

It was the year 1901. The first-aid station at the Pan-American Exposition in Buffalo, New York, was a big and busy one, equipped with everything from bandages to an operating room. It was fortunate they had an operating room the day Bill, a 58-year-old man, was brought in. He had taken two bullets at close range.

In surgery, the doctors saw that the first shot had grazed a rib and deflected. The second wound was right in the stomach, and there was no exit wound. The bullet was still inside.

Rapidly yet carefully the surgeons repaired the damage that had been done. They knew they should also remove the bullet to prevent infection, but they could not find it within a safe period of time before Bill had to be brought out of anesthesia.

They closed him up—no drainage—and hoped for the best. Bill was taken to a private residence in Buffalo to recuperate. But a week later he was dead.

"If" is a big question here, but if the doctors had been able to locate and remove the missing bullet, Bill might have lived. If only the doctors had used all the help available. If only they had used a new invention on display not far from the scene of the shooting—a revolutionary device called an X-ray machine—that could have located the missing bullet. But they didn't know how well it worked. They were not accustomed to using it.

In the last days there will be those who are not accustomed to leaning on God, who try to do everything for themselves. They will not be at peace. But those who are familiar with trusting Jesus will be joyful. They'll know what to do. And He will help them. You can be one of those. Invite Jesus to share every moment of your day.

WHY DO YOU LOVE JESUS?

Not everyone who says to me, "Lord, Lord," will enter the kingdom of heaven, but only he who does the will of my Father who is in heaven. Matthew 7:21, NIV.

The story is told of a young lady who left her small town to go to college. While there, she met a young man who seemed so self-confident that she was certain he was very rich. Hoping to live the rest of her days in relative ease and luxury, she wooed him and charmed him to the extent that at last he proposed marriage and invited her home to meet his family. He had a happy secret to tell, he said, and he wanted to share it at the same time with all the people he loved.

She was delighted! Certainly everything was working out her way! But when she went to his home, she was appalled and shocked to see that it was no finer than her own. His family were simple farmers!

In a burst of hot anger, she accused him of misleading her, broke the engagement, and took the next bus home. Once home, the girl remembered she had not stayed at the young man's house long enough to learn his secret. That evening, bored and lonely, she tried to push the nagging curiosity out of her mind by curling up with a newspaper. It was then with a gasp that she learned the young man's secret, and she hastened to mend her ways.

He received a letter from her at the end of that week.

"My dearest darling," it began. "I'm so sorry I left your home in such a rush. It was so foolish of me, and I am so embarrassed! I hope the engagement is back on. I love you, I love you, I love you! . . . P.S: Congratulations on winning the Irish Sweepstakes!"

Do you find yourself doubting the quality of her love? What is your reason for loving Jesus? Is it just because you want to go to heaven? Or is it a little of that but mostly because He is nice to be with? Jesus loves us no matter what our motives are. Someone has said, "When I look at myself, I wonder how I can ever be saved. But when I look at Jesus, I wonder how I can ever be lost." That's the kind of person Jesus is. How can you not love Him?

WHY SHOULD YOU GO TO HEAVEN?

Salvation is not a reward for the good we have done, so none of us can take any credit for it. Ephesians 2:9, TLB.

If you were to be your own lawyer at the final judgment, what would you say in your defense? What reasons would you give God as proof that you should be saved?

You could list any number of accomplishments, of course. "I have gone to church almost every Sabbath since I've been born," you might say. Or "I have never killed anyone." Or "I love Jesus." Those are all good reasons. But they aren't good enough. They aren't good enough to convince even you that you should go to heaven, because they leave a little margin for error.

What about the Sabbath you stayed home because you overslept? Could that keep you out of heaven? What about the time you said you would like to kill someone because you were mad at him? Could that keep you out of heaven? What about the time you didn't actually say it, but you felt a little angry at God because He didn't answer your prayers in the way you expected? Could that keep you out of heaven?

Those nagging questions are the result of thinking we can get to heaven by what we do! But the Bible makes it very plain that we can't earn our way into heaven. We are not saved by works; we are saved by faith. By believing that Jesus wants to save us; by believing He loves us; by believing that heaven is real.

Jesus is the best lawyer you can have. And guess what He is going to say? You are a worthwhile, lovable person just because you exist! And you get to go out of this world to heaven just because you have reached out in faith for the gift He offers to everyone—the gift of eternal life. Heaven is yours because you believe.

SECOND CHANCES

Remember not the sins of my youth and my rebellious ways; according to your love remember me, for you are good, O Lord. Psalm 25:7, NIV.

Todd would say later that he couldn't believe he did what he did. No one else in the gymnasium that night could believe what they saw either.

Just before halftime, Todd, the best basketball player for his high school team, had the ball. He began dribbling it at center court. But suddenly he couldn't remember which basket was his. Which direction should he go? The audience was screaming wildly. Thinking they were encouraging him, he headed toward the nearest basket and dunked the ball just before the buzzer sounded.

Against a background of booing and whistling, Todd joined his teammates along the bench for halftime. It was then he learned he had dunked the ball into the wrong basket! He had scored for the opposing team.

Todd covered his face with his towel and cried like a baby. He was mortified. How could he have been so stupid? If only the floor would open up and swallow him.

The coach touched him on the shoulder. "Todd, I want you to start the second half."

"But Coach, I—" Todd stammered.

"You're our most valuable player," the coach said. "We need you to score one for us now."

Todd did. And his team won!

Have you made some pretty stupid mistakes? Just think how smart you are now because of them. Everyone makes mistakes, but only fools repeat them. Fortunately, in the game of life, God is the designer of second chances. Pick yourself up, dust yourself off, start over again, and be wise this time.

FATHER MAKES A DIFFERENCE

Let your conduct be without covetousness, and be content with such things as you have. For He Himself has said, "I will never leave you nor forsake you." Hebrews 13:5, NKJV.

Do you sometimes wonder whom you can trust? Have your friends let you down? Do you feel like giving up? If it seems there is no one you can trust, then I have good news for you! You can trust your father—your Father who is in heaven.

Most earthly dads mean well. But even the best of parents can have problems. Toby's dad grew up without love, and has a hard time showing love to his children. He does his best, and his kids are helping him a lot. Jill's dad is a lot of fun, and Jill adores him. But he's happiest when he's having a good time, and money runs through his fingers like water.

Sometimes Jill has to wait months for badly needed clothing because her dad has bought himself a new "toy."

Terry's father is overprotective, and Terry, age 12, groans because he will hardly let her cross the street by herself. Ryan's dad would rather study than play ball with his kids. But Ryan loves him anyway, and enjoys evenings spent at the library with him. None of us have perfect parents. But most of us have learned to get along with the parents we have. Even at best, however, people sometimes let you down. But God never will. He is the perfect parent and the perfect friend.

A party of botanists were exploring unexplored regions of the Alps, searching for new flowers. Day after day they searched without success. Hiking through treacherous mountains, fighting for footing on steep slopes, as the days passed they became exhausted. Suddenly one of the botanists shouted in excitement. He had seen an unknown flower of unusual beauty through his binoculars. The only problem was the flower's location. The flower was in a deep ravine, and could be reached only if someone was lowered into the ravine on a rope.

A young boy in the group, native to the Alps region, was offered a large amount of money if he would allow himself to be lowered into the ravine. The boy hesitated. He looked down into the dizzying depths and said, "Wait, I'll be back." Soon he returned with an older man. He approached the botanists and said, "I'll go over the cliff now and get the flower if you let this man hold on to the rope. He's my dad!"

It makes a difference who holds the rope, doesn't it? God has promised to hold your rope. He has said that He will never leave you nor forsake you. In 1990 you can trust in God to solve your problems.

JUNE 18

SLOGANS ARE TRICKY

As [a man] thinketh in his heart, so is he. Proverbs 23:7.

Can you finish these slogans?

"Pepsi: The Choice of . . . . . a New Generation."

"You deserve . . . . . a break today. So get up and get away to McDonald's."

"Kentucky Fried Chicken. We do . . . . . chicken right."

"Catch the . . . . . wave. Coke."

"In the land of Dairy Queen we . . . . . treat you right."

Why do you suppose businesses use slogans? Because they know that after you hear their slogan enough times you will unconsciously link it with their product. For example, if you want to be treated right, you will go to Dairy Queen. Right?

Consciously or unconsciously, we attach slogans to ourselves, too. Psychiatrists call this "self-talk." When something happens to us, we explain it to ourselves and tell ourselves something about us. Depending on what we say to ourselves, we feel good or bad about what happened.

Consider how you would handle the following situation: It's late in the morning. You've overslept, and when you finally wake up you discover that you have nothing clean to wear to school. You grab something out of the dirty clothes hamper, throw it on, and hurry off to school.

As you walk into your classroom, the loudmouth of the class calls out, "Where you been? Sleeping in the streets again?" Your best friend tells you quietly, "You're really a mess. What happened?"

At this point you can tell yourself anything and you'll believe it. How would you feel if you said to yourself, "I'm a lazy slob"?

On the other hand, how would you feel if you told yourself, "My clothes are messy today—I'll have to make sure it doesn't happen again"?

Sometimes we call ourselves names that are worse than anyone else might think of. The sad part is that we believe ourselves. We make ourselves feel very bad.

Successful people don't call themselves names. They don't expect themselves to be perfect, but they expect to do the very best they can.

What are some things you say to yourself that are bad? Take a few minutes now and write them down. They might be, "I am ugly. I am a slob. I am dumb. Nobody likes me. I'm a jerk." Now take each one and write it in a positive way.

"I am learning how to be more attractive. I am becoming more neat. I am learning how to remember things. I have two good friends. I am becoming less obnoxious."

Across your first list, write the following: "I will allow myself to be less than perfect."

Now take your second list of good things and read it to yourself in front of a mirror. Tape it to the mirror and read it every day. Slowly your mind will start to believe the good things, and a miracle will happen: you will be that kind of person.

And while you're thinking about good things, add this one:

"God thinks I'm something special." Now say it to yourself all day long.

AND THE LIES CONTINUE

The serpent was the craftiest of all the creatures the Lord God had made.... [The woman told him,] "God says we mustn't eat [the fruit] or even touch it, or we will die." "That's a lie!" the serpent hissed. "You'll not die!" Genesis 3:1-4, TLB.

The lies that Satan told Eve are still believed by a majority of very nice Christian people. Since Satan is so cunning, he makes his lies seem like Bible truths—unless you know your Bible well enough to spot them. One of his most widely believed lies is that people go to heaven when they die. Remember, he told Eve, "Ye shall not surely die."

A bittersweet tragedy happened two years ago at the hospital where I work. A lovely family came in to have their second baby. Their 4-year-old daughter was with them, accompanied by her grandma. Grandma waited outside the delivery room with the little girl, awaiting the happy news of the baby's birth. But sadly, the brand-new baby girl was born with severe deformities and did not live much beyond a half hour after birth.

The parents were distraught, clinging to each other and crying; the grandmother was crying with them, as well as the nurse, and the little daughter sat alone outside the room, clutching her brand-new doll. Big tears rolled down her face as she tried to understand what was going on.

The nurse who was taking care of the mother realized at once that the girl needed some reassurance. So she explained what she believed to the little girl. Unfortunately, what was supposed to be comforting did not sound comforting to me. The nurse said, "Your baby sister had to go back up to heaven to be with God; she couldn't stay with us. Father God needs her, instead."

The little girl listened solemnly, without saying a word. And when the nurse went back into her mother's room, the girl followed behind, clutching her doll tightly. She climbed up onto her mother's bed. "Mommy, you don't have a baby?" she asked gently. When her mother shook her head, the little girl pressed her doll into her mother's arms. "You can have my baby," she said, and then she curled up in her mother's arms next to her dolly.

I wondered what the little girl was thinking about "Father God." If I had been that little girl, I would be angry at Him for being so selfish. How could God need my baby sister more than my mother did? How could a loving God snatch babies away from families with no concern for their feelings? He already had lots of other babies. Why did He need mine?

I don't know that the little girl thought about it. But what if she did? What if she believes Satan's lie that we don't actually "die" when we stop breathing and our heart stops beating—that we go to heaven and become like God? That gives Satan a wide open door to "bring back the dead" as ghosts that then give advice, supposedly straight from God. Believing the lie makes people angry at God. And then Satan has them right where he wants them. Fortunately, the Bible tells us the truth. All of the dead, from Adam to Abel to the very last person on earth to die, will sleep until Jesus returns.

JUNE 20

ONLY THE SCARS REMAIN

If anyone can control his tongue, it proves that he has perfect control over himself in every other way. James 3:2, TLB.

Hazel Farris recalls that as a child she had a fiery temper that often caused her to say or do unkind things. One day after an argument had sent one of her playmates home in tears, Hazel's father told her that for each thoughtless, mean thing she did, he would drive a nail into the gatepost at the front of their house. But each time she did a kind thing, or said a kind word, one of the nails would be withdrawn.

Months passed. More and more nails were driven into the gatepost. Fewer and fewer were removed. Hazel just couldn't seem to control her thoughtless tongue! Without thinking, she blurted out insults to her playmates, sending them home in tears. With a pained expression, her father would trudge out to the gatepost each evening to add some more nails.

Each time she passed the gate or invited her playmates in, she was reminded of the reasons for those ever-increasing nails, until finally, getting them out became a challenge. The gatepost was looking ugly with so many gray spikes sticking out of it! Worse, fewer and fewer neighbor children would come over to play.

At last Hazel began to choose her words carefully. She made herself take a minute and whisper a prayer for help before she answered in anger. That gave her time to find the right words for what she was feeling. She shared her feelings with her friends, instead of blindly insulting them or reaching out and slapping them.

"You are making me mad," she would warn them, instead of blurting out a bad name. Sometimes they would stop what they were doing, and sometimes they would just leave. But at least no more nails were added to the post.

Finally Hazel began gaining the victory and creating a new character. And at last, through many kindnesses and thoughtful deeds, Hazel succeeded in removing all of the nails. As her father pulled the last nail out of the post, Hazel danced around proudly, clapping her hands. "Oh, Daddy, look! The nails are all gone!"

Drawing Hazel close to him, Father gazed at the post as he thoughtfully replied, "Yes, the nails are gone—but the scars remain."

"No man is rich enough to buy back his past." Even though you may apologize for an unkind word or deed, the pain you have caused leaves a scar on that other person's life. If you have insulted someone, a corner of his heart believes that he deserved it. When you are finished being angry, you will regret that you caused another person pain. How much better to live without regrets and "bite your tongue" instead.

JUNE 21

HE FELL FOR THE TRAP!

For God shall bring every work into judgment, with every secret thing, whether it be good, or whether it be evil. Ecclesiastes 12:14.

A man we'll call Bill owned his own construction firm. Bill was a rich man, for his company did well. And now the most important, most income-producing job was up for grabs, the construction of a new bridge across a river uptown.

Bill took painstaking care in writing up his bid for the job. His major competitor—Joe's construction—was bidding against him. Bill wanted the job more than he had ever wanted any job before. It was such a big project, it would assure him an income for two whole years!

The day of his appointment arrived. Bill put on a suit and tie— unusual for him—and found the high-rise office building without any problems, driving by the proposed site for the bridge one more time. He whistled softly as he walked toward the building, his papers in a large, brown envelope under his arm. He had done a good job, and he was counting on winning the bid!

As the elevator doors slid open, Bill stepped aside. With a start, he recognized Joe.

"Well, hello, Joe!" Bill said. "What are you doing here?"

"Same thing you're doing, I assume," Joe replied tersely.

"Good luck." He walked briskly toward his car.

Once inside the engineering office, Bill made himself comfortable and began explaining his bid, answering questions, and enjoying himself. Then the telephone rang. The engineer was called out of the office.

Bill had noticed that Joe's bid was lying on the engineer's desk, under a can of pop. He knew he shouldn't look, but he was so curious, he stood up right next to the desk, bending his neck so he could read Joe's estimates. It was difficult, for the can of pop was in the way.

And then Bill made the mistake that blew the job. Carefully, quietly, he lifted the can of pop. In that instant, he realized his mistake. The can had no bottom in it. Noisy BBs fell out of the bottom of the can, scattering noisily over the glass-topped desk and onto the floor, bouncing all over the place.

Hearing the commotion, the engineer returned and surveyed the bouncing BBs wordlessly. "Bill, your company is one of the best. We had hoped we could use you. But I can see we can't trust you, so we won't be needing your services at all. Good day."

Bill learned the hard way that "the measure of a man's real character is what he would do if he knew he would never be found out." Even grown-ups have to contain their curiosity sometimes.

JUNE 22

WHO STOLE THE PAPER?

Some men enjoy cheating, but the cake they buy with such ill-gotten gain will turn to gravel in their mouths. Proverbs 20:17, TLB.

Tracy just wasn't good at writing English papers. She was afraid to see her final grade, for she knew her parents would be upset. If only she could write a really good paper for this last assignment—it might bring her grade up to passing, at least! Maybe her roommate could help her! Her roommate was the English teacher's student aide.

When Tracy brought her problem to Heather's attention, Heather had an instant suggestion. "I happen to know for a fact that in the bottom drawer of Mrs. Baxter's file are old papers from years ago. You could borrow one of those, type it up fresh, put your name on it, and turn it in as your own—she'll never know! It's probably older than she is, anyway."

Tracy loved the idea. "Can you get one for me tomorrow?"

"No problem," Heather promised. She chose a paper that seemed like something Tracy would write about and tucked it under her arm as she left the office for the dorm. Whoever the person was who wrote it had gotten an A+! That should help poor Tracy a lot.

Right after supper Tracy began typing the paper. It took her an hour. By the time she had finished, she was nearly as proud of that paper as if it were her original composition! When she turned it in the next morning, she could hardly keep a straight face. She was bursting with foolish pride.

The next week the grades came out. Tracy opened her report card with a pounding heart and gasped. She had failed English! How could she, with an A+ paper? But how could she prove it was a good paper without revealing her secret? She didn't have time to worry. Mrs. Baxter called her into her office that day.

177

Mrs. Baxter was very eager to talk. "I know that's a good paper, Tracy, but you did not earn the A," she said somberly. "Someone else did."

Tracy was aghast. How did she know?

"That paper you turned in belonged to my sister, who graduated from here eight years ago. I typed that paper for her. The minute I began to read it, I knew it was not yours. You have three days to write your own."

While everyone else enjoyed the school picnic, Tracy sat in the library frantically doing research and writing her paper. She passed English, and she learned about honesty. And she also learned that no matter what her grade, it felt better when she had earned it herself!

JUNE 23

LEARNING FROM EXPERIENCE

King Rehoboam consulted the elders . . . and he said, "How do you advise me?" 1 Kings 12:6, NKJV.

There's a story about a young bank cashier who was named successor to the retiring bank president. One day he went to the senior officer and said, "As you know, I'm going to follow you as president, and I'd be grateful for any advice you might have."

The president said, "Son, sit down. I've got two words for you. Just two words: *right decisions.*"

"That's very helpful, sir," replied the young man, "but how does one go about making right decisions?"

"One word—*experience.*"

"That's also helpful, sir, but how does one gain experience?"

"Two words," said the older man. "*Wrong decisions.*"

Growing up means learning to make decisions. You've already made a lot of decisions this morning. Can you remember two of them? How many more do you think you will make before the day is over? Fortunately, we make habits out of many of the daily decisions we must face, so we barely have to think about them.

You are going to make your share of good decisions in life. You are also going to make a number of wrong decisions. Because of those wrong decisions, you will have to give your share of apologies. The best apologies are done right away. Don't give an excuse, and include some mention that you have learned your lesson.

Mistakes make us uncomfortable, but they are not the end of the world. Don't let the fear of making a mistake prevent you from trying new things! Ford forgot to put a reverse gear on his first automobile. Thomas Edison once spent $2 million on an invention that proved of little value.

One night Mr. Edison's shop caught fire. As he helplessly watched it burn, turning his costly experiments into ashes, he called to his son Charles. "Come!" he said. "You'll never see anything like this again!"

Then he called to his wife and brought her out to see it. As the three of them stood gazing at the fire, Edison said with almost a touch of excitement in his voice, "There go all our mistakes. Now we can start over afresh." In two weeks he started rebuilding the plant, and it was not long before he invented the phonograph.

Cy Young, the great baseball star, won 511 out of the 906 games he pitched in, a record that has never been equaled.

Young won just a few more than half his games! Even so, he was a success. To be an outstanding success in any endeavor, it isn't necessary to be right all the time. If you're right more than half the time, you're doing an excellent job. The important thing is to keep pitching.

WHAT'S YOUR THEME?

Wist ye not that I must be about my Father's business? Luke 2:49.

Since Christians are humans, we come in a variety of colors, shapes, and sizes.

A lot of Christians are like wheelbarrows—not good unless pushed.

Some are like canoes—they need to be paddled.

Some are like kites—if you don't keep a string on them, they fly away.

Some are like kittens—they are more contented when petted.

Some are like a football—you can't tell which way they will bounce next.

Some are like balloons—full of wind and ready to blow up.

Some are like trailers—they have to be pulled.

Some are like lights—they keep going on and off.

And there are those who always seek to let the Holy Spirit lead them.*

Which kind of Christian are you? Which kind of Christian do you think Jesus was?

Whether or not we are aware of it, each of our lives has a pattern to it—a theme that we sometimes follow subconsciously. Some people carry a grudge and are always suspicious of others. Some of us live to serve. And some people just live, with no goals, no plan—they just let life happen.

If we listen to the things we say, we can come up with a pretty clear picture of the theme of our lives—whether we think positively or negatively, and whether or not we are an uplifting influence or a depressing one.

Not surprisingly, the first and last recorded words of Jesus show that His life was focused on one thing: doing the will of God. What are the first recorded words of Jesus? "I must be about my Father's business."

And what are His last words? "It is finished."

To do God's will should be the focus of our lives, too. What have you done, or what will you do today, that nobody but a Christian would do?

*From Paul Lee Tan, *Encyclopedia of 7,000 Illustrations.*

JUNE 25

PROUD CHRISTIANS

Now when a man works, his wages are not credited to him as a gift, but as an obligation. However, to the man who does not work but trusts God who justifies the wicked, his faith is credited as righteousness. Romans 4:4, 5, NIV.

If I knew all your secrets, you would be in trouble! Everybody has secrets that he is ashamed of, things that would embarrass him if anybody knew. The worst thing about these secrets is that they make us afraid of what people would think of us if they knew what we'd thought or done.

There is Somebody who knows all your secrets. But don't bother to look around, for He isn't visible. He knows everything about you: everything you've done, and everything you've thought about doing. The amazing thing is that He knows all this, but He still thinks you're terrific.

Sometimes we think we're not good enough to be loved by God. We picture God with a long face, staring glumly at us, frowning! We feel that we're not what God wants us to be, so surely He cannot love us or save us. Satan is happy when we think these thoughts, for he wants us to see God as harsh, unloving, and unforgiving.

Several years ago a dirty street urchin in England stopped a man who was known for his kindness to orphan children. "Please, sir, won't you take me into one of your homes?" he pleaded. His big, round eyes were luminous in his grimy, sunken face.

The wealthy man looked down at the child. His eyes were kind. "But I know nothing about you," he said. "What do you have to recommend yourself?"

The little boy looked down at his ragged pants, his dirt-crusted jacket. "I thought these would be enough," he said, holding out his filthy clothes.

The rich man gathered up the little guy in his arms and took him home.

In our text today, Paul calls God the one who "justifies the wicked." Paul is saying that God makes the guilty "not guilty." You thought that your bad thoughts and actions would keep you away from God, but the Bible says that because you sin, you are just the kind of person God loves and saves.

God is your friend. You are worth more to Him than all the riches on earth. He is the one person you can trust with your secrets. And He wants to take you home.

WHAT IS THE MOST PRICELESS GIFT YOU OWN?

For God so loved the world that he gave his only Son, that whoever believes in him should not perish but should have eternal life. John 3:16, RSV.

There's an old story about a little orphan boy who was playing on the banks of a large river one afternoon. Soon some rich kids sauntered down to the river too. The orphan, dressed only in a ragged shirt and pants a size too small, kept his distance. He watched these rich boys roughhouse together as their parents picnicked a short distance away. From time to time the boys would run up to their parents and then return, munching happily.

The orphan's stomach knotted in hunger. He edged a little closer just to smell the food. Soon he stood just a few feet from the boys, his hands clasped behind his back, watching silently with a shy smile on his face.

"Let's go swimming!" one of the boys suggested to the others.

"I wouldna' if I was you," the orphan said suddenly, surprised at his own voice.

"Why not? It doesn't look dangerous to me."

"Oh, but it is. There's hidden rocks in there, and giddy pools. I had a friend once was sucked down in one of them pools."

The rich boy surveyed the orphan coldly. "Maybe he was and maybe he wasn't. Probably wasn't smart enough to get out on his own. I am!" And with that, he pulled off his shirt and jumped in.

Moments later his arms flailed in panic, and he disappeared downstream.

The children ran screaming for the grown-ups, who raced to the riverbank, wringing their hands with concern. The orphan boy was nowhere to be seen.

Then a shout was heard downstream. "Hold on to my hand!" Waist-deep in the water, one hand gripping an overhanging branch, the orphan reached out as far as he could toward the struggling boy. As the boy splashed and clawed toward him, the orphan pulled him to safety. The boy lay on the bank, exhausted, and the orphan crept away.

The grown-ups dashed toward the boy.

For several minutes the crowd's only concern was for Billy. And then someone noticed the orphan huddled, shivering, and wet under a nearby tree, watching Billy and his mother. "There's the boy that saved him!" they cried.

"Let's take up a collection for him. Sure looks like he could use it!"

And so they collected a sizable amount of money for the orphan.

"Here, boy," one of them said, huffing with pride at their generosity. "Go and buy yourself a new set of clothes."

The orphan stood quietly. "I don't want your money," he finally said. He pointed to the tender scene of Billy and his mother. "I just want someone to love me like Billy over there."

Love is a priceless gift. Cherish those who love you.

JUNE 27

THE SHEPHERD'S SECRET

My sheep hear my voice, and I know them, and they follow me. John 10:27, RSV.

A tourist visiting in Palestine observed several shepherds and their flocks at a watering hole. The cobblestone square was a solid mass of shaggy sheep with wet, black noses jostling each other for a chance at the water trough. With some difficulty, the shepherds squeezed their way between the sheep, briskly calling their names above the sheep's murmur, to keep them in line.

At last one of the shepherds was near enough to the tourist that he could ask a question. "I see that there are many flocks combined here. How do you separate the sheep when it is time to go home?"

"Not difficult," the shepherd said lightly. "My sheep know my voice!"

"So they always come when you call them?"

"But of course!" His voice dropped. "Unless they are sick."

"And what happens then?" the tourist wanted to know.

"When my sheep are sick, they will follow anybody."

The shepherd turned then, and called to his sheep. Sure enough, as his dusty feet began the long walk home, one sheep after another twitched its leaf-shaped ears, looked up, and hurried through the milling throng to follow him. The illustration Jesus had used in Bible times was still true in this century.

How do you know if you are a "sick" sheep or a "well" one? What does it mean to follow Jesus?

I think it means we live like He did—to respect others and do all we can to spread happiness.

Following Jesus means we believe that He is real, that He is the Son of God. It means we believe He loves us and will come again to take us beyond the stars.

"But it's so hard to believe," someone says. "I don't know what it feels like to believe."

Believing is not a feeling; it is a choice. For some people it is easier to say "I choose to believe in Jesus" than "I believe." Right now, say out loud, "I choose to believe in Jesus."

When you follow Jesus, you will hear His voice over the din and clatter of a thousand distractions. And no matter what, you will follow Him.

FLYING FEATHERS

A gossip goes around spreading rumors, while a trustworthy man tries to quiet them. Proverbs 11:13, TLB.

A little girl came to her mother with an urgent request. "Please, Mom, may I take a bath every morning instead of at night before bed?"

"But why? You're not dirty in the morning!" her mother replied.

"I know! But every morning my teacher asks who has taken a bath that day, and we're supposed to raise our hands. I haven't been able to raise my hand for three months, and everyone thinks I never take a bath!"

It's easy to jump to wrong conclusions. Too often our wrong conclusions lead to unkind, vicious rumors that destroy people.

In a small German village, a woman differed with her minister and became so angry that she began spreading ugly rumors about him around town. As fate would have it, she eventually became gravely ill and called on the minister to pray for her. He came gladly, and she asked his forgiveness of her gossiping.

"I will grant you forgiveness," the minister said, "but there's something you must do."

"I'll do anything," the woman said.

"Go pluck the feathers from a black chicken and put them into a basket, and bring them to me."

The woman did so and presented them to the minister the next day.

"You did well," the minister said. "Now take this basket of feathers and scatter them in the corners of the marketplace and from the towers of the church. Scatter them throughout the town. Then return to me."

So the woman did. She walked from one end of town to the other, scattering the feathers. Then she returned to her pastor. "I have done as you asked," she said.

"Very well. Now take your basket and collect all the feathers. Make sure not one is missing."

"But that is not possible!" the woman said with a choking cry. "The wind has carried many of them away!"

"So it is with your words," the minister said. "While I have gladly forgiven you, do not forget that you can never undo the damage your untrue words have done."

JUNE 29

HOW DEATH SNEAKS UP ON YOU

Though evil is sweet in his mouth . . . it becomes cobra venom within him. Job 20:12-14, NKJV.

A tragedy happened in Georgia, at Stone Mountain, the largest boulder in the world. A young man was walking along the curve of the boulder several years ago, oblivious to the gradual, almost imperceptible, downward curve of the domelike mountain. Suddenly he realized that he was powerless to retrace his steps back up the curve to safety. He had gone too far down.

Horrified onlookers heard his piteous crying. "Help! Help me!" But they could do nothing. As they watched, he hurtled over the edge of the mountain to his death.

Stone Mountain is not the only place where "entertainment" can kill you. One of the places we think of as safe is the most dangerous—our homes.

Are there some TV programs you have watched in the past week that made you edgy, ready to switch them off immediately if the doorbell rang or your parents came home? Have you watched lying, murder, and immorality? Have you watched rock videos, unmindful of the beat or the suggestive words? Have you watched a "true story," a historical movie, but one that glorified or entertained with evil?

Because they entertain us, these programs make it easy for us to find pleasure in viewing the very things God hates. As a result, our sensitivity to sin is dulled.

It's rather like the ants that have a passion for a sweet substance given off by a certain kind of caterpillar. The ants enjoy the juices so much that they stupidly bring the caterpillars home so they can have their fill of this sweet substance. They seem almost addicted to it! Never mind that while they are enjoying the sweets the caterpillar is quietly eating up the next generation—the baby ants.

Television can inform and educate as well as entertain. And to be entertained isn't always bad. But we must control the knob. We must keep our hearts sensitive to programs that treat God lightly, to stories about people that use bad means even to achieve something good. What we watch *can* become bitter if it dulls our sensitivity to wrong and makes us lose eternal life.

JUNE 30

HOW TO BE A HAPPY OLD PERSON

Fear not; you will no longer live in shame. The shame of your youth . . . will be remembered no more. Isaiah 54:4, TLB.

The difference between youth and old age is that when you're young you spend your time dreaming about what life is going to be like; when you're old your time is spent in remembering it. People in nursing homes spend a lot of time remembering. And though it is hard to imagine, someday even you might be an old person chomping on your dentures, remembering how it was when you were young; remembering today.

The grouchiest people in nursing homes are those who never learned how to be happy. Many of them remember only the disappointments in their lives. Either they have few happy memories, or they think they have to remember their mistakes to be "humble." They torment themselves, going over and over their bad decisions.

Two men were deep in conversation as they walked along a country road. Deciding to take a shortcut home, they cut across a pasture, where several cows were grazing peacefully.

So engrossed were they in conversation that they forgot to close the gate behind them as they left the pasture. A quiet lowing of the cattle arrested their attention, and one of the men hurried back to close the gate.

"That reminds me of something my grandfather told me a few days before he died," the man said to his friend. "He very wisely said, 'As you go down the pathway of life, remember to close the gate behind you.'"

What the grandfather meant, of course, is that every life is like a multifaceted diamond. In your life, there will be times of disappointment, times of boredom, times of great excitement, times of grave mistakes. When you meet these times, recognize them as such. "So this is one of my disappointments," you may say after meeting one. Then go on, knowing that something else will be next on your journey. Maybe one of your greatest joys will happen next.

If, instead, you experience a grave mistake, learn your lesson and close the gate behind you. You are a different, much wiser person today than you were two years ago. Don't punish yourself today for who you

185

were then. God willingly forgets the mistakes we make because of inexperience. After a mistake, get on with your life. It's a good habit to develop. "To make a success of old age, you have to start young."

JULY 1

HOW TO GET GOOD GRADES

As your days, so shall your strength be. Deuteronomy 33:25, RSV.

It was the beginning of the semester. Mrs. Barnes, the English teacher, was giving her introduction to the class. "And at the conclusion of the semester, I will expect you to turn in a 25-page term paper, double-spaced, with documented research, footnotes, and a bibliography," she said.

A low moan rose from the class, and Donna began worrying.

"How am I ever going to find time to do research?" she complained to her best friend, Stacey, at lunch. "I have so much homework to do already."

Stacey leaned back in her chair. "Well, I figure I have 12 weeks to do it in. I'll take two weeks to do my research, two weeks to write the first draft, four weeks to let it sit, and I'll still have the next four weeks to go back to it and polish it up!"

"That doesn't work for me," Donna sighed. "I work best under pressure."

By the time Stacey had finished her research, Donna still hadn't chosen a topic. When Stacey had written her first draft, Donna was trying to decide between two topics. And four weeks later, while Stacey was relaxing, letting her rough draft sit, Donna started her research.

Soon it was the day the papers were due.

"Coming to lunch?" Stacey asked Donna after class.

"How can I?" Donna groaned. "I still have to type my paper! Plus I have to finish my algebra! I'm so worried. I have so much to do, I'm going to go crazy!"

Sound familiar? What was Donna doing to herself? She was lumping several days' work into one, procrastinating so much that there was no way she could get everything done.

The best way to get good grades is to be neat and precise, and get each day's assignment in on time. When you put things off, you set yourself up for worry. God promises you enough strength for each day.

A wise person once said, "If I shirk today's tasks, I increase tomorrow's burdens."

HOW TO GET THROUGH TODAY

Will all your worries add a single moment to your life? ... Don't be anxious about tomorrow. God will take care of your tomorrow too. Live one day at a time. Matthew 6:27-34, TLB.

Shannon flopped down wearily on her bed. "I'm so worried!" she moaned to her roommate. "The boys' club banquet is coming up in just two weeks, and I haven't been asked yet!"

"I thought you heard Steve liked you," her roommate replied.

"That's what my brother said, but I'm afraid Steve's too shy to ask anybody."

"Then tell your brother to tell Steve that you want to go with him!"

"I can't do that! A girl has to play hard-to-get, you know."

"Fine, then. But I've seen that oddball Nathan making eyes at you. If you don't let Steve know you want to be his date at the banquet, Nathan might ask you first, and if you turn him down, Steve might hear of it and be afraid you'd turn him down, too. Then you wouldn't have a date at all!"

"I know, I know! That's why I'm worried!" Shannon moaned. "Time is running out, and somehow I have to get Steve to ask me first, so I can turn Nathan down graciously. Odd though he is, I don't want to hurt his feelings. I have to have a good reason for turning him down."

"You've got a problem, all right," her roommate agreed.

Have you ever worried about something similar? The fact that we worry about something usually means that it is important to us, or that we don't have any control over it.

Are the things that you are worrying about things you can change? If so, change them! Set aside a certain hour each day when you do your worrying, and come up with creative solutions to the things that worry you. Write them down. Then you can stop worrying about them.

If you can't change something, worrying about it isn't going to do a bit of good anyway. Will your parents divorce? Will you be in a serious accident? Nobody but God knows the future. Put those worries in Jesus' hands. When they creep back into your mind, remind yourself that you're just not going to worry about them. Ask yourself, "What is the most important thing for me to think about now?"

Jesus promises you enough strength for today. Today is the tomorrow you worried about yesterday. Did any of that worrying change a thing?

DAY-TIGHT COMPARTMENTS

Give us our food again today, as usual. Matthew 6:11, TLB.

In 1913 Sir William Osler stood on the bridge with the captain of a great ocean liner. The captain was understandably proud of his ship, and he wanted to show his guest everything it could do.

"Now these buttons are probably the most important feature of this vessel," the captain said, indicating large, shiny buttons to his right. "Listen!" He pressed one of the buttons. Immediately, there was a clanging of machinery as giant steel doors in various parts of the ship were shut off from each other into watertight compartments.

"If one part of the vessel should fill with water, we can protect the rest and stay afloat."

"Marvelous!" Sir Osler exclaimed.

Several months later, when he addressed the students of Yale University, he remembered that experience and drew on it in his talk.

"Each one of you," he told the students, "is bound on a longer voyage than that ship. What I urge is that you so learn to control the machinery as to live with 'day-tight compartments' as the most certain way to ensure safety on the voyage. . . . Touch a button and hear, at every level of your life, the iron doors shutting out the past—the dead yesterdays. Touch another and shut off, with a metal curtain, the future—the unborn tomorrows. Then you are safe—safe for today!"

Many years before, a penniless Philosopher gave a speech on the top of a hill that said pretty much the same thing. "Don't worry about tomorrow," Jesus said. "Live today the best way you can. Tomorrow has enough troubles of its own."

Jesus repeated His advice again in the Lord's Prayer. We are to ask for today's supply of bread. Not tomorrow's, not next week's—just today's.

We can't eat the whole day's supply of food at one sitting. And we can't develop a satisfying friendship with Jesus by merely going to church on Sabbath and ignoring Christ and the Bible the rest of the week.

Your whole body requires refilling of one sort or another. One breath doesn't last a lifetime. You sleep one night at a time, and work one day at a time. You get through the day one prayer at a time.

In the little things you do each day, from brushing your teeth to making up your bed, to saying morning and evening prayers, you weave a pattern in your life that you cannot reweave. Weave carefully today.

STRANGERS DO IT BETTER

Then Jesus told them, "A prophet is honored everywhere except in his home town and among his relatives and by his own family."
Mark 6:4, TLB.

Joe and Mary Carpenter had a large and active blended family, including children from Joe's first marriage, his wife's son, Joshua, and several children they had together.

The usual competitiveness existed between the children. Each child was touchy about everything being even, hoping he was loved as much as the others. There was also a bit of jealousy between the children. Josh was lucky. Mary and Joe had married a short time before he was born, and Joe had adopted Josh as his own. To Josh, Joe was a real father—not a stepfather.

From the time Josh was old enough to toddle around, he followed Joe everywhere. Joe often took the little boy to his shop, where Josh played with wood shavings and sawdust, and with the little wooden people and animals his father carved for him.

As Josh grew, he and his brothers learned cabinetmaking too. Their mischievous banter made Joe smile as he observed them out of the corner of his eye while he did work of his own. Since it was a small town, you can imagine how the townspeople talked when Josh left on a journey no one fully understood.

When he returned home several months later, he was different. He could touch sick people and make them well! It was almost spooky. His first Sabbath home, Joshua (the Hebrew name for Jesus) gave a testimony in church and said He had found out who His real father was—God in heaven. And He said He had come to save the world!

The people in town bristled. "He's just a carpenter! He built the cabinets for our new home," they muttered. "I watched Him grow up. Where does He get the authority to preach at us like that? He's always been just Mary and Joe's kid. He's no better than we are!"

And because of their unbelief, Jesus couldn't do His miracles in their town. Jesus was hurt, but He tried to understand. As He explained to His mother: "It's hard for people at home to stop thinking of Me as 'chubby little Josh Carpenter.' "

If your family rejects Jesus regardless of your witness, don't feel guilty that you're not witnessing well enough. Jesus was a perfect witness, yet people closest to Him didn't believe.

DREAMS

Forgetting what is behind and straining toward what is ahead, I press on toward the goal to win the prize for which God has called me heavenward in Christ Jesus. Philippians 3:13, 14, NIV.

She's 4 feet 11, weighs 85 pounds, and has a big dream. Melissa Marlowe wants to be in the Olympic games. She is a gymnast. She flies through the air, twisting and turning, somersaulting through impossible routines on the balance beam and the uneven parallel bars. Her balance and confidence take your breath away, while her happy enthusiasm inspires and amuses you. You wish you could be a gymnast like her. What does it take to be one of the best gymnasts in the world by the time you are 16?

Melissa's father and mother divorced when she was 2. Sometimes people believe they can't amount to much because they don't come from the perfect family, but that's not true. Melissa didn't let that stop her. She began playing around with gymnastics in the gym when she was 9 years old.

"It was just something to have fun with on a Saturday afternoon," she says. A year later, at the age of 10, she was in the Utah State Gymnastics Championships.

The six years since then have been filled with a lot of sacrifices and hard work. Each day begins with classes at a special school in Salt Lake City, then Melissa trains in gymnastics from 1:00 to 6:00 p.m. She confesses that she has never had a boyfriend. Her dream demands her total attention. "To be a gymnast, you have to be married to the sport 365 days a year," she says.

"You can't wake up with the attitude, 'Well, I think I'll just bag practice today and lounge around in front of the television with a bowl of potato chips.' " However, there are rewards for her dedication. She gets to travel to exciting places, and she enjoys competing and winning. By the time you read this, you will know whether or not she won a gold medal in the 1988 Olympics.

Do you have a dream? Do you have a dream for your future? Does that dream allow you to include God in it? No dream is worth dreaming unless it does. Are you willing to do everything you can to ensure that you are a winner, and that you succeed in reaching your dream? In 1990, stretch for your dream. You will find lasting satisfaction as well as success if you put your trust in God and live to bring Him glory by being the best you can be.

THE SUPERNATURAL

Jesus told him, I am the Way—yes, and the Truth and the Life. No one can get to the Father except by means of me. If you had known who I am, then you would have known who my Father is. John 14:6, 7, TLB.

I believe in the supernatural. The Bible is a book filled with supernatural events, beginning when God spoke our world and everything in it into existence. Then there was the talking snake in the tree—a snake that could fly, by the way! And when Adam and Eve were driven out of the garden, angels holding what appeared to be flaming swords guarded the entrance. This is real stuff—not fairy tales!

But believing in the supernatural is scoffed at today. People who believe in UFOs, or who say they have seen ghosts, are considered to be a little crazy. But what happens when we scoff at every "supernatural" story we hear? It is easy to doubt that the supernatural events in the Bible actually happened. The stories may seem to be fairy tales. Do you see how clever Satan is? He uses his own supernatural powers to reveal himself to a few, who tell their stories to others, who in turn say the believers are crazy.

It is a law of physics that "for every action, there is an opposite and equal reaction." When a pendulum swings one way, it swings the same distance the other way; it has an opposite equal to it.

I believe that the supernatural also has two equal opposites. I was fortunate to have grown up overseas, where supernatural evil is very evident. I have seen heathen "camp meetings," at which people run through coals without getting hurt, or sew lemons to their arms and backs and walk on nails without bleeding. I have seen them stick thin, eight-inch spears through their cheeks and tongues before dancing for their evil gods, and I have seen them jerking and bucking as the spirit left them when the dance was over. I have seen their glazed eyes. I *know* there is a "dark side" of the supernatural. I have seen people possessed by the devil.

And I have also seen that there is also a "good side" of the supernatural. God is that good side. And He is with us, night and day, forever and ever. He is coming soon to destroy the dark side of the supernatural and to take us out of this world.

THE SOLDIER'S CHOICE

And all who trust him—God's Son—to save them have eternal life. John 3:36, TLB.

What would you do if you learned this morning that the entire world was at war, and you had to make a stated choice to be on one side or the other? If you said, "I don't know. I can't decide!" someone else would decide for you. Would you let him?

If you tried not to make a decision for yourself, you would, in reality, be making a decision to let someone else choose your destiny. It wouldn't keep you from being part of the war. You would still have to fight, maybe against something you believed in! Would you still let someone else choose the side you want to be on?

Believe it or not, a worldwide battle is going on right now. In fact, it's bigger than worldwide, for it involves heaven and earth. It's a battle between supernatural powers—God and Satan. And the Bible is a record of the beginnings of that battle, with guidance on how to know the difference between the two sides, and a forecast of which side is going to win.

For those of us who've studied the Bible from the time we were in cradle roll, the special reason the Bible was given to us may become blurred. God's promises may become something we take for granted.

Why do you suppose God chose a book as His method of informing us about His plans? What if a glowing, translucent, giant angel suddenly appeared in your room in the middle of the night and told you all the promises of the Bible in one hour? Would you be scared? Would you remember it all? Would you be able to share it with others?

The Bible is the best way God has to give us encouragement without scaring us. And a book can be picked up and put down, read at your leisure, read anytime of the day or night. Also, a book is an easy way to share information with a friend.

The Bible promises that when the two supernatural beings are finished fighting, the good side will win. The Bible helps us identify the sides so we know which side to be on. If we don't choose God's side, Satan will decide we should be on his side.

Right now, say out loud, "I choose to believe that Jesus Christ is the Son of God." As you say it, you are choosing your side—the winning side! Doesn't that make you happy?

WHAT TO DO ABOUT GUILT

Oh, do not hold us guilty for our former sins! Let your tender-hearted mercies meet our needs, for we are brought low to the dust. Psalm 79:8, TLB.

In what way are boats, trains, cars, horses, bicycles, and airplanes alike? They all provide transportation. They all need energy to make them go.

Which one of them is different from all the rest? The airplane. Do you know why? Boats, trains, cars, horses, and bicycles can come to a standstill without any problem. They can reverse and go backward. But the airplane cannot fly backward. It cannot come to a standstill. If it loses its momentum and forward motion, it crashes.

We are more like airplanes than the other forms of transportation. As Christians, we must keep a forward, upward motion. If we take our eyes off Jesus and His love, or if we go backward and fall back into old, sinful habits, we are in danger of crashing.

Are you a kinder person today than you were last year at this time? Do you know more things? Is Jesus more real to you now than He was last year? I think most of us can answer yes to all of those questions. Learning new things and controlling our responses to our feelings are part of growing up.

Your parents won't spank you today because you wet your diapers when you were a baby, will they? They don't punish you today for the kind of person you used to be. And you don't need to spank yourself and hate yourself for the mistakes you made when you were younger. You're growing and changing.

If you can remember specific things you did in times past that you feel you should apologize for, then do so. That in itself helps you to grow. But if you can't find the person to apologize to, or if you have apologized and made everything right, then apologize to God for bringing pain to someone else, make a decision not to do it again, and then forget about it.

Keep going forward and upward. Don't look back, except to remember how God has led you and cared for you. And when 1990 is over, you can be an even stronger Christian than you were when it began.

ARE YOU PROUD TO BE YOU?

My son, give me thine heart. Proverbs 23:26.

A teenager whom we'll call Betsy was shopping with her mother. As they walked through the mall, Betsy's mother looked in one store window after another, searching for the specific items they were there to buy. But Betsy kept looking at the people they passed. Many people smiled broadly whenever Betsy looked at them.

"Mom," Betsy mumbled under her breath, looking down at the floor in front of her, "what's wrong with me?"

"What do you mean?" her mother asked.

"Is my hair out of place? Do I look funny?"

Her mom stopped and looked her over briefly. "I don't see anything strange. You look pretty to me. Why do you ask?"

"Because people are smiling at me. I don't know if they're laughing, or what." Betsy's teeth were clenched, so nobody could read her lips.

"They're probably smiling at you because they think you look nice or they wish they had a daughter like you," her mother returned with a light laugh.

With that thought in mind, Betsy returned the smiles of everyone she passed from then on. And she treated her mother kindly, smiling at her warmly, so that people who wished they had a daughter like herself would see why.

Was that a fakey thing for Betsy to do? Was it wrong? The Bible tells that we become what we think about and look upon. If you decide that you will be a blessing to everyone you meet today, what will you do? You'll smile at people. You'll help them whenever possible. You'll say something nice to them. And as you're busy thinking up nice things to do, you will become a nicer person.

When Jesus asks for our hearts, He is asking for our thoughts. He is asking that we study His example and treat others as He did. It may seem unfamiliar at first, but after a while it "becomes you" and it's just the way you are! By acting the way Jesus would act, by actually treating people the way Jesus would treat them, we will become like Him. Jesus wants us to forget *who* we are and concentrate, instead, on *whose* we are. And that will make all the difference in the world.

SURPRISING CONCLUSIONS

And note this: some who are despised now will be greatly honored then; and some who are highly thought of now will be least important then. Luke 13:30, TLB.

Have you ever won something by default? If your teacher grades on the curve and yours is the highest score, even if it's not very good, you earn a high score by default, because nobody did better than you. Some people think we get into heaven by default. Some people say we have to be as good as Bible characters if we want to make it there. Do you agree? Are you as strong in your faith as Daniel was? Are you willing to be stoned for your faith like Stephen?

Winning by default doesn't feel very good. I remember when, as a teenager, I won something by default. I was a sophomore at Auburn Academy in Auburn, Washington. My family and I had just arrived back home in the States after being missionaries in Ceylon for several years, where I had taken most of my elementary school by correspondence. I had spent my ninth grade in a boarding school in India where there were 10 kids in my class. Now I was in America—the "new kid" at Auburn Academy, a school of nearly 500 students! Fortunately most of the kids were accepting and friendly, and before too many weeks passed I had made many good friends.

The months flew by quickly, in spite of agonizing homesickness during the first few weeks. Soon it was time to elect new officers for the student body. I was shocked when they invited me to run for student body secretary! I mean, I had lots of friends, but I was under no delusions that I knew enough kids to win in an election! And my opponent was a well-known girl a year older than I, who'd attended Auburn for almost three years. I envied her. She had the most current hairstyle, a beautiful wardrobe, and bunches of guys hanging around her locker. She was a member of the in crowd. Next year she would be a senior!

I didn't know what to do. I was honored to have been asked to run, but it would also be humiliating to lose! "I don't know enough kids," I said. "Why should they vote for me if they don't know me?"

"This will help them get to know you," I was told.

I talked to my roommate and closest friends about it. They encouraged me to run, promising not to laugh if I lost!

My mom encouraged me to take the risk, too. And so I agreed to be on the ticket for ASB secretary. To my surprise, I won! When the votes were counted, they showed I had won by a fairly large margin!

I was surprised and very happy at first, but then my "victory" turned sour. I learned that my name was put on the ticket because the girl I was running against had a lot of friends on the nominating committee. They thought that since I was new to the school, no one would vote for me, and it would be an "easy in" for the other girl.

"Then I wasn't asked to run because I would do a good job, but because they thought I would automatically lose," I told my roommate. "And the kids who voted for me didn't really want me to win. They just didn't want the in crowd's choice to win the election."

"Well, certainly many of us who voted did want you to win," my loyal roommate told me with a smile.

It was embarrassing, and certainly very humbling, to know I had won by default. But I did my best. And after my name and face became more familiar, I had the chance to make many new friends.

I mentioned earlier that some people think we get into heaven by default. They tell us that if we can be better than anyone else, we'll earn our way into heaven. But the Bible tells us not to compare ourselves to each other! When we look at each other we lose sight of the prize. There are going to be some surprising conclusions when Jesus comes. Fortunately, heaven is not just for people of the in crowd. You don't have to beat anyone else out of Heaven to get there. You don't have to be famous. You don't have to be a Week of Prayer speaker. You don't have to be the pastor of your class, or give Bible studies.

But you do have to love and obey Jesus. That's all it takes to go to heaven.

JULY 11

WHO HAS YOUR LOYALTIES?

Then Jesus told him, "You believe because you have seen me. But blessed are those who haven't seen me and believe anyway." John 20:29, TLB.

In the January 1988 edition of *Moody* magazine, author Sheldon Vanauken tells of standing on the bridge of a destroyer "steaming under a million stars in the Far Pacific" on his way to war. He thought uncomfortably about the Christian faith he had abandoned just as he had forsaken the tooth fairy and the Easter bunny as a child. It made him uncomfortable to know that he didn't believe in God anymore. "Should I have another look?" he wondered. "Many brilliant men believe in God. They wouldn't do so if there wasn't a good reason to believe."

But he put off finding reasons to believe in Jesus until many years later. Through his studies, he learned to love the man Jesus, who was always kind and thoughtful and really cared about other people. That Jesus truly lived on earth was undoubtedly true. Secular historians recorded the life and times of Jesus Christ, and the calendar as we know it is based on His birth. Jesus Christ was a very real man who had a very real impact on our world. But was He a supernatural being in human flesh? Was He really God's Son?

How could a man—merely a man—tell people, "I forgive your sins" and "he that hath seen me hath seen the Father"? Was He a madman? Or was He really God's Son?

Sheldon had to choose. Not to decide is to decide. He felt love for Jesus, but who did he say that Jesus was? Whichever way he chose, there would be no certainty. If Sheldon chose to believe, there would be doubts: "Perhaps it's all a lie and He was just a man." But if he chose not to believe there would also be doubts: "What if I have rejected my God?"

Either way, Sheldon felt he would be gambling, betting his life that Jesus was God—or betting that He was a madman.

Then Sheldon had a thought. If the whole world went to war, he would have to choose a side without knowing which would win. If one side were commanded by Christ the King, wouldn't he choose to be on that side? The Bible identified the sides. Anyone who would choose wrong had to choose deliberately. So Sheldon chose. He chose God to be his king and to have his loyalties. Every day he says out loud, "I choose to believe that Jesus Christ is the Son of God."

Try closing your eyes to shut out any distraction and saying to yourself, "I choose to believe that Jesus Christ is the Son of God." The more you say it, the more you find yourself believing it. It's the truth!

JULY 12

MORE SPECIAL THAN ANYONE ELSE

My son, if your heart is wise, then my heart will be glad. . . . There is surely a future hope for you. Proverbs 23:15-18, NIV.

Robert Orben, a well-known humorist, says, "Who can ever forget Winston Churchill's immortal words: 'We shall fight on the beaches, we shall fight on the landing-grounds, we shall fight in the fields and in the streets, we shall fight in the hills.' It sounds exactly like our family vacation."

Why do brothers and sisters fight? Nobody knows for sure. But usually we fight because someone damages something that is ours, or takes something that is ours—especially the feeling that we are the most important person in our parents' lives.

It is normal to want to be your parents' favorite child. But there's a funny thing about wanting to be the most favored. While you are dreaming about being the favorite, you hope your parents don't abandon the others entirely! It can get to be a scary thing sometimes!

The best way to get over feeling jealous of brothers or sisters is to recognize your special talents. Do you know what they are? You can begin to find out by doing things that interest you. Maybe you will discover that something you thought you were interested in isn't so fun, after all. But maybe you'll discover that you are really good at it! Maybe you can't play the piano as well as your sister can, but maybe you can play the guitar. Maybe you can't paint as well as your brother can, but maybe you can put your thoughts on paper and write well. Maybe you can't play baseball very well, but are good at gymnastics or swimming instead.

When I first began to write stories, I worried that someone else might write a similar story before I got to it, and then nobody would want to read what I wrote. But then I discovered that even though others might write a story with the same title and even the same plot, our stories would never be exactly the same, because we would each write in our own style.

You have a style of your own that you may just now be discovering through the way you fix your room, the clothes you choose, the way you comb your hair, and even the way you do your homework! Listen to yourself, and your mind will tell you what kind of person you are. When you need directions to go somewhere, do you prefer that someone draw a map for you, give you landmarks to watch for, or tell you the exact names of the streets you are to look for? Do you learn best by studying diagrams or by reading descriptions?

Hold your thumbs out in front of you. Is one thumbnail larger and more developed than the other? That one is probably the one on the hand you write with the most. The right thumb of right-handed people is usually larger than the left thumb, and vice versa.

Your body has started talking to you already. Listen to the messages you tell yourself today when you choose your clothes, or when you do your homework, or when you raise your hand to answer a question in class. Find out just what a special and unique creature you really are!

When you get to heaven, God won't ask you, "Why weren't you like your sister?" "Why weren't you Elijah?" or "Why weren't you Daniel?" But He will ask if you used the talents He gave you. You can't use them if you don't know what they are. Find out! And then use them for God's honor and glory.

JULY 13

HOW TO GET TO HEAVEN

The one who obeys me is the one who loves me; and because he loves me, my Father will love him. John 14:21, TLB.

Dr. Joe Galusha, biology professor at Walla Walla College, tells the story of how, when he was 10 years old, he learned, wrongly, about how hard it is to get to heaven.

It seems that in Joe's Sabbath school, there was a contest for all the boys and girls to earn Investment money. Those who earned $10 all by themselves would be rewarded with an overnight camping trip. Joe was excited. He found his name on the chart and vowed that his ribbon would go all the way to the top before the quarter was over! He would work harder than anybody to earn $10 for Investment!

So the next day Joe vacuumed the whole house for his mother. And he earned a dime. He helped with the dishes and earned some more money. He washed the car—more money. His mother baked some bread, and Joe took it around to the neighbors in his wagon and sold it for money. Each week he turned in his profits from the week before, and smiled happily as his ribbon was pinned a little higher than it was the week before!

Soon the vegetable garden began to produce. Joe faithfully tended the garden, not minding the scratches and scrapes he got from picking prickly cucumbers to sell. He earned a lot of money, but still needed to earn more.

Before long it was the Friday before the end of the quarter. Again Joe took his cucumbers around to his neighbors. Some neighbors bought them, but others were sick of cucumbers and turned him down. By the time the sun was beginning to go down, Joe was still 40 cents short of reaching his goal. But Sabbath was coming, so he took his wagon home. He was sure someone would chip in and give him the 40 cents he needed in order to go on the camping trip! He prayed for it and went to bed confident he would go.

But the next morning in Sabbath school, when Joe turned in his money and admitted that he was only 40 cents short of $10, nobody offered to make up the difference. He had to do it on his own; and he had failed.

Many of the others went camping—but Joe was left behind. He hadn't done enough to be rewarded.

Through academy and college, Joe determined not to miss out ever again. He volunteered for community service; he had prayer for dorm worship; he preached at the Week of Prayer. Surely God would take note of everything Joe had done for Him and would let him into heaven on all his good deeds! He didn't want to miss out on that trip, but he was getting exhausted trying to earn his way into heaven.

Finally, a friend explained that Joe had learned the wrong lesson from his Investment money. If Jesus had been the Sabbath school leader, He would have made up the difference and given Joe the 40 cents!

In the story of the rich man's banquet, Jesus explains that the only requirement for going to heaven is knowing that we can't get there on our own. Nobody who came was good enough to come as he was, but the rich man made up the difference! The rich man—Jesus—provided the clothes. And any friend of Jesus' is a friend of God's.

THE SECRET OF BEING RICH

He who loves pleasure will become poor; whoever loves wine and oil will never be rich. Proverbs 21:17, NIV.

Wouldn't it be great to have a million dollars? What would you do if you suddenly became rich? Would you be happy? "Of course," you say. Would your dreams come true?

The other day I heard about a woman who won a million dollars. Overcome with excitement, she felt certain that all her dreams would come true. She'd never have any more worries. However, six years later she was hopelessly in debt, divorced, and suffering from a severe back disability. During her television interview, she shook her head and sadly regretted the day she won a million dollars.

Of course, it wasn't the *money* itself that had brought sorrow. It was how she had reacted to sudden wealth. Quitting her job, she bought every expensive thing she'd ever dreamed of owning. Unfortunately, *things*, even expensive things, wear out in a few years. Then she had nothing left but payments on the things she had bought on credit.

She and her husband let their sudden wealth change their lifestyle so much that it led to misunderstandings, then fighting. When their marriage ended in divorce, she was ordered to pay her husband alimony. He sued for custody of their daughter and won. She was ordered to pay child support. During a struggle with her husband over their daughter, she fell down and injured her back, making it impossible for her to go to work.

Six years ago she won a million dollars; but today she is poorer than she has ever been. She spent all her money on pleasure and expensive things, and now she has nothing.

Solomon was right when he wrote our text for today. "If you want to be rich," he said, "learn to live simply, to deny yourself, and to work hard." If you do this, you will keep your conscience clear, you will like yourself, and you will be successful in 1990. True riches have to do with character, not dollar amounts.

BE A CROWD-PLEASER

Therefore, since we are surrounded by such a great cloud of witnesses, let us throw off everything that hinders and the sin that so easily entangles, and let us run with perseverance the race marked out for us. Hebrews 12:1, NIV.

It's called the Ridge to River Race, and it happens every spring in the Wenatchee Valley of Washington State. One year several of our church school students from Cashmere, Washington, one of their teachers, and I formed a team and entered the race. It's a relay that begins on skis in the mountains and ends with a canoe run down the Wenatchee River.

Our team's participation in the race began with a cross-country ski run by one of our students. Another continued the race through a downhill slalom course. A student's mother jogged six miles in the next leg of the race, then a student bicycled for 12 miles. The final leg of the race consisted of the teacher and me struggling through several miles of the turbulent Wenatchee River in a canoe. At the end of the canoe run, our whole relay team carried the canoe together for one mile and across the finish line.

I'll never forget what it was like finishing the race. We were all tired, the canoe was heavy, but as we ran down that final mile we were urged on by shouts of encouragement from spectators lining the street. People we didn't know were cheering for us as we came by. Though we were exhausted and felt like slowing to a walk, the crowd urged us on, and we accomplished more than we thought possible.

The Bible tells us that we have a crowd of witnesses urging us on to eternal life. Are you tired? Does life seem hard? Don't give up! You have a crowd of witnesses cheering you on so you can accomplish the impossible by becoming all that God wants you to be in 1990.

SUPERNATURAL WARRIORS

And the Lord opened the young man's eyes so that he could see horses of fire and chariots of fire everywhere upon the mountain! 2 Kings 6:17, TLB.

Have you ever heard your radio send out a signal that is used in emergencies only? Were you put on "red alert"? I will always remember when I was in the seventh grade at a boarding school for missionaries' children in India and we were put on "red alert." The school had been literally cut out of the side of a mountain in the foothills of the Himalaya Mountains. A narrow, curvy road ran down one side of the mountain, but to get to the road, we had to climb up and over our side of the mountain along a rough, mile-long trail.

China lay just over the mountains, and at that time there were hostilities between America and China. If China wanted American hostages, there was a large group of us isolated on the mountain that they could go for!

At one point, we were on "red alert." The American Embassy sent word that if China should attack, they would airlift us off the mountain by helicopter to safety.

When word of the "red alert" first reached us, I was very scared. The thought of being under attack 2,000 miles from our parents and being airlifted to an unknown destination was unnerving! We were not allowed to hike into town on our monthly "town day." We had to stay on campus, where we could be gathered quickly if necessary.

Fortunately, nothing ever happened. The Chinese never attacked, and in time life went on as usual and the "red alert" was called off.

But I often wondered what could have happened if we hadn't believed the embassy's warning? We couldn't see the Chinese Army! We could have brushed their warning off as nothing. But fortunately, we believed, and we were ready to be taken to safety if necessary—even if we never saw the enemy soldiers for ourselves.

The battle that God is waging with Satan is very similar. We can't see Satan's army, either, but it is a certain threat to our lives. Jesus has told us to be on "red alert" to Satan's army. Someday Jesus will lift the curtain of secrecy under which they now hide, and we'll see how we have been surrounded by Satan's evil host. We will also see, like Elisha and his servant did, how we are being protected by God's angels.

Angels are real, whether or not you can see them. They're fighting a war with Satan's army, and we are caught in the middle. If you don't believe that there's a real supernatural war going on right now, watch out! God might end the war before you know it, and it will be too late to believe.

JULY 17

WHY DO I FEEL SO BLUE?

The Lord will command His lovingkindness in the daytime, and in the night his song shall be with me. Psalm 42:8.

At her desk one evening, Laura fidgeted nervously with her pencil, tapping it against her math assignment paper. She couldn't concentrate. She turned to her radio on the shelf beside her, and turned it on to her favorite radio station, breathing a sigh of relief when she heard one of her favorite songs come on. She turned the radio on loud so she could immerse herself in the music—that would help her concentrate! But it didn't. She still felt a brick in the bottom of her stomach. Why was it that way so much lately? She felt anxious about something, but she didn't know exactly what it was. She just felt nervous and uneasy.

Have you ever felt that way? What do you do when you feel uneasy? Some people eat; some people sleep (or try to); some people sit like zombies, listening to rock music; some listen to slower, more relaxing music. What works the best?

Mrs. Dorothy Relallack, at Temple Buell College, wondered what effect rock music might have on plants. So in the laboratory of that college she placed various plants in front of stereo speakers, in prime growing conditions. She cared for each set of plants in the same way. The results of her experiment were surprising: the plants that were in front of the stereo speaker that played only mild, relaxing orchestrated music thrived, becoming tall and sturdy plants in a month's time.

The plants that had sat in front of the rock music speaker? The squash plants became shriveled, the philodendron plants flattened, and the corn crumpled—in less than a month!

How about you? Maybe you feel anxious because your mind is being filled with pounding, depressing music. Maybe you need to try something more relaxing instead. Maybe you need a strong dose of uplifting music—maybe religious music that reminds you that God has things under control, rather than music that mourns about how bad things are in the world—how hopeless everything is—how mistreated you are. Things are bad, but God is working things out for a thrilling conclusion! That's something to be excited about!

Do your own experiment! Next time you feel down—and most people feel the most depressed at night—try singing one of "the Lord's songs" to yourself. Have you heard the one that goes,

"He didn't bring us this far to leave us,
 He didn't teach us to swim, to let us drown,
 He didn't build His home in us, to move away,
 He didn't lift us up, to let us down."

The Bible says that whatever we think in our hearts, we become. Before Jesus went out to be crucified, He sang a song with His disciples in the upper room. Jesus was probably using music to find strength.

If you fill your mind with songs that urge you to give up, or to think that everyone's out to get you, that's how you will feel. But if, on the other hand, you fill your mind with songs that pick you up and encourage you to keep going, that's how your day will go. Have a good day!

HOW MUCH TIME DO YOU HAVE?

Walk in wisdom . . . redeeming the time. Colossians 4:5.

If you live to be 75 years old, you will have spent about 25 years of your life sleeping. If you are now 15, you have been awake for only about 10 of those years—you spent at least five of them doing nothing but sleeping!

In a book by Dr. Leslie Weatherhead called *Time for God,* a lifetime of "threescore years and ten" has been compared with the hours of a single day from seven in the morning to eleven at night.

If your age is 15, the time is 10:25 a.m. At 10:25 in the morning, the day has barely begun.

So you stand at the beginning of your life. Your job right now is to learn things. You don't go to school so you can give the teacher answers to things he or she already knows—you go to school so you can learn things for yourself and understand things. Learning things makes you feel good about yourself. It helps you to be less dependent on others. You go to school so you can give intelligent answers and have an educated opinion about what's going on. In short, going to school means you have the chance to improve how you feel about yourself.

An 11-year-old girl I read about has a guaranteed income in patents for life because she went to school and learned things. She studied about phosphorescence in science class one day. Phosphorescence, as you may know, occurs when something glows green in the dark after being exposed to light. This little girl used what she had learned to invent something: she invented writing paper lined with phosphorescent lines so people could see to write in the dark!

Learning involves "hooking facts together." Learning means you don't have to make the same mistakes others have made. As you learn, don't learn things for your teacher. Don't learn things for your parents, or for anybody else. Do your best in school and learn everything you can for yourself! That's the best way to make the most of your life.

WEAVING A GOOD LIFE OUT OF BAD

Who hath saved us, and called us . . . according to his own purpose. 2 Timothy 1:9.

Karen wiped her little brother's runny nose with a tissue and sent him back outside to play. It was hard to keep her mind on her homework when he came running in so often for something or other and disturbed her concentration! It really wasn't fair that she had to baby-sit every single evening while her mother worked in the hospital until midnight. Karen was the one who put her brother to bed every night and made his lunch every morning before walking him down two blocks to the baby-sitter's house so her mother could go back to sleep. Other kids got to hang around together more. It wasn't fair!

At church, Karen had heard that "God has a plan for every person's life." "What is His plan for me?" she wondered. "Does He think it's good for me to be a live-in baby-sitter for my little brother, instead of having fun like other kids?" There was nothing noble about being a baby-sitter for your little brother! Karen decided that God might have a plan for other people's lives, but He didn't seem to have a plan for hers!

Several years went by. Karen's mother got a job on the day shift at the hospital and was home every afternoon and evening. From listening to all the interesting stories her mother told, Karen decided she wanted to be a nurse too. She discovered, much to her delight, that her classes on how children develop and how to care for childhood illnesses were easy for her because of all her experience taking care of her little brother. She became a pediatric nurse, and soon earned a reputation of being one of the best nurses in the department!

Did God have a plan for Karen's life? Does "having a plan" mean that God makes our decisions for us, and we just have to fit into His plan, like little robots? I don't think so. I think God keeps an eye on all the experiences that happen to us, and He says, "If she'll let me, I can help her remember what she's learned from that experience so she can use it for the rest of her life."

Rugmakers in China make beautiful Oriental carpets from the wrong side—working from the back of the loom. Sometimes they make a mistake and weave in the wrong color. The supervisor can see this from his side. But rather than let this mistake ruin the whole carpet, he alters the pattern to make the mistake a useful part of the design.

Sometimes it may seem that you are working from the back of the loom in your life and pulling up the wrong threads too. Things may not seem very beautiful right now, but don't let your troubles overwhelm you. Talk to an adult you trust. A good friend, like the supervisor, can help you see how God can make beautiful things out of the not-so-good things in your life.

God's long-term plan is for you to be out of this world in heaven with Him forever. You are a very special person, with a very special life. You are one of a kind!

DOES DOING THE RIGHT THING ALWAYS MAKE YOU HAPPY?

Blessed is the man that walketh not in the counsel of the ungodly. Psalm 1:1.

Johnny Urso was only 9 years old. Young as he was, he knew about the dangers of electricity. But his friends dared him to climb up a utility pole near his home in Halifax, Nova Scotia, and touch a 23,000-volt transmission wire.

Johnny refused.

"You're nothin' but a sissy," his friends sneered.

"Yeah! Johnny is a sissy, Johnny is a sissy," they began to chant.

"I'm not a sissy!" Johnny cried.

"Yes, you are! You're afraid to climb up that pole and touch the wire!"

"I'm not afraid—it's just dangerous, that's all," Johnny said, hoping they would agree.

"You'd do it if you weren't such a chicken," the boys said. "Come on, let's go! Johnny's no fun."

"Can I come with you?" Johnny asked eagerly.

"Nope! We don't want sissies playing with us. But if you climb that pole and touch the wire, you can be in our club."

Johnny anguished over his decision. He was quite certain that it was very dangerous to touch the wire. But he didn't want to be the only boy in Halifax without a friend! With a shout, he began to stride toward the utility pole. "I'll show you I'm not a sissy," he declared as he climbed up the pole.

The boys below began to cheer, and Johnny grinned. He actually felt proud of himself for being so brave! When he got to the top, he looked down at his friends and waved victoriously. Then he reached out and touched the wire.

The shock threw Johnny several feet into the air, and he landed on the network of live wires. His friends ran, horrified, for help. It took emergency crews a full hour to get him untangled from the wires, and they rushed Johnny to the hospital.

He died the next day from third-degree burns all over his body.

Many people have grieved for Johnny, even people who didn't know him. We can all understand how young Johnny felt, and why he let himself be bullied into something that took his life. It doesn't feel good to be taunted by friends. And it doesn't always feel good—right away—to do the right thing and say no. But in the long run, doing the right thing really makes you feel good! And the long run is the most important run there is.

SKELETONS IN THE CLOSET

As Jesus was leaving her home, two blind men followed along behind, shouting, "O Son of King David, have mercy on us." Matthew 9:27, TLB.

A quiet teenage boy sat in a soft, upholstered chair across from his pastor. He shook his head in despair. "I'm ashamed to be who I am," he said quietly. "My stepfather wants to adopt me. I don't know if I should or not, but I'd like to change my name. My real father is immoral—he has hurt a lot of kids. He's an alcoholic. He just went to jail, and all my friends know about it now. I feel so ashamed of what he's done—like I'm guilty too, or something. And when I look at Jesus, He's so pure that I don't see how He could possibly want to love me. My family probably makes Him sick."

The pastor reached out to touch the boy's arm. "It's true, Jesus never sinned. But He had a lot of skeletons in His family's closet too. He can identify with you—perhaps even more than I can."

"What do you mean?" the boy asked in surprise.

The pastor opened his Bible to the first chapter of Matthew. "Have you ever read this list of people in Jesus' family?" he asked.

The teenager shook his head. "It's boring."

"Yes, it's boring, unless you know who the people are in the list. Women weren't generally listed in family trees back in Jesus' time, but women are included in this list. Let's find out who they are: Tamar, Rahab, Ruth, and Bathsheba. Tamar was molested by her brother; Rahab was a prostitute; Ruth was a child of incest between Lot and his daughter; and Bathsheba committed adultery with King David. That's a lot of skeletons—and the people of Jesus' time knew about the skeletons. Jesus had a family to be ashamed of. But because the people knew that, they called out, 'Jesus, Son of David, have mercy on us!' They were saying, in effect, 'Jesus, You know how it feels to have sin in the family—please tell us You understand. Please tell us we're OK in spite of what our families have done!' And that's just what Jesus did. Jesus identified with them because He was one of them."

The teenager sat quietly for several moments, studying the toes of his shoes. "He knows what it's like to have a stepfamily too, doesn't He?" he said softly as a smile broke slowly on his face.

"Yes. Joseph was His stepfather. And Jesus was accused of being 'illegitimate.' He understands how it is," the pastor agreed.

"Thank you," the teen said softly. "I guess I can trust Jesus to understand me, after all."

Isn't it great to have a Friend who really understands?

WHAT SCARES YOU?

Perfect love casteth out fear. 1 John 4:18.

What are you most afraid of? Why? *Time* magazine reports that a nationwide survey of more than 2,200 7- to 11-year-olds, released by the Foundation for Child's Development, indicated that most children feel good about their lives, their families, and just being themselves. But more than two thirds of the children said that they are afraid that someone "bad" is sneaking around their houses and neighborhoods, waiting to break into their homes and attack them.

What do you think makes children so scared? The study showed that those who watch more than four hours of TV each day or those who attended movies on a regular basis were the most frightened.

The story is told of a Frenchman named Charney who got placed on Napoleon's blacklist and was put into a dungeon. He was forgotten and soon became very lonely. Using a stone, he scratched the words "nobody cares" on the wall of his cell. And he continued to feel lonely.

But one day a little green plant pushed its head up between a crack in the stone of the floor of Charney's cell and reached up toward the narrow shaft of light that came in through the window, high up at the top of the cell. Charney saved a portion of his daily serving of water to pour onto the plant, and within a few weeks the plant bloomed with beautiful blue flowers.

Charney was less lonesome now. He scratched out the words "nobody cares" and replaced them with "God cares."

But that wasn't the end of Charney or his plant. The man in the cell next to Charney's had a small daughter who visited him often and made friends with Charney. She told someone about Charney's flower, and word reached the amiable Empress Josephine. Josephine signed legal documents to release Charney from his prison cell. "A man who devotedly tends a flower cannot be a bad man," she said.

So Charney was set free. And he took his plant with him. It had taught him about God.

If we fill our minds with only the evil in this world, we will be frightened and alone. But if we fill our minds with God's words of love and encouragement, we do not have to be afraid. We will love Him. And "perfect love casteth out fear."

HOW TO KEEP YOUR PAIL FULL

My voice shalt thou hear in the morning, O Lord; in the morning will I direct my prayer unto thee, and will look up. Psalm 5:3.

Why do you have worship each morning and evening? Most people have worship so they can remind themselves who really is in charge of their lives. That person is God. A little talk with Jesus every morning and every evening encourages us and even feels good! I like knowing that I have given my problems over to a supernatural God who can even change people's minds, if necessary, to work things out for the best. It's good to know that He works round the clock for me!

A little girl was sent to the garden hose to fill up her friend's pail with water. She stood patiently beside the pail, guiding the water into it until it was right up to the top! Then she walked back to the faucet and turned the water off. When she returned to the pail, it was only half full.

She looked around to see if her dog had lapped up the water. But no dog was in sight.

Again she left the bucket, went over to the faucet, and turned the water on. By the time she got back to the bucket, it was entirely empty. Patiently she filled it up again, then left it to turn off the water. When she got back to the bucket, guess what had happened—it was empty again.

As you can guess, the little girl's friend soon got tired of waiting. "Where's my bucket of water?" she shouted from the sandbox.

"It won't stay full!" the little girl shouted back. "The only way I can keep it full is to keep it under the tap!"

And that's the same reason we have worship—to keep ourselves full of God's love. We are all broken, imperfect vessels. But if we fill ourselves up with God's love—whether by reading a devotional or just praying to Him at the start and close of the day—we stay under the tap. We remain full of His love.

And that's a wonderful way to be out of this world!

GOD'S LITTLE CHICKEN

And the woman fled into the wilderness, where she hath a place prepared of God, that they should feed her there a thousand two hundred and threescore days. Revelation 12:6.

From the first time she heard about the "time of trouble" at the end of the world, Natalie began to have bad dreams. She worried about what might happen to her during that awful time. Her worries clouded over the happiness of each day to the point that she dreaded going to sleep at night, and then she dreaded waking up in the morning and thinking about it again.

Her father noticed the change in her and asked what really bothered her the most about the last days.

"How will I know if I am going to be saved—if God will protect me from Satan's people?"

"The time of trouble will be hard on everyone—the good and the bad," her father said. "But we are promised that none of God's people will die during the time of trouble. It won't take long to know that you are one of the saved. When you see others around you getting sick but you don't, or when you hear soldiers looking for you in the forest, perhaps, and they don't find you—even if you aren't hidden that well.

"I think the time of trouble might even be a little exciting," her father said, "as we see the myriads of little miracles God will do for us."

You remember the ravens that God used to feed Elijah? That actually happened! And during the Reformation, John Brenz, a friend of Martin Luther's, was in danger. The king wanted him killed because of his preaching.

Pastor Brenz wondered what he should do. He prayed fervently that God would impress his mind with a plan. And it came almost as a command: he should take a loaf of bread, head out of town, and go into the first open door he saw.

Most of the doors he passed were closed against the king's messengers; people everywhere were afraid. But as Pastor Brenz passed a barn, he noticed that the door was open, so he went inside. A ladder led up to the loft, and from the loft Pastor Brenz found a small opening under the roof where he crawled in to hide.

Each day he nibbled on the loaf of bread, waiting to hear the town crier's good news that the king's men were gone.

At last, after 14 days, he heard the call, "They're gone! They're gone!"

Pastor Brenz climbed down from the loft and went to the farmhouse to confirm the news.

The farmer was surprised to see him. "And on what have you survived?" he asked in wonderment.

"I had a little bread and an egg every morning," Pastor Brenz said with a smile. Each day a hen had come into the loft, laid an egg without cackling, and then left.

Was it God's hen? Perhaps. But most important, it did what God impressed it to do. Maybe someday you will see some of God's miracles for yourself as His return draws closer. If you have stayed on good terms with God, the last days will be the most exciting time of your life!

CLIMBING INTO GOD'S HANDS

[He] brought them out, and said, Sirs, what must I do to be saved?
Acts 16:30.

A famous evangelist was in town for a series of meetings many years ago. Unfortunately, his arrival was not advertised very widely, and it wasn't until the day he was to leave town that a young soldier heard that he was there.

"Where can I find the evangelist?" the young man asked the hotel clerk.

"Well, try the train station—I know he was headed there!"

The soldier hurried to the train station and found the evangelist on the train.

"Please!" the young soldier called through the window. "Please tell me how to keep straight with God!"

The train began to move. The evangelist pulled a pencil from his pocket and laid it on the palm of his hand. "Can this pencil stand up by itself?" he asked.

"No," said the soldier.

The train gave a jerk, and he began to run along beside it.

The evangelist held the pencil upright on his palm.

"Yes!" the soldier called. "It's upright, but you are holding on to it!"

The evangelist nodded. "Exactly! Your life is like this pencil—strong but helpless. And Christ is the hand that can hold you."

The soldier could not keep up with the train's speed, but as he waved goodbye, he saw the evangelist's hand out the train window, still gripping the pencil in an upright position.

How does God hold you up? By promising you protection from Satan. By promising you that your life can have a glorious tomorrow. By giving you a peaceful today. But you can't be held by God unless you go to Him and put yourself in His hands. Do it now.

DO YOU KNOW IF YOU'RE SUCCESSFUL?

Be thou faithful unto death, and I will give thee a crown of life.
Revelation 2:10.

Bertie's parents were worried about him. At 4 years of age he should have started talking, but he hadn't. He was quiet and reserved, watching the world silently without saying anything to anybody about it. When he finally started talking during that year, his parents were delighted, though they wished he would talk more than he did.

Two years later it was time for Bertie to go to school. He didn't do well. He was quiet and very strange. The other kids made fun of him and rarely asked him to play. His teacher had a discussion with Bertie's parents and suggested that something was the matter with him. "He is very slow," the teacher said. "I'm not sure he will ever make it through school."

But Bertie did make it through, though far from the top of his class. He applied for college entrance and failed the exam. A year later he took the test again, and passed. Still he observed the world quietly through intense, searching eyes.

At last all his years of observation and thinking paid off. Bertie—better known as Albert Einstein—shared his observations and thoughts with the whole world, which earned him a reputation as one of the greatest scientists of all time. He is considered a successful man.

Do you think you are successful in school? Does being successful mean that you always make the highest score? Unfortunately, not everyone is good at taking tests. But here is a secret. Those who do take tests well know that a test is not the end of the world—it's the end of a chapter! Reminding ourselves of that fact takes away some of the tension, which helps our brains work better in remembering what we have learned. You may be doing the best you can, but still you don't get anything more than a C grade. Does that mean you're dumb? Does that mean you're unsuccessful in school? Of course not. And neither does it mean you will be a failure in life! Maybe you are a person like Einstein, and your natural talents will show up later in life.

Take a look at these other people who could have given up on being a success. Napoleon was number 42 in his class. Sir Isaac Newton was next to the lowest in his class. He failed geometry because he didn't do the problems according to the book; he had his own philosophy about it, which worked just as well.

You don't know what kind of grades your doctor made, do you? You don't know what kind of grades your pastor made in school. You don't know what kind of grades your teacher made, either, when she was your age. Some doctors, teachers, and pastors made average grades—but they still finished school and are successful.

Everyone wants to be a success, but not everyone understands what it is. Success is not wealth. Success is not a permanent attainment. Successful people are also failures in some things.

Success is knowing that you have done the best you could. Success is learning something from your failures. Consider how different it makes you feel to say "I am a failure" as compared with "I have failed three times."

Maybe you did poorly yesterday. That was yesterday. Today is a new day. Make it a successful one! Do your best!

THE CURSE OF THE RICH

It is easier for a camel to go through the eye of a needle, than for a rich man to enter into the kingdom of heaven. Matthew 19:24.

Do you know whose face is engraved on the penny? Abraham Lincoln's. Do you know why such a great president as Lincoln has his face engraved on such a humble coin as a penny instead of on a larger, more valuable coin? Here's the story.

Mr. David Brenner was born to a very poor family in Russia. They were only one of thousands of poor families. It seemed as though everyone they knew was poor. Many times David went to bed with his stomach growling and knotted with hunger. He was forbidden to talk about his hunger. His parents were forbidden to discuss the shortage of food with each other or with their neighbors for fear that someone would turn them in for criticizing the government. As punishment they would be thrown into prison.

When David Brenner became a man, he learned how to carve, and became a sculptor. In time he came to America and became an American citizen. He studied American history, and identified with President Lincoln most of all because of Lincoln's own childhood as a poor boy.

One statement of Lincoln's—that common people must be the best, because the Lord makes so many of them—stayed with Brenner. And when Brenner was chosen as the sculptor to design the face of a president for a coin, he chose to put President Lincoln's face on the penny because there would be more pennies minted than any other coin. And consequently there would be more pennies in the pockets of the common people.

The Bible warns us often of the dangers of being rich. Do you know why? I think one of the reasons is that rich people have it so easy here on earth that they become too comfortable and forget that this life is going to end someday. Too often rich people think they became that way by themselves. They think that they don't need God—that He just gets in their way.

But even worse, the wealthy man is never sure that he is loved for himself.

God loves you because He created you. Your value is not in your money, but in your humble heart. Jesus' face is more often seen in the common people than in the great. So don't worry about not being rich—it could be the worst thing to happen to someone!

WHAT MOTIVATES YOU?

Who may climb the mountain of the Lord and enter where he lives? Who may stand before the Lord? Only those with pure hands and hearts, who do not practice dishonesty and lying. Psalm 24:3, 4, TLB.

It was the day of the annual kids' picnic in Colley Reserve, a park in Glenely, Australia. All day long a mass of several hundred children participated in relays and ate their picnic lunches, including candy bars, soda pop, and anything else they could find to snack on. And being in a perpetual hurry to move on to the next fun activity, many of the children didn't worry about where they threw the food wrappers—they just dropped the litter on the ground.

By the end of the day the park was a mess. But before the children went home, they picked up every single bit of trash and rubbish they could find. The park looked even more beautiful at the end of the picnic than it had at the beginning.

Can you guess why? Are the children of Australia more concerned about the beauty of their parks than children of other countries? What would you need as reason enough to clean up a park before you went home?

Here's what happened in Australia: after the last game was over, the picnic sponsors gathered all the children together and made an announcement. They had marked two pieces of the trash lying around. The two children who found those pieces of paper could turn them in for a brand new bicycle!

That was the motivation that spurred hundreds of Australian children to clean up the park so thoroughly after they had messed it up.

Have you messed up your life? If you've made some bad decisions and now are having to live with the unhappy results, you may feel as if your whole life is trash. Clean it up. Doing the right thing and keeping your conscience clean from now on is the best prize there is. It's out of this world!

WHAT YOU NEED TO DO FOR YOUR FRIENDS

Let us not neglect our church meetings, as some people do, but encourage and warn each other, especially now that the day of his coming back again is drawing near. Hebrews 10:24, TLB.

It was the kind of moment that has even scientists holding their breath! Several years ago, buried in peat in a dry, desolate area of China, scientists found dormant seeds of lotus plants. Further study indicated that the desert area had once been a lake bed, perhaps covered with lotus blossoms. After several tests, it was determined that the seeds were several thousand years old.

Then someone had an idea. What would happen if the seeds were planted under the best possible conditions. Would they sprout? Could it be possible that the ancient, dry seeds could still contain life? No one knew for sure, but scientists were making bets both ways.

"Possible."

"No, impossible!"

Each day they checked the planting bed for signs of life. Could a seed that was thousands of years old actually sprout?

At last a tiny green sprout broke through the fine crust of the planting bed—and then another. Miraculously, the little grass seeds awakened to the rain and sunshine as if it were just another morning! God's power had never left the little seeds, even though they had been buried for thousands of years!

I don't know if those scientists were Christians or not. And I don't know if any became Christians as a result of those little seeds. But I know that when I read that story, my faith in God's power became stronger.

It isn't always the big things that strengthen our faith. Sometimes all it takes is a kindness from somebody, or an encouraging word, or the words and music of a song that increases our faith and trust in God.

You may be only a child, but you can help someone else's faith grow stronger. You can pray for your parents and your friends. You can discuss current events with your friends, reminding them that everything points to the return of Jesus. Your belief in the Bible can strengthen someone else's.

More personally, something wonderful happens when you share your confidence in God with others—your own faith multiplies!

JULY 30

COULD YOU GET A JOB AT DISNEY WORLD?

Don't copy the behavior and customs of this world, but be a new and different person with a fresh newness in all you do and think. Then you will learn from your own experience how his ways will really satisfy you. Romans 12:2, TLB.

Are you good enough to work at Disney World? Two hotel clerks at the Disney World Hotel in Florida were fired recently because they would not shave off their beards. A spokesman from Disney World explained it like this. "At Disney World we hold high standards for our employees. We want them to maintain our belief in clean living. That's why we have a dress code that states that our employees will not have excessively long, painted fingernails, will wear little or no jewelry, modest necklines and hemlines, and will keep their hair neatly trimmed without looking 'mod,' and will not wear beards."

Alcoholic beverages are not allowed in Disney World. And furthermore, the people who roam the park dressed as Disney characters are forbidden from talking to anyone who is smoking.

That sounds almost as strict as an Adventist school, doesn't it? It should make us proud of our values.

Why do you suppose teenagers who apply for a job at Disneyland or Disney World agree to the rules, while some teenagers who apply for admission at an Adventist school break the rules or make fun of them? Many of the rules are the same.

Perhaps the difference is in their attitude. The Disneyland employees feel honored to be able to work there. Sadly, not every Adventist teenager feels honored to be attending a private school of such high standards.

In non-Adventist circles, children who attend private schools are considered rich and pampered. If you attend a church school, you are one of the rich and pampered kids of the world.

So as you walk through the doors of your school this morning, look around you at the other pampered kids there and be thankful that your school has classy rules that demand that your classmates can't wear their hair like creatures from outer space, that they be clean and cooperative, that they not smoke or use drugs, that they not drink alcoholic beverages, that they be polite—and Christlike. Those aren't just Adventist values —they're the values of anyone who is worth knowing.

JULY 31

THE ROBBERY THAT SURPRISED THE ROBBERS

"But if we have bad consciences and feel that we have done wrong, the Lord will surely feel it even more, for he knows everything we do." 1 John 3:20, TLB.

The burglars left without a trace. By a robber's standards, it might be considered a first-class robbery. But the robbers got more than they bargained for.

They must have been fairly softhearted, because they robbed a pet store. But they weren't after puppies and kitties. These men were after a very expensive breed of parrot.

Evidently they had visited the store on occasion to map out the location of doors and windows in relation to the parrot's cage. They seemed to know exactly the best way to get in and out again.

As I said, it was a robbery without any misfortune—except one.

When the pet store owner opened the store the next morning, he discovered his most expensive parrot had been stolen. And while he was unhappy about it, he knew that his insurance would pay for a replacement. What concerned the owner the most was that the parrot was not well. He was under treatment for a very contagious disease common in South America, and could infect the robbers and anyone they came in contact with. In short, because the parrot was gone, an epidemic of this painful disease was possible.

Word was sent to all the radio and TV stations in the area, warning of the infected parrot.

I haven't heard the end of this story yet. I don't know if the robbers got caught, or whether or not they killed the parrot. But I can imagine if they intended to sell him to another pet store in another town, their plans were ruined, because every other pet store owner in the area was on the alert for the stolen parrot.

Many people are as foolish as those robbers. They think immorality, drugs, jewelry, and other "pleasures of this world" will be the answer to their search for happiness. They're in for a surprise. The "pleasures of this world" are infected; and they're infecting far too many people with guilty consciences, broken homes, selfish pride, self-hate, and even death.

If your friends suggest doing something that makes you feel uncomfortable, it's probably wrong. Listen to your conscience. Don't do it.

You can find the world's shortest sermon on a thousand traffic signs: "Keep Right."

AUGUST 1

HOW DO YOU SERVE CAKE?

For I am not ashamed of this Good News about Christ. It is God's powerful method of bringing all who believe it to heaven. Romans 1:16, TLB.

At the last meeting of the June 1987 camp meeting of the Kentucky-Tennessee Conference, a small table on the platform was draped with a beautiful lace cloth and four china plates. The youth speaker told the audience that he had a special surprise for them.

"I wish I could share this surprise with all of you, but unfortunately I can't. I need to choose four of you to receive the surprise on behalf of the others. Are there any volunteers?"

It seemed to be a good thing for which to volunteer. So four willing participants raised their hands.

When the four were seated around the table, the minister took a white cake box from behind the pulpit and opened it to reveal a beautiful German chocolate cake! The participants began to lick their lips. They smiled happily in anticipation of the treat.

The minister took the cake out of the box and placed it in the middle of the table. "Go ahead. Help yourselves," he offered.

The volunteers laughed self-consciously and searched the sides of their plates for some silverware. There was none.

"Oh! I guess they forgot!" the minister said. "Well, that's OK. I'll just serve it up for you." And with that, he thrust his fingers deep into the cake and pulled out a hunk of it, dumping it onto one of the plates. He smiled at the closest volunteer. "Go ahead."

Nobody moved, and the speaker continued to dig into the cake with his hand, slinging pieces onto the plates. None of the volunteers began eating. They sat around the table laughing in disbelief.

At last the lesson was over. The minister stepped back to the pulpit with a satisfied look on his face. "So you see," he said thoughtfully, "like that beautiful cake, we may have the most beautiful message of hope, we may have the most beautiful relationship with Jesus, but unless we serve it to others in an attractive manner, they will want none of it."

Do you think you present an attractive picture of Christianity to others? Do you serve up your church to others in a way that makes them want to know more—or do you make it seem unappealing? What would you change about your approach?

AUGUST 2

THE STORY THAT *STAR WARS* COPIED

Watch out for the false leaders—and there are many of them around—who don't believe that Jesus Christ came to earth as a human being with a body like ours. 2 John 1:7, TLB.

It's an exciting story—and one not so far off from modern science fiction. A supernatural Being from afar places a Child within an earth woman, and this Child also has supernatural powers. He uses these powers not for personal gain, but to bless others.

218

During His time on earth the supernatural Child reveals a great secret. A dark supernatural rival wants to take the people of earth hostage and kill them all, but if they only ask for assistance from His Father, the people of earth can resist the dark side and win.

Have you heard that story before? It's not another *Star Wars*. It's not *Superman*. It's from the Bible. And it's true.

What year is this? If you said A.D. 1990, you are correct. It's evident that Jesus made quite an impact on this world, because our calendar system is based on Jesus' birth date. Do you think we would count the years according to His birth date if He weren't a real person? Do you know how B.C. and A.D. dating came about?

For about 500 years after Jesus was born, the world followed the old Roman calendar. However, in A.D. 532 a man named Dionysius Exiguus computed the birth date for Jesus. (More recent evidence has shown that the date was only about five years off.) Dionysius estimated that Jesus was born in the Roman year 754, and he adjusted the Christian calendar to begin with that year. The years before Jesus were counted backward (B.C. means "before Christ").

The years after Jesus were counted forward (A.D. refers to the Latin words *anno Domini*, which means "in the year of our Lord"). So it is now A.D. 1990. It has been about 1,990 years since Jesus was born.

Many authors write about Jesus in much the same way as authors write about newsmakers today. They record historical events and the people involved. Many of them were not Christians and were not writing for the Bible collection.

The July 1988 issue of *National Geographic* magazine includes a story of a recent archaeological dig of a Grecian city named Kourion, which was destroyed by an earthquake in A.D. 365. Among the finds is a stone from the marketplace on which someone scratched the words "Oh, Jesus . . . of Christ." No doubt, they had heard His story from their grandparents, who had heard it from their grandparents, and perhaps they had heard it direct from one of Jesus' disciples.

We can be confident that the stories of Jesus' birth and His miracles are not just legends, because the Bible was completed within 100 years after Jesus died—not enough time for Him to become a legendary figure.

Jesus is real! Unlike the *Star Wars* stories, Jesus actually lived! I have seen some of the streets He walked on, and some of the hillsides and lakes He looked at. Someday we'll see Jesus with our own eyes. That will be a moment that's out of this world!

EVEN PEARLS NEED LOVE

Dear friends, let us practice loving each other, for love comes from God and those who are loving and kind show that they are the children of God, and that they are getting to know him better. 1 John 4:7, TLB.

We often say that God speaks to us in nature. What we usually mean is that by seeing how things work together in nature, we can see God's way of doing things. For example, the leaves on certain trees turn beautiful autumn colors and then fall off, only to be replaced in the spring with new growth. This shows God's power to re-create and restore life after apparent death. It makes us think of how the world will be after sin is destroyed and God makes all things new.

We see an example of God's love and concern in the way a mother cat takes care of her babies and protects them so faithfully. God protects us and cares about us even more than animals care about their babies.

But God's hand in nature is not seen just in trees and animals. God's hand is also seen in rocks and precious jewels. Consider, for example, the following story about a pearl necklace:

It was a beautiful necklace of 146 rose-pink pearls, which belonged to a wealthy woman named Madame Theirs. When it was donated to the French Republic, the necklace was placed in a museum and never worn. In time the pearls lost their luster and became dull.

What should they do? What could be done to restore the pearls' luster? Fortunately somebody knew what to do. A woman was found and given a very special job as "pearl mother." For several hours each day, under the watchful eyes of armed guards, this woman came to the museum to hold the pearls and wear them around her neck as she wandered through the museum. After several weeks of this tender, loving human touch, the pearls became beautiful and lustrous once again.

What does that teach you about God? That He made us to need each other. We are kept alive by human contact. Your friends need to hear from you that you like them. Your parents need to hear that you love them. Sometimes they need hugs, too.

Even God needs our contact and communication. Tell Him you love Him—right now!

WHAT THE WORLD NEEDS

The greatest want of the world is the want of men—men who will not be bought or sold, men who in their inmost souls are true and honest, men who do not fear to call sin by its right name, men whose conscience is as true to duty as the needle to the pole, men who will stand for the right though the heavens fall. Ellen G. White, Education, *p. 57.*

He that speaketh truth sheweth forth righteousness: but a false witness deceit. Proverbs 12:17.

The neighborhood boys were playing ball in Paul's front yard. The game was going along well until Jack slid into second base and Fred tried to tag him out. You can guess what happened. Jack stood on base insisting that he was safe, and Fred argued loudly that Jack was out! Soon the boys' teammates joined in the argument. There was yelling and pushing and name calling until Bill made a suggestion.

Looking at Paul, who was standing apart from the melee, Bill suggested, "Let's have Paul decide. He always tells the truth."

The other boys quickly agreed, and surrounding Paul, they asked him for a decision. When Paul said he thought Jack was safe, the other boys accepted it, and the game continued as though nothing had happened.

That is, it seemed as if nothing had happened. Actually a wonderful change occurred in that afternoon game. Paul played with a new sense of joy and dignity. You see, Paul was the worst ball player in the neighborhood. He was the only Christian in the neighborhood, too, and the boys had teased him relentlessly because of that. The only reason they even let Paul play with them was because his yard was the only yard big enough for a game.

It had been rough on Paul. Sometimes he'd felt as though he'd do almost anything to be like the other guys, but now he realized the importance of being different.

The world needs people who aren't afraid to stand for what's right. The world needs people who are willing to be different. Are you brave enough to be what the world needs? Ask Jesus to help you be all that He has in mind for you to be in 1990.

IS LIFE "EATING YOU UP"?

It is better to be slow-tempered than famous; it is better to have self-control than to control an army. Proverbs 16:32, TLB.

I like this story about Alexander the Great. A wise man once gave Alexander a special gift of three brave dogs. They were some of the man's favorites, but he wanted to show his affection and respect for Alexander by giving these dogs to the great leader.

Alexander accepted the dogs graciously, but he wasn't much of an animal lover, and when he was told that these dogs were very bold and courageous, he was skeptical. He decided to test them.

First, he had his servants bring a full-grown stag into the park to see what the dogs would do. They did nothing—they just observed the stag with tongues hanging out and tails wagging.

Alexander snorted. He sent for antelopes to be brought to the park, thinking that maybe sheer numbers would arouse the dogs. But the dogs were unaffected by the presence of the antelopes, too. They did absolutely nothing but lay in the sun, wagging their tails and licking their jowls.

Alexander was furious. Thinking that the dogs were worthless, he ordered the servants to kill them—and it was no sooner said than done.

A few weeks later the kind man who had given the dogs to Alexander returned to see how his favorites were doing. When he found out that the dogs had been killed and why, he was upset. He cried out, "Oh, mighty Alexander. You are a great leader, but you are a foolish man! You brought a stag and a herd of antelope into the park, and the dogs did nothing; but if you had set a lion or a tiger loose on them, you would have seen what brave dogs they were!"

Are you like those dogs? Or do you let yourself get upset over every little thing that happens? If you blow up a lot, it might be time to find out why. Each day has its own share of frustrations and worries, but not every one is worth getting upset over. Some things will never change, some aren't worth trying to change, and many change on their own, whether or not you worry about them.

For your own peace of mind, be concerned with the important things today; don't worry about whether or not someone smiled at you in class, or whether or not your hair is perfect, or whether or not your parents love you as much as they do your sister. If you save your strength for really big things such as doing your schoolwork or getting to know Jesus as a friend—for things that have an effect on the rest of your life—you'll find yourself worrying less and enjoying life more.

WHAT'S GOOD ABOUT MAKING MISTAKES?

Wisdom is a fountain of life to those possessing it, but a fool's burden is his folly. Proverbs 16:22, TLB.

Medical school is a very demanding time for young, aspiring doctors-to-be. Their professors demand near perfection from them. They are required to become so familiar with medical complaints and preferred medical treatments that they don't even have to think about what to do—it is supposed to just come naturally.

In one such class the professor asked one of his students what was the average dose of a certain kind of medicine for a certain kind of complaint.

The student replied promptly, "One teaspoon, sir."

The professor made no comment—he just went on with his lecture. Fifteen minutes later the student raised his hand.

"I'm sorry, sir, I believe I made a mistake in my answer a few minutes ago. That should be half a teaspoon, rather than a whole one."

"It's too late," the professor snapped, opening a large gold stopwatch and staring at it thoughtfully. He raised his eyes to the student's and said with a solemn air of finality, "Your patient died 14 minutes ago."

I'm sure that student never forgot the correct dose of that medicine!

Everyone makes mistakes. When human lives are at stake, mistakes become more costly and are sometimes irreversible. Thankfully, you probably don't have those kinds of serious mistakes to be concerned about at this point. But growing up means that you take on more and more responsibility; you make more and more of your own decisions, and you live with the consequences of those decisions.

I made good grades when I was in school—but I didn't get straight A's. Straight-A students do have a disadvantage, though. They don't have particular facts burned onto their memories as often as those of us who don't always make a perfect grade. I know that I remember better the questions I got wrong than the ones I got right!

Perhaps you can remember some foolish answers you gave on some tests. Don't forget them. The only complete mistake is the one we don't learn anything from.

TALKING TO THE ANIMALS

Then the Lord caused the donkey to speak! "What have I done that deserves your beating me these three times?" she asked. Numbers 22:28, TLB.

Perhaps you have heard of Koko, a gorilla that has learned sign language. Some years ago Koko astonished the scientific world when she began to respond to the sign language her keepers had been trying to teach her. She understood not just words, but feelings, too. Seeing a horse with a bit in its mouth, she signed, "Horse sad." When asked why the horse was sad, she signed "Teeth." Shown a photo of the famous albino gorilla Snowflake struggling against having a bath, Koko, who also hates baths, signed "Me cry there" while pointing at the picture.

Unfortunately Koko also loves an argument, trades insults, and will lie her way out of a jam. One day Koko signed "That red" as she made a nest out of a white towel. The person watching her tried to correct her and signed that it was not red but white. Koko insisted it was red—"red, red, *red*"—and finally held up a minute speck of red lint that was clinging to the towel. She was grinning.

Another time, while Koko's trainer was writing, the gorilla snatched up a red crayon and began chewing on it. "You're not eating that crayon, are you?" her trainer asked. Koko signed "Lip," and began moving the crayon first across her upper then her lower lip as if applying lipstick.

As I write this, Koko has astonished the scientists again. For some time she has had a pet kitten and a baby doll. One day recently Koko signed, "Koko want baby." Her keepers gave her her doll. She cuddled the doll for a few minutes and then put it down.

"Koko want baby," she signed again urgently.

Her keepers again gave her the doll and signed "baby."

Koko threw the doll down and signed, "Koko want real baby."

Are you able to talk to your pets? In a way, if we know our pets well enough, we can tell if they're hungry or tired or sick or afraid just by looking at them, can't we? And though we can't actually speak their language, we can communicate by touch and tone of voice.

Perhaps in heaven we will truly be able to talk to the animals. Koko has shown us that some animals think much the same as we do. When a reporter asked Koko if she was an animal or a person, Koko replied instantly, "Fine animal gorilla."

Isn't heaven going to be fun?

GROWING PAINS

Train a child in the way he should go, and when he is old he will not turn from it. Proverbs 22:6, NIV.

In the highest branches of a tree that hung out over a yawning chasm, a mother eagle carefully created a nest for the eggs she would soon lay. First she chose thorny twigs from the blackberry bushes in the valley, placing them at the very bottom of her nest. Then she brought up the sharpest stones she could find from the dry riverbed below.

When she was satisfied that the nest had enough of these discomforts, she prepared the next layer, covering the thorns and rocks with a thick layer of feathers and the softest fur from rabbits and other animals that she had killed. Now she had a warm, comforting bed for the eggs she was ready to lay.

The young eaglets enjoyed their pampered life at first, waiting snug and warm next to one another for the food their mother untiringly brought to them.

But when they were old enough, the mother eagle began removing the feathers and fur from the nest. With her sharp talons, she pulled up the thorny twigs and sharp rocks so they would poke into her young ones. In time the young eaglets became so uncomfortable and unhappy in their nest that they broke free and flew away to make homes of their own.

Would you say that the mother eagle was cruel, or helpful? Her efforts to make the eaglets dissatisfied with their old life of ease gave them the motivation they needed to grow up and find places of their own.

As humans, we are a little bit that way too. If you are a teenager, maybe you can relate to the eaglets' desire to get away and be on their own and make their own decisions. Life's like that. God has made you to question your parents' beliefs in the process of finding your own.

When you find your parents frustrating, just remind yourself that you are experiencing "growing pains." A little bit of distress actually makes the inevitable business of moving away less painful. After you are grown, you may be surprised to find out just how much you actually have in common with your parents, and how wonderful they really are.

AN EASY $50,000!

If anyone publicly acknowledges me as his friend, I will openly acknowledge him as my friend before my Father in heaven. Matthew 10:32, TLB.

It all started in the summer of 1987. Disney World began an all-out push to make their amusement park one of the most popular ones around. They wanted famous athletes to help them. And so it was that Frank Viola, pitcher for the Minnesota Twins, was surrounded by cameras and cheering fans as he left the baseball field at the end of the World Series. It was a prearranged exit.

As the cameras started to roll, a voice called out from behind one of the cameras.

"Frank Viola! You've just won the World Series! Where are you going now?"

Without missing a step, Viola replied, "I'm going to Disney World!"

The cameras stopped rolling. And Frank Viola was given $50,000 for his "pitch."

There were other prearranged conversations. After winning the Super Bowl football game in January of 1988, Washington Redskins quarterback Doug Williams left the stadium amid flashing bulbs, video-cameras, and cheering fans. Before he had gone far, one of the Disney World cameramen called out, "Doug Williams! You've just won the Super Bowl! Where are you going now?"

And Doug shouted back happily, "I'm going to Disney World!"

They gave him $50,000 and free passes and hotel accommodations just for acknowledging that going to Disney World was one of his desires.

After the 1988 Winter Olympics, as America's gold medal skater Brian Boitano left the rink amid a similar crowd of fans, flashing lightbulbs, and videocameras, someone called out, "Brian Boitano, you've just won a gold medal! Where are you going now?"

And Brian Boitano called back with a smile, "I'm going to Disney World!"

Fifty thousand dollars became his instantly.

I wish they would ask me where I'm going! Someday someone may ask you where you're going. Do you know? God promises you wealth untold and certain happiness in a place that isn't just a man-made fantasyland. God's place is a place where the happiness goes on and on, a place that you never will have to leave, a place where you never get bored of the rides, a place where everything is free. Someday God will say, "[insert your name]! You've just won a battle against Satan! Where are you going now?"

All you have to say is "I'm going to heaven!" And then reach out and take your prize. Heaven is yours! And it's out of this world.

WHAT'S WRONG WITH CRUCIFIXION?

Then [Jesus] told them, "My soul is crushed with horror and sadness to the point of death . . . stay here . . . stay awake with me." Matthew 26:38, TLB.

There is something wrong with almost every picture ever painted of Jesus' crucifixion. Do you know what it is? I'll tell you in a few minutes. But first a story.

Many years ago a budding artist painted a picture of Jesus hanging on the cross. He was very pleased with himself and took the finished canvas to the writer Tolstoy for his opinion.

Tolstoy studied the canvas silently for several minutes. Then he pointed to the figure of Jesus. "You do not love Him," he declared.

The artist was stunned. "But . . . but that is Jesus Christ!" he stammered.

"I know," Tolstoy replied. "But if you loved Him, you would paint Him better."

We have to personally appreciate what Jesus did for us before we can love Him as He deserves. Sometimes He seems almost unreal and unacquainted with the problems we have today. But the Bible tells us that Jesus was tempted in all points as we are, yet without sin. That doesn't necessarily mean that He was tempted to do every bad thing there is in life, but He was tempted generally in all points as we are: He was tempted to overeat, to be proud, to be immoral, to be jealous, to take something from somebody else, to be conceited, and so on.

Since Jesus was a red-blooded teenager, He probably longed to have a girlfriend, get married, and have a family just as you do. Yet He knew it could never happen because of His mission in life. No doubt there were many women who would have loved to be His girlfriend, but He couldn't let Himself love them that way, because in the end it would cause them more pain when He left. And what about the children He would leave behind without a father? Jesus had to deny His inborn need for the special love of a wife.

It is often said that when Jesus was crucified, He gave His all for us. Have you ever thought about what all He gave for us? He gave His life, yes. He gave up the right to defend Himself. He gave up the right to call on the angels to deliver Him. But perhaps even more than that, He gave up His right to modesty.

You see, the way most artists paint the Crucifixion incorrectly is that out of love and respect for our precious Friend, Jesus, every artist paints Him with a white cloth tied around His waist. He is shown dying modestly. But a crucifixion was a shameful death. People were actually crucified without their clothes on.

The Crucifixion was an ugly, embarrassing, horrid experience for Jesus, just as it would be for you if you had to hang naked in front of your friends. But Jesus did it willingly for you because He wants you to be with Him in heaven. You are special; you are worth dying for. What a terrific Friend Jesus is!

AUGUST 11

DANGERS OF PLAYING IN SATAN'S PLAYGROUND

Can a man hold fire against his chest and not be burned? Proverbs 6:27, TLB.

In some Eastern countries it is not unusual to behead a criminal for misconduct, rather than sustaining him in prison for years and years.

One day a criminal was brought before a king to hear his sentence. The criminal's heart thrashed loudly in his ears as he stood like a small chessman on the massive black-and-white tile floor and heard the solemn words regarding his execution. He dared not think much about whether or not it would hurt or whether it would be a quick death.

"Is there one last request you would like to make?" the king asked, as he usually did.

The criminal swallowed, his mouth dry. "If you please, sir, I would like just a drink of water."

The king ordered the glass of water brought to the man. But the man's hands were shaking so badly, he could not bring the glass to his mouth.

The king was annoyed. "Don't let yourself tremble so!" he cried. "Your life is safe until you drink that water!"

For a brief moment the criminal lifted his eyes to the king's as he pondered the king's words. Then in an instant the man opened his hand and let the glass drop to the floor. It shattered into several pieces. The water glimmered in puddles on the slick marble squares.

The guards shifted nervously.

Raising his head and looking boldly into the king's face, the condemned man claimed the royal word. "You said my life was safe until I drank the water, sir. I cannot drink it now."

The king smiled bitterly. "You have won your life," he said. "I cannot break my word, even to you. You are saved."

In a way we are like that condemned man. Our lives and our consciences are safe until we take sin into our bodies. We have God's word on that. But once we choose to do something that we know is wrong, we burn ourselves. Our consciences become singed.

Throw away any sin that might keep you away from God. The fleeting thrill of sin is not worth risking your eternal life and your good conscience for.

AUGUST 12

LOST SOMETHING LATELY?

And now, my little children, stay in happy fellowship with the Lord so that when he comes you will be sure that all is well, and will not have to be ashamed and shrink back from meeting him. 1 John 2:28, TLB.

Have you ever lost something that you really cared about? Can you remember the feeling of butterflies in your stomach as you frantically searched high and low for it, hoping that you'd find it soon?

It's painful to lose something. Psychologists tell us that loss of one kind or another is the cause of most mental illnesses. What are some things you might lose that would make you feel terrible? Among your list might be the loss of a family member; the loss of a friend either through death, moving away, or betrayal; the loss of a pet; or the loss of prized possessions. Even the loss of a good reputation—through poor choices, poor companions, or malicious gossip—can literally make you sick.

Being a teenager is one of the hardest phases of anyone's life. You're almost an adult, and because of the tremendous supply of hormones surging through your body, you feel each of your feelings very keenly —perhaps more so than you will later on in your adult life.

Some of the choices you make now will affect your adult life, whether you realize it or not. This is the story of a friend of mine, an Adventist boy who lives just down the street. We'll call him Tyler.

I always thought well of Tyler. He often played with my own little boys, and his sister did some baby-sitting for me on occasion. I thought he was growing up to be a nice young man with a bright future.

But Tyler chose friends who were looking for excitement. As I understand it, first they began skipping school. Then someone said marijuana was fun. From there they went on to harder stuff. And finally they went so far as to steal equipment from the church school to get money to pay for more drugs.

They were arrested and charged with felonies. They brought shame on their families and a cloud over their futures. At one time they could have been anything they wanted to be when they grew up. But now that they have a felony on their records; they can never hold a job for which they must be bonded and licensed. They don't have as many choices of what they can be for the rest of their lives, for they have records that will always follow them.

I still like Tyler. I feel sorry for him and his family because they must all be feeling a very deep sense of loss for something that can never be found—the feeling of a good conscience; the happy, peaceful feeling of having no regrets; the best of opportunities for a happy and productive life.

Are there some things you have been thinking of doing that might cause you to lose something precious to you? Don't do it. Some things can never be found again.

AUGUST 13

THE CADILLAC COFFIN

And what profit is there in gaining the whole world when it means forfeiting one's self? Luke 9:25, TLB.

My dad used to tell a story in one of his sermons that I have remembered to this day. It took me a while to understand what it meant, but it is now one of my favorites.

It seems that a very rich man had died. In his last will and testament were instructions on how he wanted to be buried. It had to be a very large grave because the man wanted to be buried in his $50,000 brand-new, air-conditioned Cadillac.

It took the gravediggers several days to dig a hole the right size and to rig up the special cranes needed to lower the car into the grave.

Ordinarily gravediggers don't attend the funerals, but this one they had to see!

It was a beautiful car—white and silver, with a plush steel-blue interior. And as the car was lowered slowly into the grave with the dead man at the wheel, white leather driving gloves on, one of the gravediggers gave a low whistle and said to the other, "Man, that's really living!"

Was it living? What good is that Cadillac going to do that dead man? Not a thing! He even missed out on seeing everyone's reaction to his elaborate funeral!

In just a short time you will have to make a decision on what kind of work you want to do for the rest of your life. Perhaps you already know and are working toward it now. What was it that attracted you to your choice of a career? Was it how much money you could make? Was it how much prestige you would get? Was it how much you could help others? Did you think about whether or not that career would cause you Sabbath problems? Are you ready and willing to go to court or lose your job in order to get Sabbaths off?

No job is worth losing your good relationship with God. No amount of money is worth the risk of narrowing your vision of being God's helper. The most important questions you should be asking are "Will this job allow me to help others?" and "Will this job conflict with my Christian conscience?"

You have some exciting yet difficult choices to make in the next few years. Don't make those choices alone. Tell your parents or some other trusted adult that you just want to discuss all the pros and cons of a particular job to help you make your decision. Also, ask God to help you know what to do. And then pick a job that won't prevent you from going out of this world.

AUGUST 14

FILTHY RICH—BUT DEAD!

For the love of money is the first step toward all kinds of sin. Some people have even turned away from God because of their love for it, and as a result have pierced themselves with many sorrows. 1 Timothy 6:10, TLB.

There's an old story about the gold rush days in the Klondike that is said to be true, though it is very bizarre.

Several years after the gold rush, a mining party, pushing deep into the wilderness, came upon an old cabin hidden among overgrown bushes. There was a dense layer of moss on the roof, the windows were cracked, and the boards were weather-beaten and bare.

The mining party pushed open the creaky door, and what they saw made them stop in their tracks. There in front of them, as though placed by a movie crew, were the skeletons of two men sitting on two sides of a rickety wooden table. On the table, between the skeletons' bony arms, was a huge pile of gold nuggets—and a letter.

With their hearts in their throats, the miners approached the skeletons cautiously, and one of them pulled the letter from under an armbone and began to read. The letter said it all. The two men had been lucky to find so much gold. Each day that they went out they found more gold than they had found the day before, and they couldn't make themselves stop panning for the precious ore. They were so eager to get rich that they had forgotten about the early onset of winter in that northern territory.

One morning they awoke to find a severe snowstorm in progress. They couldn't get out of their cabin. Their meager supply of food eventually ran out, and still the storm raged. At last they sat down and died—among all that worthless gold. Their greed had killed them.

What is the difference between greed and goals? Greed means you want to have more than your share of something at any expense; goals are something of value that you are willing to work for—something that will help you grow and become a better person.

Close your eyes and think of Jesus as a 12-year-old boy in His father's workshop. He was a boy just like you. What are some things that He might have had as His goals? What are some things that He might have been tempted to be greedy about? Aren't you glad He didn't give in to the temptation to be greedy? Giving His life for us remains the most loving thing that anyone has done for a friend.

An anonymous writer has given us the following thoughts about money:

"Money will buy:
A bed but not sleep.
Books but not brains.
Food but not appetite.
Finery but not beauty.
A house but not a home.
Medicine but not health.
Luxuries but not culture.
Amusement but not happiness.
A crucifix but not a Saviour.
A church pew but not Heaven."
Don't let a love for money kill you!

AUGUST 15

SOMETHING IN COMMON

Let this mind be in you, which was also in Christ Jesus. Philippians 2:5.

Think for a moment about your special friends with whom you feel most comfortable. Can you remember the first time you met them? Do you know why we feel comfortable with some people and not quite so comfortable with others?

Scientists have conducted tests to find out what it is that draws us to some people and not to others. They arranged blind dates for several hundred college students, interviewing them before and after their dates to see how it went. Each student participated in the study voluntarily, and most of the students had fun at it.

Through the interviews with the students after the dates, scientists discovered that feeling comfortable with others depends to a great degree on whether or not you have something in common with them. The scientists found this out by telling each student a little bit about his date before he met her. Not everything they said was entirely true. If they knew a guy wanted to be a veterinarian, for example, they would tell him that the girl he was about to meet raised horses, or some other kind of animal, and also wanted to be a vet when she grew up. They would clue the girl in to what she was supposed to be like so she could play along.

In almost every case, when the couples had something in common, they reported having a much better time together than if they were complete opposites. So much for the theory that "opposites attract"!

Perhaps you are not dating yet. That's OK. Better yet, you probably have a lot of friends with whom you do things in a group. Can you identify the things you have in common with those friends? If you don't have much in common, why do you hang around with them? Is their influence going to be a good one for you, or will you have to sacrifice your standards to be more like them?

Jesus wants us to be like Him. We have to raise our standards to be like Him, and that's good; and the more we have in common with Him, the closer and more precious a friend He becomes.

What do you have in common with Jesus? A kind disposition? A love for God? High morals? Honesty? See if you can think of other characteristics Jesus has, and pray that you can be more like Him today and every day.

AUGUST 16

THE BIRTHING ROOM

Jesus replied, "With all the earnestness I possess I tell you this: Unless you are born again, you can never get into the Kingdom of God." John 3:3, TLB.

They were just a poor and lowly migrant family from Mexico. I was working the night they came to the hospital to have their baby. It should have been Christmas Eve, because they looked the part of Mary and Joseph at the inn.

She had long black hair in a thick braid that hung clear down her back, almost to her feet. He was just barely taller than she was, with a short beard and curling hair that came just to his shirt collar. His were working hands—calloused and stained, with yellow fingernails that he reached out to caress her shoulder, but withdrew when he saw me looking at them. His dark, almond eyes bore the strain of the anxious hours he had spent getting her to a safe place to have her baby.

An interpreter pieced the story together for us. She had gone into labor early that morning as they passed through northern California. They had relatives in Oregon and were driving up to pick strawberries with them and stay with them. When the labor pains became more intense, the anxious father-to-be had exceeded the speed limit, hoping a policeman would stop him for speeding and tell him where to find a hospital. But no policeman came.

They sped on up the highway, much faster than they should have, until they reached Hillsboro, Oregon, where their family was living. And they reached our hospital just in time. As I helped the shaking woman get into her hospital gown and climb into bed, I sensed that we didn't have long till her baby would be born.

Other nurses readied the birthing room and called a doctor; but before he got there, I was privileged to deliver the woman's baby—a warm, wet, healthy baby boy.

As the baby let out his first gurgling cry, the new father wrapped his arms about his wife's shoulders, put his head against hers, and blinked back a rush of tears. He wiped at his eyes with the back of one of his dirty hands and smiled, "He is American! My son is American!"

I thought about Jesus' words to Nicodemus that we must be born again. Our hearts are the "birthing room." When we choose to believe in Jesus, we are born into God's family. We become born into a new land, as it were—we become citizens of heaven; our birthright is that glorious place where our Father lives. God wants us to be assured that we are citizens of heaven—born again to a land that's out of this world!

AUGUST 17

WHAT COMES FIRST?

But seek ye first the kingdom of God, . . . and all these things shall be added unto you. Matthew 6:33.

Doug plopped himself down on his bed and sighed heavily. He had to clean his room—again. And it was a horrible mess—again. It was such a mess, in fact, that he didn't know where to start! He was sure he would never finish.

Mother stuck her head in the door. "How's it going?" she asked cheerfully. Then she stepped into the room and looked around. "Why, you haven't even started yet!" she said, disappointed. "What's keeping you?"

"I don't know where to start!" Doug complained. "I've been putting some things away, but it doesn't look any different than it did 15 minutes ago!"

"Well, then," Mother said, "let me tell you a secret. In every room of the house there's one main thing that either makes it look messy or clean. In the bedroom it's your bed. If you start by making up your bed, you'll get a big jump on the job; a messy-looking bed is the main reason a bedroom looks bad."

Doug nodded. "What are the other things for the other rooms?" he asked.

"In the kitchen, if the counters and the table are wiped off and set in order, dirty dishes in the sink aren't so obnoxious. And in the living room, if things on the floor and the couch are picked up, the room looks better—even if it's not vacuumed or dusted."

Doug gave it some thought. When his mother left for chores of her own, he made up his bed, curious to see if his mom's method worked. Sure enough, it was almost magical. Once the bed was made up, the room looked at least 90 percent better!

Jesus must have known the law of "first things first." When He was here, He said that if our main goal in life is to love and trust God, everything else that we want in life will fall into place. People who love and trust God are honest; they are peaceful; they don't feel isolated and alone; they know that someday they will have a second chance at having a life of their dreams.

People who love and trust God are happy and hopeful; they do their jobs as though they were working for God, and that makes them enjoy even the most mundane of tasks.

People who love and trust God know what to do first. And now you do too.

THE BOY WHO SUED HIS PARENTS

Be a good workman, one who does not need to be ashamed when God examines your work. 2 Timothy 2:15, TLB.

Recently I ran across a story about a teenager who was suing his parents for having had him. He alleged that life was hard, that it wasn't fair that his parents had not asked him whether or not he wanted to be born. And since he had discovered how tiring and difficult living was, he was angry that he had to do it.

No one would argue with him that life is hard. Many times it *is* hard. But the opposite is also true. Life is also enjoyable—often more so after a difficult task has been done.

If there's one thing you can count on in life, it is this: circumstances are continually changing. Nothing stays the same. Some of the friends you have now will develop different interests and drift away from you.

Many of the concerns you have now will be replaced by others as you grow through life. The steady progress of life is this: from ages 1 to 21 you do what somebody else tells you to; from ages 21 to 65 you do what you have to do; and from age 65 on you do what you want to do.

It has been said that life is a paradox. Each of us is born helpless, totally dependent on somebody else to figure out what our needs are and then to meet those needs. As babies we were carried around by somebody else, fed by somebody else, clothed by somebody else, warmed and kept covered by somebody else. At first glance that can seem like a rather blissful existence—we don't have to be responsible for one thing! But at second glance it seems like a drag—perhaps even risky if you don't trust the person who is caring for you!

So God lets us grow up. Growing up means taking increasing responsibility for our lives: feeding ourselves, dressing ourselves, thinking for ourselves—eventually working for our own money and for our own satisfaction.

Perhaps that boy who was suing his parents for having given him life didn't understand how life changes. Perhaps he was still expecting his parents to do everything for him and make him happy. No wonder he thought life was hard! Nobody can make you happy. Happiness comes from being true to yourself, from choosing to make the best of whatever life dishes out to you.

Some grown-ups seem to agree with the boy; they have decided not to have children because of the condition the world is in. But children who are not born do not have a chance for a life in heaven, either.

So thank your parents for giving you life. Take up the challenges of life with eagerness. When you meet an obstacle, don't look for someone else to change things for you; look for the things *you* can do to overcome it.

As you take on more and more responsibility for your life, resolve never to do anything that would make you want to hide from God. Grow up! And enjoy it!

AUGUST 19

DISHONORABLE PARENTS

Honour thy father and thy mother: that thy days may be long upon the land which the Lord thy God giveth thee. Exodus 20:12.

How do you honor parents who are dishonorable? How do kids honor parents who continually beat them, or belittle them, or molest them? Do such parents deserve honor? If those "parents" are not honored, will their children die? They might—as a result of abuse.

Several years ago the headlines of nearly every newspaper in the nation carried the story of a teenage brother and sister who killed their father. After their arrest and trial, they had a chance to tell their story.

Ever since they could remember, their father had beaten them several times a day with his hands, his belt, brushes—whatever was available. He molested his daughter daily. He would not let the family have a telephone in the house. Everyone except the father was a prisoner in the house—a tortured prisoner.

The brother and sister talked to a school counselor, but without offering any protection to the children, she called the authorities, and a social worker made a visit to their home. The dad acted really nice while the social worker was there, but when she left, he beat the children until they passed out. Their mother never stepped in to protect them.

At last the children could take it no longer. They felt that they had to kill their father if anything was ever going to change. So one day when the dad came home from work, his son was waiting inside the garage with a rifle. He shot his father there.

The boy went to jail. After a year when he was released on probation, he had this advice to give: "I want to tell other kids who live as I did, don't let your helplessness go on so long that you get as desperate as we did. Tell somebody about it, and ask for shelter! The death of my father brought an end to the abuse he gave me; but it also brought the beginning of heavy guilt. I don't know which is worse."

The home is supposed to be a place where family members feel safe, both emotionally and physically. An unhealthy family has the motto "Don't talk, don't trust, don't feel."

In contrast, a healthy family shares feelings with each other in an atmosphere of caring and growing. Members of a healthy family are honest with one another. In a healthy family, members don't pick on one person and make him feel bad. A healthy family takes the "kindergarten approach": everyone holds hands and crosses the road of life together. Unfortunately, healthy families are becoming more and more rare as the end of the world approaches.

Is your family healthy? If not, does an abusive parent deserve honor? What does honor mean? For one thing, it means that you don't talk disrespectfully to your parents. But telling your pastor or a counselor that you don't feel safe at home is not dishonorable. You deserve to feel safe. You deserve to feel cared for. If somebody is hurting you and warns you not to tell, that's your first clue that you *should* tell somebody who can help—maybe a friend's parent or a favorite teacher or your pastor. And keep on telling until somebody listens and does something to stop the hurting. That person won't judge your family or withdraw from you. He will help your family start healing.

A parent who abuses his own child is not like our Father. God is a perfect parent. God is nurturing and loving, even while He asks for obedience. That is what a real parent should be.

BEST-KEPT SECRETS

Wine gives false courage; hard liquor leads to brawls; what fools men are to let it master them, making them reel drunkenly down the street! Proverbs 20:1, TLB.

Do you remember some of the rules your family had when you were younger? Perhaps they were like these: "Never cross the street alone"; "Be in bed by eight o'clock." Do you cross the street alone now? Are you always in bed by eight o'clock? If not, are you breaking your family rules? Probably not, because while we call those "family rules," they are actually "family principles."

Your parents didn't want you to cross the street alone because they knew you didn't know enough about traffic safety to get across without danger. As you grew up, you learned to look both ways and cross the street safely by yourself. Now you are adding more and more to that knowledge—perhaps you are learning how to drive *in* the street!

What was the principle behind the rule to get in bed by eight o'clock? That's right—the principle of sufficient rest for a growing body.

Adventists have many health principles that people of other religions are just now recognizing as excellent rules. Scientists have compared the lifestyle and principles of Adventists with those of others and have concluded that Adventists who follow the health principles given to us by God through Mrs. White live an average of five years longer than other people!

As a result of those studies, health maintenance has become a national obsession. You've seen the increase in caffeine-free beverages; there are nonsmoking areas in restaurants and even nonsmoking flights in airplanes! High school students are encouraged not to smoke or drink—athletes in most high schools may be kicked off the team for drug use! Fast-food restaurants now offer salad bars for healthy fast food. Whole-grain breads and cereals with nuts in them are available everywhere. A burger stand in my town even offers vegetarian hamburgers!

The ironic thing is that while the world is adopting these health principles as a new thing, many Adventists who have known about them for so long are giving them up! Vegetarian, non-cola-drinking Adventists are becoming more and more rare these days. And sadly, even moral purity is getting harder to find.

I'm sure Satan is pleased. In time our minds and our consciences will be dulled, and we will be the weak ones, while his people are the strong.

God speaks to us through our minds. He gave us principles of healthy living so that our minds will be alert and receptive to His messages. If we dull our minds through lack of sleep, drugs, alcohol, or illnesses caused by unhealthy living, it is harder for God to get through to us.

Healthy living is God's idea. God's people knew about it first. What are you going to do about it?

HOW TO GET ANYTHING YOU WANT!

No matter what you ask for from the Father, using my name, he will give it to you. John 15:16, TLB.

The story is told of a beggar in a large city who caught the sleeve of a wealthy lawyer as they passed on the sidewalk.

"Got a quarter?" the dirty beggar asked with doleful eyes.

The lawyer glanced at the beggar's face briefly and started to brush him off. But something about that face stopped him. "Don't I know you from somewhere?" the lawyer asked, puzzled.

"Of course! We were in college together—remember English lit, Main Hall, second floor?"

The lawyer remembered. He cried out his friend's name and clapped him on the back. "Why, sure, I remember!" And taking in his friend's ragged condition, the lawyer pulled out his checkbook and wrote out a check for $100.

"Listen, friend," he said, "I don't care what has happened to you in the past; it's the future that counts. Take this check and make a new start for yourself." He pressed it into his friend's hand and, with a friendly handshake, hurried on his way.

The beggar stared at the check. He wandered down toward the bank and stood at the window for a few minutes, studying his reflection. Inside, the tellers were well dressed and clean, a contrast to the beggar's rumpled clothes, unshaven face, and tattered felt hat. The beggar looked down at the check again. Should he cash it? Would they believe it was real? He looked again at his reflection. No. They would probably think he had forged it and would arrest him on suspicion of forgery.

With a sigh, the beggar folded the check, stuffed it into his jacket, and wandered on down the street.

A few days later the lawyer sought out his friend on the same corner. "Hiya, friend!" he called. "Did you cash the check? Get yourself some new clothes and a hot meal? Gamble it away?"

The beggar shook his head and stared down at his dirty toes. "I didn't cash it," he said. "They would take one look at me and decide I had forged it."

The lawyer wrapped an arm around his friend's bony shoulder. "My friend," he said warmly, "what makes that check good is not your clothes or appearance, but my signature. Go on! Cash it!"

Jesus says the same thing to us. Going to heaven does not depend on how we look or how good we are; it depends on knowing Jesus as our friend. His signature on the record books of heaven gets us in.

Satan wants us to think that it's hard to be saved. Jesus came to show us that Satan is wrong.

AUGUST 22

ARE YOU WASTING JESUS' TIME?

If all the other events in Jesus' life were written, the whole world could hardly contain the books! John 21:25, TLB.

Young Jesus of Nazareth smiled dreamily as he carried in the family's wash from the bushes outside. His mother was teaching Him stories of their people. He was fascinated by the miracles Moses had performed for the pharaoh before the Israelites were released from slavery. Jesus had learned them in order. He could hardly wait to show His mother how well He remembered them. And then there were the Ten Commandments, which Moses had brought down from Mount Sinai—the rules that told how to live to be happy, including keeping God's holy day. Tomorrow was Sabbath. Jesus always helped His mother and father prepare the house for Sabbath before the sun went down each Friday. It was the rule!

But some of the rules about Sabbath bothered Jesus. A Jew could not light a lamp on the Sabbath. A Jew had to keep track of how far he traveled on the Sabbath. A Sabbath day's journey was two thirds of a mile, at which time a good Jew would stop and eat. Then he could continue for another two thirds of a mile before he stopped again.

A good Jew would not spit on the grass on the Sabbath, for that was the work of irrigating.

It was not right to carry anything on the Sabbath, for that was work.

When Jesus grew up, He must have been uncomfortable about keeping those man-made Sabbath rules. He knew they weren't what God had in mind for His holy day. Sometimes He healed people on the Sabbath—the priests said that was breaking the Sabbath. Sometimes Jesus picked wheat from a field and ate it—the priests said that was breaking the Sabbath. Do you think He was? No, Jesus wasn't breaking God's Sabbath rules. Instead He was breaking the restrictions that people put on the Sabbath. Jesus needed to show us how to get on track and keep Sabbath the way God intended it.

Someone has suggested that Jesus was a radical character, deliberately healing people on the Sabbath to cause a ruckus and then leaving town. I don't think so. The Bible tells us that when Jesus passed through a town, He healed everyone in it! To do that, Jesus must have healed people every day, but the Sabbath healings caused the most commotion, so those are the ones that were often recorded.

Seventh-day Adventists go to church on Sabbath because that is the day Jesus went to church. And that is the day God rested after Creation. And it is the day we will worship with Jesus in heaven. Jesus came to earth to get us back on track. If we don't get back on track, then Jesus' sufferings were a tragic waste.

WHAT IS THE BIBLE ALL ABOUT, ANYWAY?

Then the angel said to me, "These words are trustworthy and true: 'I am coming soon.' " Revelation 22:6, 7, TLB.

True or false: The Bible is about Seventh-day Adventists.

The answer is false. Nowhere in the Bible is the term *Seventh-day Adventist* mentioned. Jesus was not a Seventh-day Adventist. He was raised as a Jew, but He realized that the Jewish religion misunderstood much of what God intended for His people. Jesus might be considered a "Jew on strike."

In showing the people God's true plan, Jesus offended many Jewish leaders who thought they knew better than Jesus what God wanted them to do. They were jealous of Jesus and killed Him. That divided the Jews. Those who knew Jesus remembered what He had told them about God. They started a new religion called Christianity. But they weren't Seventh-day Adventists. Seventh-day Adventists have been around for less than 150 years; Jesus died nearly 2,000 years ago!

So where do we fit into the Bible? I like to think of the Bible as a pyramid. Most of it—the broad base—is about the Jewish people; it's a history book. But as with all pyramids, it gets narrower at the top, and something has to be chipped away.

A smaller portion of the Bible is about Jesus' followers—the Christians. You can read about the beginnings of Christianity in the New Testament. It used to take a lot of courage to be a Christian; now it's an accepted way of life.

An even smaller portion of the Bible—like gold dust that has to be filtered through, but that sparkles here and there throughout the Bible—contains the beliefs of our young religion, called Seventh-day Adventism.

We are told that someday, just before Jesus comes, there will be an even smaller group of people taken to heaven without dying. Perhaps you will be one of those people!

As I write this, the nurses at the hospital where I work are on strike. They are refusing to work until a better agreement is made for higher wages and better working conditions for patient care. A strike is a scary thing. Emotions and angry feelings run strong. But there is also a feeling of support, unity, and fearlessness when everyone is in it together!

I think that someday God's people will have to go "on strike" for religious reasons. Though the government will decree that we have to worship on Sunday, we will refuse. There will be pressure on us from non-Christian friends to give in and worship on Sunday. But we won't give in. We'll support each other. It's going to feel really good as the excitement of what's really happening begins to sink in—as we realize that we are experiencing the actual end of the world! As we actually see the little black cloud coming out of the east, and our smiling Jesus sitting on a throne, with billions of angels blowing their trumpets, we will begin to fly!

It's going to be really exciting! It's going to be out of this world!

AUGUST 24

DO YOU PING OR DO YOU ZING?

Even a child is known by his actions, by whether his conduct is pure and right. Proverbs 20:11, NIV.

It's bright red with black stripes, wide tires, and fancy shiny wheels. It's my new car, and boy, does it go fast! However, when I first bought it I thought something was wrong with it, because it would barely run. When I pushed the pedal to the floor, the engine coughed, spluttered, choked, and wheezed. Going up hills, the engine made loud pinging noises. It's terrible to have a new racy car that barely crawls down the road.

At stoplights people would look over and admire my car because it was so pretty. But when the light turned green and my car choked through the intersection, their looks of admiration changed to smiles and laughter. My car had a lot of flash on the outside, but inside it was a dog!

Solomon said that people can sometimes be like my car. We can look really good on the outside, but when someone watches how we act, he gets to know what we're really like on the inside. What do people see in you? How smoothly are you running?

I found out that my car's problem had to do with the kind of gas I put in it. I stopped using "regular" and began filling it up with "super." When I put in higher quality gasoline, my car performed as well as it looked like it should.

If your performance isn't what it should be, consider what you are putting in your mind. Are you filling your mind with good things, lovely things, positive things? Fill yourself up with Jesus by thinking about Him and how much He loves you. Put some zing into your life. Run as exquisitely as you look!

AUGUST 25

THE PROFESSOR'S SURPRISE

But suddenly the food he has eaten turns sour within him. Job 20:14, TLB.

A biology professor walked into the classroom with a brown bag in his hand and a twinkle in his eye. He grinned impishly, obviously relishing the delight of teaching his squeamish students the fine art of animal dissection.

He placed the sack on the desk and strode in front of the desk, announcing, "As a special treat for you, I have in this bag a fresh pond frog that we might inspect together. First we will examine the outside of the frog, and then"—he raised his eyebrows ominously—"we will dissect it."

The bag rustled as he reached inside. He pulled out a waxed-paper bag and carefully opened it. For a moment he stared silently at the thing in his hand: a cheese-on-rye sandwich.

"That is strange," he murmured to himself. "I'm quite sure that I already ate my lunch!"

Of course, the professor was only kidding. But some of his students never knew that; they thought he was really absentminded! They thought he was a fool.

In Australia a 31-year-old nurse became ill because of her bizarre habit of eating paper. She started eating paper when she was 12. First it was small amounts of blotting paper and sheets from exercise books. During her nurse's training she stopped her habit, but after she got married, she took it up again. At last her diet of 5 to 10 sheets of Kleenex and half a page of newspaper each day made her sick.

Whatever we take into our bodies has the potential of helping or hurting us. Bad things can make us sick, even in small doses.

A person who feeds on evil sooner or later realizes what a fool he has been. The damage can't always be undone. Girlie magazines cheapen boy-girl relationships. Drugs and alcohol affect your memory and your concentration—sometimes permanently.

It's never too late to change. Are the things you have been taking into your body pure and true and honoring to God? It's not just a slogan that "you are what you eat." You are what you *think*, too.

AUGUST 26

HOW DO YOU KNOW A BLESSING FROM A CURSE?

We know that all things work together for good to them that love God. Romans 8:28.

The story is told of a man in China who raised horses for a living. When one of his prized stallions ran away, his friends gathered at his home to mourn his great loss. After they had expressed their concern, the man raised this question: "How do I know whether what happened is bad or good?" Nobody had the answer.

A couple days later the runaway horse returned with several strays following close behind. The man's same acquaintances came again to his house—this time to celebrate his good fortune.

"But how do I know whether it's good or bad?" the old gentleman asked them again. Nobody had the answer.

That very afternoon the horse kicked the owner's son and broke the young man's leg. Once more the crowd assembled—now to express their sorrow over the incident. "But how do I know whether this is bad or good?" the father asked again, and again nobody had the answer.

Well, only a few days later, war broke out. The man's son, however, was exempted from military service because of his broken leg. His friends gathered—and you know what the man asked them. Nobody had the answer.

Maybe you are going through some tough times right now. Maybe it seems as if nothing good will ever happen to you. But according to Romans, all things have a beneficial ending for those who love God. God can turn around the tragedies in our lives that Satan causes, and make good come from them. Some of the best counselors have themselves been through hard times. Some of the best mothers and fathers have experienced loneliness as children and have learned how best to help you. But most of all, when things are going bad and all we can do is ask Jesus to help us hold on, He becomes a truly special friend—the only way out of this world.

244

IT'S A MYSTERY

I and my father are one. John 10:30.

It is said that Saint Augustine, one of the early church fathers, was walking on the shore of the ocean one day, pondering the mystery of the Trinity—how there could be three Gods with the one name. He came upon a little boy who was playing with a seashell. The youngster would scoop a hole in the sand, then go down to the waves, fill his shell full of water, and pour it into the hole he had made.

Augustine said, "What are you doing, my little fellow?"

The boy replied, "I am going to pour the sea into that hole."

"Ah," said Augustine, "that is what I have been trying to do. I have been trying to fit God into my limited understanding of Him."

Doesn't it make sense that the God we worship and to whom we entrust our lives should be vastly greater than our limited ability to understand Him? If you find it difficult to understand some things about God, such as how He has existed forever or how He can live in your heart, don't feel alone. Lots of people feel the same way. It is unrealistic to expect to understand all the teachings of Jesus fully, but that doesn't mean you should toss the Bible aside as worthless. I don't understand how computers work, and I couldn't make one if I wanted to. But that doesn't mean that my computer is worthless. Even though I don't understand everything about it, I have found that my computer still works for me! And even though I don't understand everything about God, He still works for me too.

THE GOOSE THAT MADE HIM DO THE DISHES

There was a time when I wouldn't admit what a sinner I was. But my dishonesty made me miserable and filled my days with frustration. . . . I finally admitted all my sins to you. . . . And you forgave me! All my guilt is gone. Psalm 32:3-5, TLB.

Many years ago, in the early 1900s, a renowned preacher confessed that when he was 12 years old, he had killed one of the family geese by throwing a stone and hitting it squarely on the head. Figuring that his parents wouldn't notice that one of the 24 birds was missing, he buried the dead fowl, dusted off his hands, and considered the matter closed.

But that evening his sister called him aside. "I saw what you did," she said quietly.

"What do you mean?" the boy asked, trying to bluff his way out of it.

"I saw you kill Father's goose," his sister said again. "And I even know where you buried it. And if you don't offer to do the dishes tonight, I'll tell Mother."

Frightened, the boy did just as she said. He washed all the dishes by himself. The next morning his sister gave him the same warning. All that day and the next the frightened boy felt bound to do the dishes. His mother couldn't help wondering about his sudden interest in a chore that previously he had done his best to get out of. As they finished the dishes on the third day in a row, the boy and his mother began to talk.

The following morning the boy surprised his sister by telling her it was her turn to do the dishes. With the raise of an eyebrow and the flick of her head, she motioned him outside. "Remember, I'm going to tell Mother about the goose," she quietly reminded him.

He replied calmly, "I've already told Mother, and she has forgiven me. Now you do the dishes. I'm free again!"

It's always hard to admit our mistakes. We are afraid of what others might say and do, and whether or not they will still care about us. If those other persons are parents, you can be certain that they will still love you—even if you've made a mistake!

Sometimes it is best to begin the confession with a statement that shows you have learned your lesson already—for example, "I've done something really stupid, and I want to talk with you about it. Please let me finish, and don't be angry with me."

How good it feels to make things right! When we try to hide the mistakes we have made, we become slaves to the mistakes. Confession brings release from that bondage.

AUGUST 29

TWO HUNTERS AND A BEAR

The day of the Lord is darkness, and not light. As if a man did flee from a lion, and a bear met him. Amos 5:18, 19.

What would you do if you met a bear in the forest? One sunny day two hunters trudged through a forest in search of game. Dry twigs snapped under their heavy boots as they stalked their prey. Suddenly, on the other side of a huckleberry bush, a grizzly bear stood up on his haunches, front paws waving in the air, shiny black nose twitching, massive head shaking, as it searched the air for the scent of the men.

The men ran for cover. One man climbed the nearest tree, scooting up into the highest branches amid a noisy rustle of leaves. The other man, seeing a cave to his left, ran into it to hide.

The grizzly seemed puzzled by the action and in no hurry to eat. He dropped his front paws to the ground, snapped at the air, and sat down between the tree and the cave to reflect upon his good fortune.

Suddenly, and for no apparent reason, the hunter in the cave came rushing out and almost ran into the waiting bear. He hesitated, and then dashed back in again.

Breathlessly the hunter in the tree watched his friend, thankful that the grizzly did not follow. The same thing happened a second time; the hunter dashed out from the cave, hesitated, and then dashed back in again. When he emerged for the third time, his companion in the tree frantically called out, "Woody, are you crazy? Stay in the cave till he leaves!"

"I can't," Woody panted. "There's another bear in there!"

The Bible says that a similar kind of dilemma will someday come upon the godless. They will find trouble in the very place they run for safety. According to the prophet Amos, these people may be religious, and even long for the coming of the Lord, without realizing that His arrival will present for them the greatest problem of all—judgment of their wrongdoing.

Who are the godless? They are the ones who love evil rather than good, and who expect the Lord's protection without ever doing what is necessary to qualify for it.

Remember this: There is a way to stay out of eternal death, but no way to get out of eternal death.

AUGUST 30

THE TRICKY PHONE BOOTH

And when thou hast shut thy door, pray to thy Father. Matthew 6:6.

There are many things that people who live in America take for granted. I'll never forget when we came to America in the early 1960s on furlough and saw an automatically opening door for the first time. Doors weren't opening automatically when my parents left America for Burma, but when we returned five years later, they were! I remember sitting in the car with my brother and sister while my parents ran into a grocery store to pick up a few things for supper. They returned a short time later with grocery bags in hand, laughing hysterically. It seems my mother had nearly fallen through the door as she leaned into it and it opened

247

automatically. Of course, we all had to get out of the car and try those fancy doors for ourselves! What fun!

In a letter to his friends, hymnwriter Wendell P. Loveless related this story about someone else's introduction to something unfamiliar. One evening a European tourist in New York entered a telephone booth to make a call. To his dismay, he found the phone booth to be much different from those in his own country. He couldn't get the light to go on. It was beginning to get dark, and he was having difficulty finding the number in the directory. He kept looking up at the dark bulb in the ceiling, and reaching for it. Then he tried to step outside with the phone book. But the phone book was chained to the phone, and the chain was not long enough. The dark bulb seemed to mock his efforts.

As he tried again to find the number in the fading twilight, a passerby noted his plight. "Sir," the kind passerby called out to him, "if you want to turn the light on, you'll have to shut the door."

To the visitor's amazement and satisfaction, when he closed the door, the booth was filled with light. He soon located the number and completed his call.

Does that remind you of a spiritual lesson? If we want our time with Jesus to light us up, we have to close the doors. That means that while you are having worship or praying to Jesus, you must really think about what's going on. Put the TV schedule out of your mind; don't think about what you're going to wear to school; don't even think about the upcoming test; just concentrate on talking to Jesus. Make your worship time quality time.

To turn on the light, you have to shut the door!

AUGUST 31

DELINQUENT STUDENTS OF RENAISSANCE HIGH

For our transgressions are multiplied before thee, and our sins testify against us. Isaiah 59:12.

The Bible teaches that we cannot hide our sins. We may be able to cover them for a while, and even get away with them for an extended period of time. But the time will inevitably come when we must face up to them, either in this world or in the next.

This truth was illustrated by what happened to a group of students at Renaissance High School in Detroit.

The Detroit *News* reported that the young people cut classes to attend a rock concert in Hat Plaza. I'm sure they felt they had gotten away with it. They had a marvelous time—they even got up close to the stage! But the next day, when the Detroit *News* appeared on the newsstand, it carried a color photo of the concert. And right there—on the front page, in living color—were the delinquent students of Renaissance High, easily recognizable by anyone.

The eagle-eyed assistant principal, Dr. Elijah Porter, spotted the students. They were called into his office. There was nothing they could say. Their sins were found out.

Perhaps you have some secret sin that you are hiding. Confess it and stop doing it! Or maybe you are gradually being drawn into a situation that you know is wrong, but you're tempted to pursue it because you think you won't get caught. Go no further. Your picture may not appear on the front page. You might think you are getting away with something, but the Bible says you won't get away with it!

You may sow seeds of wrongdoing in secret, but the harvest can't be concealed.

SEPTEMBER 1

MIRACLES STILL HAPPEN

For we are his workmanship, created in Christ Jesus unto good works. Ephesians 2:10.

Have you ever heard the phrase "What you are speaks so loudly, I can't hear what you're saying"? Do you know what it means? It means that those who know us best can tell whether we practice what we preach. Yours is a Christian home. Do your neighbors know it? Or is it off to church every Sabbath (what you preach) and then home to fuss and fight and annoy your brothers and sisters (what you practice)?

A self-righteous, pompous Sunday school teacher was trying to explain to his class the importance of living in holy obedience to Christ. With head held high and chest thrust outward, he strutted impressively back and forth across the room, saying arrogantly, "Now boys, why do people call me a Christian?"

There was a momentary silence. Then one of the boys slowly raised his hand.

"Yes?" boomed the teacher with a knowing smile.

The boy responded, "Probably because they don't know you."

Every Sabbath we all walk in the doors of the church with our Sabbath smiles and our best clothing. We don't mean to deceive each other—we just want to be pleasant. But if you go to church with a heavy heart and see everyone else there smiling, it's easy to think that you're the only person in the world who has problems. We can talk ourselves into feeling really bad if we judge ourselves by others.

But when we really get to know each other, we realize that all of us struggle with nearly the same things. There is no such thing as a perfect family, whose members never get angry. Family situation comedies on TV give the false impression that all families joke and laugh together, that everyone is quick-witted, and that families solve their problems in a mere half hour. But real problems often last much longer than a half hour. Real families don't always have a quick retort to everything that is said. Real families don't always know just what to say to help each other. Real families laugh and cry and sometimes even hurt each other. But they also apologize to each other.

There is no such thing as a perfect person who always does what is right. Those who think they are perfect show by their pride that they are not.

The Bible tells us that all of us have sinned. But little by little, as we learn how much God loves us and how imperfect we are, our lives change. God's love changes us. It's a miracle!

SEPTEMBER 2

JESUS WAS ONCE 13

I drew them with gentle cords, with bands of love. Hosea 11:4, NKJV.

The naturalist S. L. Bastian tells of a certain kind of spider that builds its nest in the branches of a small tree or bush. In this delicate enclosure the baby spiders are hatched. If the nest is disturbed in any way, the little spiders will all rush out in fright. At once the mother goes to their side. She is alerted to their potential danger in a most unique manner.

Each of the young ones has a thin silky strand attached to it, and all of these threads are joined to the body of the mother. When the babies are threatened by an enemy, they naturally scurry off, giving their lines a sharp tug. This is instantly felt by the adult spider. Within seconds she pulls them back to the nest, where they are protected from harm.

We too are linked to God with eternal cords that cannot be broken. When danger affects us, Jesus' attention is drawn to us in a special way because of the bands of love between Him and us. Remember, Jesus was a teenager on this very same earth. He struggled with wanting to be like His friends and sometimes having to make a choice to be different when they chose to do evil. No doubt Jesus walked away from a fight, rather than getting into one. No doubt He had to endure wisecracks from the other kids about Joseph not being His real father. No doubt He had friends who drank wine and tried to push it on Him. No doubt when He refused, He was accused of being a goody-goody.

And no doubt He helped His mother with the dishes, and even carried out the garbage, and probably He even swept the floors—all before a game of kickball in the street with His friends.

Jesus was a real flesh-and-blood Palestinian teenager. He remembers how it is to grow up. Even before we sense our trouble, He is hastening to give us His assistance. God loves everyone as though there were but one of us to love!

A ROOM IN THE PALACE

In my Father's house are many rooms. . . . I am going there to prepare a place for you. John 14:2, NIV.

A pastor in Ireland went to visit a poverty-stricken Christian woman. She had only one room, but by hanging up sheets and blankets, she divided the area into a bedroom, a living room, and a kitchen. She explained to her visitor, "This is a very poor place. I hope you don't mind coming here."

The minister assured her that it was his privilege to be in her home.

"Well," she said, "it is a poor place, but a King's daughter lives here!"

There is royalty living in your home, too. I like to think of my home on this earth as a rental unit that I'm living in until my room at the palace is finished. Our text today says that God's home in heaven has many rooms. I like that! He isn't going to make us live outside His house—we will actually have our own rooms in our Father's house! He will be right there with us!

And since Jesus knows us so well, I'm sure He is planning each of our rooms just according to the things we like. If you like window seats, there will probably be one in your room. If you like secret passages, there will probably be one of those, too. Jesus knows just what you like, and He is making your room just perfect for you.

Until we get to heaven, we have things to do here. We have been put on this earth to share our faith and the good news about God with others. There are very good things to enjoy on this earth. But we shouldn't love the things of this world so much that we don't look forward to heaven.

As the wagon train cowboys used to tell the settlers: "Don't drive your stakes too deep—we're moving in the morning."

GOD DOESN'T MAKE JUNK

God created man in his own image. Genesis 1:27.

After drill practice, a line of green-suited Army recruits stood side by side at attention, waiting for their next order. The drill sergeant had been insulting them for a full hour—his way of teaching them how to march. At last, after inspecting the soldiers nose-to-nose, he barked out, "OK! All you dumbbells fall out!"

All but one recruit did so. That one recruit remained at attention, his eyes staring straight ahead.

Angered by what he thought was defiance, the sergeant marched up to the rookie and growled, "Well?"

But the young man held his ground. With a steely stare straight ahead, he said, "There certainly were a lot of them, weren't there, sir?" and saluted.

It's not wrong to affirm your worth. God wants you to know that you are special; that's what is going to get us through the rough times at the end of the world. People who know they are special experience three basic emotions: they have a sense of belonging, a sense of worthiness, and a sense of inner confidence. Christianity gives us all of these.

But sin undermines these emotions. When you do something you know is wrong, you have a sense of guilt, fear, and hostility at those who haven't made the same mistakes. At that moment Satan has you right where he wants you. He makes you shout to yourself, "I am such a dummy!" He wants you to think God doesn't love dummies.

But that's when God says, "You are special. I made you in My image. And I don't make junk."

GETTING THINGS STRAIGHT

But now we have been delivered from the law . . . so that we should serve in the newness of the Spirit. Romans 7:6, NKJV.

It was an icy-cold day in North Dakota. A boy and his friend were hitchhiking home from school, having a good time sliding along the blue-white frozen puddles beside the road. It didn't matter—at first —that no one stopped to pick them up. But soon they were cold and hungry, and every car that passed them by, blowing cold air in their faces, was an assault on their courage.

Then Jesse saw a familiar car. It was his married brother's car, heading in the same direction they were. "Oh, boy!" he said, waving at the car. "We'll get a ride now."

His sister-in-law was driving. She smiled and waved back, but to his surprise, she kept on going.

"I don't believe it!" Jesse cried. "My brother's own car, and it passed us by!"

The boys ended up walking all the way home. Jesse went straight to the phone and called his sister-in-law. "You passed me and my friend walking along the road—why didn't you pick us up?" he asked, puzzled.

"You know how your brother is," she explained. "Larry told me never to pick up hitchhikers." She was so intent on obeying her new husband's every regulation that she missed his overall intent.

Sometimes we do that with Christianity. We get so busy keeping all the regulations that we forget God's overall intent of loving obedience to Him. Our love for God is the reason we go to church, it's the reason we help others in need, and it's the reason we want to go to heaven.

SEPTEMBER 6

TRUTHFUL LYING

Though his hatred is covered by deceit, his wickedness will be revealed before the whole congregation. Prov. 26:26, NKJV.

All lies are sinful, but some are more damaging than others. It's much more harmful to say something untrue about a person than to claim that a fish you caught was huge when it was no more than 8 inches long. Perhaps the worst kind of lie is the one that is intended to destroy the character of another. It can even take the form of telling the truth, but doing so in a way that suggests something false.

Two men worked on a large oceangoing vessel. One day the mate, who normally did not drink, became intoxicated. The captain, who hated him, entered in the daily log: "Mate drunk today." He knew this was the man's first offense, but he wanted to get him fired.

The mate was aware of the captain's evil intent and when he saw what was written, he begged him to change the record. However, the captain replied, "It's a fact, and into the log it goes!"

The mate determined to get even. A few days later he was keeping the log, and concluded it with: "Captain sober today."

Realizing the implications of this statement, the captain asked that it be removed. In reply the mate said, "It's a fact, and in the log it stays!"

If you really want to hurt somebody, you can repeat something he said and distort the meaning. In fact, you can be entirely accurate, but imply a falsehood. That's mean. And it isn't a very nice reflection on you.

253

If you earn the reputation of always saying something unkind about others, even your friends will wonder if you do the same to them. But those who insert an honest compliment about somebody else into their conversations will be trusted and respected. It makes you feel good, too.

SEPTEMBER 7

SEARCHING FOR TREASURE

Be content with such things as you have. Hebrews 13:5, NKJV.

Sometimes, instead of being grateful for what God has given us, we look around and want everything that everybody else has, too. We become covetous. As a result, we miss seeing how fortunate we really are.

An ancient Persian legend tells of a wealthy man by the name of Al Haffed, who owned a large farm. One evening a visitor related to Mr. Haffed tales of fabulous amounts of diamonds that could be found in other parts of the world, and of the great riches they could bring him. The vision of all this wealth made Mr. Haffed feel poor by comparison. So instead of caring for his own prosperous farm, he sold it and set out to find these treasures.

But the search proved to be fruitless. Finally, penniless and in despair, he committed suicide by jumping into the sea.

Meanwhile, the man who had purchased Mr. Haffed's farm noticed one day the glint of an unusual stone in a shallow stream on the property. He reached into the water, and to his amazement he pulled out a huge diamond. Later, when working in his garden, he uncovered many more valuable gems.

Poor Al Haffed had spent his life traveling to distant lands seeking jewels when on the farm he had left behind were all the precious stones his heart could have desired.

Discontentment makes rich men poor, while contentment makes poor men rich. God wanted to spare us from discontentment when He gave us the tenth commandment which says: "Thou shall not covet . . . any thing that is thy neighbour's." That isn't a threat. It's a secret of happiness. We aren't happy when we continually want what someone else has. Isn't God a good counselor?

SEPTEMBER 8

OLYMPIC WISDOM

You will keep him in perfect peace, whose mind is stayed on You. Isaiah 26:3, NKJV.

As Christians, we are to be self-disciplined not only in our physical appetites but also in our thoughts. To lose control of our minds is to fall prey to Satan.

The difficulty of controlling the mind is underscored by Lanny Bassham, an Olympic gold medalist in shooting the small-bore rifle. He wrote, "Our sport is controlled nonmovement. We are shooting from 50 meters—more than half a football field—at a bull's-eye three quarters the size of a dime. If the angle of error at the point of the barrel is more than .005 of a millimeter (that is, five one thousandths), you drop into the next circle and lose a point. So we have to learn how to make everything stop. I stop my breathing. I stop my digestion by not eating for 12 hours before the competition. I train by running to keep my pulse around 60 so I have a full second between beats. . . .

"You do all of this, and you have the technical control. But you have to have some years of experience in reading conditions: the wind, the mirage. Then you have the other 80 percent of the problems—the mind!"

Our thoughts begin to drift into forbidden areas, and we let them go. We are lustful. We think proudly. We give in to self-pity. Race-car driver Sterling Moss once said of driving at high speeds: "It's necessary to relax your muscles when you can. But relaxing your brain is fatal!" It's the same in the battle with Satan.

Learn to control your mind. "He who will not command his thoughts will soon lose command of his actions."

SEPTEMBER 9

KEEPING COOL

A wise man controls his temper. He knows that anger causes mistakes. Proverbs 14:29, TLB.

Natalie Miller, a student in Eugene, Oregon, was the proud owner of a spirited horse named Shiloh. He stayed in a pasture near her house and she would often ride him home during the lunch hour. While Shiloh munched on the sweet grass in the front yard, Natalie would dash inside and make a quick sandwich for herself.

One day when Natalie hurried outside with her sandwich in her hand, she discovered in dismay that Shiloh had taken off down the street and was galloping at a fast pace, mane flying freely in the breeze.

Natalie chased after him. But her pace was not fast enough. She lost sight of the horse after only two blocks. She began walking, calling his name, whistling, making all the sounds he was familiar with.

After several minutes, she saw a boy leading Shiloh out of a garage, just as a man with a horror-stricken look pulled into the driveway.

Speechless, the man stared at the boy and the horse, then slowly opened the door of his car and stepped out on unsteady legs.

Natalie ran up to them before the man could say anything. She thanked the boy for her horse, and then started a long explanation about how the horse had gotten away from her.

The man listened quietly.

When Natalie had finished explaining, the man wiped his brow with a heavy hand.

"Thank you for telling me that," he said slowly. "Just last week I told my son that he couldn't have a car and would have to find some other way to get around!"

Things aren't always what they seem, are they? Suppose that father had started yelling at his son for buying a horse without permission before he knew the whole story? It would have caused needless friction between them. It's better to remain calm and find out the whole story before reacting than it is to react first and have to back down later and feel like a fool.

Next time something happens that you don't understand, stay cool. Ask questions. Find out the whole story. Then decide if it's worth getting angry about.

SEPTEMBER 10

HEROES AROUND US

Anxious hearts are very heavy, but a word of encouragement does wonders! Proverbs 12:25, TLB.

A man stood at a drugstore checkout counter leafing through a teen magazine while he waited for his turn in line. "This is terrible! Just terrible!" he muttered to himself. Then he nudged the woman in front of him. "Just look at the kids on these pages. Nothing but trash. Kids don't have anybody to look up to these days."

A boy behind him heard the conversation and cleared his throat. "Excuse me, sir," he said, "but I disagree with you. Not all kids are into the kind of things you're seeing in that magazine. And we still have heroes. My dad is a hero to me and I've got a couple teachers who could make a lot more money than they do if they weren't so interested in working for kids. We've got heroes. You've just got to look around."

There is a myth floating around that parents like to go to work, that parents enjoy getting up every morning, that parents don't get tired. It's also a myth that parents enjoy emptying the dishwasher and cleaning up the house and doing the laundry. Parents don't enjoy doing those things any more than you do—but they do them anyway, because they have to be done.

Many fortunate parents have jobs that they enjoy; many do not. But if they don't work, there is no money for a house, church school, new clothes, vacations—the list could go on and on. And so they go to work faithfully, day after day, because they care.

Being responsible for you is a burden that your parents took on willingly. They probably had no training in how to parent. They're learning, even as you are learning how to be a teenager. It's all by trial and error. But even though they love you, being your parent is often a little scary and exhausting. A word of appreciation from you can do wonders to lift your parents' spirits and send them back to work with more energy than they had yesterday. Why don't you thank your parents right now for working so faithfully so you can have the things you need—and the things you just have to have. And thank them for being your parents!

Will Rogers once said, "I can live a whole week on one compliment." Appreciation works the same way.

IS YOUR HAMPER OPEN?

Despise God's Word and find yourself in trouble. Obey it and succeed. Proverbs 13:13, TLB.

If I were to open the door to your room right now, how would it look? Is your bed made? Are your clothes picked up, or are they lying all over the floor? Is your homework done and neatly stacked on your desk, ready to be taken to school? If so, good for you! If not, then here's a story you can probably identify with.

A teenage boy had a hard time keeping his room looking very neat. He seemed to think that the floor of his room was his closet. He would drop his pants and let them lie there until he needed them again. His shirts sometimes made it to the closet—not to the hangers, but to the floor of the closet, in a heap. Underwear and dirty socks, unfortunately, made little stinky piles on the floor, under the bed, and all around it, which this boy stepped on or around, depending on how much energy or how dirty the items were.

In desperation the boy's mother bought a clothes hamper for her son. She painted it his favorite color and, with much ceremony, placed it in her son's room in a spot specifically chosen by him.

She hoped his room would look different from then on. But she was disappointed. In less than a week the little gray piles of dirty socks and jeans were back.

The boy's mother was exasperated. "Why didn't you use the hamper?" she asked him.

"But Mom," the boy replied, "it's never open!"

We have a marvelous Book—the Bible—that can help us keep our lives clean and happy. But like the clothes hamper, the Bible doesn't open all by itself—we have to open it. And unless we open the Bible and *use* it, it doesn't do us any good.

Choose one Bible principle—honesty, integrity, kindness, trust in God—and be aware of how you use it today.

SECRETS OF TRUE GREATNESS

The more lowly your service to others, the greater you are. To be the greatest, be a servant. Matthew 23:11, TLB.

What makes people great? Can you think of someone that you know personally, about whom you could say "He's great"? What are the qualities that make someone outstanding? Is it looks? Is it grades? Is it clothes? Probably not. True greatness can be summed up in the words "and then some."

James E. Byrnes, secretary of state from 1945 to 1947, said this about greatness: "I discovered at an early age that most of the differences between average people and great people can be explained in three words—'and then some.'

"The top people did what was expected of them, and then some. They were considerate and thoughtful of others, and then some. They met their obligations and responsibilities fairly and squarely, and then some. They were good friends to their friends, and then some. They could be counted on in an emergency, and then some."

A story I heard recently describes this quality well. The parents of a girl whom we'll call Ardis were getting a divorce. When they told Ardis, she got a sick feeling in the pit of her stomach that she was sure would never go away. She cried off and on for days. She was angry; she felt betrayed; she wanted to die. She felt so alone!

When her friends heard about it, many of them put their arms around her and told her to call if she ever felt lonely and they would come over. Ardis thanked them, knowing she could never call somebody up and say, "I feel like crying; please come over and be with me."

But one friend seemed to know the best way to help. She didn't tell Ardis to call her. This friend showed up at Ardis' doorstep each morning and walked with her to school, and then home again. On Father's Day, when Ardis was home alone with her mom, this friend knew it would be an especially lonely day for Ardis. She walked over to Ardis' house and rang the doorbell, and when Ardis opened the door, her friend told her cheerily, "I've come to shine your shoes!"

They both knew that Reeboks don't need shining, but it gave them both something to laugh about together, and Ardis felt better. Her friend was a friend—and then some.

You can be great too!

GOD AND YOU, TOGETHER

But they that wait upon the Lord shall renew their strength.
Isaiah 40:31.

There are two conflicting statements that I've often heard about life—maybe they confuse you, too. They are "The Lord helps those who help themselves" and "Wait on the Lord and let Him work things out for you." How do you know when to "help yourself" and when to "wait on the Lord"?

Fourteen-year-old Jeff was bored. And hungry. Since Mom had started to work and Grandma had moved to Florida for the winter, it seemed that he never got anything homemade to eat. Oh, he could make chocolate-chip cookies with the best of them. And Mom was careful to keep fresh fruit in the house. But for the past several weeks he had been hungry for homemade bread. And Mom had been too tired to make it.

It was Sunday. Mom had gone for her hospital shift before the sun came up, and Jeff faced a day alone. He tried not to feel sorry for himself. Mom didn't usually work Sundays, and he wasn't often neglected. But he wasn't in the mood to read, it was too cold to go outside, and for a variety of reasons, all of his friends were occupied and couldn't come over. Jeff picked up a cookbook and leafed through it. His eyes fell on a recipe for easy-made bread, and he thought, *I could bake some bread and surprise Mom.* He grinned. He'd kneaded the dough lots of times, even though he had never made up a recipe from scratch.

So Jeff got out the bowl and measured the warm water. He remembered to test the yeast in a little bit of water and sugar—it was alive and growing. He mixed in the salt, sugar, oil, and flour, and stirred until the spoon wouldn't move. Then he scraped the sticky dough onto the flour-covered table. So far, so good. He was a little clumsy, but he managed to knead in enough flour so that the dough grew elastic and handled easily. Then he put it on the countertop to rise.

Now, what Jeff hadn't counted on was the fact that the kitchen in their drafty apartment was so cold that even fruit left out on the counter would not ripen. An hour passed. The dough lay in the bowl in a hard lump. Jeff poked at it. Nothing. Another hour passed. It was already noon. The dough had hardly risen a bit.

Jeff knew that his yeast was alive, and being the kind of kid who liked to work out problems, he put his mind to work on this one. Gazing absentmindedly out the window, he noticed that the sun shone with a winter brilliance, which gave him an idea. Jeff picked up the bowl and took it outside, setting it on the back porch in the warm sunlight. Within minutes it began to rise, and an hour later Jeff kneaded the dough into two fat loaves.

Later on, as he thought about it, Jeff realized that he had learned something from that bread. He had learned something about what happens when his will meets up with God's. His efforts didn't make that dough rise. But on the other hand, the dough couldn't have risen if he hadn't mixed the water, flour, and other ingredients together in the first place.

The Lord honors honest efforts—even honest mistakes. And if you do your best to lay a good groundwork, the Lord will often make good things out of it.

SEPTEMBER 14

IMPOSSIBLE PROJECT

Do you know a hard-working man? He shall be successful and stand before kings! Proverbs 22:29, TLB.

It was a horrible tractor accident. Young Morgan Rowe was the worst injured, eventually losing one arm and severely damaging his other one. One evening as he dozed in the hospital, he overheard his parents discussing how they would ever pay their $30,000 hospital bill. Morgan opened one eye.

"Don't worry; I'll help," he promised.

Three months after leaving the hospital, he began to scour his neighborhood in Valdosta, Georgia, for returnable bottles and cans. First he paid the $455 ambulance bill, and then he put $2,500 toward his hospital bill.

The hospital leaked Morgan's story to the press, and when officials at the recycling center of Reynolds Aluminum heard about Morgan, they put him in touch with the Bear Archery Company in Gainesville, Florida, where the family had moved.

Morgan explained what his project was, and Bear Archery began to donate all spare metal from aluminum arrows to Morgan's scrap drive. Soon other people were also helping. Morgan kept on collecting aluminum cans on a full-time basis.

At last, five years after his accident, Morgan presented a check to the hospital in Valdosta for $17,713—the final installment of his $30,000 medical bill.

Although the hospital bill is now paid, Morgan plans to continue raising money for a wing at a hospital in Atlanta, Georgia, where he also was a patient.

How old is Morgan? Eleven. He was 6 years old when he made the promise to his parents that he would help pay his own hospital bill.

Now, is there anything you have to do that seems impossible? You can do it! Just get started!

THE BOXER WHO WAS A SOFTIE

But whoever slaps you on your right cheek, turn the other to him also. Matthew 5:39, NKJV.

He was a big man, this wrestler. Years of weight training had turned the muscles of his arms into ropes as hard as the bark of a tree. He could lift more than 150 pounds without any problem, easier than you or I can lift a pound of potatoes.

One day this big, strong man was driving to an appointment when he misjudged the speed of a small red car coming behind him, and pulled out in front of it. What do you think happened? Well, the offended driver of the red car turned his lights on the high beams, leaned on his horn, yelled obscenities, and tailed the wrestler's car until he forced it off the road. When the wrestler stopped, two men jumped from the little red car, ran to the wrestler's car, and began pounding on it with their fists. The wrestler was going to apologize, but the men gave him no chance.

While all this commotion was going on, another car came speeding along the road and sideswiped the red car, knocking it off the steep shoulder of the road.

What would you have done if you had been the wrestler? Fortunately for the owners of the red car, the wrestler was a Christian. He was just about ready to get out of his car and defend himself when the accident happened, taking the attention of the attackers from his car back to theirs.

They hurried away from the wrestler to see about their own car. As they stood silently gawking at their car, scratching their heads and wondering how to get it back on the road, the wrestler walked over to the highway's edge and looked the situation over for himself.

Then, flexing his muscles, he stooped and lifted the little car back onto the road as easily as if it were a sack of flour. The men were amazed, then chagrined.

"Thanks," they said gruffly.

"Hey, no problem," the big man replied. "Sorry about pulling out in front of you. It was a miscalculation on my part."

261

With a wave, the men hopped in the red car and sped away.

Have you ever been confronted by a really angry person who hurt you physically or just hurt your feelings? It's natural to want to get revenge and hurt him back. But while getting revenge may make you even with your enemy, forgiving him and keeping your cool keeps you *ahead* of him. Try it next time. It's God's way.

SEPTEMBER 16

ARE YOU A PIG OR A CHICKEN?

And the Lord replies: I will be your lawyer; I will plead your case.
Jeremiah 51:36, TLB.

The story goes that a pig and a chicken wandered around the farm they lived on, discussing something the farmer had announced recently.

"I think it's a great idea," the chicken clucked. "He wants us all to feel involved in making a go of our farm."

The pig grunted. "He wants to sell bacon and eggs," the pig grumbled. "For you, that's being involved. For me, it's commitment."

Would you say Jesus was "involved" in showing us how much God loves us, or was He "committed"?

What kind of friend are you?

Joel, a ninth grader, moved to a new school. It was not far from his old school, but the new school was much larger. To his happy surprise, he found that one of his friends, whom he hadn't seen in five years, was a student there too.

Joel thought his old friend would be happy to see him; he wasn't. Instead, Joel's friend joined the other students in making fun of Joel's plaid pants, crew cut, and cowboy shirts and boots. How do you suppose Joel felt? What should his friend have done differently?

A story about Jackie Robinson, the first Black baseball player to play in the Major Leagues, illustrates true friendship. While he played with the Brooklyn Dodgers, Jackie faced venom nearly everywhere he traveled —fastballs at his head, spikings on the bases, insults from the stands. During one game in Boston the taunts and racial slurs seemed to reach a peak.

In the midst of this, another Dodger, a Southern White named Pee Wee Reese, called time-out. He walked from his position at shortstop toward Jackie at second base, put his arm around Jackie's shoulder, and stood there talking with him for what seemed like a long time. The gesture spoke more eloquently than the words—"This man is my friend."

When your name comes up in the judgment, Jesus will be standing right there beside you with His arm around you. That gesture will tell the whole universe, "This person is My friend."

ARE YOU SMART?

Jesus answered, My kingdom is not of this world. John 18:36.

This is a test. Think a minute before you answer each question. The answers could be much different than you think!

First question: How much is half of eight?

Second question: What is one and one?

Third question: Can you think of a word that is the same, whether it's spelled backward or forward?

Now for the answers. If you said that half of eight is four, you are wrong. Half of eight is three! Here's how: As you know, a figure eight is composed of two small zeros one on top of the other. Draw a figure eight on a piece of paper. Now draw a line down through the figure eight, exactly in the middle. You have created two threes standing face-to-face.

If your next answer was that one and one are two, you are again wrong. One and one makes 11. My son Marc taught me that answer when he was just a little guy of 4 or 5. He drew a figure 1 on a piece of paper, and then he drew another figure 1 right beside it—1 and 1, the way he figured it, made the number 11!

And now for the last answer. No doubt there are several words that are the same spelled backward or forward, but the one I had in mind is the word *racecar.*

How did you do? Experts tell us that the key to intelligence is not in how well we can memorize facts, but in how well we can creatively use those facts to see things differently.

Christians have to be intelligent. Jesus talked in parables when He was here. Some people couldn't comprehend what He was saying because they couldn't think in different terms than they were used to.

We have to think of events in this world differently than non-Christians. When we hear of wars and starving people and new diseases, we don't just pass them off as something the governments have to take care of; we see them in a different way. We see them as signs that sin has just about played itself out on this world, and that Jesus will come very soon!

COURTESY OF SIN

For if you live according to the sinful nature, you will die. Romans 8:13, NIV.

Perhaps you remember the terrible earthquake that struck Mexico in 1985, when live satellite coverage brought the pictures of the devastation to the whole world almost as soon as the tragedy happened. While amid fire and smoke, dust, and broken concrete the rescuers dug frantically into the rubble, we who were not victims of the earthquake watched our TV sets in stunned silence.

Then suddenly the following words flashed across the bottom of the TV screen: "Courtesy: SIN."

The letters SIN actually stood for Spanish International Network, but how appropriate they were at the bottom of scenes of total devastation and agony!

While we know it isn't emotionally healthy to dwell on the ugly aspects of our life in this world, it doesn't hurt to realize that all the misery we experience is the result of *sin*. We know that sin separates us from God because we feel guilty and unworthy and unlovable, That isn't God's estimation of us—that's ours. And if we keep on making bad choices and feeling more and more guilty, we end up telling ourselves that it's useless to hope that God loves us. Then we give up trying, and sin really gets a hold on us, placing us in danger of being eternally lost.

Since we know that all human suffering is the result of sin, why do we treat sin so lightly? Why do we go after it and try to be a part of it, instead of fleeing from it in revulsion, knowing how much pain it is going to cause?

Listen to your conscience. If something makes you feel the least bit uncomfortable, then don't do it. Leave the room. Say something to lighten the situation or to defend what you know is right. Ask God to help you run away from doing something you would hate yourself for doing. He'll help you. He wants you with Him—out of this world!

SEPTEMBER 19

TURTLE LEGEND

Can a man hold fire against his chest and not be burned? Proverbs 6:27, TLB.

The story is told of a turtle who stood on the bank of a big river, testing it with his toe, waiting to go across.

A scorpion reached up and tapped on his shell with a front leg. "Please, sir, won't you let me ride on your shell across the river?" he asked. "I have urgent business on the other side."

The turtle looked back in horror. "If I let you ride on my back, you will sting me. And then I will die." He edged closer to the river, but was stopped by the scorpion's shrill voice.

"Please. I must get across the river. I promise you that I won't hurt you. I give you my word."

The turtle cocked his head to one side, thinking. "You give me your word?"

"Yes. I give you my word that I won't hurt you."

"All right. Climb up."

And so the scorpion climbed on the turtle's back, and the turtle swam into the water. The current was strong, and the scorpion clung to the turtle's shell for dear life. At last the turtle, weary from swimming, made his way up on the far shore. At that moment when they were on dry land, the scorpion flipped his curved tail against the soft skin of the turtle's neck and stung him! Then he hopped to the ground.

"Why did you do that?" the turtle gasped as pain shot through his body. "You promised—"

"You knew what I was when you picked me up," said the scorpion as he scuttled away.

You also know right from wrong. You know that drugs are dangerous. You know that promiscuity doesn't bring happiness. You know that God can be trusted. If ever you choose to ignore God's warnings and tamper with sin, remember the words of the scorpion: "You knew what I was when you picked me up."

SEPTEMBER 20

DOES GOD PLAY FAVORITES?

Again I looked throughout the earth and saw that the swiftest person does not always win the race, nor the strongest man the battle, and that wise men are often poor, and skillful men are not necessarily famous; but it is all by chance, by happening to be at the right place at the right time. Ecclesiastes 9:11, TLB.

A bank teller received a call one afternoon from a little old lady. "I need some help," she said in a soft, quivery voice.

"I'm sorry, but I can't help you right now," the teller replied.

"But this is urgent. You see, I received a letter informing me that my account was overdrawn, but I'm sure that I deposited my Social Security check last week—"

"Ma'am," the teller cut in, "I can't help you right now."

"But I'm worried!" the woman snapped. She began to berate the bank teller and threatened to complain to the bank president.

"I'm worried too," the teller said softly. "This bank was just robbed."

The most harmful assumption we can make is that everyone else is doing OK and we're not. The more we compare our lives with others, the more dissatisfied we can become—especially if things aren't going too well for us at the time. We want to be happy, but playing the "martyr" role doesn't help. When you feel sorry for yourself and shut out the world, you lock yourself in.

We've gotten ourselves into a bit of a problem by believing that if things aren't going well for us, we are not blessed by God and He isn't taking care of us. It's easy to say carelessly, "God has been good to me and has given me good parents." Does that mean that God hasn't been taking care of those poor children who have been brought up by abusive parents? Does that mean that God doesn't love *them*, that He decided they shouldn't be blessed? Of course not!

God isn't a mad scientist, controlling a great switchboard, deciding whether it's time for one person to be blessed and another to be abused. God does not choose certain disasters to come to us. Disasters are a fact of life. But when they come to us as a result of poor choices (our poor choice, or someone else's), God helps us through them. He promises that He is working overtime to bring good out of evil and to bring sadness to an end.

Even though we all walk around with cheery faces in public, no one has ever been without hurts of some kind. Your teacher may be hurting or afraid, even though she greets you with a smile on her face. Your classmates may be worried and scared, even though they say nothing about it.

God created people to need people. We need each other's smiles. We need each other's encouragement. We all have problems. Why don't we share more happiness with each other?

SEPTEMBER 21

WHAT ARE YOU LEARNING?

To learn, you must want to be taught. To refuse reproof is stupid. Proverbs 12:1, TLB.

The story is told of a meeting in heaven just days after everyone had arrived from earth. Old friends and relatives were meeting each other, and excitement was everywhere.

Then the angel Gabriel announced that it was show-and-tell time. "Is there anyone who would like to share a story with the group to illustrate how bad things were on earth?"

One man volunteered instantly, raising both hands and jumping up and down. "I will! I will!" he said, smiling. "I can tell about the awful flood of 1829!" He turned arrogantly to the man next to him. "Wiped out the whole city!"

x

Gabriel made his way toward the man. "So you want to tell about a flood?"

"It's a great story!" the man gushed.

"OK," Gabriel allowed. "But remember that Noah is in the audience."

That man's flood story was nothing compared to the one Noah could have shared. Mrs. White tells us that when we get to heaven, we will try to recall the trials we endured for our faith here on earth, but they will seem like nothing. No matter how bad your problems, there will be someone there whose experiences were worse than yours.

Troubles come to everyone. When your troubles are heavy, your best friend's troubles might be light. But that means that yours will get lighter too in time. Psychologists tell us that whenever we feel uncomfortable, it is because of growth. We feel uncomfortable because we are learning something. No matter what the situation, in time we get comfortable with it. That's good if we are making good progress and learning good things. But it's bad if we are making bad decisions and feeling comfortable with them.

But when bad things happen to us, we must be careful that we don't shut out the whole world and label it "unsafe." In the book *Following the Equator,* Mark Twain is quoted as saying, "One should be careful to get out of an experience only the wisdom that is in it, and stop there, lest we be like the cat that sits down on the hot stove lid. She will never sit down on a hot stove lid again, and that's well; but also she will never sit down on a cold one anymore."

Next time you begin to worry about something, ask yourself why you are uncomfortable. Are you going to learn something good and be helped to grow by going through this trial? Then bear with the temporary discomfort. Identify the good things you can learn. There is no mistake so worthless as the one we learn nothing from.

SEPTEMBER 22

COSTLY MISTAKES

A fool thinks he needs no advice, but a wise man listens to others. Proverbs 12:15, TLB.

As I write this, the last part of the 1988 Tour de France bicycle race is on TV. My husband and sons are watching the race, and I'm trying to ignore the commentator and do my work to meet a deadline. But something the commentator just said has captured my attention. I find myself staring at the TV to watch the instant replay of what must have been the most awful experience of the lead biker's life!

The Tour de France, as you may know, is a bicycle race across France on country roads and through small towns. The race takes about four weeks to finish, but each day's winner is recorded, and the biker with the most winning days is awarded the prize money.

There aren't many spectators along the country roads—a few scattered bunches sprinkled here and there. But in the towns the route is crowded with cheering spectators held back by ribbons and whistle-blowing policemen. A motorcade leads the way. There is no way any biker could go the wrong way. There should be no excuse for a mistake. But as we watched, the biker in the lead just a few miles from the finish line—the evident winner—did not follow the leading motorcade. Instead, when the motorcade turned left, the biker went straight. He whizzed past the whistle-blowing policeman who stood in the street waving his arms to the left to show him the way!

The next biker, just a few feet behind, followed the motorcade and the policeman's directions—and won the race.

Was it the motorcade's fault that the first biker didn't win? No. They both had studied the maps.

Was it the policeman's fault that that biker didn't win? No. The policeman waved his arms continuously, giving the same signal, while all the bikers came through town.

Was it the first biker's cycle that made him lose the race? No. His bicycle was not broken. It was under his command.

It was the biker's own fault that he lost the race. It was his own fault that he lost the prize of several thousand dollars. He wasn't paying attention. Maybe he had put his mind on "automatic" and had stopped thinking. Or maybe he thought he knew the route better than anyone else.

It's easy to question that man's intelligence. But how many of us are ignoring the signs and signals that tell the direction our lives should take? How many of us think that we know the way better than anyone else? How many of us have even stopped thinking about it? It's a dangerous thing to do—to stop thinking. Our race is one that cannot be run again. There will be many winners, but there will be just *one* Second Coming. If you miss out on it, you lose everything!

SEPTEMBER 23

THOSE TEMPTING SCHEMES

Thou shalt love thy neighbour as thyself. Mark 12:31.

Joey and Nathan were taking their dog for a walk one day when suddenly the dog got away from them and ran into the garage of Mr. Watson, their neighbor. While they were retrieving their pet they noticed that Mr. Watson had a neat-looking pair of skis hanging on a side wall next to his lawn mower.

Several weeks went by. Then one morning the two awoke to a winter wonderland! The ground was covered with snow, and school had been canceled for the day. The snow was deep enough that they could go sledding or skiing on the hills near their home—if they had any skis.

"Hey, let's use old Mr. Watson's skis," Joey suggested.

"He's not home, remember? He always leaves for work before we get up," Nathan reminded him.

"Well, he's so nice that I'm sure he wouldn't mind if we just went into his garage and borrowed them, as long as we put them back," Joey insisted. "I know right where they are."

"So do I," Nathan said. "But that wouldn't be right just to take them without asking."

As luck would have it, their mom walked into the room just about then. "You boys and your crazy schemes!" she said. "What would you want someone to do if you were Mr. Watson?"

Joey shrugged, his face warm. "I guess I'd want to be asked."

Mother nodded and left the room.

When Mr. Watson returned home from work that evening, the boys went to his home and asked if they could borrow the skis the next day. "Of course," Mr. Watson said. "In fact, I have another pair of skis in the shed. You can use both pairs so you can ski together."

Joey and Nathan felt good. Things had turned out much better than they could have imagined—all because they had put the Bible's rules into practice.

SEPTEMBER 24

DOES GOD LOVE YOU WHEN YOU'RE BAD?

But it displeased Jonah, . . . and he was very angry. And he prayed unto the Lord. . . . I pray thee, O Lord, was not this my saying? . . . I knew that thou art a gracious God, and merciful, slow to anger, and of great kindness, and repentest thee of the evil. Jonah 4:1, 2.

How would you feel if you had to come face-to-face with someone who had the reputation of being very dangerous? Would you want to try to strike up a friendship, or would you want to stay as far away from him as possible? If you knew that this person was about to be punished for his wrong deeds, would you be glad or sad?

If you had been Jonah, how would you have felt about the people of Nineveh? Let me tell you a little bit about them. Their reputation for being fierce and evil was well deserved, for they had been known to skin their enemies alive. The mere thought must have made Jonah shudder.

But God asked him to go to these terribly cruel people to warn them of their sure destruction if they did not change.

Warn them? Why should God warn them? They deserved to be destroyed! Shouldn't God be willing to destroy such people? Doesn't God hate sinners?

You remember how Jonah went reluctantly to Nineveh and preached, even though he didn't really want the people to be saved. Jonah hated them too much. He preached because God told him to do so, but he didn't expect any results and didn't want any. He fully expected them to be destroyed.

Can you imagine a preacher telling people to change their ways when he is actually hoping they won't? I wonder how Jonah preached. Not very enthusiastically, I can imagine. I don't picture him standing on the street corner shouting the warning. I picture him shuffling down the street, speaking in a voice just loud enough for others to hear, "In 40 days Nineveh will be overturned."

Why might Jonah have been afraid to tell the message out loud and clear?

Because as our text for today says, Jonah knew that God is a loving and forgiving God. He knew that God will forgive people if they ask Him to—even people as wicked and heartless as the people of Nineveh!

Sometimes Satan tries to make me believe that I'm too bad to be forgiven. I imagine he does the same to you. When he suggests to us that God is angry with us and doesn't love us, let's just tell him to stop wasting his time. Our God is a loving God. The God who forgave Nineveh will forgive us, too.

SEPTEMBER 25

HOW TO HELP A DROWNING MAN

Let each of you look out not only for his own interests, but also for the interests of others. Philippians 2:4, NKJV.

Things weren't going well for Max. His business was in financial trouble, his family life was a mess as a result of the pressure, and he realized that financially he was worth more to his family dead than alive.

One day as Max drove home alone in his car, he slowed down on the bridge near his home and finally stopped. He sat silently for a few minutes, listening to the roar of the river below, and then he opened the door of his car and got out. With his mind seemingly on automatic, he walked to the side of the bridge, climbed over the railing, and jumped.

Another man, coming in the opposite direction, saw what Max did. Horrified, he slammed on the brakes, jumped out of his car, loosened his tie, and dashed in after Max. But this man couldn't swim. He thrashed his arms in the water, floundering desperately, realizing too late that his efforts were in vain and that he himself was drowning.

Max *could* swim. Contrary to his expectation, the jump did not kill him. And as he watched the other man—a total stranger—struggling helplessly against the current in an effort to save him, something stirred in Max's heart. Summoning all his strength, he swam over to the man and rescued him. Saving that stranger who had attempted to save his life brought new hope and meaning to Max.

Do you sometimes feel as if you're drowning in problems? Psychiatrists agree with Jesus that the best treatment for anyone who feels he is going to suffer a nervous breakdown is to find someone who is worse off than he is and help him. It really works.

SEPTEMBER 26

JESUS IS A SMART GARDENER

Do not be deceived, God is not mocked; for whatever a man sows, that he will also reap. Galatians 6:7, NKJV.

There is a fable about a farmhand who worked for an evil master. One day the master told the farmhand to plant a field of barley. He acted immediately, preparing the soil, planting the seeds, and cultivating the crops.

After a few weeks, the evil master asked his servants to carry him out to the fields to see how his crop was coming. Astonished to see oats growing instead of barley, he called for the farmhand at once. "You idiot!" he shouted. "I asked you to plant barley, and you planted oats instead. Can't you tell the difference between the two?"

"Oh, yes," the farmhand replied. "But I didn't think it would make any difference what I planted. I figured that even if I planted oats, barley would come up if I wanted it to."

"You're crazy!" the evil master screamed at him. "Where on earth did you get that ridiculous idea?"

The farmhand replied quietly, "I got that idea from you, sir. I've been watching the way you live. I've noticed that even though you are constantly sowing seeds of evil, you expect seeds of virtue to come up."

Someone has said that the cost of living may go up or down, but the cost of sowing wild oats remains the same. You take all of your relationships with you through life. The things you do with your boyfriend or girlfriend will remain in your memory even after you are married, bringing either remorse or joy. Guard your future happiness by sowing the right crops today. Take care of yourself!

271

LIVING WITH A THIEF

Thou shalt not steal. Exodus 20:13.

What would you do if you found a roll of $100 bills lying on a city street? What if you found them on the floor of a department store? What if you found them in the forest? Sometimes it's not easy to know how to make things right. But when the answer is not so difficult, it really feels good to know you're an honest person.

A janitor working in a bank late one night found a small pack of bills lying on the floor, underneath the counter. He picked it up and discovered to his delight that he'd found $1,000. What a find! Was this an answer to his prayer that God would help him support his family? They were in dire need of money!

What do you think the man did? He kept the money. Gratefully he stuffed the pack into his pocket, finished his work, and went home.

When he got home, he went right to bed. But he couldn't sleep. All the things his mother had taught him about honesty kept passing through his head. The next morning when the bank opened, he hurried downtown and rushed into the bank president's office, demanding an appointment.

Throwing the pack of money on the president's desk, he breathlessly told him the whole story. When he had finished, he felt a tremendous sense of relief.

The bank president had listened quietly. Finally he asked, "Why did you return this money? It's not likely we could have traced its loss to you. You could have gotten away with this bonus."

"I am a Christian," the janitor replied, "and even though you might not have known about it, God would have. And besides"—the janitor straightened proudly—"I didn't want to live with a thief!"

THE OWL THAT WINKED

But why do you judge your brother? Or why do you show contempt for your brother? Romans 14:10, NKJV.

It's easy to criticize other people. It's easy to dissect the decisions they make and the things they do. Unfortunately, the person who earns a reputation as a faultfinder also earns a reputation of being insecure and jealous of others. Eventually this bad habit is going to backfire on him.

Consider a young man in New York City who stood outside a taxidermist's store, waiting for a bus. In the window of the store was an owl. It was a beautiful animal, its eyes staring silently out the window at passersby. Without saying a word, the man studied the owl, admiring its beauty. But then a young lady came over to look in the window too.

"Nice owl," she said conversationally.

The man shrugged. "It's not bad. But if that was as good as I could do, I'd find another job."

"What do you mean?" the young lady asked.

"Well, look at it. The head is out of proportion to the body, the pose of the body is unnatural, and the feet are pointing in the wrong direction. I've seen better work than that."

And as they both stared at the bird, it turned its head, ruffled its feathers, and gave the young man a broad wink. The young lady he was trying to impress had the last laugh as the man slunk away.

It's no shame to admit you don't know everything. Rather, it gives other people a chance to share what they know with you! The most popular people are those who encourage others to shine.

SEPTEMBER 29

STRUGGLE FOR LIFE

The hour is coming in which all who are in the graves will hear His voice and come forth. John 5:28, 29, NKJV.

In Hanover, Germany, is the grave of a woman who died before World War I. An atheist, she did not believe in God or the resurrection. She believed that each of us lives only this life, and that is that. Afterward we become litter or garbage.

But perhaps there was a tiny seed of hope in her heart, because in her will she left instructions that her grave was to be covered with granite and marble cemented together and bound by heavy chains. And on her gravestone were inscribed the words "This burial place must never be opened." She almost dared God to resurrect her. What she had not reckoned with was the power God has to give life.

In time a little acorn fell to the ground near the woman's grave. The rains came, the sun shone, and the outer shell of the acorn decayed. The seed sprouted, and a new life—an oak tree—began to grow. Today a massive oak tree stands where that woman's grave is. That massive oak broke the chains that bound the granite and marble together, and moved the stones aside.

God is all-powerful. Someday He will even give life back to that unbelieving woman. Imagine how shocked she is going to be!

273

HOW TO CONQUER SOMETHING DIFFICULT

The steps of good men are directed by the Lord. He delights in each step they take. If they fall it isn't fatal, for the Lord holds them with his hand. Psalm 37:23, 24, TLB.

No doubt you have heard of Anne Morrow Lindbergh, the wife of Charles Lindbergh. She was famous in her own right for her many accomplishments. Perhaps her parents had been able to teach her how to conquer difficult things as a result of something they had learned from a 12-year-old boy.

Mr. and Mrs. Morrow enjoyed traveling through Europe. One day in Rugby, England, they lost their way to the train station to return home. After wandering through the streets for nearly an hour, they realized that they were hopelessly lost. Nothing looked familiar to them; there were no landmarks, nothing.

Mr. Morrow stopped a little boy who was passing by them. "Could you tell us how to get to the train station?" he asked. The boy's reply formed one of Mr. Morrow's guiding principles in his life.

"Well, you turn to the right there by the grocer's shop and then take the second to the left. That will bring you to a place where four streets meet. And then, sir, you had better inquire again."

To Mr. Morrow the boy's answer was a parable of life: "It is best to advance, if only a little way, in the correct, rather than the incorrect, direction." In other words, break up larger tasks into smaller ones.

Studying for a test becomes easier if you break it up into segments: first you have someone quiz you to help you find out what you don't know. Then you make out flash cards for yourself. Then you drill yourself. And then you take your test.

Nobody expects you to know a whole year's work on the first day of school! You take the school year one day at a time, one subject at a time, one chapter at a time, one page at a time, one minute at a time. You can do it, and you can do it well!

IS FORGIVENESS TOO CHEAP?

So overflowing is his kindness towards us that he took away all our sins through the blood of his Son, by whom we are saved. Ephesians 1:7, TLB.

In a rural mining town a minister was once approached by a young man who said he would give anything to believe that God would forgive sins.

"But I cannot believe He will forgive me if I just turn to Him. It's too easy, too cheap," the man said miserably.

"Why do you expect forgiveness to have to hurt?" the minister asked. "You were working in the mine today. How did you get out of the pit?"

"The same way I usually do. I got into the cage and was pulled to the top," the man answered.

"How much did you pay to be pulled out of the pit?" the minister asked.

"I didn't pay anything."

"But weren't you afraid to entrust yourself to that cage? Wasn't it too cheap?" the minister asked.

The man shook his head. "Oh, no! It's a reliable elevator. The company put a lot of money into it, but it was cheap for me. It cost me nothing." As he said it, he realized that it cost God an awful lot to send us Jesus. And because of the investment God has made in us, forgiveness costs us nothing. Even if we don't believe we are forgiven, we are! We can trust Jesus to save us even more than the young miner trusted that elevator to bring him up out of the mine.

OCTOBER 2

ALL THINGS CONSIDERED

Oh, don't worry, I wouldn't dare say that I am as wonderful as these other men who tell you how good they are! Their trouble is that they are only comparing themselves with each other, and measuring themselves against their own little ideas. What stupidity! 2 Corinthians 10:12.

A Peanuts cartoon strip shows Charlie Brown working on a carpentry project one day when Lucy comes by and asks him how the birdhouse is coming along.

In Charlie's inimitable style, he tells her that he's a lousy carpenter, he can't saw or nail straight, and he always splits the wood. Besides that, he says that he is stupid and lacks confidence and good taste and that he has absolutely no sense of design. At last he concludes that all things considered, it's coming along OK.

I would say that given all the things he isn't, it's a wonder he decided to build a birdhouse in the first place! Good for him for trying, anyway.

Have you ever compared yourself to others and felt that you weren't "good enough"? We often think that everyone else seems to have it so much better than we do. They have more money, or better looks, or more self-confidence, or they know the "right people"—and everything seems to be going well for them. They probably seem to be the best Sabbath school leaders, too! Everything—even their Christian life—is going well!

God must be really proud of them, we think. Nearly every Sabbath they praise God by singing solos and performing in duets and trios. They can read Bible texts in class out loud without stumbling. They can give the mission story well. We never get a chance to say anything. We're just too stupid.

Fortunately, God, knowing our history and the history of our ancestors, looks at us and says something like this: "Considering that you are the first person in your family to finish high school, you have a remarkable sense of determination and self-confidence. Everything is going OK." Or He may say, "Considering that your parents were not raised as Christians, you have a remarkable sense of faith in God. All things considered, things are going very well!"

The fact that you are concerned about how well you know Jesus is a good sign. But don't compare yourself to others. They might fail. Nobody becomes a Christian and stays there. He has to choose over and over, day after day, for the rest of his life, to do the "Christian" thing. Christianity is a journey, not a destination. Welcome aboard the most exciting venture of your life!

OCTOBER 3

TOTAL OPPOSITES

I would have you learn this great fact: that a life of doing right is the wisest life there is. Proverbs 4:11, TLB.

When Leonardo da Vinci was painting his masterpiece *The Last Supper,* he searched carefully for a man whose face most closely resembled his vision of what Jesus must have looked like. At last he chose a man by the name of Pietri Bandinelli, a chorister with the Milan Cathedral.

Day after day Pietri sat for Da Vinci, not moving a muscle, staring at one spot on the wall so that the great artist could get every detail perfectly, from the shadows on the face to the folds of the garment. When the artist had finished painting the figure of Jesus, he paid Pietri for his time, excused him, and began searching for other models for the disciples.

The searching and painting went on for several years. At last there was just one character left to paint—the figure of Judas.

Da Vinci again went out into the streets to find a model for Judas, searching each face he passed, looking for someone who most resembled this twisted betrayer. At last he saw a man shuffling along the streets of

Rome with shoulders bent toward the ground, an expression of cold evilness on his face. Da Vinci introduced himself and asked the man if he would mind earning a little money as a model. The man nodded brusquely as Da Vinci gave him the address of his studio.

The morning he arrived at the studio, the bum took his place on the appointed stool and began to look around, as if recalling events of days gone by. Finally he turned, and with a look that told how hard it was to realize the change that had taken place, he said, "Maestro, I was in this studio 25 years ago. I then sat for Christ."

What a wasted life! Poor decisions had aged the man, taken away his purity and his self-confidence. The sadness and remorse stooped his shoulders and changed his image entirely. How important it is to choose carefully. Your future happiness is under your control.

OCTOBER 4

SOMETHING YOU CAN'T IGNORE

May your roots go down deep into the soil of God's marvelous love; and may you be able to feel and understand, as all God's children should, how long, how wide, how deep, and how high his love really is; and to experience this love for yourselves, though it is so great that you will never see the end of it or fully know or understand it. Ephesians 3:17, 18, TLB.

Mr. and Mrs. Robert White, of Advance, Missouri, were traveling through Baton Rouge, Louisiana. As they drove along the highway and up the Mississippi River Bridge, their attention was arrested by a large billboard standing high above the city. On it was a picture of Jesus hanging on the cross, head bowed. And underneath the picture was the statement "It's Your Move!"

What are you going to do about the gift Jesus gave to you? Are you going to take it? Or is it going to be for nothing?

Sadly, many people today don't even give the Crucifixion a thought. A woman stopped by the jewelry section of a New York department store to buy a necklace for her niece. She asked the clerk to show her what they had.

"Do you want a plain gold chain," the clerk asked, "or do you want the one with a little man on it?"

How would you feel if you had done what Jesus did and nobody believed it really happened; if nobody said thank You; if nobody seemed to care? Jesus isn't touchy or proud about what He did, but remember that He is still partly human. He loves you. In fact, you could say that He's crazy about you. He doesn't want to lose you. He might even be wringing

His hands over you, hoping you will move toward Him, wishing He could force you to love Him. But He doesn't force anyone. It's your move.

IT'S ALL IN YOUR HEAD

I have loved you even as the Father has loved me. Live within my love. John 15:9, TLB.

For centuries doctors have known that much of our sickness is all in our heads. Some perfectly healthy people actually do feel sick unless they are taking some sort of medication. When I worked as a psychiatric nurse, it was not uncommon to give patients what is called a placebo—a pill that is nothing more than sugar, or a shot that is often nothing more than salt water.

I remember one patient who came in again and again, complaining of back pain. He was a man in his 40s, with scars and tough areas all over his arms, legs, and hips where shots had been given for years. He had eventually become addicted to pain shots, and would come in complaining that his back was killing him when he actually just wanted more pain shots.

At last his doctor decided he was going to cure this man of his addiction. Rather than actually giving him a pain shot, we tried a saline, or salt water, injection. It was hard for me to look serious as I gave my routine explanation that I had given him his shot and that it should start working within 10 minutes. I felt a bit dishonest. He was no dummy. The first time he got a shot, he commented that it didn't sting. I brushed it off lightly with a joke about my technique being very good. But when the next shot didn't sting either, he became angry and demanded to talk to the doctor.

The doctor changed the shots to plain sterile water. Those shots stung. For about three days we got by with making the patient think that the water shots were helping his pain. But then he guessed our trick, and they didn't "help" anymore. That was 18 years ago. I don't know what ever happened to him, but he clearly didn't need the medication; he just wanted someone to care.

There are lots of things in life that we think we need. Most of them are just placebos. They don't bring real happiness or relief from this world's pain. The only real cure is faith in Jesus and a friendship with Him.

THE BEST ADVERTISING

We talked to you as a father to his own children—don't you remember?—pleading with you, encouraging you and even demanding that your daily lives should not embarrass God, but bring joy to him who invited you into his kingdom to share his glory. 1 Thessalonians 2:11, 12, TLB.

A number of years ago, near what is known as the Kingsport Press in Tennessee, the southbound bus made scheduled midday stops of 20 minutes so that passengers might freshen up and get a bite to eat.

As he brought his bus to a stop, one driver said, "Folks, we'll be stopping here for 20 minutes. This line makes it a strict policy never to recommend an eating place by name, but if anybody wants to see me while we're here, I'll be eating a wonderful T-bone steak with french fries at Tony's first-class, spotlessly clean diner directly across the street." With that remark he slowly sauntered into the tiny but tidy restaurant.

Naturally, many of the passengers on the bus took his advice and went into the eating establishment. It came as no surprise to them that the meals they ordered were very good.

You are a walking advertisement for your religion. If you walk happily into your church on Sabbath morning, your neighbors can see that you highly recommend your religion. But if you fuss and fight as you get into the car on your way to church, and then again when you arrive home after church, they may wonder if it did you any good after all. People are watching, whether you know it or not. You are a walking advertisement for your God.

NUMBER MAGIC

[Jesus] created everything there is—nothing exists that he didn't make. John 1:3, TLB.

I've got this crazy habit of adding up numbers. Whenever I see a license plate, I automatically add up all the numbers to see if they equal an odd or an even number. People with even totals on their license plates are supposedly good people, but you have to watch out for the odds! I also watch for number sequences. For instance, I really get excited if I see one license plate with, say, the numbers 689 driving right next to a license plate with the numbers exactly in reverse—986—or some other similar sequence!

I don't know when I started doing this, but I have discovered in the process that numbers are fascinating! There is a spiritual lesson to be derived from numbers, too. It's a fact that when you add up two odd numbers, you will always come up with an even number. That translates into "all things work together for good to them that love God," as far as I am concerned. The odd numbers equal things in life that aren't even or fair. They have their place. When they are all added together, they come out OK in the end.

The number 9 has always been one of my favorite numbers because my original name, Nancy Beck, has nine letters in it. I have discovered something interesting about the number 9: you can't sink it! If you write out your times tables for nine (9 X 1 = 9, 9 X 2 = 18, 9 X 3 = 27, and so on), you discover that when you add the individual numbers of the total together, they equal nine. For example, 9 X 2 = 18, and 1 + 8 = 9; 9 X 3 = 27, and 2 + 7 = 9. Isn't that fun?

Now what would you think is God's favorite number? I think one of God's favorite numbers is 7. The number 7 is for the Sabbath. That is also the number of clean animals Noah took into the ark. That is the number of times Joshua walked around the city of Jericho. That is also how many days it is going to take us to get to heaven after Jesus comes. And there's more!

Dr. George A. Miller, conducting a study for the Office of Naval Research, discovered that the average person can remember accurately only seven items on any list read to him.

Dr. Miller offers this intriguing suggestion: Perhaps since the human memory is limited to seven items, this might explain why the number 7 crops up so often—the seven wonders of the world, the seven notes of the musical scale, the seven seas, the seven deadly sins, seven ages of man. I think it shows that God is a God of order and that He is in charge. How about you?

OCTOBER 8

YOUR WEIGHT IN DIAMONDS

"They shall be mine," says the Lord of Hosts, "in that day when I make up my jewels." Malachi 3:17, TLB.

A personal notice in the Dayton *News* shared this exciting announcement: "The staff of LeRoy's Keepsake Diamond Center wishes to congratulate our office girl on the birth of her baby boy, who weighed in at 18,176 carats." That was a valuable baby boy!

And I think that God looks at us in similar terms. We are not just humans—we are jewels to Him! Even though we may think we are of no value.

A gentleman who went to church every week became seriously ill. But as he lay in bed, he worried that he didn't feel much love for God in his heart. He searched for some feeling that he loved God. But there was none.

With that thought on his mind, he welcomed his best friend into his home and immediately shared his concern with him. "I don't know how to love God," he worried.

The friend smiled. "When I go home from here, I expect to take my baby on my knee, look into her sweet eyes, listen to her charming prattle, and tired as I am, her presence will rest me, for I love that child with unutterable tenderness. But she loves me little.

"If my heart were breaking, it would not disturb her sleep. If my body were racked with pain, it would not interrupt her play. If I were dead, she would forget me in a few days.

"Besides this, she has never brought me a penny, but is a constant expense to me. I am not rich, but there is not enough money in the world to buy my baby.

"How is it? Does she love me, or do I love her? Do I withhold my love until I know she loves me? Am I waiting for her to do something worthy of my love before I give it to her? No, I love her simply because she is mine."

The sick gentleman closed his eyes as a tear slipped out from under his lids. "I see," he whispered. "It is God's love I should be thinking about now, and not my own. And when I realize how fully He loves, I cannot help loving Him back!"

God loves you. Whether or not your life is lived for Him, He will always love you. Whether or not you feel that you are loved by God, you are! Love is not a feeling, it is a decision. God has chosen to love you. You are a valuable jewel that He does not want to lose!

YOU CAN'T EXHAUST GOD'S STOREHOUSE!

And because of Abraham's faith God forgave his sins and declared him "not guilty." Romans 4:22, TLB.

When the famous preacher Charles Spurgeon was riding home one evening after a heavy day's work and was feeling very weary and depressed, the verse "My grace is sufficient for thee" came to him. How could God's grace be so grand? Surely he would at last come to a point at which he would make one mistake too many and God would say "Sorry! That's more sins than I can forgive. I have just run out of grace."

But then Spurgeon thought of all the little fishes in the Thames River. "Why, I am being as ridiculous as an apprehensive little fish who worries that he will drink the river dry," he said. "It's as if the River Thames said to me, 'Drink all you want, little fish! My river is sufficient for thee.' And so it is—I cannot drink the river dry."

And then he thought of a little mouse in the granaries of Joseph in Egypt, afraid lest it might—by daily visits to the corn bins—exhaust the supplies and starve to death. Joseph would stand by the bins and say with a smile, "Eat up, my little friend. My bins are sufficient for thee!"

Or suppose he was a mountain climber breathing heavily as he neared the top, fearing he might consume all the oxygen in the air if he breathed too fast. And God would say, "Breathe away! Fill your lungs! My atmosphere is sufficient for thee!"

And Spurgeon smiled a deep, satisfied smile. He saw that God does not get exhausted. God never runs dry; He creates more and more of what is His. His forgiveness never runs out. As a bumper sticker said so well: "A Christian is not perfect; he is forgiven."

Adapted from Paul Lee Tam, *Encyclopedia of 7700 Illustrations.*

OCTOBER 10

DISGUISED KINDNESS

We can justify our every deed but God looks at our motives. Proverbs 21:2, TLB.

The Highway Department of the state of Florida is supposed to keep its roads beautiful and maintain the trees and shrubs planted along the major highways. When they discovered one morning that vandals had destroyed some expensive palms in front of one of the billboards, the supervisor of the department was angry. Because of budget cuts, there was no money to replace the palms. There was no money even to remove the ugly stumps and clean up the place.

The story was carried on the evening news, and donations and volunteers were requested to clean up the mess. To the Highway Department's delight, Eastern Airlines offered to pay the entire cost of cleaning up the debris and replanting new palms where the old ones had stood.

The job was done quickly. The new palms were even bigger than the old ones. The new palms were so large, in fact, that they effectively blocked out the billboard on which a rival airlines was advertising at the time!

Do you think Eastern Airlines actually meant to help? Or did they see an opportunity to seem caring while actually being selfish? Have you ever done that? Have you ever helped someone else make a fool of himself and then laughed at him afterward?

Dope peddlers do this. And anyone who urges you to drink alcohol really wants to laugh in your face. Anyone who tells you to *prove* your love only wants to laugh at you later.

Real friends don't make you prove anything. Real friends don't enjoy watching you make a fool of yourself. Real friends watch out for each other. Real friends are few and far between, but each one is a treasure!

OCTOBER 11

JIMMY'S SURPRISE

For long ago the Lord had said to Israel: I have loved you, O my people, with an everlasting love; with lovingkindness I have drawn you to me. Jeremiah 31:3, TLB.

Have you ever been in an actual hurricane? In the area around the Philippines they have *typhoons*, severe windstorms that are similar to hurricanes. During a typhoon the wind blows in from the ocean with such tremendous power that small fish are blown in with the water and end up in shallow pools that are formed around the exposed roots of trees and other low-lying, bowl-shaped areas.

A typhoon can destroy an entire village of thatched-roof huts in minutes. But along with the destruction comes a blessing—the hundreds of fish so conveniently waiting to be caught. As the grownups rebuild their thatched huts, the children take baskets throughout the village and pick up the fish from the muddy holes.

One day a little boy named Jimmy was busy going from mudhole to mudhole, feeling all around for the fish. He had a technique of reaching for the fish's tail first, and then feeling along the fish's body for the gills. Hooking his fingers in the gills, he would pull the fish up out of the mud and place it in his basket.

In the muddy pool around a big jackfruit tree, Jimmy felt what seemed to be an unusually large fish. He began to feel around in the mud for the fish's tail. There was none. Carefully he squeezed what seemed to be the fish's body, following it closer and closer to the tree, feeling for the gills. There were none! But when he got right up to the trunk of the tree, he discovered, to his horror, that the ugly face of a python was staring right into his! The huge snake's black forked tongue darted wildly in and out of its brown, scaly mouth! Its body was coiled around the trunk of the tree. And its tail, which Jimmy had been squeezing, had disappeared into the mud.

283

Jimmy screamed. Then, leaving his basket behind, he raced for home to find his mother. She was a devout Muslim. Upon hearing Jimmy's story, she declared that Jimmy's life had been spared by Allah for a special purpose. Jimmy searched for that purpose as he grew up. He felt very special. He wanted to really make something of his life—and he did. He became an Adventist minister.

Your life is just as sacred, just as special. You are somebody to God!

POOR LITTLE COW

Here on earth you will have many trials and sorrows; but cheer up, for I have overcome the world. John 16:33, TLB.

Connie Beck, one of my favorite cousins, was lucky enough to grow up on the Beck family farm with three sisters and one brother. Each time we would visit North Dakota, we would make sure we stopped at Uncle Benny's farm for some real farm life—horseback riding, wild potato digging, cow milking, hay climbing, and weiner roasting. I loved being with all my cousins, but Connie was special because she made sure that we all got to do a bit of everything; she was the "activities director" of our stay.

It was Connie who patiently showed me how to milk a cow. It was Connie who rode the horse double with me because I wanted to see what it felt like to gallop but was afraid to do it alone. And it was Connie who assured me that her pet cow was safe to ride.

I was scared of cows. But Connie's pet was gentle. She had been treated like a puppy since she was born. Her tail had been accidentally pulled off by the kids but she was still gentle and let us ride her. I could see by the way she responded to Connie that the two of them had a very special relationship.

I never knew what happened to that cow until a family reunion in June 1988. Connie and I were talking about our visits to the farm. When I asked about the cow, she said that because of that cow, she became a vegetarian. She had come home from school one day and had gone out to the barn to see her pet cow, but she was gone. The cow never wandered away, so Connie flew back into the house to ask her mother where it was. Hesitantly, her mother told her that the cow was dead. Her father had decided that the cow had outlived its usefulness as a pet and must now become food for the family.

To Connie, the thought of eating her pet was enough to make her swear to vegetarianism from that moment forward. When the family ate steak—her pet cow's contribution—Connie couldn't stand to be at the table. Suddenly meat eating became a terribly cruel thing to do.

Think for a moment about Adam and Eve when they killed their first lamb. What an ugly moment that must have been—a difficult and excruciatingly painful moment—as they killed a trusting lamb they had cared for since it was born. Death is the result of sin. Sin is ugly—and painful. But someday it will be gone for good.

WHAT TO DO IF YOU MAKE A MISTAKE

Young man, it's wonderful to be young! Enjoy every minute of it! Do all you want to; take in everything, but realize that you must account to God for everything you do. Ecclesiastes 11:9, TLB.

One of the exciting benefits of growing up is learning to make decisions and to take responsibility for the consequences. It's always easier in the short term to blame somebody else for your mistakes. But in the long view those who blame others without taking responsibility for their own actions will never be leaders. And worse than that, they won't enjoy living with themselves.

A student nurse was awakened from sleep one night during World War II and told that she had to assist in surgery right away, as there were some casualties coming in.

She dressed quickly and rushed to the hospital. Throwing on her surgical clothes, she hurried to set up the operating room. The patient was already being wheeled in, and the doctors were impatient. It was an emergency, and tensions were high.

"Wash the wound!" the surgeon yelled over his shoulder as he rushed from the room to scrub his hands.

The young girl opened a bottle of sterile water and poured it into the nearest basin. Picking up some gauze, she turned to wash the wound as the doctor had demanded. But suddenly she realized that she had poured the water into a nonsterile basin! The rules of surgery and infection control forbade her from using it.

Her heart pounded in her ears. Nobody would know she had used a contaminated basin. She paused only a moment. But she would! As she hurried past the surgeon to the cupboard for a new bottle of water and another basin, she tried to explain what she had done. "I'm sorry, sir. I have to get another basin of water. I haven't washed the wound yet."

The surgeon reacted just as she'd feared. With an oath, he shouted that she was incompetent. But he couldn't send her away, for no other nurse was available.

Surgery was delayed by only a few minutes. The doctor was quick and skilled, and the student nurse stood at his side, handing him instruments. It wasn't until surgery was over that she had a chance to see the patient's face. She gasped and her breath caught in her throat, for the patient was her mother, the one who had taught her through childhood to keep a clear conscience, no matter what the cost.

How do you suppose the student felt? How would she have felt if she had simply gone ahead and used the contaminated water to clean the wound?

Admitting your mistakes is embarrassing. Sometimes, admitting your mistakes is downright disgraceful. But in the long run you will be trusted and respected. But more important, you will like yourself. And that's a good way to feel.

OCTOBER 14

DRAMATIC CONCLUSIONS

But the Holy Spirit tells us clearly that in the last times some in the church will turn away from Christ and become eager followers of teachers with devil-inspired ideas. 1 Timothy 4:1, TLB.

Twelve-year-old Jason knew the plots of all the latest movies in town. One day as he explained each one to his mother, she listened in surprise. "How do you know all this?" she asked. "We don't go to movies!"

"Oh, all my friends at school go, and they tell me. It's cool, Mom. I don't want to be totally square, you know, and since you won't let me go, I have to find out somehow!"

"Why do you have to know the plots and imaginations of movie-makers?" his mother teased. "You have the best imagination I know. You come up with some pretty good stuff yourself."

Jason lifted the lid on the cookie jar. "Oh, it's OK, Mom. Don't worry."

But Mom worried. In the next few days she thought about the movies Jason had told her about. All of them treated immorality lightly, as though it were something to be winked at. They were filled with swear words and took the name of God in vain. The heroes took all the credit for their conquests. If they'd had to use and abuse other people to get to the top, it was OK—something they had to do. Each characteristic was directly opposite Jesus' example. Silently, subtly, the devil's philosophies were being planted in the minds of those who watched.

Mom had to agree that many TV programs were just as bad. In fact, some movies were less objectionable than many TV shows. So it wasn't so much a matter of where you watched a movie as what you watched. Even the best stories totally left God out of their plots. Friendships were mended, problems resolved, all without God's help. But paying to watch a movie added the sting of expense to the undermining of a pure character.

Jason's classmates hadn't always gone to movies. But once they began going, they became more and more careless about what they saw. Now they went regularly to every new movie that came to town. Few bothered to consider the content. Few stopped to think about the violence and silliness they saw week after week. Why did that always happen? Where would it end?

Nobody knows right now. The end of the story hasn't been written yet, but the "dramatic conclusion" is coming soon. Have movies been distracting you from getting ready to be with Jesus? Will what you watch on TV or in the theaters be a burden on your conscience during the time of trouble? It's your choice. You control the knob. You control your feet.

A FEW GREAT PEOPLE

Trust in the Lord with all your heart, and lean not on your own understanding. In all your ways acknowledge him, and he will make your paths straight. Proverbs 3:5, 6, NIV.

How would you feel if you were made president, or prime minister, or chancellor of your country? Have you ever thought of yourself as the leader of your country? Of course, you would have to be a few years older than you are now, but someday, if the world lasts long enough, you could be . . . who knows? Does this thought scare you, or delight you?

The Bible tells us about a young man who was out looking for his father's donkeys when the prophet Samuel told him he would be the new king of Israel. Saul was such a timid young man that when the people tried to make him king, he hid behind their suitcases. He did not feel qualified for the job.

Saul did not feel as if he was great enough or special enough to be king, for he knew that he was just an ordinary man. Yet as long as Saul did not trust in himself but trusted in God, great things were accomplished through him.

You may not feel very great. In fact, chances are, you feel very ordinary. But don't forget that you are made in the image of God! You are special, and if you trust in God, He will do something great through your life. You don't have to be talented. You don't have to be slim. You don't have to be handsome or beautiful. You don't have to be popular. All you must be is committed to your Friend Jesus, and be willing to do the great things He has in mind for you.

Let this year, 1990, be a year of discovery, when you discover each day what great things God has in mind especially for you!

FIND OUT WHO YOU ARE

For you created my inmost being; you knit me together in my mother's womb. I praise you because I am fearfully and wonderfully made; your works are wonderful. I know that full well. Psalm 139:13, NIV.

Our text today says that when you think you aren't special, you are insulting God. That's right, God is insulted when you put yourself down. You see, you are His creation, and when you say "I'm not very good," or when you look at someone else and say they aren't very good, you are saying that God's creation is not very good.

Once there were three cars parked side by side in a parking lot. Strange as it may seem to you, these cars were discussing the meaning of life. The car on the left tooted his horn to get the attention of the others and then asked what they thought was the greatest achievement in life.

The car on the far right crouched low to the ground and purred a quick answer. "Life has meaning," he said, "when you are racing down a deserted freeway at 250 miles per hour. The wind tugs at your hood, and you feel as if you are literally flying. If you can't do that, then you really aren't worth anything!"

The car in the middle jiggled up and down in disdain. "That's a rotten answer," he said. "It's too limited. Where are you going to find a deserted freeway, anyway? Real living means that you get away from freeways and highways and test yourself against the rugged natural land. You really know how tough you are when you cross swift rivers and climb steep mountains. When you roll over logs and tip sideways going over rocks. That is what separates the cars from the go-carts!"

The car that had first posed the question sighed a deep sigh of superiority. His windshield wipers swiped back and forth as he said, "You two really have shallow values. Whatever happened to service and love? Real meaning in life comes from belonging to a family. It comes from taking kids to school and from hauling groceries home. Real meaning in life is when you take the family to the beach for a picnic on a nice summer day. Life is lived through relationships and belonging!"

Now, breaking away from the cars, let me ask you, which car was right? Which car had the right idea of what life was all about? Did you say the last car?

Actually, all three cars were correct. You see, the first car was built and designed for racing. The second car was a four-wheel-drive high-clearance vehicle designed for off-road driving, and the last car was a beautiful four-door station wagon.

The racing car was great at high speeds, but terrible off the road. The four-wheel drive vehicle was great off-road, but unstable at high speeds. And the station wagon was great for hauling things around, but it couldn't race or drive through the woods very well. Each car was created for a different purpose and therefore was made differently.

God made you for a specific purpose. You are not like anyone else. You have gifts and abilities that God needs to make His work here on earth successful. So stop looking at others and wishing you were more like them. Praise God for who you are. Find out what it is He has designed you for, and become all that God has in mind for you to be.

OCTOBER 17

WHAT KEEPS PEOPLE OUT OF HEAVEN?

Listen now! The Lord isn't too weak to save you. And he isn't getting deaf! He can hear you when you call! But the trouble is that your sins have cut you off from God. Isaiah 59:1, 2, TLB.

She was a sprightly little woman in her 70s with an estate-type mansion overlooking beautiful Green Lake in Seattle, Washington. She needed summer help, and I, at 17, needed a job. She was looking for someone like me to be her companion, to drive her to town for groceries, and to drive her around in the evenings in her antique Cadillac convertible. She was offering $100 per week to the lucky young woman who would accept the job.

My mother went with me for an interview. We found all the furniture in her black-tiled drawing room covered with white sheets, but when she heard I played, she pulled back a corner on the sheet covering the shiny grand piano and suggested I could give her concerts some evenings if we had nothing else to do. She took us upstairs and showed me the room that would be mine. It held a canopy bed and a high, soft mattress that reminded me of the legend of the princess and the pea. The room had its own covered balcony, which overlooked the lake.

All the time the little lady showed us around, she kept saying, "Aren't we having fun?" with a little giggle. I wondered if she said that all the time.

She seemed a very dear person, but in the end I decided not to take the job. I preferred to spend the summer at home, since I'd been in boarding schools since the eighth grade.

I suppose it would have been different if I had known and loved the funny little lady, if she'd been part of my family. But I didn't know her. So no matter how lovely her house or how much money I could make by living there, and no matter how much fun it would have been to cruise the streets in her Cadillac convertible, I wouldn't have been happy there.

I think that's why God, in His love, will choose to take only those who love Him out of this world to heaven. The others, who hate Him or don't have time for Him, won't be happy there. It's not unfair that they won't get to go. It's giving them what they want. Like a doting parent, God wants to give you what you want. Which will it be?

OCTOBER 18

YOU DON'T NEED POINTS

Salvation is not a reward for the good we have done, so none of us can take any credit for it. Ephesians 2:9, TLB.

The famous artist Degas witnessed one of his pictures being sold at an auction for $100,000. When asked how he felt, he replied, "I feel as a horse must feel when the beautiful cup is given to the jockey."

There's no greater letdown than anticipating an honor and then being left out.

When I was little, my Sabbath school teacher spent a lot of time stressing that every soul we won to Christ would be a star in our heavenly crowns. She often asked, "How will you feel if someone else has more stars than you do? In heaven everyone will know how active you were for Jesus."

Many years have passed, and today I disagree with her. How could heaven be a happy place if we're jealously comparing crown size and number of stars with each other? There won't be rivalry in heaven. And besides, getting there doesn't depend on how many souls we've won to Christ. But perhaps my teacher's philosophy still lurks somewhere in my subconscious, as evidenced by the following story.

I was the cradle roll Sabbath school leader at the time, and we had a routine of having a short program for our babies and then an adult lesson discussion while the babies played on the floor. I led out in the lesson, and after each one, a certain young woman expressed her appreciation and said she always felt as though she understood God in a new light as a result of the day's discussion.

After some months, she asked the pastor for Bible studies and eventually planned to be baptized. I was so happy! This was the first person I felt I'd had a direct influence on—the first known "star in my crown."

Before her baptism, the pastor read a list of people this young woman wanted to thank for leading her to Christ. These people were to stand. I got ready, but my name wasn't called. I'm ashamed to say that I felt like the horse must feel when the cup is given to the jockey! All those months of leading meaningful Sabbath school discussions, and I didn't get even honorable mention! It didn't seem fair.

But as I often do, I thought about it and decided it was best that I was not mentioned, because my motives were wrong. I wanted to be given credit for leading her to Jesus, but He was the one who had done the work. Thank God, I can still go to heaven if I love Him. We're not saved because we are good, but because God is good.

THANKS, BUT NO THANKS!

If a man loudly blesses his neighbor early in the morning, it will be taken as a curse. Proverbs 27:14, NIV.

When is a door not a door? Think about it for a minute. When is a door not a door? When it's ajar, of course! When is a car not a car? Ah, yes. When it turns into a driveway!

That's enough of those silly riddles. But there are times in life when things really are not what they seem to be. For instance, when does something good become bad?

As you think of our text today, can you picture a man getting up early in the morning, before anyone else is awake, then walking down his neighborhood street, shouting at the top of his lungs, "Good morning, neighbors!"

Later that day, in court for disturbing the peace and being a public nuisance, our friend the early bird whines, "But Your Honor, I was just being friendly! Since when is it a crime to be friendly to your neighbors?"

Is it wrong to say "Good morning, neighbors"? Is it wrong to wish your neighbor well? No, of course not, unless you forget to think about their well-being when you do it. Even acts of kindness can become cruel if they are done at the wrong time or in the wrong place.

Learn to think before you act. Try to imagine what it must feel like to be the kid who sits next to you in math class. What is your grandma's life like today? What does she need or want? If you were in her shoes, what would you need or appreciate? When you know that answer, you are ready to be a real friend.

When does something good become something bad? When that something good makes someone sad.

When does something good become better? When that something good creates a memory you treasure. Do good things at the right time in 1990.

WHY DO BAD THINGS HAPPEN TO GOOD PEOPLE?

For when I am weak, then I am strong—the less I have, the more I depend on him. 2 Corinthians 12:10, TLB.

Sometimes when troubles come, our first reaction is to ask "Why me?" We imply "Why is God against me? Why is He hurting me like this?" as though God strikes people at random with pain or sorrow just because He feels like it.

When good things happen, however, it's easy to forget God's help and care. When we make a good grade or hit a home run, how often do we say "Why me?" Do you ever question why you should be so lucky as to have so many good things happen to you? Is it because you have earned it?

Do you deserve to be happy because you go to church regularly? Do you deserve to be happy because you're good looking or are nice to others? Whatever good things you may have done, my guess is that every reason you may give for deserving happiness should have applied to Jesus, too. Certainly He didn't deserve to be unhappy or ill-treated—but He was.

Whether or not a life is filled with one good thing after another has no bearing on whether or not a person is close to God. Even healthful-living Adventist Christians get sick and die before they have lived to old age. Christians have house fires and lose their children. Does that mean God isn't with them? Of course not! The only difference between a Christian and a non-Christian in tragedy is how he or she responds to God. Ever since Job had his problems and his wife told him to curse God, Satan has been trying to make us all blame God for the world's troubles. It's not fair. Satan brings the trouble, and God gets the blame.

When I have trouble and discouragement—and believe me, adults have discouragements too—I try to see through it to the cause: Satan is trying to turn me against God. And though I may not feel as if God is near me at all, I make myself get down on my knees and I pray. We are told that Satan flees when he sees us praying. The result has been that when I am discouraged, I spend more time with God than when things are going well. In that way, "when I am weak, then I am strong."

When I get up off my knees, I don't always feel any different; but I know I have shown Satan whose side I am on. And I have shown myself, too. That makes me happy, and I see my problem in a new light. Though it may still be there, I know I'm not the only one carrying it. It feels good to depend on God. We all need a little help from Someone "out of this world."

ARE YOU A GOOD FRIEND?

A friend loves at all times, and a brother is born for adversity. Proverbs 17:17, NIV.

Have you ever felt lonely? Have you ever felt that nobody cared about you? That nobody would ever like you?

One day Ralph was riding his bicycle down a long hill near his house. Sometimes Ralph amused himself by seeing how fast he could pedal down that hill. His bicycle tires hummed comfortably as he pedaled hard. The crisp fall wind pulled at his hair, and hot tears stung his eyes.

Ralph was lonely. His family had just moved to a new town, and Ralph didn't know anybody! Sure, Ralph had fun riding his bike. But he missed his old friends.

Suddenly he heard something. His feet swung backward, locking up the rear brake. His back tire squealed as it traced a curving black line on the road behind him. Was someone calling his name? Yes, he heard voices yelling "Ralph! Ralph!" For a moment he was back home again, and his friends were calling for him to come play ball. Then Ralph snapped back to reality. Nobody around here knew his name. He was alone—and so lonely! But there it was again. Someone was yelling his name!

Ralph turned his head to look behind him. There in that ball field beside the church were about 20 kids his own age. They were waving to him and calling his name. One of the kids had met him, he realized, and had told the others his name. "Hey, Ralph! Come play ball with us."

Ralph smiled. Suddenly he didn't feel lonely anymore. Why not look for someone lonely today and be a friend to him? How many friends can you gain in 1990?

I HATE TO BE SHY

If there is any excellence, if there is anything worthy of praise, think about these things. Philippians 4:8, RSV.

Jan was considered by the girls at school to be one of the wittiest, most likeable kids around. For Jan Rowland had a quick—and funny—retort to almost anything. She was genuine, too, just the kind of friend who could cheer anybody up! That's how her girlfriends knew her. But when she got around the boys, she couldn't think of anything to say.

"I hate to be shy!" she would moan afterward.

Shyness comes in varying degrees. Some kids are so shy, they won't ask the librarian for help in finding a book. On the other hand, some don't mind asking for help in the library, but they wouldn't think of talking to someone they don't know very well. Others can strike up a conversation anywhere, but when they get around someone they really want to impress, they don't know what to say.

Sometimes even famous people are shy! Experts tell us that shyness is caused by thinking that everything we do is a performance. Shy people feel that the whole world is their judge, and they are afraid that those with whom they come in contact aren't going to like what they do or say. So they find it hard to say anything.

If you are shy, you need to give yourself a "love pat." Remind yourself that you have value independent of your latest achievement, your looks, or your parents' income. Jesus died for you. You are special! Then think on the bright side. Rather than imagining what you'll do if someone doesn't return your greetings, picture them smiling at you and thinking how friendly you are. Remind yourself of past successes. Can you remember the time you spoke to a little child and his mother beamed? Can you remember a time you just smiled at someone without saying anything and his or her eyes lit up? That is a feeling that is out of this world.

You'll always find someone who is more scared than you are, someone who is shier than you, someone who needs *your* smile. Find that person. Don't say negative things about yourself; say positive things—about yourself and others. Then think about those things. That's how you can get over being shy.

OCTOBER 23

CONFIDENCE IN GOD'S LOVE

For I am convinced that neither death nor life, neither angels nor demons, neither the present nor the future, nor any powers, neither height nor depth, nor anything else in all creation, will be able to separate us from the love of God that is in Christ Jesus our Lord. Romans 8:38, 39, NIV.

In the evening I would walk over to meet her. My step was quick; my heart was light. She was the love of my life. She would be practicing the piano, and I would quietly watch her from the door. I loved her adorable little nose, so cute and pointed. She had pretty blue eyes and such a slim little waist. I really liked her!

After a few minutes of watching from the door, I would enter the practice room and slide next to her on the piano bench. My arm would almost automatically slip around her waist and sometimes I would lean over and whisper those three special words into her ear, the words she loved to hear: "I love you."

She'd finish practicing, and we'd walk together from the music building toward the cafeteria and supper. As we walked, I remember wondering to myself exactly what I meant when I said "I love you." Did it mean that I was proud of her, that she made my heart beat faster and my palms sweaty? Did it mean that she made me feel different than I'd ever felt before?

Since those days I have discovered what love means. When I tell my wife "I love you," I am saying that she is as important to me as I am important to myself. When she is happy, I am happy; when she is sad, I share her sorrow. When something hurts her, it hurts me, too. I live for her, and I am dedicated to her well-being.

Jesus showed us what love means by dying to save us. Now He shows us what love is all about by caring for our needs and sharing our joys and sorrows. Whether or not we love God, He keeps on loving us.

In fact, there is nothing that can separate God's love from you—He loves you, no matter what you do!

MENDING BROKEN FRIENDSHIPS

If your brother . . . repents, forgive him. If he sins against you seven times in a day, and seven times comes back to you and says, "I repent," forgive him. Luke 17:3, 4, NIV.

A funny thing happened at the skating rink in January of 1986. I fell and broke my elbow. It wasn't funny to me, of course, but I'm sure that seeing a grown woman thud on the floor like a sack of potatoes must have been amusing to those watching! Luckily, it didn't hurt too much. In fact, after I fell, I got up and skated some more, and it wasn't until I tried to put on my coat and go home that I realized I couldn't straighten my arm. After some consideration, we decided to go to the hospital, where X-rays confirmed a broken elbow.

It wasn't a good time for a broken right arm! I had just given my word that I could have this book finished in eight months, and I lacked 30 pages of being finished with another book that I wanted to complete first. But with a broken right arm, that meant that all typing had to be done with one hand—my left one!

Well, I won't bore you with details except to say that I did get the other book typed—in three days, no less—and I discovered all sorts of other new ways to do things: like buttering toast by holding the knife in the hand with the splint and moving the toast around and around with the other hand. My kids had to tie my shoes, cut my baked potato, and take on many more chores.

Since I'd never broken a bone before, the splint was a bit of a novelty at first, but I soon became tired of it. I missed my strong right hand! The doctor said I might not have full use of it even after the bone had healed—that it might never straighten at the elbow like it used to.

I guess whenever things change dramatically in our lives, we tend to get philosophical about it, and I found all sorts of philosophical things to which I likened the situation. But most of all, I was reminded of how the loss or estrangement of a friend feels. Sure, you can go on with your life, but it's just not the same. And to wait while the break heals is sometimes harder than anything else.

Trust is a gift that we and our friends loan to each other. If one betrays that trust, it isn't always easy to get it back. We watch the friend cautiously, and the relationship goes back to "first base" until the trust is reearned. And that happens through an apology and consistent kindness.

It is a divine thing to say "I'm sorry." We don't do it naturally, but God puts the need in us to make things right. If you need to make something right with a friend, don't resist God's reminder. Do it today.

OCTOBER 25

THEY'RE WATCHING YOU!

For He shall give His angels charge over you, to keep you in all your ways. Psalm 91:11, NKJV.

Just because you can't see something doesn't mean it's not there. Angels are unseen yet present, and I take God's word for it that they're there—something like radio waves or magnetism. It won't be until we get to heaven that we learn of the many times our angels took special care of us. I have often wondered how it would be if our angels talked with us now. Can you imagine hearing a chuckle after a near calamity? "Whew! That was a close one!" your angel might say.

This reminds me of a couple stories I've heard about human "angels."

Melody sat on her front porch steps, head in her hands. Behind the open screen door, people talked in hushed voices. Her mother had explained it, but it didn't make a lot of sense to Melody. While away on a business trip, Daddy had been in a terrible accident, and he wouldn't be coming home anymore.

Cars drew up in front of the house and women carried in covered dishes. Some of them patted Melody's shoulder or ran their hands through her dark curls. Several told her that she should be brave, that she was her mother's big girl now. But Melody didn't feel big. She felt scared and alone. Other people hurried past as though she didn't exist.

"Melody!"

She raised tear-brimming eyes at the sound of her name. Her best friend, Jennifer, stood before her, tears streaming down her cheeks. "I'm so sorry, Melody," she whispered. "I just heard about your daddy."

Without another word, Jennifer sat on the steps beside her friend and stayed there all afternoon. She didn't talk, for she didn't need to. Years later Melody told the story. "She comforted me in a way that nobody else did. She cried with me. She cried with me all afternoon."

Melody couldn't see her angel's tears, but she could see Jennifer's. And she was comforted.

Bobby ran around the playground from slide to seesaw, from swing back to slide. New to town, he'd been at his new school a week and still hadn't made any friends. He went up and down the slide until three tough-looking boys raced up; then he ambled over to sit on the ground under a big tree. Most of the kids were playing kickball, but they hadn't played that at his old school and he didn't know how. Besides, no one had asked him to play.

A shadow fell across his face, and a moment later an acorn shot into his lap. Bobby jerked his head up, scowling, wondering who was teasing him now. "Hey, Bobby, you want to play catch?"

The red-haired, freckle-faced boy tossed the ball into the air, expertly catching it in his glove.

"I'm not real good at catch." Bobby stood up, wiping his hands on his jeans. "There weren't many kids at my old school, and most of them were girls. We didn't play much ball."

"That's OK. I'll teach you."

And so Bobby and his freckle-faced "angel" spent the next 15 minutes throwing a ball back and forth while the heavenly angels smiled.

HOW VALUABLE ARE YOU?

Again, the kingdom of heaven is like a merchant looking for fine pearls. When he found one of great value, he went away and sold everything he had and bought it. Matthew 13:45, 46, NIV.

I remember it so clearly, the panic as I ran from room to room, calling out, hoping somebody would answer. I remember the fear that began to chill my 8-year-old heart. A little voice deep inside whispered, "Your family has left you. They went back to America and left you here. And there's no one to care for you."

We were missionaries in Sri Lanka. One day after spending some time at a friend's house, I came home to find my family gone. That's when I panicked, fearing I'd been left behind. Of course, soon my parents came into the house from wherever they'd been, and everything was all right.

As I think back on these brief moments of panic, I wonder why I was afraid. If I'd only remembered how much my parents loved me, I would not have even imagined that they would ever leave me behind. I was too important to them—too valuable.

In the text above, Jesus teaches us something about how valuable we are to God. You are pearls of great price. God gave up the dearest Person in the universe—Jesus—in exchange for you. You are too important for God to leave behind. Your freedom from sin has cost too much for God not to care about you. This year and every year God is beside you, caring for you. He'll never leave you alone.

Every day, take time to remember how important you are to the King of the universe. You are a special treasure! God is coming back for you.

OCTOBER 27

SHEEPISH OR BETRAYED?

And [Jesus] will reply, "I tell you, I don't know you. You can't come in here, guilty as you are. Go away." Luke 13:27, TLB.

My friend Lois and I used to like to go upstairs in the church where her dad was the pastor, go through a tiny secret door at the rear of the balcony, and step out onto a small hidden porch. I don't know what it was actually intended for, but as our parents stood around talking after prayer meeting on those hot tropical Ceylon evenings, Lois and I would sneak out onto our cool little porch and watch everyone from above. Nobody knew we were there, which made it all the more fun!

One evening as we passed through the pews in the balcony and headed for the secret little door, our way was suddenly blocked by a tall teenage boy. We knew him, but at ages 10 and 11, Lois and I were very much intimidated by him. Suddenly he twisted up his face and hissed, "Vanish from my sight!"

Neither one of us knew how to vanish. We stood in stunned silence, unable to move. Did he think the balcony was his? Did he know something we should know? Maybe he should vanish instead!

At length we tried to explain that we meant him no harm and just wanted to go to our little door, but he leered at us and repeated his demand: "Vanish from my sight!" He said it with such venom that our bluff was called, and we turned and "vanished"—not because our feelings were hurt, not because we didn't know him, but because we felt sheepish at being caught.

I have never forgotten his words, and I have never been asked to vanish since then. I'm glad for that! But the Bible tells us that someday God Himself is going to tell some people to vanish from His sight, and I surely don't want to be one of them.

I used to think that when Jesus says "Go away from Me, I never knew you," it would hurt the feelings of those people and they would feel betrayed. After all, they've done good things in Jesus' name. But now I don't think so, for they are impostors. They will know that their motives for doing good in Jesus' name were not love and kindness, but peer pressure perhaps, or a desire to say and do things that were socially acceptable. Perhaps they were baptized just because they thought it would look good or help them get a better job. Or they said "Praise the Lord" all the time because they wanted to sound sanctimonious. We have no way of knowing who they are, and it's not our place to judge. But they know who they are. They'll feel sheepish because they've been found out. They won't feel betrayed.

Of course you don't want God to say, "Vanish from My sight, for I don't know you!" And when you have followed Him out of love and gratitude that overflows in kindness to others, He won't, for God will know you as one of His children! In fact, He has known you long before you were born, and He is glad that you love Him, too.

OCTOBER 28

HOW TO TELL WHEN YOU ARE LOVED

For long ago the Lord had said to Israel: I have loved you, O my people, with an everlasting love; with lovingkindness I have drawn you to me. Jeremiah 31:3, TLB.

Are you loved? Take a moment to think about that and ask yourself who loves you and why. How do you know?

There is always the danger that by defining love, we inadvertently put limits on it, so a definition of love can be considered only partially true. That is, if I were to say that when God sends a sunny day He is saying "I love you," then it seems as though rainy days mean "I don't love you." But I believe rainy days say "I love you" too. If we say that when we are happy, it means God is blessing us, then we may think that just because we're unhappy, God has pulled back away from us. But I believe God is with us all the time, and many times I have found that I have felt more of a blessing in times of sorrow than in times of joy. God feels closer when you're down and out and He's the only one you can talk to. You talk to Him more often then.

So then how can you tell when you are loved? Since I work as a nurse in obstetrics, I have the opportunity to see love in action every day I go to work. Mothers love their newborn babies, although that is only the beginning of a lifetime of care and concern. Most mothers want to get their hands on their babies as soon after birth as possible. Many new mothers keep their babies in their rooms with them. And it doesn't matter if the mother is asleep or awake—when the baby cries she gets up and tends to her baby's needs even at the expense of her own.

Mothers smile at their babies and spend a lot of time just looking at their faces and into their eyes. Sometimes we must give the newborns necessary medications or do necessary procedures that cause them pain. During these times the mothers almost always ask, "Can I hold him while you do it, or right afterward?" Mothers hurt for their babies when their babies feel pain.

God loves us in the same way. He wants to be with us, to have us lean on Him when we are troubled or distressed. He wants us to look into His face and spend time with Him.

The best way to know when you are loved by someone is if that someone makes you feel good about yourself. And no one does that better than Jesus. Look around you today at the things He has created to make the world beautiful. And as you observe the variety of color and size, imagine Jesus whispering to you "I love you."

Do you feel good about yourself when you think about how special you are to Jesus, how He longs for you to love Him and choose to go to heaven? Of course you do! And that's how you know He loves you.

OCTOBER 29

FROM MUMMIES TO MOSES

The whole Bible was given to us by inspiration from God and is useful to teach us what is true and to make us realize what is wrong in our lives; it straightens us out and helps us do what is right. 2 Timothy 3:16, TLB.

One of the most fascinating things I've ever seen were the glass cases of mummies in the Cairo, Egypt, museum several years ago. All the generations of King Tut were there, wrapped in dirty white bandages, with prunelike faces. It's incredible that they have been so well preserved.

As I looked down into those mummy faces, I couldn't help thinking about Moses. He was adopted into the royal family, you remember. If he hadn't obeyed God's call to lead God's people, he would be a mummy now, instead of a living person up in heaven.

It is because of Moses' story in the Bible that the Standard Oil Company discovered oil and is operating oil wells in Egypt.

You will remember the story that to prevent the soldiers from killing their baby, Moses' family made a basket of bulrushes and daubed it with pitch to make it watertight before floating it on the water. The *pitch* was a black, oily slime that seeped up through the ground and floated on top of the Nile River, sticking to the bulrushes along the shore.

The people of that day didn't know where the slime came from, but they knew it was water-repellent. Can you picture Moses' mother frantically smearing the pitch on the outside of her baby's basket, praying the whole time and watching furtively for soldiers?

And the slime worked. The basket floated. The baby was found by the pharaoh's daughter, and the rest is history.

Now back to the Standard Oil Company. One of the directors of the Standard Oil Company happened to be reading the second chapter of Exodus, and the third verse caught his attention. It said that the ark of bulrushes that Moses' mother made for him was daubed with slime and pitch.

"Where there's pitch, there must be oil," he said to himself. "And if there was oil in Moses' time, it must be there now." So the company sent out its geologists and oil experts, who discovered that, sure enough, there was oil.

When Moses wrote Exodus, he had no way of knowing that pitch indicated the presence of oil underground. The fact that pitch was mentioned and that oil has been found right there proves to me that the Bible is not a book of make-believe stories. It isn't coincidence that the story of baby Moses happened at the Nile. It isn't fiction, either.

Moses is a real person. I have seen the mummies of his adopted family. I know they were real. The oil underground is real too.

You can trust the Bible.

OCTOBER 30

WHAT'S SO BAD ABOUT OUIJA BOARDS?

Their king is the Prince of the bottomless pit whose name in Hebrew is Abaddon, and in Greek, Apollyon. Revelation 9:11, TLB.

Laura, a young woman in my church, had a personal experience with a ouija board just a few years ago, before she became a Christian. She and her sisters were playing with one, asking it questions. Then Laura asked, "Who is moving the pointer?" The board spelled out the words "I am."

"Who are you?" Laura asked again.

And the pointer spelled "I am Satan, also known as Apollyon."

Laura and her sisters put away the game immediately. It had stopped being fun. But the devil had already gotten his grip on Laura, and over the next few years she found herself drawn irresistibly toward the occult.

When she became a teenager, Laura became a Buddhist and tried transcendental meditation. One day as she was meditating, she saw as in a dream a vision of tiny doors in front of her. To her astonishment, a person smaller than a Barbie doll came walking toward her, through door after door. The little person was her!

When she recognized herself, Laura was frightened. She immediately stopped meditating and got up off the floor. The vision vanished.

Laura called her meditation teacher. "What happened?" she demanded of her teacher. "What was going on?"

The teacher said slowly and ominously, "You are very special, Laura. Your spirit guide has a message to give the world through you."

Laura remembered her experience with the ouija board. She didn't want to have anything to do with that "spirit guide." She began searching for answers, for someone to affirm her suspicions that this spirit guide was not someone she should listen to. She found her answers in Christianity.

Laura is now a Seventh-day Adventist—in fact, a pastor's wife! Her message to all of us is that it is very easy to speak to the devil. The devil is showing himself and taking over the world more openly than God is right now. But once we make that first contact with the devil, we can escape only with Jesus' power.

The best thing to do is to stay far away from anything that seems even remotely occult—such as the New Age crystals and pyramids, horoscopes, chants, and tarot cards, which fortune tellers use to predict futures. Laura says she would avoid having these things in her house because of their connection to the occult.

The devil will use anything he can to get you under his control. Are there some seemingly harmless things you have or do that he might use as his entering wedge? What will you do about them? The devil plays for keeps.

OCTOBER 31

BEWARE! GHOSTS ARE FOR REAL!

You have let me sink down deep in desperate problems. But you will bring me back to life again, up from the depths of the earth. Psalm 71:20, TLB.

I believe in ghosts. Do you? But I don't believe ghosts are the spirits of dead people. I trust the Bible when it tells us that people who have died stay dead until Jesus comes. But I believe that Satan and his angels make themselves into ghosts to deceive people.

One of the most dangerous things to believe is that the supernatural doesn't exist, that it's child's play. As Christians, we have to believe in the supernatural to believe in God. God, Jesus, the angels, and the Holy Spirit are supernatural beings. The Bible is filled with all sorts of stories about the supernatural world.

But if the devil can make us regard the supernatural as a hoax or a silly game or something harmless, it is easy for him to make us scoff at the Bible stories and begin to doubt the existence of God.

Tonight is Halloween. Do you know anybody who is dressing up as a red devil with a pitchfork? The devil loves that kind of costume. He wants to be considered a joke. He doesn't want us to know how serious he is about deceiving us. He doesn't want us to know how powerful he is, how real and how capable he is of turning us against God.

So why is it so easy to hear the devil but so hard to hear God? Because God speaks in a still small voice. God doesn't push Himself on us like Satan does.

I like to think of the earth's history as a big roller coaster. God is the tracks, but Satan makes the dips. At the beginning of the ride God spoke to Adam and Eve in person. It was easy to hear Him in the quiet garden. Then the activity began. The first dip was during Noah's time. Satan pushed people down, away from God. All except Noah and his family fell off the roller coaster and were lost.

While Satan retreated to plan another approach, God brought His people back up to Him. Things were sort of OK for a while, with little dips and recoveries.

Then Jesus came to be with us—and the earth had a flesh-and-blood connection to heaven. With Christ's death, Satan pushed the earth into a devil's spin. But God helped us recover.

There have been dips and climbs since then. Now we are into the deepest, most heart-stopping dip of all. Satan is pulling us down, trying to make us think the dip is fun. People are frightened, but they don't want to admit it. They're trying to have a good time. Satan and his people are making so much noise that it's hard to hear God's still small voice. But God is still there, guiding the car, ready to put on the brakes and bring the ride to an end. The last words in the Bible promise God's deliverance.

Hold on! Don't get off before the ride is over.

YOU CAN BE ANYTHING!

For as [a man] thinketh in his heart, so is he. Proverbs 23:7.

If someone had told me nine years ago that I would write a junior devotional someday, I would have laughed out loud and kept on laughing through the night. Because nine years ago I was not a writer. I had stories in my head that I wanted to share, but I thought no one would want to hear what I had to say. I thought that somewhere there was a group of "chosen" people who did all the writing, and since no one had asked me if I wanted to be part of them, I couldn't expect to join their ranks.

Then one day I sent a two-page story to *Our Little Friend,* and they bought it! What elation! And a whole $7! Next I decided to try writing a book. I wrote down my outline and two chapters and mailed them to an Adventist publisher. The editor wrote back, asking to see the whole thing.

Two and a half years later, after rewrites and additions and numerous mailings back and forth, that book became *No More Alphabet Soup.* With more than a little discomfort, I endured the family's bantering about how they finally had an author in the family. But I felt no different inside than before I'd written my book. I also knew that having a book published didn't mean I was a better writer than anyone else.

Other people can tell a story better than I can. Some of them do it, and others just dream. Maybe you are one of the future authors the world is waiting for. The rest of us can't go on forever. But unless you take the time to learn the techniques of good writing and then sit down and tell the stories inside your head, you may never become a writer. And the rest of us will miss the blessing of what you have to say.

You can do just about anything you set your mind to do. And while writing a book for Adventist young people certainly didn't bring me prosperity, it did bring the feeling of satisfaction that comes from achieving a goal, from doing something I thought only others could do.

Is there something you think is beyond you? Conquer it! Think positively. Tell yourself, "I can do it." Imagine yourself having already done it. And before you realize it, you have.

NOVEMBER 2

WHAT MAKES A GUY LOVABLE

Kindness makes a man attractive. Proverbs 19:22, TLB.

He was not the most handsome guy in school, but Cindy knew that she wasn't the most beautiful girl, either. She felt she was lucky just to have a date to the banquet—she wouldn't worry about whether or not someone else wanted to go with him. But Cindy's image of Harvey changed that night—even before he gave her the corsage. In one small moment Harvey became the most desirable guy on campus!

The girls' dorm lobby was crowded as the guys came calling for their dates. Cindy waited nervously upstairs for the monitor to page her name. At last she heard it: "Cindy, you have a caller in the lobby."

Cindy took one last look at herself in the mirror. She smoothed the satiny folds of her red evening gown and then closed the door behind her as she headed down the hall. She didn't know Harvey very well, and she hoped the evening would not be too boring.

Cindy's eyes scanned the milling crowd below as she started down the stairs. Suddenly, in one awful moment, she lost her balance and fell, rolling like a duffel bag, over and over, to the bottom!

The lobby became tensely silent as everyone watched in open-mouthed horror at the sight. Only Harvey moved, pushing his way toward Cindy. It was then that he became, to Cindy, the most handsome guy on campus. For in that fragile moment, when Cindy's self-esteem was most vulnerable and she looked up at him from the floor, Harvey made it seem intentional, by exclaiming, "Wow—there's no way I can top that! Hey, you're all right, aren't you?"

And while everyone else concluded that the fall had been on purpose, only Cindy and Harvey knew how his quick thinking had spared her a humiliating moment.

They had a wonderful evening, and Cindy discovered what makes a man attractive: a real man takes advantage of every situation he can to help others feel good about themselves. And isn't that what Christianity is all about?

NOVEMBER 3

WATCH OUT FOR "IF ONLY"

Get all the advice you can and be wise the rest of your life. Proverbs 19:20, TLB.

One of the hardest parts of growing up is to be plagued by the "if onlys." When you become a teen, just venturing out for the first time from under your parents' wings, everything is fresh and new. You have no haunting memories of poor decisions you've made in the past, for most of your decisions have been made for you by your parents. But now that you are making more of your own decisions, be careful. As a young parent, it occurs to me that the main challenge in life is to get from birth to old age with as few "if onlys" as possible.

Of course, you want to have a happy adulthood, everyone does. And what teenager has not prayed "Dear Jesus, please come soon . . . after I get married and have a family?" The irony of this is that while we're young, dreaming about and planning for the future when we'll be grown, we don't often take care to prevent "if onlys" from marring our future happiness. Let me explain.

For example, everyone wants to be happily married. But many teenagers go steady with the first person who asks them to, and even though they may not really enjoy being with that person, and their friends may advise them to break up, they don't do it. It hurts too much to break up, they say. And what will people say if they don't have a date for Saturday night? Eventually, without a lot of thought, they get married. And they learn that divorce hurts much more than breaking up with a boyfriend or girlfriend ever could.

Or some teenagers drop out of school because they are bored with it and want to jump into life now! Gone are the dreams of being a teacher or an engineer or a doctor. Everything seems OK at first. None of the bothersome homework that others are struggling with. High school dropouts even have money—at first. But a few years down the road, when they see their friends (the businessmen of the community) with better-paying and more rewarding jobs, the dropouts see, too late, the foolishness of their decision, and they say, "If only I had stayed in school."

Some may say, "If only I hadn't given in to the pressure to try smoking or drugs," as they struggle to get over an addiction they now regret.

If you have a decision to make, talk it over with someone you trust. Pray about it. Consider the worst thing that could happen regarding whichever direction you may choose to take, and ask yourself if you could live with that. Or would that become a haunting "if only"?

Jesus wants you to be happy. He wants your life to be "out of this world." There are so many people who really care about you. Talk to one or more of them and prevent as many "if onlys" as possible.

NOVEMBER 4

HOW TO DESTROY YOUR ENEMIES

There is a saying, "Love your friends and hate your enemies!" But I say: Love your enemies! Pray for those who persecute you! Matthew 5:43, 44, TLB.

It will happen to you sooner or later. Someday someone is going to start a rumor about you that will not be true and that will not be fair, and those who do not know any better will believe it.

Sometimes grown-ups cringe at the forthrightness of children, though their honesty is admirable. When a child doesn't like someone, he tells him so—to his face. But when a grown-up gets mad, he starts rumors —behind that person's back.

You stand at the threshold of being a grown-up, and someday your enemies will stop telling you they don't like you. Instead, they'll spread rumors about you behind your back in an effort to turn others against you. When you hear about it, you will be hurt. You may think everyone believes it, and you may feel like getting even.

Don't! The best way to refute bad gossip is to be such a nice person that those who hear the rumor can't believe you are capable of doing anything so evil, and will see through the rumor and rally to your side. Here is where your reputation is so important. Everything you do, every look on your face, shapes your reputation. And a person with a good reputation is next to impossible to lay low.

Abigail Van Buren says a person's true character is shown in what he does when he thinks nobody's looking, and in how he treats someone who cannot fight back.

The person who starts bad rumors is a person to be pitied. He feels so overpowered by how good you are, or by how many friends you have, that he wants to do something—anything—to get your attention. Give it to him! If you can find out who he is, seek him out and take him to lunch. Tell him he has hurt you and that you know that neither one of you is happy with feuding. Tell him you want to be his friend! And if he accepts your offer, you will have one of the most loyal friends you could ever ask for.

Abraham Lincoln is reported to have been asked by an elderly woman: "How can you speak kindly of your enemies when you should rather destroy them?"

"Madam," he said, "do I not destroy them when I make them my friends?"

That's what Jesus wants us to do.

NOVEMBER 5

A DATE WITH A KING

If you keep the Sabbath holy, . . . enjoying the Sabbath and speaking of it with delight as the Lord's holy day, and honoring the Lord in what you do, . . . then the Lord will be your delight. Isaiah 58:13, 14, TLB.

How do you feel about the Sabbath? Is it a day to be "endured," or a day to look forward to? Why? Seventh-day Adventists have a whole day set aside to worship God and reverence His monument of Creation. People who join the church often remark about how wonderful it is to have a whole day to spend in nature or Bible reading and not feel guilty that they aren't out mowing the lawn or doing the laundry. They do not see the Sabbath as a burden, but as a delight. Happiness in life is more often the result of attitude than of circumstance.

Richard had looked forward to his school's annual ski trip for weeks. A fine skier, he simply enjoyed the sport, zooming down the mountain-side with absolute freedom and grace.

Unfortunately, just after noon that first day Richard fell, tumbled several feet, and had to be carried off the mountain by the ski patrol. Richard had broken his leg.

307

He was stunned. He'd never broken anything before and had been in fine shape. In fact, the regional basketball games were coming up, and he was captain of his team. He spent the rest of the afternoon in the lodge, quiet and sober. That evening Richard went into the hospital for surgery.

He woke up the next morning with his leg covered in a heavy cast, suspended by traction. He was depressed. "Might as well shrivel up and die," he muttered. Everything was going wrong.

Friends and classmates soon started coming, some of whom he hardly knew. They brought flowers, cards, candy, and a huge banner that reached clear around his room, proclaiming their admiration for him. The biggest surprise was a visit from the Harlem Globetrotters, in town for a game! "We visit all team captains," they explained, eyes twinkling. By the time that first week was over, Richard had to admit that it had been one of the most exciting of his life. His cast, once a heavy eyesore, was now something he cherished—decorated with signatures, notes, and drawings from people who cared about him.

Suddenly Richard didn't mind the cast. Because it now stood as a symbol of love, it changed from a burden to a delight.

The Sabbath is like a date with God, a symbol of His love and power. The Sabbath means 24 hours of no homework, 24 hours with which to remember how special God is and how much He loves us.

We're getting ready to go out of this world. Why not prepare by getting accustomed to heaven's schedule? In heaven the angels worship God joyously on the Sabbath.

NOVEMBER 6

WHAT A BROTHER!

There are friends who pretend to be friends, but there is a friend who sticks closer than a brother. Proverbs 18:24, RSV.

I don't have an older brother. But what I understand of older brothers is that they seem to have a certain sense of humor. To break the ice and make others feel better, they sometimes pretend to be ignorant in certain situations. A couple of stories in the Bible seem to show this type of humor in Jesus' dealings with people. I like it. To me, Jesus is a big brother who is fun to be around. Let me explain.

You remember the 10 lepers whom Jesus healed? Before they were healed, they may have approached Him timidly, almost stalking Him, calling out for Him to heal them, but unsure that He would. To their surprise, Jesus greeted them and told them to go and show themselves to the priests. All 10 of the lepers headed down the trail, leaping and dancing for joy as they saw that they had been healed. Only one stopped and, minding his manners, remembered that he hadn't thanked Jesus for the miracle.

I can see that one leper kneeling at Jesus' feet, his hands clasped together, thanking Him. And even though Jesus must have been saddened by the ingratitude of the other nine, I can see His eyes sparkle as He smiles fondly at the leper and tells him how special he is for returning, then bids him get up and hurry to catch up with the others.

The Jesus I know is not the classic serious-faced person, always gazing sadly up into heaven. He had many serious moments, of course. But most of the time I think His eyes sparkled and danced with humor. Good humor—not the kind that belittles, but the kind that unites, the kind of humor that endeared Him to the ones He shared it with.

There is a special kind of humor between two people who have shared the same experiences. I can't wait to spend eternity with Jesus, laughing at His jokes and hearing Him laugh at mine! Jesus is the kind of big brother you can have fun with. He's "out of this world," and He wants to spend time with you because you're special to Him. Get to know Him and see what I mean!

NOVEMBER 7

FORGIVE YOURSELF

He knoweth our frame; he remembereth that we are dust. Psalm 103:14.

It's easy to be too hard on ourselves. But everyone makes mistakes!

In *The Camera Never Blinks*, Dan Rather relates a lasting memory of a time he was reminded how human he is. During the 1968 elections Rather had his first assignment as a CBS analyst of the elections. He was getting nervous about this assignment—he'd have only one chance to do it right—so he decided to fly home to be with his wife the evening before the final rehearsals. The producer told him to be sure he was in New York by 10:00 the next morning.

When his plane landed at La Guardia at 8:40 the next morning, Rather complimented himself on his timing and decided he even had extra time for a shoeshine before he had to be at the studio.

The shoeshine man couldn't help commenting on Rather's shoes. "Well," he said, "it's been a long time since I saw this! One black shoe and one brown." It was not a dark brown, either, but almost a tan. And there was no time to buy another pair!

Rather hurried to the studio with one thought on his mind: to get to his desk as inconspicuously as possible. But when he opened the door, he saw the producer waiting for him with four other men—the "big brass" of CBS. All he could hear was the echo of his footsteps as he approached them.

No one mentioned the shoes. The chairman of CBS asked Rather how he was. Standing on one foot with the other behind him, Rather gulped, "Fine, Mr. Chairman," and hurried to sit down. Whether they noticed his shoes or not, Dan Rather will never know. Nobody ever said a thing about them. "But whenever I feel that I am taking the star treatment seriously, I remember the black shoe and the brown shoe. And the feeling always passes," Rather writes.

Everyone makes mistakes at one time or another. My mother always told me, "It's not so important whether or not you make mistakes as it is whether or not you learn from your mistakes."

Be easy on yourself. God knows how hard it is to be human. The next time you make a mistake, pick yourself up, fasten what you have learned in a corner of your mind, and go on. Forgive yourself.

NOVEMBER 8

ARE YOU LISTENING?

But if anyone keeps looking steadily into God's law for free men, he will not only remember it but he will do what it says, and God will greatly bless him in everything he does. James 1:25, TLB.

Every message has both a sender and a receiver. This old story, which still makes the rounds, illustrates that point well. It seems that a woman went to a lawyer and told him she wanted a divorce. The lawyer got out his notepad and began to ask questions.

"Do you have any grounds?" he asked.

"Oh, yes," she nodded. "About three quarters of an acre."

The lawyer looked at her. "What's wrong? Do you have a grudge?"

"No, but we've got a carport."

The man paused again, puzzled. "Does he beat you up?"

"No," she retorted. "I'm up before him every morning."

Finally the lawyer blurted out, "Lady, why do you want to divorce your husband?"

"Because," she explained, "it's impossible to communicate with that man!"

God is trying to get a special message to us: "I love you. And because I love you, I want you to have freedom of choice. But because I love you, I want to give you warnings about things that will hurt you. Don't worship other gods. Come visit with Me one day a week. Treat your parents with respect. Don't steal or kill." And more.

But too many times we garble the message. "It doesn't matter if I keep the seventh day holy or not. My parents are just trying to make my life miserable. Stealing and killing mean just that; but cheating isn't stealing, and hating isn't killing." And far too many of us are dissatisfied with what we have, wanting instead what our friends have. What we find in the end is that we are not happy.

"God doesn't know what He's talking about!" we shout in frustration. But have we really been listening? God is trying to say "I love you. You are special. And until I come, I want you to be as happy as possible on earth. Remember Me."

And if we really are listening, we will do something about what we hear. And we will be happy because we will be right with God.

NOVEMBER 9

MOON POWER

Where is the one who has been born king of the Jews? We saw his star in the east and have come to worship him. Matthew 2:2.

The story is told of an airline passenger who sat beside a sad young woman. She poured out her heart to the other passenger, explaining that she and her boyfriend had had an argument and now he wasn't speaking to her.

A half hour later a male voice came over the public address system. "Ladies and gentlemen and young lovers," the voice said, "on your left, we bring you the moon."

All the passengers turned to look at the brilliant golden moon shining luminously outside the windows. Immediately the sad young woman smiled and seemed happier through the rest of the flight.

When the plane landed, she walked into the terminal hand in hand with her boyfriend—the copilot.

The moon is given a lot of credit for making people feel romantic. It's hard to know whether we feel romantic about the moon because it does have special powers, or if we just think we should feel that way in the moonlight because we have been told that's how it should be. Who really cares? The moon is given a lot of credit for making people restless and crazy when it is full. I work as a nurse in obstetrics, and we have found that more babies are born around the time of full moon and new moon than during the other phases of the moon.

It is a known fact that the moon has an effect on the tides, though. So maybe it does affect these other aspects of our lives, too. But we may never know for sure. For me, the power of the moon lies in its reminder that man is a created being. No one can convince me that the sun, moon, and stars just happened by chance and continue their orderly progression in the heavens, on time and flawlessly, without design.

I believe there is a Creator. And as I see the passing seasons, the autumn leaves falling to the ground and becoming nourishment for the trees that bud in the spring, I believe that God can make good out of evil. When you feel alone, just look up past the moon at the stars and talk to God.

NOVEMBER 10

THE TROUBLE MAT

Cast your burden on the Lord, and He shall sustain you. Psalm 55:22, NKJV.

Ted McMurphy had a new job, a good job, a job that he enjoyed and that had a lot of room for advancement. His boss was pleased with his work too. The problem was that nothing in Ted's background had prepared him for learning to use a computer, for keeping accounts and a hundred other details in the precise way this company wanted it done.

Ted put in a lot of 9- and 10-hour days learning the ropes. And when he came home at night, all he wanted to do was drop in a chair and "die" until bedtime. His wife, Suzie, and his two little boys had other ideas.

"Daddy's home! Daddy's home!" Sometimes he could hear his boys' shouts even before he put his key in the door. It was hard to straighten his shoulders and put a happy smile on his face when all he could think of were the problems he faced on the morrow.

And then Sue brought home a new doormat. The mat was shocking red, and the word "welcome" blazed across it in white letters. Just seeing it gave him such a cheerful feeling that he had an idea.

The next evening as he got home from work, he paused at the mat. Slowly he wiped his feet across it, then straightened his shoulders and opened the door. No one saw him, and no one wondered why he had wiped dry feet on a new mat.

Several weeks later, however, Sue was looking out the window when Ted came home and saw him wiping his feet on the mat. "What were you doing?" she laughed, opening the door. "I'm not that fussy about dust in the house."

Ted grinned a little sheepishly. "If you really want to know, it's my trouble mat. Every day when I come home, I wipe my troubles from work onto that mat. And then I forget about them. I used to try to pick them up in the morning, but I've discovered that by morning they don't seem nearly as important."

Maybe you need a trouble mat. I'm sure that we could all use one. However, we have something better than a trouble mat. God has offered us His strength, His shoulder, to lean on. Sharing our problems with God helps us know Him better. It increases our faith and trust in Him, too, because we can see how He has helped us through the bad times. Telling God about our problems doesn't change the problem, but it changes *us*. Take your troubles to God and see how many He takes away.

WHEN YOU WERE A CHILD

Unless you change and become like little children, you will never enter the kingdom of heaven. Matthew 18:3, NIV.

Perhaps you can't remember what you were like when you were a little child. I can guess that you probably had a good imagination and were sometimes painfully honest.

In his book *Elephant Bones and Lonely Hearts*, former biology teacher Ronald Rood tells of a visit he made to a second grade as a guest speaker. He had shown slides of a Hawaiian volcano pouring molten red lava into the sea. When the lava poured into the ocean, the kids could almost hear and feel the white clouds of steam. Afterward Mr. Rood passed around a chunk of lava. One of the last children to hold it returned it to Mr. Rood almost reverently, cradling it gently in his hands. "Mr. Rood," he said, his eyes wide with wonder, "it's still warm."

To another classroom Mr. Rood brought a boa constrictor named Julius Squeezer for the children to hold. As he explained that snakes need love just as all animals do, he allowed the children to pet the snake. Afterward he asked the kids what they thought about snakes since meeting Julius. One little girl said wisely, "I can't really tell about snakes, because Julius isn't an ordinary one. He's—well, he's Julius." Her prejudice toward snakes had changed since she knew one firsthand.

To get to know someone so well that you take them off their pedestal is a sign that you are friends. A young boy whom Mr. Rood had known for a long time wrote to the biologist with this problem: "Our teacher says we should write to someone important, and if not someone important, someone interesting. So I thought of you. Do you know anybody?"

I think God wants us to do that with Him, too. God wants us to think of Him as a loving Father and not as a cold and distant judge. He wants us to feel comfortable telling Him just how we feel, whether it's to say "I'm mad that You're not doing more miracles for me" or "I'm having a hard time feeling close to You." Or maybe God would like for you to put your imagination to work and put your arm around an empty chair, saying, "God is right here next to me." It's OK to be a child forever where God is concerned. Children are some of His favorite people!

313

THEY'RE ON YOUR SIDE

There will be more joy in heaven over one sinner who repents than over ninety-nine just persons who need no repentance. Luke 15:7, NKJV.

It would be wonderful if everything we tried to do turned out perfect, if we could be the absolute best at everything we tried to do. But as long as we live on this earth there will always be people who do something better than you do it; someone who can ride a bike faster, sing higher or lower, draw better, memorize more than you can. On the other hand, there will always be someone who cannot do everything as well as you can. Life is like that. It balances out.

It feels good to be a winner, and it's fun to cheer a winner. But it's good to cheer a loser, too. In fact, the angels know how that feels.

In the 1980 Olympics held at Lake Placid, New York, America's star speed skater, Eric Heiden, skated off with five gold medals. Five hours after Heiden had skated to a new Olympic world record in the 10,000-meter race, skaters were still competing in the event. But their times were growing longer; obviously no one else was going to beat the new world record, and spectators began to leave the stands.

Then someone pointed out that in the final heat, which wouldn't start for another hour, there was only one skater. That lone skater was a 17-year-old South Korean boy who was skating in his first Olympics. If everyone left, not only would he be skating alone, but no one would be there to watch him.

As the word drifted back through the crowd, several hundred people sat back down to wait. And to watch.

They started cheering when the gun went off, and kept up the shouting through each lap. The young boy skated his heart out, coming close to beating Heiden's time for a brief while. Still the crowd cheered. They were not cheering for a winner, but for someone who needed their support.

Have you heard any cheers lately, maybe in your spiritual race? Maybe you haven't been much of a spiritual giant recently and have fallen behind. Don't stay there. All heaven is watching you, cheering for you, just waiting for you to ask for help as you pick up the pieces of your mistakes and keep on going. You're not a hopeless case. You're a reason to cheer.

"BUT I'VE BEEN SO BAD!"

Salvation is not a reward for the good we have done, so none of us can take any credit for it. Ephesians 2:9, TLB.

Do you ever feel like such a bad person that you wonder how anyone—especially God—can love you?

On a quiet afternoon three Englishmen sat inside a quaint English tea shop having tea. Their young waiter, new at his job, scurried around, trying to do everything just right. As he hurried to the men's table to refill their cups, he tripped on his own feet. The tray and teapot went flying into the air, landing at last against the wall, where the tea splashed onto the unfinished wood and sank into its thirsty fibers.

It left a large stain. A huge, ugly brown stain on the wall.

All afternoon the waiter watched helplessly as the stain dried. At last he realized that it was there for good. The sight of it made him feel sick. And he dreaded telling his boss about it.

The same three men returned the next day, and when one of them asked about the incident, the waiter showed him the stain. "Do you know how to get it off?" he asked desperately. "My boss hasn't seen it yet, but I have to tell him about it soon."

The man shook his head. "No, I'm afraid I don't know how to get it off, but I think I can fix it up for you. Let me talk to your boss."

The waiter was hesitant, but at last he agreed and showed the man to the office to speak to the boss.

The man returned a few minutes later, smiling. And as the waiter watched, he took a charcoal pencil and outlined the stain, then shaded and sketched for several minutes. What emerged was a breathtaking sketch of a flying horse that seemed almost to leap out of the wall.

The waiter was amazed. But he understood when he read the artist's signature. He was one of England's best artists. Through the man's skill, that wall, instead of being a silent reminder of the waiter's clumsiness, became instead a beautiful work of art.

God can do the same with your mistakes. As far as He is concerned, there are no bad people—there are only good people who make bad decisions. Sometimes those decisions leave ugly scars. But when they help us appreciate the miracle of God's love, the stains become more beautiful.

ONE FOOLISH LITTLE TOWN

*Wherefore let him that thinketh he standeth take heed lest he fall.
1 Corinthians 10:12.*

A certain little town in a remote part of the country had a problem. It seemed there was a high bluff at the edge of town where people would go to watch the sunsets, and for some reason many of them would fall off and get hurt. Some of them even died, because there was no way to get to them quickly after they fell.

The town fathers discussed what should be done about this problem. "Perhaps if we had a road to the bottom of the bluff, we could save their lives," they said. And so a road was built, and sure enough, some lives were saved. But some of the people who fell still died.

The town leaders felt they needed something more. "If we had an ambulance in town, we could get these people to the hospital sooner," they decided. And so they bought an ambulance, and the situation became better. Now when someone fell, the new ambulance could get to them quickly on the new road and whisk them off to the hospital. Fewer lives were lost. The town fathers were happy.

But one man was not content. At the next town council meeting he made a suggestion. "I think there is a better solution," he said. "If we could prevent people from falling off in the first place, it would be better. Why not build a fence at the top of the bluff? Then nobody would be able to fall off at all."

It was a novel idea, but they tried it, and nobody fell off the bluff again.

There are many people who are scarring their lives with the results of poor decisions. They have no fences to protect them, no guidelines for happiness. But God has a plan. Though He *can* pick up the pieces after we have hurt ourselves, He would rather prevent scars in the first place. And that's what His fences—the Ten Commandments—are for you.

HOW TO KNOW YOU'RE RIGHT WITH GOD

*[Jesus] said, "Unless you turn to God from your sins and become as little children, you will never get into the Kingdom of Heaven."
Matthew 18:3, TLB.*

I attended almost every revival meeting my father ever held. When he asked people to make a decision to follow Christ, I always made sure that he wouldn't feel like a failure. With the tender heart of an 8-year-old, I'd go up if nobody else did. Or if I didn't think enough people had responded, I'd join their group at the front of the altar. You could say that I was continually giving my heart to Jesus.

I listened to the sermons, too, of course, and in time I had every inflection in my dad's presentation memorized. I knew just when to put away my books and listen up for the appeal. The thing that concerned me most was the emphasis on making everything right with God, that our sins had separated us from Him.

At that time my gravest sin was getting fighting mad at my brother and sister, and I'm not sure now that that was a sin anyway. I kept all the Commandments; I didn't swear or kill or worship idols. I thought everything was right between me and God, but when I heard sin stressed time and time again, I wondered if I was missing something.

I don't think I was. I think any child who sincerely loves Jesus and confesses his sins is—yes—ready to go to heaven. I think that's why Jesus said adults should become like little children.

As we grow up, we encounter more of the sins mentioned in the Ten Commandments, the stealing and lying and committing adultery. The reasons these things are sins is because they are hurtful and harmful. Afterward we feel guilty and unsure of God's love, and we find that, yes, sin has separated us from our heavenly Father.

But when you're a child and you have always loved Jesus, you can stand clean before Him with confidence, no matter what you have done. And you can thank God for that confidence that everything is right between you! Remember how it is now, and as you grow and meet more serious temptations, resolve not to let anything come between you and Jesus to mar that special relationship you have with Him.

A man on his deathbed was asked if he had made everything right with the Lord. "I don't remember that we ever quarreled," he replied.

If you feel that you are right with God, then you probably are.

HOW TO GET YOUR TEACHERS TO LIKE YOU

When a man is gloomy, everything seems to go wrong; when he is cheerful, everything seems right! Proverbs 15:15, TLB.

There's usually at least one student in every class who can make the teacher's face glow. You've seen them. This student can answer nearly every question put to him with the kind of ease and detail that makes the teacher smile proudly and look around the room as though to say to the others "Isn't he marvelous?"

What makes a student a teacher's pet? What is the secret to getting along with teachers and making them like you? I think I know.

First, you have to understand that teachers become teachers because they feel they have something they want to share with others. They like to explain things. They usually like the subjects they teach. But most of all, teachers like students who like what they have to say. A math teacher, for example, likes students who share his love of math, or those who at least try to like math. It's just like any other friendship—we become friends with the people who share our interests.

It isn't necessary to make the best grades in class for your teacher to like you. As long as he knows you are doing your best, he will respect you for it. Let him know you are trying. Stay after class and tell him that what you are studying is hard for you to understand. Ask him if he can give you any extra help after school. Ask a friend who understands it to explain it to you. Then do your best. As long as a teacher sees that you are trying, he will like you.

Don't ever say "I'll never learn this stuff," because your mind believes what you tell it. Think positive thoughts. Then say "God is helping me learn this." And He will. Try it today!

NOVEMBER 17

THE STUBBORN MULE

Simply let your "Yes" be "Yes," and your "No," "No"; anything beyond this comes from the evil one. Matthew 5:37, NIV.

Expletives: those testy little four-letter words that seem to show up when people are angry or frustrated. Are they really necessary? Have you thought about the real meanings of some of the "OK words" that we use? What about "goodness" or "my word"?

I'll admit that using expletives is a hard habit to break. And some people have adapted their language to omit the expletives but leave the choice of the four-letter word up to the listeners. Sort of like a multiple-choice exclamation. "Blank you!" The listener can put in his own oath, as it were.

Sometimes we can let off steam before it bursts into an expletive by warning, "Irritation is rising." Just saying it feels good and sounds so funny, you might burst into laughter instead of an oath.

It reminds me of a story I once read about an elderly farmer. One chill morning he needed to harness his old mule Sally so they could begin plowing. But what the soft-spoken farmer had in mind and what long-eared Sally had in mind were two different things. Sally lay on the warm straw in her stall munching away drowsily while her owner tried to get her up. She turned her head to the side and gave the farmer a baleful stare as he pulled on her harness.

"Get up, lazy Sally—get up, get *up*, tch-tch," he said gently, very well controlled.

But Sally did not get up.

The old farmer planted a shoe firmly on Sally's rump in an effort to shove her to her feet, but even that didn't work. Still the old gentleman did not lose his cool. No expletives, no shouting, just calm perseverance.

At last the gentle farmer stooped down, tapped Sally on the head with his hat, and offered this ultimatum: "Sally, I'll not cuss you or kick you, but I will twist your tail."

An expletive is nothing more than a release valve for our emotions. But there are other ways to release frustration. Next time you get upset, try saying out loud, "Irritation is rising." And then when frustration subsides, state that, too: "Irritation is falling."

God's name is too wonderful to be used in vain. Angels bow when they say it. Why should we spit it out in anger? And try doing something about your problems instead of just complaining about them.

DON'T BE OFFENDED

Great peace have they which love thy law, and nothing shall offend them. Psalm 119:165.

When he was chosen by his teacher to be the restroom monitor, Donavin felt special. It was a responsibility given only to a few students who could be trusted. As monitor, Donavin had to be in the boys' restroom after recess to make sure the boys in his class put their paper towels in the litter bin and to remind them to go straight back to class after they finished drying their hands.

Donavin was lots of fun to be around, and he could have had lots of friends, but he took everything he did seriously, including his friendships. He was a true friend to those who were his friends. But Donavin also took his job seriously, and if anyone threw his paper towel on the floor or started punching somebody in the restroom, Donavin didn't hesitate to use his authority to tell that person to stop. Of course, the boys were acting up on purpose, but they got angry when Donavin did his job.

How would you feel about someone in your class who had the authority to boss you around? Well, many of the boys didn't like Donavin while he was restroom monitor. The next year, when someone else had the job, Marc discovered how much of a friend Donavin could be, and now they're as close as brothers. If Donavin were to become restroom monitor again, that wouldn't change how Marc feels about him, because they're friends.

Sometimes people think of Jesus as someone who tells them what they can and cannot do. If you don't know Jesus, you might get angry. But when Jesus becomes your friend, you understand how seriously He takes His job of warning you about unhappiness. When you do as He says, you like yourself. And that is a feeling that is out of this world!

IS JESUS FOR REAL?

The fool says in his heart, "There is no God." Psalm 14:1, NIV.

When I was a teenager, *Time* magazine ran a cover page that pronounced, "God Is Dead." It raised quite a commotion, needless to say, but it is something that every person must straighten out for himself.

I think it is important to have a good reason to believe that Jesus came to earth as a baby, that He grew up to be a real man, and that the Bible can be trusted. Do you believe it? Do you wish you had proof that the Bible is true?

There is proof! Archaeologists have found ruins of cities mentioned in the Bible, right where the Bible says they were, complete with such architectural novelties as Babylon's hanging gardens and underground water tunnel. I have been lucky enough to see these ruins for myself.

As with any history lesson, much of it has to be taken on faith. I have to believe there was a World War I and World War II, because I am told it happened. I can't prove there was a real General MacArthur, but people who saw him tell me he was real, so I choose to believe.

I can't prove there was ever a Man named Jesus, but other books besides the Bible talk about Him. A Jewish historian by the name of Josephus has written about the history of the Jewish people, and he talks about Jesus and His good works. You understand that historians don't make up stories. They are like reporters. They have to tell about real events, not dreamed up-ones.

We believe historians. We believe the history stories of our country; why not also believe what historians say about Jesus? He is a real man. He is alive. And the Bible, a history book about Him, tells us that when He was here, He promised that He would come back and take us out of this world. The Bible also says we are foolish if we don't believe.

ESCAPE!

There hath no temptation taken you but such as is common to man: but God is faithful, who will not suffer you to be tempted above that ye are able; but will with the temptation also make a way to escape, that ye may be able to bear it. 1 Corinthians 10:13.

Spiders who live with me are lucky! I really don't like them at all, but I'd rather see them alive—and out of my way—than smashed and dead.

The other morning while emptying the garbage sack in the kitchen, I noticed a spider crawling around over the corn husks and corncobs inside the sack. I'd planned to tie the sack closed and put it outside in the garbage can, but I couldn't stand the thought of the spider discovering he was tied inside and suffocating! I didn't have enough nerve to pick him up, so I just took the whole garbage sack outside and left it open, leaning against the picnic table, with a corn husk "bridge" that the spider could crawl up and out to freedom. When I have found spiders stranded in my sink, I've placed the dishcloth at an angle so they could crawl up and out to safety, and they usually do. I was sure this spider would do the same.

I was busy inside for about an hour. When I went to check on the spider to see if he had escaped, I noted with dismay that he hadn't. He was still exploring what he evidently thought was a wonderful "playground."

I moved the corn husk bridge closer to him, hoping he would crawl onto it, then I went back inside the house. If only I could talk to the spider and warn him of the coming danger!

Another hour went by, and still the spider stayed inside the sack. By that time I had given up on him, so with a horrible feeling in the pit of my stomach, I went ahead and tied a knot in the sack and put it in the garbage can. However, I left a little gap in the top of the sack, and I hope the spider found the way out.

If God could put a yearning in my heart to hope that a little spider would be smart enough to escape danger, how much more of that same quality does God have for you and me? Perhaps that is why Jesus became a person—so He could warn us in our own language about what was coming. You are so very special to God. Take the bridge He has provided for you—Jesus Himself—and get out of the traps Satan would have you in. God wants to see you saved!

THE BLESSING OF "UNANSWERED PRAYER"

Don't be weary in prayer; keep at it; watch for God's answers and remember to be thankful when they come. Colossians 4:2, TLB.

One Sabbath for the children's story in church, our pastor told us about a little girl who always threw one of her shoes under her bed before she crawled in at night. Her mother watched the little routine without question for several nights, and then she finally asked, "Honey, why do you do that?"

"My teacher said to do it," the little girl replied.

"She did?" the surprised mother asked. "Did she say why?"

"Oh, yes! She said we should throw one of our shoes under the bed every night, because then, in the morning, while we are on our knees looking for the shoe, we'll already be in a position to pray."

Not a bad idea!

Everyone loves stories of miraculous answers to prayer. When I was growing up, these were the only kinds of prayer stories grown-ups told. No one ever mentioned the many prayers that seemed to go unanswered. And so in time, when my prayers were not miraculously answered as I had requested, I came to believe that God listened to everyone else, but must be ignoring me. *Why bother to pray?* I wondered.

As I grew up, I didn't take as many things to God in prayer as I had before, although I still prayed about the big things. But even though I'm sure God often spoke to me with guidance, I more often than not went ahead with what I wanted to do instead of what I should have done. And when those decisions led to unhappiness, I blamed God.

"I prayed about this," I lamented, not admitting that God's answer had been no. But since I had wanted it to be yes, I had gone ahead with my plans as though they were God's leading. But no is as much an answer as yes. And sometimes no is more loving than yes.

Perhaps we need to change our whole perspective on prayer. Rather than thinking of prayer as a "wish list" for God, we also need to think of it as a chance for God to talk to us. Maybe as an excuse to just talk to each other! You don't give your other friends a wish list each time you talk, and then expect them to grant every one. You just share feelings. Make it the same with your best Friend, Jesus. And as you do, you will have a peace in your heart that is out of this world.

ARE YOU LISTENING, FATHER?

If you, then, though you are evil, know how to give good gifts to your children, how much more will your Father in heaven give good gifts to those who ask him? Matthew 7:11, NIV.

Do you sometimes wonder if God is listening to you? Many times we try to get someone's attention, but nobody will listen.

The Jacobs family sat around a long table eating Thanksgiving dinner. It was such a wonderful occasion. Relatives were visiting from far away, everyone was happy, and the dinner was delicious! Suddenly in the middle of all the jolly talk and laughter a shrill voice screamed, "Somebody pass me the butter!" All the family members became quiet, and all eyes turned toward Nichole, the screaming butter eater. With a stern face, Mother ordered Nichole to her room until she could be more polite. Nichole burst into tears and fled.

Soon things returned to normal around the table. The laughter was heard again, Nichole was allowed to come back and finish dinner, and everything seemed to be going well. However, Nichole's mother had lingering questions about her behavior. Why had she been so rude?

After dinner, Uncle Charles played back the video he had made of their Thanksgiving together. Everybody sat quietly, enjoying the happy scene again. Then they heard Nichole's little voice, almost lost in the laughter around the table, ask politely, "Please pass the butter." Again Nichole's voice asked politely, "Please pass the butter." Finally they heard Nichole shriek, "Somebody pass me the butter!"

Sometimes people may ignore you. Perhaps people who care a lot about you will accidentally let you down, but God is different. God is the best friend you will ever have. He is listening for your faintest whisper. He is eager to answer.

IT DOESN'T PAY TO CHEAT

What the wicked dreads will overtake him. Proverbs 10:24, NIV.

It was probably one of the best lie detectors ever invented. In India several hundred years before Christ, a system was devised that would show if a suspected criminal was guilty or not.

The suspect was taken into a darkened room along with an interrogator and a donkey. The suspect was told that he would be asked several questions about the crime and that he must hold the donkey's tail as he answered, for the donkey would bray if he told a lie.

What do you suppose a criminal did? He simply didn't hold onto the donkey's tail. In the darkness of the room, the interrogator couldn't see what he was doing, and assumed the suspect was following directions. Nobody would know for sure . . . or would they?

What the criminals discovered was that they came out from the dark room with clean hands. You see, they were not told that soot had been rubbed onto the donkey's tail. If they had followed directions, their hands would be covered with soot. But by not touching the donkey's tail and then lying about it, the criminals sentenced themselves—guilty.

There is nothing more uncomfortable than a guilty conscience. In fact, the Bible tells us that the wicked flee when no one pursues them. Feeling guilty, they think everyone is after them.

When Jesus comes, sinners will finally realize that what they didn't want to think about has really happened. They will try to get out of having to look God in the face when He pronounces them eternally lost. They will cry for the rocks and the mountains to fall upon them, but instead they must face God. The nagging fears they've been carrying around will overtake them at last. What a horrible realization, that they are eternally lost. Forever.

Do you have a nagging fear that something you're doing is not right? Then stop doing it. Keep your conscience free. That is the best present you can give yourself.

NOVEMBER 24

HONEY ON THE HOUSE

For everything there is a season, and a time for every matter under heaven. Ecclesiastes 3:1, RSV.

A family we'll call the Howards, of Los Angeles, California, had a problem. One summer they began to notice an unusual odor throughout their house. It was very faint at first, and they attributed it to years of cooking, thinking that perhaps the walls were getting permeated with oils and odors.

It was not an obnoxious odor at first, because it was so faint, and the Howards couldn't tell exactly what it was or where it came from. But then the smell became stronger and more pungent—especially in the living room. It was a sweet smell—almost like honey.

The neighbors who came over laughed at the odor and suggested that the Howards had a real "home, sweet home!"

Months went by. By now the smell was obnoxious, almost over-whelming. But the Howards had no idea of its cause until one night that will forever "stick" in their memory!

Fortunately no one was in the living room when it happened. Without warning, the living room ceiling collapsed and fell with a thud to the floor, oozing with sticky, sweet honey! The ceiling tiles were saturated with honey. The support beams dripped honey. It was the biggest honeycomb that anyone had ever seen! It must have been there for years, unnoticed but silently saturating the structures.

You can imagine what a mess it was to clean up! The carpet and furniture were totally ruined by the sticky, oozy mess. Everything that wasn't washable had to be replaced.

Now, I'm sure the Howard family liked honey, but on toast—not on the house!

The Bible tells us there is a time for everything, and a place for everything too. No matter how sweet honey is, we don't want it in our hair or matted in the rug. And no matter how sweet love is, there are certain things that are not sweet until the right time. Don't let the sweetness of grown-up love be ruined by a bitter memory of something you know you shouldn't do now. Your conscience is worth looking out for, and no one can take care of it any better than you!

NOVEMBER 25

YOU ARE WHAT YOU THINK

He will keep in perfect peace all those who trust in him, whose thoughts turn often to the Lord! Isaiah 26:3, TLB.

Have you ever chewed yourself out for something you did? Have you ever said "I can't believe I did that! How dumb!" Have you ever called yourself an idiot? Does it make you feel any better, or does it make you feel worse?

All of us do what psychiatrists call "self-talk," which influences how we feel. It is believed that our feelings come through a three-step process: first something happens, then we self-talk, and then our feelings come, based on what we tell ourselves. For example, if you do well on a test, you subconsciously tell yourself that you're smart, and then you feel good about yourself. If you make a bad grade, you tell yourself you're dumb, and that makes you feel bad.

But just because you did poorly on one test doesn't mean the next test has to be the same. If you do poorly, don't tell yourself you're dumb. Instead, tell yourself that, yes, you did poorly on the test, but next time you will do better.

No one understands the human mind better than God. He tells us we can always be at peace (feel good about ourselves) if we keep our minds on Him. That doesn't surprise me, because when I think about God, I think about how special He thinks I am. And when I tell myself that God thinks I'm special, it makes me feel good inside.

Have you told yourself something good about yourself today? Don't call yourself bad names. God wants you to feel happy. When you have done something stupid, maybe something that could deserve a bad name, stop, don't do it. Ask forgiveness instead. God has told you in a thousand ways that you're special, but only you can tell yourself that. Do it now! Do it often! And you'll have a day that's out of this world.

NOVEMBER 26

HOW DO YOU SOUND?

A good man's speech reveals the rich treasures within him. An evil-hearted man is filled with venom, and his speech reveals it. Matthew 12:35, TLB.

I have been fascinated with words for a long time. It amazes me at how quickly we can choose our words—special combinations of letters—and string them together to make sentences. I am also amazed at how people do things or avoid things or feel better—simply because of how we join words together. Two people can say the same thing in two different ways, and one will sound argumentative, and the other gracious.

For example: if someone is telling you something you don't understand and you say "You're not making any sense," he will probably get mad at you. Can you guess the reason? Of course, you seem to be attacking him. On the other hand, if you say "I don't understand what you're saying," he will think you are polite and will likely rephrase his statement. The difference? Your choice of words.

Everyone is a little insecure, and we are continually asking ourselves whether we are likable or not, according to how others respond to us. Quite naturally, we don't like to be with people who don't make us feel good about ourselves. And that is the secret of popular people—they make us feel good. Rather than attacking what we say or what we do, they graciously share their interpretation of what we're saying or doing.

If you don't like arguments, then don't tell someone else that he's saying something wrong. He will want to defend himself. Instead, tell him how you *feel* about what he said. Nobody can argue with feelings! "I don't think I can agree with you on that" sounds so much better than "You're wrong!"

If we keep in mind the fact that everyone we meet wants us to make him feel better, it makes even the most casual or brief exchanges important. As Christians, we should look out for each other, "in honour preferring one another." I think God is pleased when we can disagree without being disagreeable.

A gray-haired, distinguished gentleman arrived at the door to an office building at the same time as a young woman and held the door open for her.

"Don't hold the door open for me just because I'm a lady," she said crisply.

The man was silent for a moment, then replied, "I didn't open the door for you because you are a lady. I opened it because I'm a gentleman."

Maybe our rule should be that we don't speak graciously to others because they deserve it, but because we are Christians.

NOVEMBER 27

GOD, WHY DO YOU LET US HURT?

So Satan went out from the presence of the Lord and afflicted Job with painful sores from the soles of his feet to the top of his head. . . . His wife said to him, ". . . Curse God and die!" Job 2:7-9, NIV.

Have you ever wondered why there is so much suffering in the world? Since God is a God of love and gentleness, how can He stand by while people hurt each other? How can our loving God allow the devastation of earthquakes, floods, tornadoes, and other natural disasters?

Perhaps you've wondered how you can trust God with your life when He lets such terrible things happen. Is God trustworthy? Does He really care?

Our text for today speaks to these questions. Imagine for a minute that you are Job. You have everything anybody could desire. Besides that, you are a moral and just man. People respect you and are awed by your success.

You are in town one day, visiting with friends, when you hear a knock at the door. A messenger rushes in to tell you that you have been robbed of all your oxen and donkeys (your sports cars and bank account), and all your servants have been killed.

While this messenger is still speaking, another one runs up. He tearfully describes how fire has just fallen from heaven and destroyed your sheep and your shepherds (your cattle ranch estate).

As you sink weakly into a chair, your head spinning in disbelief, two more messengers arrive. One tells you that your camels (your fleet of motor homes) have been stolen. The other messenger, however, has the worst news of all—all of your children have been killed in a tornado!

You wonder why God is doing this to you. While you wonder, you break out with large, painful pimples all over your body—not a speck of skin is unaffected. As the days pass, while you are trying to settle where you can live and bury your dead children, the pimples open into large, weeping sores. Whatever is God doing to you? Can you trust Him?

Read the story of Job and answer three questions: first, who blessed Job with such great wealth and a wonderful family? Yes, God did! Second, who took everything away? Yes, Satan. Now one final question. Who got all the blame from Job's wife and friends? You'll find the answer in his wife's words, found in Job 2:9.

Do we, like Job's wife, sometimes blame God for the heartache that Satan causes? God is not responsible for the suffering in this world. He wants to bring the suffering to an end. But Satan wants to test us. He wants to try to make us hate God. Since Satan can't ever go back to heaven, he doesn't want us to go either. He wants us to hate God.

Don't let that sly serpent, Satan, con you. Put the blame for disaster on Satan's shoulders—not God's—and let 1990 be the year you love God even more.

NOVEMBER 28

WHOM ARE YOU GOING TO BELIEVE?

In the beginning God created the heavens and the earth. Genesis 1:1, RSV.

So what are we going to do if this story about God and creation turns out not to be true? What if there is really no heaven? Believers and atheists have been debating this for years. Is there any way to prove there is a God?

A minister and his friend, an evolutionist, were walking along the beach one overcast afternoon. The evolutionist was expounding his favorite theory, that man and matter just happened to evolve to the state they now are.

The minister listened politely, but he couldn't agree. *How am I going to get through to this guy?* he wondered silently.

By and by his toe bumped against something hard, half buried in the sand. He stooped to scrape away the sand and picked it up. It was a large, old-fashioned watch, still ticking. The minister immediately had an idea.

"Friend," he said, shaking off a few wet grains of sand that still clung to the watch, "look what I found!"

"Why, it's a watch!" the man replied.

"Yes! I wonder how it got here!" Taking out his pocketknife, the minister pried off the back of the watch to expose the ticking gears and fine movement inside. "I'm surprised it still works. Amazing, isn't it, how all these gears work together so well?"

"Why, of course. Someone planned it well," the evolutionist replied.

"And then he made it," the minister said.

His friend nodded.

Slowly the minister closed the back of the watch and slipped it into his pocket. "My friend," he said gently, "how is it that you can concede that someone had to plan the function of the watch and then made it, but you insist that man—who is much more complex than a watch—just happened?"

The evolutionist had no reply.

In the end, when all the discussion is over, you have to believe someone. Will you believe the words of another mortal man, or the words of an immortal God?

NOVEMBER 29

LOSERS CAN BE WINNERS

A good name is to be chosen rather than great riches, and favor is better than silver or gold. Proverbs 22:1, RSV.

The story is told of gold medalist Al Oerter and Rink Babka, teammates in the 1960 Olympics in Rome. They were expected to dominate the field in discus throwing. But the night before the competition Babka came down with a severe case of dysentery; his belly hurt and he could eat nothing. Many feared that he would not be able to compete in the next day's events, but he did, even in his weakened condition, and he made it through the qualifying round. But many then wondered if he could again compete that afternoon in the finals.

When his name was announced that afternoon, Babka was there, though he was pale and obviously not feeling well. In spite of his setback, however, he gave a strong performance, staying in the lead after three rounds. But his teammate, Oerter, was not doing as well. Babka watched on the fourth throw as Oerter's discus landed far short of his potential.

On the fifth round Babka was still in the lead. But when Oerter stepped into the circle, spun, and threw the discus, it landed much farther than any other discus that day. Oerter ended up with the gold medal, and his friend Babka got the silver.

What nobody knew till later was that Babka had helped his friend win. After the fourth round, Babka had noticed a small flaw in his friend's throwing technique. He had taken Oerter aside and suggested that he hold his throwing arm a little higher during the spin. Oerter did, and he won. And though Babka's kindness resulted in his getting the silver medal instead of the gold, certainly no one would call Babka a loser!

Sometimes it may seem as though Christians are losers when they try to be kind. Others may take advantage of those who are kind. Maybe for this reason you are having a hard time justifying a Christian lifestyle. Maybe it seems as though kids who don't worry about religion and church are having more fun than you are.

Sometimes it does seem as if people of the world get all the breaks—money, fame, travel. But the game's not over yet. The stories have not all been told. Maybe nobody knows about the times you were a winner and helped somebody when you knew you wouldn't benefit from it. Maybe nobody knows—yet. But in time everyone will notice that the pattern of your life is one of kindness and respect for others. That's how a reputation is made—by life's small events. And a good reputation brings more happiness than silver or gold.

NOVEMBER 30

SECRET CODES

A cheerful look brings joy to the heart, and good news gives health to the bones. Proverbs 15:30, NIV.

Have you ever made up a secret code that just you and a few close friends shared? My son Marc has one in which certain numbers stand for certain letters in the alphabet. The messages are written in numbers, rather than in letters, and only those who know the code can read the messages.

I used to write secret letters to my friend Lois by using lemon juice and a toothpick. When Lois got the note, she held a burning match under the paper, just close enough so it scorched the lemon juice, and then she could read the note. It was a poor way to get messages across, though, because there was always the big chance that someone else knew how to make the letters appear, or that the message would get burned up during the process!

All of us send secret messages to each other, in another way. It's called "body language." If you watch closely, you can tell a lot about people just by watching what they do. For example, if a person has a long, unsmiling face, you can guess that all is not well with him. Either he is sad or sleepy or worried about something. And if he drags his feet as he walks, you can be even more sure that something is wrong.

I learned just recently that horse statues in parks are fashioned in code. Traditionally, when all of the horse's hooves are on the ground, the rider died a natural death. Two hooves in the air indicate the rider was killed on the battlefield. If just one hoof is raised, the rider died from wounds suffered in battle.

Sometimes our faces reflect how we feel inside, but the reverse is also possible. We can start feeling good inside if we turn our lips into a smile, whether we feel like smiling or not.

Try this experiment. Put a frown on your face and say "Go away!" Now smile and say the same thing. Keep it up! Keep smiling the rest of the day.

WHAT DO YOU LEARN FROM CHRISTMAS?

Dear friends, let us practice loving each other, for love comes from God and those who are loving and kind show that they are the children of God, and that they are getting to know him better. 1 John 4:7, TLB.

It was the first day of December, and Mother set out the wooden Nativity set on the mantel, placing the Baby Jesus figure gently in the wooden manger.

"Poor Baby Jesus," she told the children. "He doesn't have any soft straw for His mattress. Why don't we give Him some?"

"Sure! I'll get some tissue," the littlest sister replied.

"No, why don't we give Him a soft mattress a different way, a way that will please Him," Mother suggested. "I'll put a basket of straw on the side table near the manger, and each time one of us does something kind for someone else in secret, we'll place a piece of straw in the manger. Baby Jesus should have a nice soft mattress by Christmas Day."

That afternoon the oldest brother emptied the dishwasher without being asked. His mother was surprised when she discovered it. She checked the manger, and sure enough, there she saw the first piece of straw.

There was another piece of straw in the manger that evening. Without being noticed, the oldest sister had crept into her brother's room, picked up his clothes, and turned down his bed.

The table was mysteriously set when everyone went downstairs for breakfast the next morning. Another piece of straw in the manger.

"I love you" notes began showing up on mirrors and on plates around the table. And clothes were washed and folded before Mother could get to them. The dog was fed and the mail brought in without anyone asking. The neighbor's weeds were even pulled in front of her gate. The baby was bundled up and taken for long walks, and more and more straw was placed in the manger.

By the time Christmas morning arrived, the wooden Baby Jesus slept on a thick, cushiony mattress of straw. And over the top of Him was a thin, soft sheet of tissue that the oldest brother placed for His blanket.

331

It was a Christmas that taught everyone the real reason Jesus was born.

BEING HAPPY FOR MISFORTUNES

One thing I know, that though I was blind, now I see. John 9:25, RSV.

Eddie Robinson, blind for nine years as a result of complications from a truck accident, was struck by lightning in June of 1980. "I heard a sound like a whip cracking over my head," he recalls. "Next thing I knew, I woke up facedown in the mud." Doctors estimated that Eddie was unconscious for about 20 minutes. When he regained consciousness, he made his way to a neighbor's house on rubber-like legs, then, after getting a drink of water and resting, he went home and lay down on his bed. An hour later Eddie, still incredibly thirsty, made his way into the kitchen, downed a half gallon of milk, and slumped onto the sofa. Suddenly he realized he could see the plaque on the wall.

Eddie let out a yell to his wife. "Doris, I can see!"

It was a miracle that doctors couldn't explain, but they tested his eyes and were amazed. The lightning bolt had restored Eddie Robinson's eyesight, improved his hearing, and had corrected his heart irregularity.

Eddie attributes his recovery to God. "I now appreciate the everyday wonders of life," he says. "Moonlight filtering through the leaves, the flowers in the garden, a caterpillar spinning its cocoon."

Archbishop Terence Cardinal Cooke emphasized the meaning of life in his last pastoral letter when he wrote: "The gift of life, God's special gift, is no less beautiful when it is accompanied by illness or weakness, hunger or poverty, mental or physical handicaps, loneliness, or old age. Indeed, at these times, human life gains extra splendor as it requires our special care, concern, and reverence."

Sometimes we learn to appreciate things more when we think we're going to lose them. Problems can make us focus our attention more on the life to come than on the boring round of activities here. We put things in a better perspective.

An anonymous poet said it this way:

"I asked God for strength, that I might achieve;

I was made weak, that I might learn humbly to obey.

I asked for health, that I might do greater things;

I was given infirmity, that I might do better things.

I asked for riches, that I might be happy;

I was given poverty, that I might be wise.

I asked for power, that I might have the praise of men;

I was given weakness, that I might feel the need of God.
I asked for all things, that I might enjoy life;
I was given life, that I might enjoy all things.
I got nothing that I asked for—but everything I had hoped for. Almost despite myself, my unspoken prayers were answered. I am, among all men, most richly blessed."

DECEMBER 3

FILLING IN THE GAPS

His roots shall spread out; his beauty shall be like the olive, and his fragrance like Lebanon. Hosea 14:6, NIV.

Several years ago thousands of acres of forest burned to the ground here in Oregon in what has been called the Tillamook burn. Driving through that coastal range today, you can still see occasional charred trunks above the lush, new growth of young trees.

The rejuvenation of a forest is wonderful to see. Perhaps a huge oak or redwood that has occupied a spot in the forest for decades is finally blown down in a storm, leaving an open place where it once stood. What happens? Full sunlight shines down on that once-dark area, and little bushes and trees that had been struggling to survive suddenly thrive. New growth begins, and soon the area is filled in with more trees than it had before.

Could that empty spot in the forest be like an empty spot in your life? Perhaps you have lost a good friend or a member of your family. Maybe you have lost your home and all your worldly goods to fire. It hurts to lose something you cherish. And you can either be consumed by that hurt and become rebellious, or you can allow God to "shine down on you" more during this time and fill that open space with good things. The most healing prayer to pray is "God, I'm empty; I'm devastated. Hold me up and fill me with Your love." As God warms that empty spot, your "branches" will spread. Your priorities will change or reorganize, and you will cultivate a warm relationship with God.

It's normal to mourn what you have lost. It's OK to cry and show how bad you feel. But also remember that every ending is the start of a new beginning. Look for it.

TAKE IT ON FAITH

All things work together for good to them that love God. Romans 8:28.

If you drive through Holland in late spring, you will see mounds of beautiful tulip blossoms cut from their stalks, lying in high piles as refuse. This might seem to be a crime, but there is a method in the madness of Holland's gardeners. Dutch tulip bulb growers know that if they leave the blossom untouched, too much of the plant's sap is needed for the bloom, and the bulb's growth is stunted. Also, when the tulip petals fall off and decay, they can cause mold diseases. So the growers cut off the blossoms in their prime, forcing all the plant's energies into the bulb.

Many things happen to us that we cannot understand at the time. Sometimes it takes years before we begin to see how a certain event has worked out for the best. And sometimes we won't understand until we get to heaven.

A friend of mine told me about how she met her husband. She said her boyfriend at the time, whom she was just crazy about, had broken up with her suddenly for no good reason, just before she met the man whom she married. "I was devastated at the time," she says. "I thought my boyfriend was Mr. Right, and we had been talking about getting married and everything. But then he said he didn't want to see me anymore, and I couldn't understand it. I thought I could never love anyone the way I loved him." But looking back, she says it was the best thing that could ever have happened to her. The person her old boyfriend has become is someone she knows she would not have been happy with. He has already been divorced twice and can't keep a job. "I'm so thankful that he left me before we got married," she says.

Maybe you have recently broken up a wonderful friendship. You're hurting. You think you will hurt this way for the rest of your life. But you won't. As more distance comes between you and this friendship, your wounds will heal. They may leave you a little bit changed, but that is often for the better. You are wiser now. You understand more. Perhaps you understand yourself better, too. Maybe a new door has just been opened or will open because of this experience. Try to find the joy of anticipation, the wonder of finding out what's around the corner. Remember, God has promised that "all things work together for good to them that love God."

THE DESIRES OF YOUR HEART

Delight yourself in the Lord and he will give you the desires of your heart. Psalm 37:4, NIV.

If you were to describe happiness in one sentence, what would it be? "Happiness is . . ."

I'll never forget a dream I had once when I was dieting. For some reason, every store I entered was giving away anything and everything I wanted. (Now, armchair psychologists, don't analyze this dream too deeply, though the parallels are quite obvious.) First I went into a dress store, and every dress I tried on looked wonderful on me, and was, of course, free. I came out of that store loaded with packages!

Then I went into a grocery store. Again, everything was free! I loaded up my cart, and just as I was about to leave the store, I passed by the frozen food section. I slowed at the ice-cream section. There was chocolate-chip ice cream. Was it free too?

The store manager nodded eagerly. "Help yourself! It's all free! Take what you wish!"

Now, there's a problem with helping yourself to free food. You don't want to cheat yourself by taking too little, but neither do you want to look greedy and take too much! So I didn't take any! In my dream, I couldn't put my hand in that freezer and take out any ice cream. So I left the store with everything but what I wanted most of all.

That's the problem with taking things. I'm glad God says He will *give* us the desires of our heart; we don't have to *take* them.

What are the desires of your heart? Is it to be popular? To have a good figure? To be captain of the baseball team? Why do you suppose you think that having those things would make you happy? Go ahead and imagine what life would be like if you had those things. Let's say you're the most popular student in the school; you have the best figure in the whole school; you're captain of the baseball team. How do you feel? Like someone special?

Isn't that what most of our desires boil down to in the end? Everyone wants to be special. That is the desire of our hearts. But specialness is not something that we *take*. It is *given* to us by God.

Each time the class bell rings today, hold out your hands and look at them while you remind yourself of how special you are. Jesus would have died if you were the only person who would be saved. That's how special you are!

IS YOUR STOMACH RED?

He that is slow to anger is better than the mighty. Proverbs 16:32.

How do you deal with anger? Are you annoyed quickly? Are your emotions at a sudden heat? Is your tongue quicker than your better judgment? Or do you keep your anger inside, maintaining a stoic face, seeming calm on the outside while you stew on the inside? Either way you look at it, anger is not good for your body.

When I was in nursing school, we saw a film that I'll never forget, which demonstrated how damaging the effects of anger can be. In it, a dear little man, who seemed to be about 70, had a stoma, or surgical opening, into his abdomen, which exposed a portion of the lining of his stomach. So the lining of his stomach was easily seen from the outside as a smooth light-pink ring.

As the film began, the man and his doctor discussed things of general interest to the elderly gentleman: baseball teams, his garden, his grand-children, and so forth. Eventually the discussion became heated, as the doctor argued some point with him. The man tried to argue calmly, but even as he spoke, the lining of his stomach began to turn red. The conversation soon grew very heated. And now the man's stomach lining was an angry, fiery red, the color of a lobster.

At last the doctor apologized, and the conversation returned to neutral, happy things. Slowly but progressively the stomach lining returned to its original light-pink color.

Anger is just not good for us, whether or not it gets us in trouble for what we say or do. It is physically harmful. But how can we keep from getting angry?

Sometimes it helps to empathize with the irritating individual and give him the benefit of the doubt. Try to imagine the real reason he is so irritating to you. Perhaps some family problems are bothering him. Sometimes a person who is out of sorts with the world needs someone to say, "You seem really angry about something. Would you like to talk about it?" And if he does, you will probably make a friend.

People can't make you angry unless you let them. It's your choice.

DON'T GET IN THE CAR

A wise man will hear, and will increase learning. Proverbs 1:5.

Eleven-year-old Jill panted up to the bus stop just as it drew away without her. Tears of disappointment filled her eyes. Everything had gone wrong that morning, and now she'd be late for school.

Just then a blue car pulled up to the curb, and a nice-looking young man smiled out at her. "Missed your bus, huh?" he said. "I'll give you a lift."

Jill backed off, remembering her mother's warnings about not taking rides with strangers. "No, thank you."

"Aw, come on. You can trust me," he said with a grin. "Besides, you'll be late for school if you don't."

So she got into the car with the friendly young man. But he didn't take her to school. He sped out of the city to a wooded area, where he tormented her, beat her up, and finally left her to find a way back as best she could.

Patty and Carol had a date with two boys whom they knew fairly well. But to their surprise, as soon as the boys picked them up, the girls realized that they'd been drinking.

When the boys stopped their car at a store for beer, Patty and Carol jumped out and ran to a phone booth. No one answered at either of their homes. The boys came back and promised to drive carefully, so the girls reluctantly got into the car. Soon the driver's foot got heavier on the gas pedal, and he laughed at the girls' screams.

The car sped out of control, skidded off the road, and crashed into a tree. Both Patty and Carol were killed.

These true stories were told to some elementary school students not long ago, and the question was asked "What could have been done to prevent Jill from being harmed and those girls from being killed?"

The kids were silent for a moment. Then one girl said, "They could have prayed before they got into the car."

Bad answer. Of course they could have prayed. But please listen carefully to the next thing I'm going to tell you. We live in a sinful world, and because of this, God must permit terrible things to happen. Sometimes He interferes, but more often matters follow a cause-and-effect course. In other words, if you cut your finger, you will bleed. If you step off the edge of a high roof, you will fall to the ground and get hurt.

What could Carol and Patty have done to avoid being killed in the wreck? What could Jill have done to save herself a day of terror? What can you do if you're faced with the same problems?

Don't get in the car!

OOTW-12

How can I say this so you'll remember it? I wish I could stand on a mountain and shout it, or tattoo it into your brain. Don't worry about being impolite. Don't worry about hurting someone's feelings. Don't worry that the other kids might make fun of you.

Don't get in the car!

Carol and Patty could have stayed at the store. They could have explained their problem to the manager. They might have borrowed coins from him if they ran out of money for the phone. They could have even called the police for help. If you're ever in the same situation, keep calling your parents or other friends; *just don't get in a car with drinking drivers. Don't accept rides with strangers.*

By all means, talk to God about your problem. Give Him a chance to help you out of it. But don't run ahead of Him by thinking you have to solve your problem yourself. And no matter what—don't get in the car!

DECEMBER 8

HOW TO LOVE YOUR ENEMIES

Listen, all of you. Love your enemies. Do good to those who hate you. Pray for the happiness of those who curse you; implore God's blessing on those who hurt you. Luke 6:27, 28, TLB.

Mother Teresa, the nun who has devoted her life to helping the poverty-stricken people of Calcutta, often gives people unusual advice. When a group of Americans, many of whom were in the teaching profession, visited her in Calcutta, they asked her for some advice to take home to their families.

"Smile at your wives," she told them. "Smile at your husbands."

Thinking that perhaps the counsel was simplistic, coming from an unmarried person, one of them asked, "Are you married?"

"Yes," she replied, to their surprise, "and I find it hard sometimes to smile at Jesus. He can be very demanding."

Jesus does ask us to do some pretty difficult things sometimes. For one thing, He tells us we are to love our enemies and do good to those who despitefully use us. That's hard! How can you love somebody who's being unfair to you?

I've found that it helps to imagine why the person might be acting the way he does. Give him the benefit of the doubt. People often take out their frustrations on people whom they think are inferior to themselves. But just because someone yells at you doesn't mean you deserve it. Maybe that person is struggling with a difficult decision, or maybe somebody else has just yelled at him. Maybe he's sick or worried about a personal problem. You may never know. But try to pick some reason for his crankiness and put the blame on circumstances, rather than on yourself.

If you're still upset at being unfairly chewed out, seek out a friend and talk it over. No doubt you'll feel better then.

But how do you love someone who is cranky or downright hateful? Love comes in varying degrees, but it has as its core the desire to give happiness to the loved one. Perhaps you don't want to get chummy with the cranky person, but you certainly do wish him happiness—not only for his own enjoyment, but also because that might stop his angry outbursts. When you are praying for his happiness, you are loving him. And when you see things in that light, it isn't hard to love your enemies after all.

THEY GOT CAUGHT!

Be sure your sin will find you out. Numbers 32:23, RSV.

There was a news story several years ago about two young boys who thought they could beat the system but who got the shock of their lives when things didn't turn out the way they expected!

The boys were 13 at the time. As I remember the story, they saw this sign in a local ice-cream store: "Free ice-cream cone on your birthday. Age limit, 12." The boys were one year too old! But being clever young men, they weren't about to let one year come between them and free ice-cream. So each boy filled out a card for the free ice-cream cone, but instead of putting down their real names and birthdays, they used fake names and fake birthdays, planning it so each would get a free ice-cream cone within the next few weeks. They put their correct addresses on the cards, though, so the free offer would reach them.

The fake birthdays arrived and with them the ice-cream cones, and the boys congratulated each other on being so clever. They never gave the incident another thought, until they were "18." Six years after they received the free ice-cream cones on their "birthdays," the boys' aliases received official mail from the U.S. government, telling them it was time to sign up for the draft!

Eventually the truth came out, and through some confessions and the help of their fathers, the government was made aware that the names on the cards were actually aliases. But the two had several scary weeks before everything was resolved.

Many things in life are like that. Something may seem innocent and fun at the time, but may in the long run prove no fun at all. Smoking and taking drugs may seem to be the cool and grown-up thing to do when you're young, but by the time you reach adulthood and are stuck with the addiction and bad health, it isn't fun anymore!

Messing around, doing a lot of hugging and kissing and petting, can seem like fun or the way to be popular. But in the end it will ruin your reputation and bring shame and remorse.

You've heard stories about different kids that are told in whispers or with loud laughter. Sometimes everyone knows, because you can't hide a baby. Other times an abortion is dismissed with a shrug and the comment "Well, what do you expect?" Even when kids don't get caught, the dating patterns they set will hurt their chances of having a happy marriage.

The Ten Commandments are guides as much as they are rules, guides that help us have a happy life.

LOOKS CAN BE DECEIVING

For the Lord sees not as man sees; man looks on the outward appearance, but the Lord looks on the heart. 1 Samuel 16:7, RSV.

There is a story about some tourists who were traveling through a mountain pass and came upon a spot where a little cabin was built at such an angle that it overlooked a beautiful valley and looked up toward two majestic mountains besides. As the tourists stopped there to take some pictures of the snowcapped, rugged peaks, the owner of the cabin, a bearded frontier-type, hobbled out to greet them.

"You must have planned the location of your cabin very carefully!" the tourists gushed, breathless over the panoramic view.

"Yup!" the frontiersman replied. "It has the best TV reception I could get."

Things are not always as they seem. Sometimes the people who seem to be on the mountaintop aren't really there at all, or aren't there for the same reasons we would be. Sometimes winners are actually the ones who turn out to be losers.

I have been out of high school for more years than I care to admit, but at a reunion a few years ago, I was surprised at how my classmates and I had changed. Many of the kids who had been considered popular were now divorced and unhappy, still bouncing around from husband to husband or wife to wife, much as they did between boyfriends and girlfriends in high school.

On the other hand, most of those who were quiet and stable in high school, doing their best in class and having fun with a variety of friends, are now respected businessmen, teachers, and medical personnel. They are still stable and are achieving personal satisfaction from being that way.

Stable doesn't mean boring, and stable kids can be popular, too. As we've said before, kids who make other kids feel good are the ones who are popular. But if you must compromise your moral values to be popular, don't do it. Don't sell yourself short just to have friends. Those kinds of "friends" are fleeting. There are many more years to your life than the ones in high school, and you have to live with yourself for each of them. In the end, you are the winner if you are true to yourself. You're worth looking out for!

SNEAK, PEEK, AND SHRIEK

Be sure your sin will find you out. Numbers 32:23.

It was two weeks until Christmas, and excitement was running high in the Brown household. Perhaps the most excited family member of all was Terry, the Browns' 11-year-old son. Terry was especially excited this year because he had asked his grandmother for a very special present. He had asked her to buy a Stratego game for him.

At last Grandma's presents had arrived, and sure enough, there was a box for Terry. It was just about the size that he thought a Stratego game should be, and it rattled the way he thought a Stratego game should rattle. But was it really a Stratego game? Terry wondered. He would be so much more content if only he knew for sure.

Mother put all the presents from Grandmother in the big pantry in the hall. She closed the door and locked it, leaving the key in the lock. Terry studied the pantry door as Mother walked into the kitchen, an idea brewing in his mind.

Suddenly he jumped up, turned on the light, slipped into the closet, and locked the door from the inside. Now he would not be surprised by anyone opening the door.

Terry quietly found his present and carefully peeled off the Scotch tape and wrapping paper. Soon he was looking at a brand-new Stratego game. He was thrilled! He spent a few seconds admiring it, then carefully wrapped the present back up so that no one would know it had been unwrapped.

Terry was just placing the present back in the big box when he heard Mother's footsteps in the hall, walking past the pantry. Terry held his breath. Suddenly there was a click, and Terry stood in total darkness. Mother had turned off the pantry light!

Terry panicked. Even though he could have used the key to get out, he began to shriek and yell for Mother to come let him out.

Thousands of years ago a Bible writer said, "Be sure your sin will find you out." It's almost inevitable. Someone will find out. And sneakiness is no substitute for obedience. Be good to yourself. Choose to be honest and obedient in 1990 and always.

BEFORE WE PROVED A THING

While we were yet sinners Christ died for us. Romans 5:8, RSV.

I don't remember his name, but a certain young man, whom we'll call Tim, wanted to join the Army. They wouldn't take him because of a problem he'd had with the bones in his foot; they didn't think he could endure the rigors of walking and hiking that are required of a soldier.

Tim decided to prove to them that he could stand up on his own two feet just as well as anybody else! He decided to walk from New York to Washington, D.C. The newspapers were notified about what he was doing and why, and they covered his story.

By the time several weeks had passed and Tim had walked 300 miles, the bureaucratic red tape had been cut, and the Army sent a representative to tell Tim that he could enlist after all. He had proved he could make it.

It's tough to prove things. The hardest thing of all for us to prove is that we are fit for heaven. Aren't you glad God doesn't say "If you can go for two days without being irritated at all, then I'll let you come to heaven" or "If you can make straight A's in all your classes for all four years of high school and then do the same in college, you can come to heaven"? Not many of us would make it, I'm afraid.

But those are not the requirements for heaven. We don't really have to prove a thing to God; He loves us because we are His. He made us, and that's all the reason He needs to want us to be with Him forever. The Bible says that "while we were yet sinners" Christ died for us. Before we had proved a thing, He said we were worthy.

A young woman opening her first bank account was asked to sign her name as she usually did. She wrote on the line, "Love always, Catherine."

That's how I think God signs His name too. *"Love always, God."* No matter what we've done, no matter how we feel toward Him.

CAN YOU PROVE YOU'RE A CHRISTIAN?

Since we have such a huge crowd of men of faith watching us from the grandstands, let us strip off anything that slows us down or holds us back, and especially those sins that wrap themselves so tightly around our feet and trip us up; and let us run with patience the particular race that God has set before us. Hebrews 12:1, TLB.

Ginger, age 18, took on the mind-boggling task of teaching her grandpa to drive. He'd lived in a small rural town all his life and could chug along on a tractor in a field or get where he wanted by foot. He'd never felt the need to drive before. But at age 70 he took a notion that modern life was leaving him behind, and he wanted to join it.

He didn't take to driving naturally, but Ginger proved a patient teacher. First she had him drive in level fields and then on deserted dirt roads. At last he was ready for the big time, so with Ginger sitting beside him and both of them carefully belted in, Grandpa took the car to town.

They celebrated with ice-cream sodas, then began the journey back to the farm. All was well until Grandpa made a sharp left-hand turn without warning. The car behind him was going too fast to stop. He slammed on his brakes, but hit Grandpa and Ginger broadside.

"Why didn't you signal?" The question was asked the old gentleman by several people, including Ginger.

"I've lived in this town since I was knee-high to a coon," he replied. "Everybody around knows where I live."

As Christians, we talk about heaven as our home and how we are now preparing to go there. But do people know that you're going home? Can they tell where you're headed? If you were called into court on the grounds of being a Christian, would there be enough evidence to convict you?

A man in California found himself driving behind a car sporting a bumper sticker that read "You toucha my car, I breaka your face." The message of the bumper sticker wouldn't have seemed so unusual except that the driver and her passenger were both nuns in full habit. Somehow it didn't seem right that Christians should talk that way (of course, it could have been meant as a joke), and when we do, non-Christians gloat over it. "Christianity hasn't changed them any," the non-Christians observe. "Who needs it?"

It's unfair, you say, to judge Christianity by one person? Maybe so, but many people do just that. No matter how much you resent it, others are watching you to see what God is like.

With every thought, every word, and every action, you should ask yourself "What would Jesus do?" When this is your rule of thumb, then

Jesus' character becomes yours, and Jesus' home becomes your destiny. And people will *know* that you are going home.

YOU COULD BE RICH!

When a man is gloomy, everything seems to go wrong; when he is cheerful, everything seems right! Proverbs 15:15, TLB.

A sad and lonely widow sat rocking beside the window of her home one cold and rainy evening. It was Christmas, but she didn't have a tree. She didn't even have lights up, or any of her Christmas decorations out. She just didn't feel like she had anything to celebrate that year. Her husband had died, and all her children lived clear across the country. She was all alone.

As she sat there musing about all her misfortunes, feeling sorrier and sorrier for herself, there was a knock on the door, followed by a few children's voices singing Christmas carols.

The widow got up and shuffled over to the door, glad for an excuse to stop her depressing thoughts. She invited the children in, noting that they were shivering and that their ears and the tips of their noses were bright red.

"Would you like some hot chocolate?" she asked, and the children nodded their heads eagerly. "Then come into the kitchen and stand by the stove while I stir it up," the widow said, starting for the door. The children followed.

"Now you'll have to sing for your supper," the widow commanded with a light laugh. "Sing me some more songs while I heat the milk up!"

So the children sang a few more songs, watching wide-eyed as the widow took matching silver-rimmed teacups from the cupboard, placed them on matching saucers, and filled them with the steaming hot liquid. She placed a graham cracker beside each place and invited the children to gather around the table.

The children sipped the hot chocolate quietly. Then the youngest one—a little girl about 5 years old—got up the courage to ask a question that had occurred to her. "Madam, are you rich?" she asked in a quiet voice.

The widow looked around her small kitchen and then down at her simple dress. She didn't feel rich. "Why do you ask?" she returned.

"Because," the little girl answered solemnly, "your cups and saucers all match each other."

Too soon the children had finished their refreshment and were gone. The widow looked around her living room with new eyes. *Maybe I am rich,* she thought to herself. And she began to count her blessings.

What are you thankful for today? Name three things that are going well for you. Maybe you are richer than you think, too!

WORK IS NOT A FOUR-LETTER WORD

So the Lord God banished [Adam] from the Garden of Eden to work the ground from which he had been taken. Genesis 3:23, NIV.

Work, work, work—to many, it's a four-letter word. I guess I'm a philosopher at heart, but I often find myself weighing the benefits against the losses where work is concerned. This is what I have come up with regarding work. Jobs are necessary to keep the world on track, and we all work to help each other. (Somebody has to make the trucks for the farmer to till the fields and grow food to sell to people who live in the city, who sell the food to those who make the trucks for the farmers to use, and so on.)

Jobs are necessary to give us an identity, much like education does. For example, if you say you are a nurse, people tag you with certain characteristics they feel all nurses have. If you say you are a painter or an artist, you're pegged yet another way.

Jobs give us something to get up for in the morning.

Jobs are necessary if we want to have money to buy things.

Jobs are necessary to give us a sense of accomplishment. Ideally, work should be so enjoyable that we'd rather be there than anywhere else. Sometimes jobs end up being a kind of love-hate situation. While we love the money, we hate the hours we spend making it. When we buy something with that money, we don't want to have to spend any time working on it to keep it in shape. And yet taking care of something that stays with us for years, aging but not forsaken, feels good. It feels good to work for something, to work on something. And God knew that. So He gives us work.

When Adam was sent from the garden, God didn't leave him there with nothing to do with his time. He gave Adam work to do.

While you are in school, that is your work. When you get into high school, you may add a job to your work as a student. If you are only a student, think of your schoolwork as a business—your business. Because whether your business fails or prospers, you are the one most affected. Be good to yourself. Do your best to make your business thrive!

DO THE LAST DAYS SCARE YOU?

*And surely I will be with you always, to the very end of the age.
Matthew 28:20, NIV.*

Sometimes the events of the last days on earth scare me. I don't want to hear about being persecuted and chased and frightened. That's the way one of my teachers used to put it to us. He always put emphasis on how utterly horrible the experience was going to be, and I grew so afraid that I could hardly concentrate on the daily tasks I had to do. Somewhere lurking in the future was that awful experience! I dreaded it!

And then I talked to my dad. He said that God would allow those people who were not spiritually strong enough to make it through the time of trouble to die first. And for those still alive, it was going to be rather frightening, but not only for us. It will be a frightening time for those who are chasing us too! No one is going to enjoy it. But for those on God's side, the fear that we are not right with God will be greater than the fear of pain or death. We will wonder if we have confessed every sin, if we were faithful witnesses for God, if we had learned to love Him enough to trust Him. These are the things we will fear.

It won't take long for us to know whether or not God is with us. After a while, we'll notice that though we are being pursued, the enemy cannot find us! Though they may be shooting at us, their bullets will be deflecting off of something invisible. We are told that just before Jesus comes, He will not allow any believer to be put to death, because it would not serve any purpose in helping someone else make his or her decision for God. By then it will be too late. So death will not be what we will fear; we will fear that we have not known God and loved Him as well as we could have.

We can do something to keep from being too fearful then, can't we? We can start today by being in constant communion with God. Whisper a prayer as you go between classes! Memorize the Bible text for today and repeat it again and again as you go through the day. Fill up your "data bank," and you will feel at peace. And then don't forget to trust Jesus. He promises that He will give us the strength we need when we need it. He promised! And God never breaks a promise!

MARGY'S MONEY

Your own soul is nourished when you are kind. Proverbs 11:17, TLB.

A young man, Alan by name, stood at the door of a modest brick house and gave a light knock. It was a cool, sunny day, typical of a December in Texas. A Christmas wreath welcomed all visitors, and when Mrs. Daniels opened the door, Alan saw a big Christmas tree covered with ornaments and surrounded with gifts.

"Do you have any work that I might do?" he asked politely. "I could rake leaves or do anything else you might have."

Mrs. Jones smiled, her eyes taking in his shabby jacket and the withered left arm that hung limp at his side. "I'm sorry, I just don't know," she told him. "My husband has run to the store and he'd be the one to ask about having any yard work done."

"When will he be back?" Alan persisted. "I'm trying to earn money to buy Christmas presents for my mom and my girlfriend."

"Well—" Mrs. Daniels glanced toward the window. "There he is now."

After a few moments of bargaining, Alan and Mr. Daniels agreed that he would rake the front leaves for $10. Mr. Daniels went on about his pre-Christmas chores and left him with a rake and some large plastic yard bags.

It was apparent to anyone who felt inclined to watch that the young man was having a hard time raking leaves with his one good arm. An hour passed. Mr. Daniels went out to help, and the two of them filled four large bags.

In the meantime, Mr. Daniels had asked his wife, "Do you have any oranges or nuts that you could put into a bag for this kid? He told me he was trying to earn money to buy Christmas presents." So she and her 16-year-old daughter, Margy, fixed up a big sack of winter fruits, adding a box of stationery and a bottle of cologne for good measure.

Alan left the Daniels with a big smile, carrying the bag of goodies and the pay he had earned. When the family talked about it that evening, Margy began to grin. "What's with you, Margy?" her dad asked. "Oh, I was just thinking. I wonder what Alan thought when he found the $20 bill I put in there!"

How do you suppose the young man felt when he found the extra $20? How do you suppose Mom felt when she had to replace the stationery and cologne she'd bought for Christmas gifts for friends? And how did Margy feel a couple of days later when she didn't have any more money? I think Margy received the biggest blessing of all. Have you done something lately to give teenagers a good reputation? Is there something you can do today? Think about it! Being kind is the best kind of blessing there is.

DECEMBER 18

HAPPY ENDINGS

Your Father, who sees what is done in secret, will reward you. Matthew 6:18, NIV.

The story is told of a young man who worked at an inn during college summer vacations as headwaiter. Late one evening a family came who had driven a long way and were obviously tired and hungry. And though some people were still finishing their dinner, the dining room had just been closed to new guests. The hostess refused to seat the tired family.

Overhearing the conversation and seeing the disappointed looks on their faces, the young man stepped in as headwaiter and said, "Why don't you come on in? I can't let you be disappointed. *I'll* wait on you."

Gratefully the little group accepted his invitation and enjoyed a hot meal. Before they left, they took the headwaiter's name. But he never did hear from them.

A few years later, when the young man had graduated from college and was looking for a job, he started a round of interviews. At the first one, when he stepped into the boss's office for the interview, the executive behind the desk looked up from his papers and said casually, "How's everything at the inn?"

Then he explained that he was the man who had been traveling that night with his family, and he had never forgotten the kindness of the young headwaiter. He had already made up his mind to hire him even before he received his résumé or talked to him. The young man's kindness had served him well.

Obviously our motives for being kind should not center around what others will do for us because of our kindness, but kindness should be a way of life for Christians. We are God's helpers, taking care of each other for Him. We are His hands; we are His voice. And everything God asks us to do for Him has a happy ending. Someday we will be rewarded publicly for our kindness to others: we will be summoned by the King of the universe for dinner and eternal life!

Maybe you don't feel as if you have anything to offer anybody else. Look around. There is always someone who needs something. Maybe you can be a "secret friend" and leave encouraging notes around for your friends. Maybe you can just listen as your friends talk—good listeners are far too few. Whatever kindness you choose to share, remember that kindness always comes back. And even if you don't receive public applause right now, the happiness you'll feel inside is worth every minute you spend for others.

DON'T LOOK AT ME!

Not all who sound religious are really godly people. They may refer to me as "Lord," but still won't get to heaven. For the decisive question is whether they obey my Father in heaven. Matthew 7:21, TLB.

It's easy to be let down by other Christians. Some people refuse to attend church if another member offends them. "If that's the way Christians are," they say, "then I want none of it."

How do you feel when others deface the name Christian? How do you feel when you deface the name?

To keep from getting discouraged about the things that so-called Christians do that are definitely not Christlike, we need to remind ourselves that Jesus knew this problem would come up. He warned His followers that not everyone who called Him Lord really meant it. Not everyone who attends church has been converted and received a change of heart. And if we assume that just because they say they are Christians, then everything they do is OK, we can get into trouble. Things may not always be what they seem.

Years ago a certain young woman set her eyes on a certain wealthy young man and determined that he would be the man she would marry. Unfortunately, she had a problem. She was terribly nearsighted and was afraid that if he knew that, he would not want to marry her, no matter what she did to help him fall in love. So she devised a plan to try to convince the man that her eyesight was even more than perfect. She stuck a diamond stickpin into a tree, then went to find her suitor and guided him to a bench 200 yards away from the tree.

Presently she pointed to the tree and cried out, "Look, darling! Isn't that a diamond sticking out of that tree?"

"Why, I'm amazed," he said. "How did you know? Certainly I couldn't see a diamond from this far away!"

"I'll get it for you," she offered happily and started toward the tree. But her entire plan was blown when she tripped over—a cow.

The devil would like to mislead us too. He wants us to think that everyone who attends church is a Christian. Then if we're looking at how they live, we are likely to get discouraged when they fail. Maybe we'll even stop coming to church—Satan would love it if we did that! He wants us to be confused and let down.

It has been said that the church is a hospital for sinners, not a rest home for saints, and that is true. However, if you want to get well, you have to do what the doctor says—not what other patients advise. You can get confused if you try to pattern your life after someone in church. He may trip you up. The best course to follow is to obey Jesus and look to Him as your example.

DECEMBER 20

HOW TO KNOW YOU'RE GROWING UP

It's like this: when I was a child I spoke and thought and reasoned as a child does. But when I became a man my thoughts grew far beyond those of my childhood, and now I have put away the childish things. 1 Corinthians 13:11, TLB.

Have you ever seen a tomcat that's bigger than his mother trying to act like a kitten again? We have one. He tries to nuzzle and nurse like a tiny kitten, even though he's almost twice the size of his mother! It makes her mad and me, too.

When you were a baby, everyone loved you because you were so tiny and helpless—you were a baby, and that's how you were supposed to be! And then, as you grew up, those same people celebrated your first tooth, your first steps, and the day you threw away your bottle or your pacifier.

You kept on growing and learning new things. If you ask your parents, I'm sure they will say that you grew up too fast. You know so much more today than you did a year ago!

Part of a parent's job is to help you to get along in the world as a grown-up. That's why they teach you to share and to use manners at the table, and to be clean and dress nicely. Because although they will always love you, no matter how you look, not everyone else out there will.

Unfortunately, one of the last things people seem to learn as we grow up is that we need to stop acting out our feelings like babies do. Babies do that because they can't talk. But we can. We have words to express how we feel, and it is a very grown-up thing to tell someone that you feel angry, rather than to pout and sulk and make them guess. Oh, yes, it's hard! Many grown-ups haven't learned how to do it. It may take you years to perfect the skill, but you will like yourself better when you do, because you will not only look grown-up, but will sound grown-up, too. And people will treat you with respect.

LOVE UNDESERVED

For God so loved the world, that he gave his only begotten Son.
John 3:16.

It was a foggy September morning that I got a call from the hospital. "Tell your husband to come right in. We've got a cornea." My husband, Gary, had been on the list for a donor cornea just a short time, and we were expecting a wait of several months. But just that morning a young man about Gary's age had been killed in a motorcycle accident, and his family had agreed to donate his corneas.

Gary's condition was not a life-or-death problem. He had a condition known as keratoconus. His corneas were taking on a peaked curve, and he was losing his vision in one eye because of it. The corneal transplant, it was hoped, would give him back his vision and allow his eye to be fitted with a contact lens.

The cornea was just hours old. After I called Gary at work to tell him to hurry to the hospital, the graveness of what that other man's family must be going through hit me. I sat down at the table and stared out at the white, foggy landscape and cried. I wanted to thank the parents for their son's gift. I wanted them to know we were grateful. But the doctor had told us that they did not exchange names or phone numbers between donors and recipients in the cornea donor program.

Gary's surgery went well, and the transplant was a success. But the experience was sobering. It is a sobering thought to know that a man, by dying, had given you something you otherwise wouldn't have. And it is even more sobering to know that you can never give him anything in return.

That's how God's gift of life is. Love undeserved, out of this world. A gift we can never match, but only accept with gratitude. There's not a thing we can do to make God love us.

He loves you because you *are* you. Because He made you. And nothing you do can ever make Him stop loving you. Read the text again, but put your name in place of the word "world." "For God so loved [your name], that He gave His only begotten Son."

WILL YOU GREET HIM OR HIDE?

There will be great joy for those who are ready and waiting for [Jesus'] return. He himself will seat them and put on a waiter's uniform and serve them as they sit and eat! Luke 12:37, TLB.

When you were little, did your mother ever tell you "Just wait till your father gets home"? How did you feel? Did you wait eagerly for his arrival? Did you go out to welcome him with open arms, or did you stay in your room, even hide? You probably hoped your mother would forget to tell him to punish you, didn't you?

Because my parents were missionaries, there wasn't an Adventist school near my home as I grew up, so I attended a boarding school from the time I was in the seventh grade. I know it is hard for boarding school teachers to have the kind of love and tender concern for their students that their parents usually show, and it seemed that the philosophy of many of my teachers was "Just wait till Jesus comes!" We were scared into obedience for fear of being eternally lost.

While I'll admit that fear of awful punishment is certainly a strong motivation for not doing something, it certainly doesn't foster a warm relationship between the person giving the punishment and his victim. I'm sorry for those of my teachers who held the fearful philosophy that Jesus' coming is an event to be dreaded,

Jesus seemed to know that this would be a prevailing feeling before He comes, because He said, "When you see wars and famines and men's hearts failing them for fear, look up! Don't run away! Be standing out there waiting for Me, for your redemption draws near!"

Certainly those who do not know Jesus will be fearful not only of the frightening events happening in the world, but also of the return of Jesus—because they will remember the wonderful things they heard about heaven and they will realize too late that they will never experience it.

But now, while we have the time to get to know Jesus as a friend, our motive for turning to Him and making Him our friend should not be to avoid eternal death. We respond to Him because He is wonderful and because He offers His friendship and love to us. And if we are His friends, then His coming will be something we will look forward to.

You don't need to fear Jesus' return. Talk to Him every day about everything! You don't need to hide anything from Him—even if you feel mad at Him—because He already knows it, anyway. And He still loves you. Confess your sins. Get to know Jesus as your personal friend. Then you will welcome Him with a smile and open arms when He comes to take you out of this world.

GARY'S FRIENDS

He who walks with the wise grows wise, but a companion of fools suffers harm. Proverbs 13:20, NIV.

It was a hot summer day in Spokane, Washington. Gary leaned on the handle of the lawn mower and wiped his forehead with the back of his hand. *Why did the grass have to grow so fast, anyway?* he wondered. Mowing it took up too much of his playing time.

Somebody whistled to him from across the street. It was his friend Ron. "Hey, Gary!" Ron called with a wave. "Wanna go down to the river and roll rocks?"

A steep hill dotted with large, heavy boulders rose up behind the river. Gary's friends had told him what fun it was to roll the boulders down the hill, then watch them bounce across the road and splash into the river on the other side.

But Gary had to finish mowing the yard. He had promised his mom that he would.

"Not today," Gary called back. "I've got to finish this." Ron waved and sauntered on down the sidewalk.

"He's probably going to get the other guys to go with him," Gary muttered to himself. "And here I am, stuck with the lawn!"

Late that afternoon, as Gary was playing with his friends, a police car drove slowly down the street toward them. It stopped right in front of his house, and a policeman stepped out.

"Are you the guys who were rolling rocks down the hill this afternoon?" the policeman asked.

Ron and the others nodded slowly.

"Well, one of those rocks hit my car! If I hear any more reports of you boys rolling rocks down that hill, you'll be in for some trouble," the policeman warned them.

"I wasn't there," Gary said quickly. "I was mowing the lawn."

"Really?" the policeman said, as though he didn't believe him. "We'll just check that out with your mother."

He turned and walked up to Gary's front door. Gary's mom answered his loud knock. "Hello, ma'am," the policeman said. "Could you tell me what your son was doing at about 2:00 this afternoon?"

"Yes, he was mowing the lawn." She looked puzzled, but managed a smile. "In fact, I believe you can still smell the grass."

The policeman looked around. He sniffed. "Very well. Thank you." And he turned, walked to his car, and drove away.

Gary sighed heavily, happy that he had obeyed his mother and finished his job.

Why did the policeman think that Gary had helped roll stones down the hill? Because his friends had. Sometimes even if we haven't done anything wrong, we can get a bad reputation because of the things our friends do. That's why it is very important to choose only good friends. Your parents can help you choose.

DECEMBER 24

WALK LIKE AN ANGEL

Obey me, and I will be your God and you will be my people. Walk in all the ways I command you, that it may go well with you. Jeremiah 7:23, NIV.

How do angels obey God's will? Is there anything different about the way they do what is asked of them and the way you obey God? For one thing, they do what God asks right away, don't they? They do it cheerfully and willingly. And they always do the best they can do. But most important of all, they obey without asking any questions.

Angels don't ask why before they get started doing God's will. They just get going and do it because they trust that God does not ask them to do anything they cannot do.

As a nurse, I find it fascinating to find medical reasons for some of the commands God gave the Israelites. He didn't give them any reason for His command that they circumcise their baby boys on the eighth day of life. God just told them that was the day it was to be done. And the Israelites obeyed God without asking questions. They could not know that God has made the blood clotting factor of little boys to be highest on the eighth day of life! That means they don't bleed as much when the surgery is done on the day that God commanded Abraham's descendants to do it. He obviously had a master plan.

Thousands of years ago when the command was given, nobody knew anything about the clotting factors of blood. But we know it now, so now we understand.

Another rule God gave was that the Israelites were not to take blood into their bodies. Orthodox Jews still prepare "kosher" meats, draining the blood of the animals before the meat is eaten. Perhaps God gave this warning because He knew of diseases that are passed through the blood.

The angels obey God without asking why. They know Him well. They know He can be trusted. There are many things that happen in this life that we can't understand. Sometimes we feel like mistrusting God until He can give us a good reason why bad things happen. But many of those questions will not be answered until we ask them in heaven. We just have

to trust God's track record of having good reasons that we will understand later—much later, sometimes—perhaps not until we are out of this
world.

HOW MUCH DOES PRAYER WEIGH?

Give us this day our daily bread. Matthew 6:11.

How much does a prayer weigh? The only man who tried to weigh
one still doesn't know.

It happened in 1945, a week before Christmas. A man whom we'll call
Mr. Levine owned a grocery store in New York City and was busy stacking
apples when a tired-looking woman came in and asked for just enough
food to make a Christmas dinner for her children. Mr. Levine asked her
how much she wanted to spend.

She answered, "My husband was killed in the war, and I have nothing
to offer but a little prayer."

Mr. Levine sniffed. "Write it on paper," he said, turning back to
stacking the apples. To his surprise, she plucked a piece of paper out of
her blouse and handed it to him. "I did that during the night," she said,
"while watching over my sick baby."

Without thinking, Mr. Levine took the paper from her hand. *What
will I do with it now?* he wondered. Then an idea flashed through his
mind. He placed the paper, without even glancing at the prayer, on the
weight side of his old-fashioned scales. "We'll see how much food this is
worth," he said with a sigh, rolling his eyes toward the ceiling. Other
customers were watching.

To his astonishment, when he slapped a loaf of bread on the other
side the scale did not go down. To his confusion and embarrassment, it
would not go down, though he kept on adding food. While other
customers began to gather, he grabbed whatever he could lay his hands
on and added it to the scale. Still the scale didn't move. His face got red,
and he became angry and flustered.

So finally he said, "Well, that's all the scales will hold anyway. Here's
a bag. You'll have to put it in yourself. I'm busy."

With a little sob, the woman took the bag and began filling it with
food, wiping her eyes on her sleeve now and then. Mr. Levine tried not to
look, but he couldn't help seeing that he had given her quite a big bag and
it was not yet full. Gruffly he rolled a large ball of cheese down the
counter toward the woman. Because he did not want to stare at her, he
didn't see the timid smile of grateful understanding that glistened in her
eyes at this final betrayal of his crusty exterior.

When the woman had gone, Mr. Levine looked at the scales, shaking his head in puzzlement. Then he found the solution: the scales were broken.

Mr. Levine lived for many years afterward. He never forgot the woman, though he never saw her again. And even as an old man, he still shook his head in amazement whenever he thought of her. And he always kept the slip of paper on which she had written her prayer: "Please, Lord, give us this day our daily bread."

Adapted from Paul Lee Ton, *Encyclopedia of 7700 Illustrations.*

DECEMBER 26

AFTER CHRISTMAS

Do not store up for yourselves treasures on earth, where moth and rust destroy, and where thieves break in and steal. But store up for yourselves treasures in heaven, where moth and rust do not destroy, and where thieves do not break in and steal. For where your treasure is, there your heart will be also. Matthew 6:19, 20, NIV.

You are 8 years old, and it's the day after Christmas. You have opened all your packages and played with all your new toys. Some were boring, and some are already broken. All those relatives you were forced to hug and kiss have gone home. Aunt Edith gave you a billfold with a $1 bill in it for good luck. Last Christmas she gave you a billfold, too. Next Christmas she'll get you another one. Grandma's $5 bill is in your new billfold, too, and you can't remember what her card said or even which card you took it from. Or was that Aunt Mildred's $5 bill? Even though right after Christmas dinner you thought you'd never be hungry again, you wonder what's left of yesterday's feast.

You're tired. Yet you want to stay awake and be excited even though you can't think of a reason why. You flip on the TV and see ads for the toys and electronic games that you got for Christmas. For some reason, hardly anything you see on the screen looks as big and fancy as it did a few days ago. Of course, the toys that you didn't get still look super, and you wonder if you got the wrong things, until you go to the neighbor kid's house and see how disappointing his presents are.

Even the tree that looked so beautiful yesterday looks limp and lost today. Some of the lights have burned out, and it doesn't even matter. You'll help Mom replace them next year. You change your radio from one station to another, trying to avoid leftover Christmas carols. You wander around the house, dreading going back to school, but bored with staying home. In short, Christmas has left you disappointed and unfulfilled.

This is an example of our life apart from Jesus. Anything that you are eagerly waiting for can fit into this picture. Just change the names and fill in the blanks. When you get that job, when you get that new car, when you have more money, when you finish school, when you get married, when Christmas comes . . . When, when, when. But somehow the future always seems to be disappointing when you reach it.

Learn from the day after Christmas. Next year, put your heart where the "day after" is better and more exciting than all the days that went before. Set your mind and heart on heaven. Don't be disappointed again.

DECEMBER 27

TRIED ANYTHING NEW LATELY?

I can do everything through him who gives me strength. Philippians 4:13, NIV.

"I can't do it," Sarah wailed.

"Do what?" her friend Trudy asked.

"Mrs. Beebe asked me to tell the mission story for Sabbath school this week, and I said I would, but now I'm getting scared. I'm going to do awful. I just know it!"

"Yeah. You probably will," Trudy replied, returning to her homework.

Sarah gave Trudy's arm a shove. "What do you mean?" she demanded.

"You probably will make a fool of yourself," Trudy said again, with no expression on her face.

"Hey! You're some friend!" Sarah retorted. "I thought you would tell me I'd do a good job!"

"You know yourself better than I do," Trudy said lightly. "I think you'll do a good job. But if you say you won't, then who am I to argue with you?" She chewed on her pencil for a moment, then caught Sarah's attention and held it. "If you want to know the truth, I'm a little envious of you. I've never been asked to tell the mission story. Mrs. Beebe must know you'll do a good job, or she wouldn't have asked you."

Sarah shrugged. "You won't laugh at me, will you?"

"Of course not!" Trudy assured her. "I'll be sitting there wishing I were you!"

Have you ever felt like Sarah, accepting a job in Sabbath school and then being scared when the time came? It's pretty normal. Even professional singers get a little nervous just before they go on stage. But they use that nervous energy positively, remembering past successes and telling themselves that they will do just fine.

Have you ever felt like Trudy, wanting to be asked and wondering why nobody ever did? More than likely, it's not because nobody thinks you'll do a good job. Some people seem so shy that their teachers don't want to make them uncomfortable by asking them to do something in front of the others.

No matter how good and kind or smart your teachers are, they can't read your mind. If you'd like to do something in Sabbath school, tell them! Teachers love having someone volunteer to help. It's the way to get things going, to test yourself and find out what you like to do. Maybe you'll do a good job, and maybe you'll goof up a few words. Who cares? Do it again! Remember, practice makes perfect, and God has promised to help you witness for Him. You don't know just what is waiting for you in your future—perhaps you'll be a great musician or a great preacher or a great teacher. You're preparing for that great future right now. Go on! Start practicing!

DECEMBER 28

HOW DO YOU PLAY TIC-TAC-TOE?

Be self-controlled and alert. Your enemy the devil prowls around like a roaring lion looking for someone to devour. 1 Peter 5:8, NIV.

Do you like to play tic-tac-toe? Almost everyone does, and almost every culture has a game similar to it. Why do you think we like to play it so much? Why do you like to play any game? The challenge of thinking ahead and watching your opponent's moves and planning strategy? I think so. It's fun to use your mind.

One of the most skillful strategy planners is Satan. He is no dummy. Unseen, he listens to your conversations and watches the things you look at, learning all about your weaknesses and strengths. Then he goes after those weaknesses to get to you. If he is successful in making you fail, it makes him look good to his angels—the ones who believed him when he said that we will never be good enough to go to heaven.

Does that make you feel like giving up? Don't you dare! God is an excellent strategist as well. When Satan announced that we aren't good enough to go to heaven, he didn't add that God has promised to help us. With God's help, we can be good enough to go to heaven.

If you will reread the first sentence of our text for today, you'll notice it says to be self-controlled. There's one thing Satan does not know about us, and that is our thoughts. Satan cannot read your mind. Therefore, if you control yourself and don't spout out angry words or whisper dirty secrets or watch dirty movies, Satan has no way of knowing what your weaknesses are. Pray silently about them, and your struggle will be between you and God.

You can win this battle. You can be a person who lives out of this world!

HOW DO YOU EAT POPCORN?

When you walk through the fire, you will not be burned. Isaiah 43:2, NIV.

Do you enjoy eating popcorn? Before it's popped, or after? Silly question, you say.

I like to think that we're all a little bit like popcorn, and we're all a little bit like coal. Let me explain how.

When I was a little girl in Ceylon, I used to spend hours lying on the grass, watching the busy ants that scurried in and out of their holes in the ground. Sometimes when I was not feeling at all kind, I would take a stick and open those holes just to see the nurse ants hurrying up from the dark tunnels with little white bundles in their jaws. The bundles looked like grains of white rice, but I was told that they were actually ant eggs that had not yet hatched.

One day I saw a little ant scurrying along a sandy stretch of our backyard toward his home, carrying a long piece of grass, more than 10 times his own length, above his head.

Just to see what he'd do, I dug a shallow ditch in front of him. He started into the ditch, but the piece of grass got stuck. Undaunted, the tiny ant backed out of the ditch and hurried along the side in search of another place to cross.

I was faster than he was, and lengthened and deepened the ditch.

The ant paused for a moment and went back to the place he had first tried. He hesitated only a moment, as though pondering the situation, before placing the piece of grass across the ditch and scurrying across, then lifting the blade of grass from the other side and hurrying on his way. Ingeniously, he had used his burden to make a bridge to progress.

To put that in popcorn terms, sometimes the heat of our burdens can change us into something more beautiful and desirable than we were before. A lump of coal becomes a diamond after the pressure is on. Maybe you're under pressure right now. Hang on! You can make it through! Someday you'll be a diamond that's out of this world.

WHEN HELPING ISN'T HELPING

But we also rejoice in our sufferings, because we know that suffering produces perseverance; perseverance, character; and character, hope. Romans 5:3, NIV.

It was a perfect cocoon, attached firmly to a twig, that Tracy found in the forest.

"Take it home," her father suggested. "Let's see what kind of butterfly hatches out."

So they took it home and put it in the corner of an old empty fish tank. Tracy covered the tank so that when a butterfly came out, it couldn't fly away without her seeing it first.

Every day she checked on the cocoon, looking for any sign of movement or cracks along the top. It was shaped like a flask with a narrow neck, and Tracy wondered how any butterfly could ever wriggle out of an opening that small.

At last the day came. Tracy watched in awe as the seemingly lifeless cocoon slowly moved back and forth with the unseen butterfly's struggle to be free. When she saw no progress at the end of a half hour, Tracy could stand it no longer. She hurried to the bathroom for the tiny fingernail scissors her mother often used. Then, taking the cover off the tank, she lifted out the cocoon and carefully snipped the confining threads at the narrow opening.

Before long the butterfly crawled out, but its wings never opened. It spent the rest of its short life crawling around in the old fish tank instead of flying on rainbow wings.

Tracy had only meant to be helpful. But her science teacher explained that the pressure the butterfly undergoes during its hours of intense struggle through the tight opening forces necessary fluids into its wings, stiffening them and enabling the butterfly to fly. Tracy's attempt to help had actually been the worst thing she could have done.

Sometimes living isn't easy. Sometimes it seems easier just to give up and drop out. But it's much better to hang in there and learn perseverance. Perseverance produces character, which gives us the ability to make decisions based on what's right and wrong, rather than on how we feel. And a good character produces hope, self-esteem, and positive thinking. In other words, a good character brings happiness that's out of this world!

MYSTERY GIFTS

I love all who love me. Those who search for me shall surely find me. Proverbs 8:17, TLB.

The royal castle in Dresden, Germany, contains art treasures and other costly objects. If you visit there, you may also see a big egg made of iron.

Many years ago a prince proposed to a Saxon princess, and she agreed to marry him. Some time later he sent her a gift, but she was very disappointed when she saw that it was only a big egg made of iron. In fact, being somewhat spoiled, she became so angry with the ugly present that she threw it to the floor. When it hit the floor, it sprang open. Inside was a silver egg.

Surprised and happy, she picked up the silver egg and examined it. When she discovered a secret spring, she pressed it, and the silver egg opened to reveal a gold flower. Thoroughly intrigued, the princess looked closer and noticed another little spring, which she pressed.

Now she found a little golden bird. When she touched one of its wings, the bird opened, and there was a little crown. Finally after pressing on the other wing, a diamond ring fell out—a present from the prince to his bride-to-be. This was his novel way of expressing his love to his fiancée.

The Bible too is a treasure chest that must be examined and studied to reveal its beauty.

And as you study your Bible, you too will grow more beautiful as you prepare to spend the rest of your life—out of this world!